PERSON-CENTERED AND
EXPERIENTIAL THERAPIES WORK

PERSON-CENTERED AND EXPERIENTIAL THERAPIES WORK

A review of the research
on counseling, psychotherapy
and related practices

EDITED BY

MICK COOPER,

JEANNE C. WATSON &

DAGMAR HÖLLDAMPF

PCCS BOOKS
Ross-on-Wye

First published 2010

PCCS BOOKS Ltd
2 Cropper Row
Alton Road
Ross-on-Wye
Herefordshire
HR9 5LA
UK
Tel +44 (0)1989 763900
www.pccs-books.co.uk

Person-Centered and Experiential Therapies Work:
A review of the research on counseling, psychotherapy
and related practices

A CIP catalogue record for this book is available from the British Library

ISBN 978 1 906254 25 4

Cover designed in the UK by Old Dog Graphics
Printed in the UK by PageBros, Norwich

CONTENTS

PREFACE

Since their inception in the 1940s, person-centred and experiential (PCE) therapies have, perhaps, never faced such challenges. In countries such as the UK, for instance, PCE therapies have been all but removed from lists of 'empirically supported therapies' (e.g., National Institute for Health and Clinical Excellence, 2009); while in Germany, PCE therapies has been approved by the scientific board for psychotherapy of the German government, but not by the board for national health insurance. Increasingly, there are very real concerns of moves towards a therapeutic 'monoculture', 'in which cognitive-behavioural therapy (CBT) dominates; and in which other therapeutic orientations – such as psychodynamic, person-centred and integrative – are marginalized: freely-available only for clients who actively decline CBT, or in the private and voluntary sectors' (Cooper & McLeod, in press).

To a great extent, this threat to PCE therapies is closely linked to the emergence of an 'evidence-based' agenda within healthcare commissioning and public policy circles. Increasingly, only those therapies that are considered to be of proven efficacy and financial benefit are endorsed or supported through public funding. And it is here that PCE therapies are often seen as falling short. Across settings and client groups, PCE therapists often find themselves encountering the myth that 'There's no evidence that person-centred therapy works' (Cooper, 2004).

It is this state of affairs that is the driving force behind the present project. Although it is true that, to some extent, members of the PCE community have shied away from research in the past few decades, there is vast and growing body of evidence to support a wide range of PCE practices. The aim of this project, therefore, is to draw this evidence together and to present it in an accessible and succinct manner, such that PCE therapists will be more empowered to present the facts about the effectiveness of their work.

In addition, this project aims to create a common and shared understanding of the current research findings, such that members of the PCE community can take a PCE research agenda forward. For this reason, this book not only reviews the evidence, but also reviews PCE research tools and methods, such that a more coherent and effective programme of research can be developed for the future.

Historically, this project emerged from a meeting of PCE researchers, students and practitioners at the 8th Conference of the World Association for Person-Centered and Experiential Psychotherapy and Counseling (WAPCEPC), held in Norwich, UK in 2008. Potential editors were identified who then, in collaboration with the WAPCEPC Board, proposed a range of topics to be reviewed, and contacted leading specialists in these areas to lead these inquiries. Further volunteers were then brought into many of these chapters, creating a PCE Task Force whose mission was to 'review the evidence base for PCE practice, to disseminate the results of this investigation, and also to identify key areas in which the evidence base for PCE practice needs to be developed.'

The first chapter in this book, by Elliott and Freire, provides a definitive review of the quantitative evidence for the effectiveness of PCE therapies, tracking the evolution of the data analysis since the early 1990s. This is followed by Hölldampf, Behr and Crawford (Chapter 2) who focus specifically on the evidence base for PCE therapies with children and young people. Chapter 3 (Cornelius-White and Motschnig-Pitrik) broadens the focus of these analyses, looking at the efficacy of person-centred approaches in the fields of education, parenting and management. In the following chapter (Timulak and Creaner), the *qualitative* evidence on outcomes in PCE therapies is synthesized. In Chapters 5 and 6, the focus moves away from the global outcomes of PCE therapies, to look more specifically at the effectiveness of PCE-related processes. Bohart and Tallman (Chapter 5) review the evidence for the person-centred concept of the client as an active agent of self-healing, while Watson, Lietaer and Greenberg (Chapter 6) consider a broad range of relational, affective and experiential processes and their relationship to outcomes. The next three chapters review a range of PCE-related tools, measures and research methods. Watson and Watson (Chapter 7) review measures of self- and organismic-functioning, while Freire and Grafanaki (Chapter 8) focus on PCE measures of the therapeutic relationship. In Chapter 9, Wilkins reviews a range of research methods that are closely aligned with a PCE epistemology. The book concludes with a brief chapter (Cooper, Watson and Hölldampf) in which the chapters are reviewed and key priorities for further research are identified.

Authors have specifically endeavoured to make each of these chapters as accessible as possible to a wide-ranging, non-specialist audience. However, for those readers unfamiliar with research literature, some of the terms presented in this book may seem somewhat alien or daunting. For this reason, we would strongly encourage readers new to research to read this text alongside an introduction to counselling and psychotherapy research, such as Sanders and Wilkins' (2010) excellent new *First Steps in Practitioner Research*. A more advanced introduction to research methods and concepts in the field is Barker, Pistrang and Elliott's (2002) *Research Methods in Clinical Psychology*; while Timulak (2008) gives an excellent overview of methods and findings in his *Research in Psychotherapy and Counselling*. The British Association of Counselling and Psychotherapy has also developed a glossary of key research terms and concepts that can be found at www.cprjournal.com. For a broad and accessible overview of research findings in the field, see Cooper's (2008) *Essential Research Findings in Counselling and Psychotherapy*. Key terms from the glossary of this book follow (see pp. 4–6). For the most thorough, systematic and definitive review of the evidence, see chapters in Bergin and Garfield's *Handbook of Psychotherapy and Behavior Change* (Lambert, 2004).

We would like to express our thanks to all members of the WAPCEPC Task Force who contributed to this book; and to members of the WAPCEPC Board for their guidance and input on the project. Special thanks also to Maggie Taylor-Sanders, Pete Sanders, Sandy Green and Heather Allan at PCCS Books for all their tireless work on bringing the manuscript to fruition.

Mick Cooper
Jeanne C. Watson
Dagmar Hölldampf

REFERENCES

Barker, C. B., Pistrang, N., & Elliott, R. (2002). *Research methods in clinical psychology: An introduction for students and practitioners* (2nd ed.). Chichester: Wiley.

Cooper, M. (2004). *Person-centred therapy: Myth and reality.* from http://www.strath.ac.uk/media/departments/eps/counsellingunit/Person-Centred_Therapy_Myth_and_Reality_-_Mick_Cooper.pdf

Cooper, M. (2008). *Essential research findings in counselling and psychotherapy: The facts are friendly.* London: Sage.

Cooper, M., & McLeod, J. (in press). *Pluralistic Counselling and Psychotherapy.* London: Sage.

Lambert, M. J. (Ed.). (2004). *Bergin and Garfield's handbook of psychotherapy and behavior change* (5th ed.). Chicago: Wiley.

National Institute for Health and Clinical Excellence. (2009). *Depression: The treatment and management of depression in adults (update).* London: Author.

Sanders, P., & Wilkins, P. (2010). *First steps in practitioner research.* Ross-on-Wye: PCCS Books.

Timulak, L. (2008). *Research in psychotherapy and counselling.* London: Sage.

Editors'note: In the chapters, US and UK English has been used according to the nationality of the lead author.

GLOSSARY OF KEY TERMS

(from Cooper, 2008*)

Clinically significant improvement
Movement from within the range of scores for a clinical population to the range of scores for a non-clinical population

Cohen's *d*
A commonly used effect size measure, indicating the amount of difference between two groups relative to 'background' variation: a *d* of .2 can be considered 'small', a *d* of .5 'medium,' and a *d* of .8 'large'

Control group
A group of individuals with characteristics similar to those in the 'experimental group', but who do not participate in the procedure being tested

Correlation
The degree of association between two variables, ranging from 1 (total positive association) to –1 (total negative association), with 0 indicating no relationship between the two variables

Effect size
A measure of the strength of relationship between two variables (often used synonymously with Cohen's *d*)

Effectiveness
The extent to which an intervention, when used under ordinary circumstances, brings about a desired effect

Efficacy
The potential to bring about a desired effect

Empirical
Based on concrete experiences or observations, as opposed to purely theoretical conjecture: not to be confused with 'empiricism', a branch of philosophy that considers experiences or observations as the only true source of knowledge

---

* Cooper, M. (2008). *Essential research findings in counselling and psychotherapy: The facts are friendly.* London: Sage.

Hierarchy of evidence

A means of grading the strength of evidence, based on the susceptibility of research findings to bias. The following hierarchy (in descending order of importance), outlined by Eccles et al. (1998), is used as the basis for the UK Department of Health's (2001, p. 18) clinical practice guidelines for psychological therapies and counselling, and is the approximate order of weighting for the present text:

Ia Evidence from meta-analysis of randomized controlled trials
Ib Evidence from at least one randomized controlled trial
IIa Evidence from at least one study without randomization
IIb Evidence from at least one other type of quasi-experimental study
III Evidence from descriptive studies, such as comparative studies, correlation studies, and case-control studies
IV Evidence from expert committee reports or opinions, or clinical experience of respected authority or both

Hypothesis

A tentative explanation of certain observations or facts

Mean

The mathematic average of a set of scores, calculated by summing the scores and dividing by the number of scores

Mediating variable

A factor that accounts for the relationship between two variables

Meta-analysis

A statistical procedure which pools findings from different studies to estimate overall effects

Moderating variable

Factors that affect the relationship between two variables

p-value

The probability that a particular difference between groups has come about by chance

Quantitative research

Number-based research, generally incorporating statistical analysis

Qualitative research
Language-based research, in which experiences, perceptions, observations, etc. are not reduced to numerical form

Randomization
The process of assigning research participants to treatment or control conditions by chance, to minimize the likelihood of systematic differences between groups

Randomized controlled trial (RCT)
(Aka randomized clinical trial) An experimental study in which participants are randomly assigned to two or more groups, such that the efficacy of the different interventions can be identified

Research
A systematic process of inquiry that leads to the development of new knowledge

Significant differences
A meaningful and important difference between two or more groups that is unlikely to be due to chance variations

Standard deviation
A measure of the spread of a set of data, larger standard deviations meaning that the scores are more dispersed

REFERENCES

Department of Health. (2001). *Treatment choices in psychological therapies and counselling.* London: Author.

Eccles, M., Freemantle, N., & Mason, J. (1998). North of England evidence based guidelines development project: Methods of developing guidelines for efficient drug use in primary care. *British Medical Journal, 316*(7139), 1232–1235.

CHAPTER 1

THE EFFECTIVENESS OF PERSON-CENTRED AND EXPERIENTIAL THERAPIES
A REVIEW OF THE META-ANALYSES

ROBERT ELLIOTT & ELIZABETH FREIRE

Do clients change over the course of person-centred/experiential (PCE) psychotherapies? Do PCE therapies help bring about these changes? How do PCE therapies stack up against other therapies? Are cognitive-behavioural treatments (CBT) really more effective than PCE therapies? In this chapter, we review the quantitative evidence for the effectiveness of person-centred/experiential (PCE) psychotherapies, looking in turn at what we know about each of these questions. In addition, we will also look at whether there are likely to be differences among different PCE therapies and the client problems for which PCE therapies are likely to be most effective.

Research on the effectiveness of PCE therapies can be a hard sell for many humanistic therapists, who either find it irrelevant (because they are already convinced that the therapy they do is effective) or threatening (because they fear that it will show their therapies to be ineffective). This is particularly the case because effectiveness/efficacy research is almost always quantitative, and PCE therapists are typically quite sceptical about quantitative research. Reducing rich, contradictory and often subtle client experiences to numbers is often seen as dehumanizing and un-person-centred (Elliott, 2007).

In the field of psychotherapy/counselling research, it is common to distinguish between two kinds of quantitative outcome research: *efficacy* and *effectiveness* studies. Randomized controlled trials (RCTs) are defined as *efficacy* research, while *effectiveness* research gauges how well therapy works in practice or naturalistic settings. Both approaches deal broadly with whether a type of therapy works. Both by definition involve quantitative assessment of client functioning before and after therapy, delivery of some particular version of a therapy (here PCE), and systematic statistical analyses. In addition, efficacy research adds control groups of clients who either don't receive therapy at all or who receive a different kind of therapy.

Author note. This research was supported by a generous grant from the British Association for the Person-Centred Approach. Robert Elliott can be contacted at fac0029@gmail.com; Beth Freire can be contacted at elizabeth.freire@strath.ac.uk.

questions about *how much* clients change pre- to post-therapy,
ns of the *amount of change* in clients in PCE therapy vs. no-
:r-therapy controls, are the kinds of questions that lend themselves
ntitative measurement and analysis. In fact, these questions are
difficult and cumbersome to answer without recourse to quantitative
measurement.

Fortunately, as we try to show in this chapter, the results of quantitative
outcome research on PCE therapies are primarily good news for therapists
and counsellors working within this approach. Beginning with Smith, Glass
and Miller's (1980) ground-breaking study, we will summarize the results of
six successive meta-analyses on the outcome of person-centred/experiential
therapies that focused predominantly on psychotherapy with adult populations.
A summary of these six meta-analyses can be found in Table 1 (see p. 15).

SMITH, GLASS, & MILLER (1980)

Quantitative summaries of the effectiveness of person-centred experiential
psychotherapy/counselling go back to Smith, Glass and Miller's (1980) classic meta-
analysis of 475 controlled outcome studies involving a wide variety of different kinds
of therapy and clients of all ages.

Smith et al. (1980) were pioneers in the field of *meta-analysis*;[1] their ground-
breaking study was the first major meta-analysis in the social sciences. What they did
was this: for each measure from each of the studies they analyzed, they took the average
(or mean) post-therapy score for all the clients who received a particular kind of therapy
and subtracted from it the average score of the clients in the control group on that
outcome measure (preferably in a no-treatment or waitlist condition). Then, they divided
this difference by the standard deviation[2] of the control group, producing results expressed
in standard deviation units, which puts everything on the same metric or scale, so that
results can be compared and combined across measures, studies and types of therapy.
This statistic is known today as Glass's δ (pronounced 'delta').[3]

Included in the Smith et al.'s (1980) meta-analysis were studies involving person-
centred and gestalt therapies. In this first meta-analysis, the authors were interested
in controlled effect sizes (*ES*s), that is, comparisons between clients who got therapy
and those who did not (waitlist or no-treatment controls); in order to make this
easier, they ignored pre-therapy scores and only compared post-therapy outcomes.

---

1. Meta-analysis is a quantitative analysis of bodies of quantitative research (literally, analysis of analyses).
2. Standard deviation, roughly, is the average amount of variability from the mean.
3. After Gene Glass, the second author of the study. The Greek letter delta is a common abbreviation
for change or difference in science and engineering.

Unfortunately, although this is a common practice in meta-analyses, it does not control for pre-therapy differences, which can affect outcome, even in RCTs, where clients are randomly assigned to a particular therapy vs. some kind of control group.

The mean controlled *ES* for person-centred therapy was .62 *SD* (*N* = 150 effects; we don't know how many studies these came from). The *ES*s for gestalt therapy were quite similar: Mean = .64 (*N* = 68 effects). Compared to the overall *ES* of .85 for the entire sample of 475 studies in the meta-analysis, these values were on the small side, and certainly smaller than the effects Smith et al. (1980) reported for cognitive or behavioural therapies, although they did not do any direct comparisons with CBTs.

GREENBERG, ELLIOTT, & LIETAER (1994)

The first meta-analysis specifically focused on PCE therapies was carried out by Greenberg, Elliott and Lietaer (1994) in 1991–92 as part of a major review of research on humanistic therapy for the fourth edition of the *Handbook of Psychotherapy and Behavior Change* (Bergin & Garfield, 1994). For the purpose of this and the following meta-analyses reviewed here, the authors decided to include not only therapies that were explicitly labelled as one of the main forms of humanistic-experiential therapy (e.g., person-centred or client-centred, gestalt, experiential, focusing-oriented, psychodrama, or emotion-focused/process-experiential), but also 'supportive' therapies that described the use of therapist empathy or exploration of client experiencing as an important component of the therapy. The presence of advice-giving or interpretation as a required part of the therapy was an exclusion criterion.

Within these parameters, they attempted to locate all available quantitative outcome studies in order to address the question of how much clients changed over the course of therapy. Greenberg et al. (1994) tried to find all outcome studies of PCE therapies from 1978 onward for which it was possible to calculate a change effect size and which focused on adult clients. They obtained pre–post change effect sizes on 134 measures from 36 studies, involving 1,239 clients. In contrast to Smith et al.'s (1980) analysis, effect sizes (*ES*s) were calculated by finding the difference between pre-therapy and post-therapy (or follow-up) mean scores and dividing by the pre-therapy standard deviation. This made it possible to use data from so-called 'uncontrolled' one-group studies, which are important in naturalistic settings and in the early stages of work on a new approach or client population.

The average pre–post effect size (*ES*, here Glass's δ, following Smith et al., 1980) for this sample of studies was 1.20 *SD* (this kind of *ES* is always expressed in standard deviation units). The authors were pleased and surprised by this result, since it was a large effect: it means that the average client in a PCE therapy moved from the 50th to the 88th percentile in relation to the pre-treatment population. However, they also noted that there was a large amount of variability between studies, as indicated by the standard deviation of .75.

In addition, they found few if any differences across types of client presenting problem, therapy modality (individual vs. group vs. in-treatment programme), length of therapy, or type of PCE therapy. They did, however, find slightly larger effects at early follow-up (less than a year) than at either post-therapy or longer-term follow-up, although this difference was not statistically significant.

This did not, however, satisfy the editors of the book, Sol Garfield and Allen Bergin, who insisted that these effects might have occurred in any event, without therapy (a phenomenon known as 'spontaneous remission'). Therefore, the authors looked at studies that used control groups (either 'waitlist' or 'no treatment' control groups). These studies can tell us whether clients in PCE therapies did better than clients who received no therapy or who were placed on a waiting list. Greenberg et al. (1994) then found 15 studies in which the amount of client change in the PCE therapy could be directly compared to the amount of change in clients in a no-treatment or waitlist control group. They found an average *controlled ES* of 1.24, which was nearly as large as the pre–post *ES*, and about twice the size of the controlled effects for PCE therapies reported by Smith et al. (1980). This established a causal link between PCE therapy and client outcome, at least for these studies.

This was still not quite enough to satisfy the editors, who raised the issue of whether in fact clients in PCE therapies did as well as clients in other therapies. Fortunately, the authors were able to find 26 studies in which a PCE therapy was compared to another form of psychosocial treatment (e.g., psychoeducational interventions, CBT or psychodynamic therapy). Pre–post *ES*s were calculated for the comparative therapies as well, and differences in pre–post *ES*s for PCE vs. non-PCE therapies were calculated. Effect sizes favouring the PCE therapy were given positive values; those favouring the non-PCE therapy were given negative values. The results were quite variable, ranging from –1.42 (Lerner & Clum, 1990) to 1.77 (Johnson & Greenberg, 1985); however, the average difference between therapies was .04, essentially zero.

ELLIOTT (1996)

The 1994 meta-analysis has since been extended four times by Elliott and colleagues, with increasingly large samples of studies, still focusing on adult clients, but with similar and increasingly differentiated results. The Elliott (1996) version, presented as a conference paper in Germany a year earlier, included 63 studies. Again using Glass's δ as the measure of effect size, Elliott found an average pre–post *ES* of 1.21

(N = 66 treatment groups). Pre–post effects were slightly larger for early follow-up (less than a year): 1.50 (N = 31; SD = 1.21) than for immediate or longer-term outcome. The largest effect sizes were obtained for active, process-guiding experiential therapies and couples problems.

Once again controlled effect sizes were calculated by finding the difference between amount of pre–post change in PCE therapy vs. no-treatment/waitlist control conditions. The result was an average ES of 1.04 (N = 28 comparisons). Comparative ESs[4] were also calculated as before, with similar results, an average ES of .04 (N = 37 comparisons).

Equivalence analyses. This meta-analysis added an important feature: In the first analysis, we had not shown that PCE and non-PCE therapies were *equivalent*, only that they *failed to differ* significantly. However, this time there were enough studies to allow an *equivalence analysis*, a method developed in biomedical research, recently adapted by Rogers, Howard & Vessey (1993). This involved several steps: First, the minimum clinically relevant difference was set at –.4 or .4 SD, as proposed by Elliott, Stiles and Shapiro (1993) because it was roughly midway between a small effect (.2 SD) and a large effect (.5). (Differences of less than .4 were assumed to be uninteresting from a clinical point of view.) Second, the mean and SD were calculated for the comparative ESs. Third, a statistical significance test (t test) was run on the difference between the mean comparative ES and the criterion of –.4 or .4 (whichever was closest to the obtained value).

The equivalence analysis showed that the average difference in ES between PCE and non-PCE therapies was .04. This difference was not significantly different from zero, but it was significantly different from .4, which met the definition of equivalence. The next thing was to compare the effect size of PCE therapies as a whole to CBT (N = 25; M = –.06; SD = .61), which produced the same results: equivalence. However, when the data were broken down further, the combined sample of studies labelled as person-centred or as supportive-nondirective[5] showed a small but nonsignificant disadvantage to CBT (N = 17; M = –.23; SD = .49). In an equivalence analysis, this type of result is characterized as *equivocal*: that is, it was not significantly different from either 0 or –.4, so nothing can be said one way or the other about whether the two therapies differ from one another or are equivalent. The recommended conclusion with equivocal results is that more research is needed.

Controlling for researcher allegiance. The Elliott (1996) analysis included another new feature: controls for *researcher allegiance*. The researcher allegiance effect is well-

---

4. The difference between amount of pre–post change in PCE therapy vs. other therapies.
5. The combining of PCT with supportive therapy was later called into question by Elliott and Freire's (2008) update of the meta-analysis.

established in the psychotherapy outcome literature, most notably by Luborsky et al. (1999), who showed that almost all the variance in the outcome of comparative outcome studies could be accounted for by the theoretical orientation of the investigators. This means that if the researcher is a CBT therapist, then he or she will most likely find results favouring CBT, whereas if the researcher is a PCE therapist, then PCE therapy will fare better. Researcher allegiance is particularly an issue when two active therapies are pitted against one another. In order to control for the effects of researcher allegiance, one has to measure it, which is not very difficult (usually, reading the last paragraph of the introduction section will suffice). For this purpose, a three-point scale was used: 1 = pro PCE therapy; 2 = neutral/can't tell; 3 = con PCE therapy. These allegiance ratings were then used to predict the results of the comparative outcome studies, obtaining a correlation of –.59, a very large and highly statistically significant effect. In particular, supporters of PCE therapies on average found large substantial, positive comparative ESs (M = .63; N = 10), while advocates of non-PCE therapies found PCE therapies on average to be less effective than theirs (M = –.31; N = 12). In addition, researchers with neutral or indeterminate allegiances typically obtained 'no difference' results ($M\ ES$ = –.02; N = 16).

Elliott (1996) dealt with this problem by repeating the analyses with the variance for researcher allegiance statistically removed from the comparative effects. The result was that even the relatively small but equivocal differences obtained earlier disappeared, making all the comparisons statistically equivalent.

ELLIOTT (2001)

Elliott (2001), the next iteration of this expanding meta-analysis, was published as a chapter in Cain and Seeman's (2001) *Handbook of Humanistic Psychotherapy*. This time, there were 99 therapy groups from 86 different studies, with a systematic effort to locate both older studies and German-language research. In addition to the larger sample, this meta-analysis used improved statistics, reflecting developments in meta-analytic practice, including (a) the more reliable Hedges' g effect size statistic (the difference between pre- and post-test scores was divided by the pooled standard deviation rather than the pre-therapy standard deviation) and (b) correction and weighting formulas (Hunter & Schmidt, 1990) were used to correct for small-sample bias and to provide more precise estimates.

Pre–post and controlled effects. Before correction, the average client pre–post change amounted to 1.06 (N = 99 studies). This analysis contained several larger German language studies with relatively small effect sizes, so correcting for small sample bias and weighting by sample size (larger studies counted for more) produced somewhat smaller effects: M = .80 (N = 5,030 clients). This is still considered to be a large effect. There were 36 comparisons (from 31 controlled studies) between PCE therapies and no-treatment or waitlist control conditions, with an uncorrected mean score of .99 (SD = .72); after correction and weighting, this shrank to .72 (N = 1,096 clients), again because of smaller effects in a few large studies.

Comparative effects. Forty-eight comparisons, drawn from 41 studies, amounted to an average comparative effect size of .00 (SD = .62); the corrected value was also .00 (N = 993). Once again, CBT was found to be statistically equivalent to PCE therapies, with a mean comparative ES of −.16 (N = 33; SD = .58; $t(0)$ = −1.59; $t(−.4)$ = 2.41, p <. 05). This time, however, the combination of the two forms of non-process-guiding therapy (person-centred and so-called 'supportive-nondirective') was worse than CBT (M = −.33; SD = .5; $t(0)$= −3.12 (p <. 01); $t(−.4)$ = .69). However, comparisons between CBT and pure person-centred therapy and process-guiding forms of PCE (e.g., process-experiential/emotion-focused therapies), were equivocal, meaning that no conclusions could be drawn one way or the other due to the small samples. Once again, however, when researcher allegiance was controlled for statistically, all of these differential or equivocal differences became equivalent.

ELLIOTT, GREENBERG, & LIETAER (2004)

The most recent version of the Elliott et al. meta-analysis to be published in full detail was in the fifth edition of *Bergin & Garfield's Handbook of Psychotherapy and Behavior Change* (Lambert, 2004). This involved another substantial increase in the sample of studies: For the pre–post analyses, there were 127 samples of clients seen in PCE therapies, drawn from 112 studies. Consistent with previous analyses, the overall unweighted pre–post ES was .99 (SD = .58); the weighted ES was .86 (N = 6,569). As before, controlled effects, measured against no-treatment or waitlist conditions, were only slightly smaller: unweighted: .89 (N = 42 comparisons; SD = .71); weighted: .78 (N = 1,149 clients).

Comparative effects against non-PCE therapies could be obtained from 55 studies, with an unweighted mean difference in ES of .04 (N = 74 comparisons; SD = .56); weighted: .01 (N = 1,375 clients). This was an equivalence finding ($t(0)$ = .61, ns; $t(.4)$ = −5.5, p < .01). In addition, they analyzed five studies in which more vs. less process-guiding PCE therapies were compared, for a comparative ES of .48 weighted (SD = .26) and .45 unweighted (N = 164 clients; SD = .25); even with the small sample of studies, equivalence analyses favoured process-guiding PCE therapies ($t(0)$ = 4.07, p < .05; $t(.4)$ = −.6, ns). In comparisons with CBT, PCE therapies were again statistically equivalent (N = 46; M = −.11; SD = .51; $t(0)$ = −1.49, ns; $t(.4)$ = 3.88, p <. 01).

However, when researcher allegiance was controlled for, these and other between-therapy differences disappeared and were replaced by statistical equivalence findings.

An added feature of this analysis was the identification of particular client problem types or diagnoses that had garnered enough research to meet US criteria as 'efficacious' within the revised Empirically Supported Therapies (EST) framework used by Chambless and Hollon (1998; the successor to the APA Division 12 Criteria), that is, (a) either equivalence to established treatments or superiority to another active treatment or no-treatment control; (b) in two or more independent research settings:

1. Depression. Elliott et al. (2004) reported that enough empirical research had been done on PCE therapies to support the claim that in general they were 'efficacious' (using the Chambless-Hollon criteria) for depression. Beyond this, they argued, emotion-focused therapy (EFT) in particular met a higher standard, 'specific and efficacious', based on superiority to another treatment in two or more research settings.

2. Abuse and post trauma. EFT also appeared to be 'specific and efficacious' for post-trauma difficulties including the effects of childhood abuse. However, an important limitation to this line of research according to the EST framework is that it did not look at PTSD (post-traumatic stress disorder) per se, but instead focused on client post-trauma difficulties more generally.

3. Anxiety. The existing evidence for PCE therapies for various anxiety problems was more mixed, but sufficient to warrant the lower standard of 'possibly efficacious' (multiple open clinical trials or at least one study showing rough equivalence to an established treatment). However, for panic and generalized anxiety, based on the existing research, it appeared that experiential therapies were less efficacious than CBT. Elliott et al. (2004) expressed concern about this trend in the literature and recommended more research to investigate the possibility further.

4. Couples problems. Elliott et al. (2004) also found that EFT for couples had the best track record of any PCE therapy, and met the criteria for 'specific and efficacious'.

5. Promising emerging areas. Finally, the authors pointed to several client problem areas that met the lower standard of 'possibly efficacious' and were worthy of further study. These include experiential treatments for anger and aggression (e.g., domestic violence), life adjustment in schizophrenia, major personality disorders (i.e., borderline or fragile processes), and various health-related problems (e.g., adjustment in cancer or HIV).

ELLIOTT & FREIRE (2008): PRELIMINARY CONCLUSIONS

Our intention for the latest version of the ongoing meta-analysis is to publish it in a peer-reviewed scientific journal; therefore, only a brief summary of the preliminary findings has been published to date and can be presented here. However, these results have confirmed, strengthened and extended the previous analyses, using a much larger sample of more than 180 scientific outcome studies (97% focusing on adults 18 or older; the rest involving adolescents) and thus can serve as an overall summary of what we know to date about the effectiveness of PCE therapies. These results are generally good news for therapists and counsellors working within the person-centred approach, because they provide multiple lines of evidence demonstrating that these therapies are highly effective.

Conclusion 1: PCE therapies are associated with large pre–post client change. To establish this, we looked at 203 samples of clients, from 186 studies, amounting to more than 14,000 clients. Similar to previous analyses of smaller samples, we obtained a weighted average effect size of 1.01. Social scientists consider this to be a very large effect, many times larger than effects typically found for common medical procedures or medications. In other words, on average, PCE therapies make a big difference for clients. Furthermore, this is particularly true for general symptom measures, as indicated by the two large UK-based studies by Stiles et al. (2006, 2008).

Conclusion 2: Clients' large post-therapy gains are maintained over early and late follow-ups. Next, we looked to see if clients retained the benefits of PCE therapy over time. The answer to this question is also yes. In fact, our analyses indicate that, if anything, clients in PCE therapies show slight further gains during the first year after therapy (effect size of .99 immediately after therapy vs. 1.12 for follow-ups less than a year after therapy). Furthermore, these gains are maintained beyond the one-year mark (*ES* = 1.13). This stability of post-therapy benefit is consistent with the PCE philosophy of enhancing client self-determination and empowerment, indicating that clients continue to develop on their own after they have left therapy.

Conclusion 3: Clients in PCE therapies show large gains relative to clients who receive no therapy. In order to show that there is a causal relationship between PCE therapy and client change, it is necessary to compare clients who get therapy to those who don't. These studies are most convincing when the assignment to therapy or no-therapy (or waitlist) is random (making it a 'randomized clinical trial' or RCT). This is because randomization usually (but not always) makes the two groups of clients roughly equivalent to start with.

We analyzed data from 63 studies, involving more than 2,100 PCE clients compared to more than 1,900 individuals in control conditions (waitlist or no-therapy). We found a controlled weighted effect size of .78, which is considered to be a large effect size. Clients who received therapy showed very little change: .19. About half of these controlled studies did not randomize clients to receive PCE therapy vs. waitlist/ no therapy; these studies are generally dismissed by scientific review panels, for example, those charged with developing and revising government or health service guidelines. For this reason, we ran the same analyses for the 31 randomized clinical trials within our sample (some 550 PCE clients), and found that randomization made almost no difference (controlled effect size = .78 SD). This is a very interesting finding, because many scientists believe that randomization is necessary if we want to conclude that therapy causes client change; however, our data indicate that randomization did not affect the size of the controlled ES, suggesting that randomization is not critical in this situation for inferring causal influence. Overall this body of research provides the second main line of evidence for the effectiveness of PCE therapies.

Conclusion 4: PCE therapies in general are clinically and statistically equivalent to other therapies. To answer the question of how PCE therapies stack up against other therapies, we were able to collect 109 studies, including 135 comparisons between PCE and other therapies; these studies contained data from more than 6,000 clients. As in the previous meta-analyses (except Smith et al., 1980), we first calculated how much clients changed in PCE therapy, then how clients seen in other therapies changed, and finally how much more or less clients in PCE therapies changed in comparison to clients in other therapies. The results of our analysis showed that there was virtually no difference between PCE and other therapies in amount of pre–post change (weighted comparative effect size = .00). That is, PCE therapies were neither more nor less effective than other therapies. Once again, we weeded out the non-randomized studies, leaving 91 so-called 'gold standard' RCTs involving 110 comparisons, with virtually identical results (comparative $ES = -.01$).

Conclusion 5: Broadly defined, PCE therapies might be trivially worse that CBT. As we had done in the previous meta-analyses, we next looked at 76 comparisons between PCE therapies (including either explicitly defined humanistic-experiential therapies or 'supportive' therapies) and CBT, including 63 comparisons from RCTs. When the entire sample of PCE therapies was pooled together they differed significantly from *both* 0 and −.4 ($ES = -.18$ for the full sample and $ES = -.16$ for the RCTs); in other words, as a general category PCE therapies appeared to be slightly but trivially less effective than CBT. However, this small effect disappeared when we statistically controlled for the theoretical orientation of the researcher ($ES = -.06$ for the full sample). This result was consistent with the previous three meta-analyses.

Conclusion 6: So-called 'supportive' therapies have worse outcomes than CBT but other kinds of PCE therapy are as effective or more effective than CBT. In this meta-analysis, our larger sample enabled us to look more closely at our data in order to really understand what was going on. Two unresolved questions had been, 'What is responsible for the trivial superiority of CBT?' and 'Why should controlling for researcher theoretical allegiance make it go away?' In order to answer these questions, we divided the PCE therapies into four types:

1. *Person-centred therapy*, explicitly following Carl Rogers and emphasizing the facilitative conditions in a relatively pure form.

2. *Supportive* therapies typically labelled by researchers as '*supportive*', or '*nondirective*'.[6]

3. *Emotion-focused therapy* (also known as process-experiential therapy), including individual (Greenberg, Rice, & Elliott, 1993) and couples (Greenberg & Johnson, 1988) versions, and explicit process guiding and staged therapeutic tasks (e.g., chair work).

4. *Other experiential* therapies, including gestalt, focusing-oriented, psychodrama, expressive and so on, that focus on immediate client experiencing, expression or enactment.

What we found when we analyzed separately for each of these types of PCE therapy was that the small effect in favour of CBT could be accounted for by the presence of the supportive therapies. That is, studies in which these therapies were used have substantially worse outcomes when compared to CBT (38 studies; effect size = −.35; for the 33 RCTs the effect size was −.29). Further investigation of these revealed them to be watered-down, typically non-bona fide versions of PCE therapies, commonly used by CBT researchers, especially in the USA.

In contrast, once the supportive therapies were removed, the effects of the bona fide PCE therapies could be seen more clearly: PCT appeared to be statistically equivalent in effectiveness to CBT (22 studies, including 18 RCTs, with identical effect sizes of −.09), even without controlling for researcher allegiance. Furthermore, although the number of studies is small, the newer emotion-focused therapies (EFT) for individuals or couples actually appeared to be *more* effective when compared to CBT (7 studies; effect size = .35; for the 4 RCTs the effect size was .55). Other experiential therapies were also equivalent to CBT (10 studies; *ES* = −.14; including 7 RCTs with *ES* = −.07). These results were so striking that we

---

6. Although the researchers sometimes used the label 'nondirective', these therapies do not correspond to standard definitions of nondirective client-centred therapy (e.g., Rogers, 1951).

wanted to make sure there was no error. Therefore, one of us went through the entire data set and reclassified all the studies from scratch, with the same results.

WHAT ARE THE IMPLICATIONS OF THIS SERIES OF META-ANALYSES?

The pace of research on PCE therapies continues to accelerate, making it difficult to keep up with. At this point, however, the overall findings, which have become increasingly clear with each successively larger data set, are uniformly good news for person-centred/ experiential practitioners: Clients use our therapies to make large changes in themselves; these changes are maintained over time and are much larger than our clients would have experienced without therapy. Furthermore, our clients show as much change as clients seen in other therapies, including CBT, but only if bona fide person-centred, emotion-focused, and other experiential therapies were involved.

From a policy point of view these data point to the proposition that person-centred/experiential therapies are empirically supported by multiple lines of scientific evidence, including 'gold standard' RCTs and recent very large RCT-equivalent studies in the UK (e.g., Stiles et al., 2006, 2008). This body of research suggests that the lists of empirically supported or evidence-based psychotherapies that have been constructed in various countries – the NICE Guidelines in the UK or the list of empirically supported treatments in the USA, for example – need to be updated with the type of evidence we have reviewed. PCE therapies should be offered to clients in National Health Service contexts and other mental health settings, and paid for by health insurance.

Relying on multiple lines of evidence, such as provided in the present study, provides a sound basis for establishing public mental health policy. In the UK, for example, the shortfall in the availability of psychological therapy in the National Health Service could be instantly resolved if health authorities were to draw upon the large body of trained PCE counsellors and psychotherapists.

For those of us in the PCE therapy tradition, the moral of this story is that we do not need to be afraid of quantitative research, either outcome research or RCTs. However, if we let others define our reality by studying watered-down versions of what we do, we are going to be in trouble. For this reason, it is imperative that as PCE therapists we do our own outcome research – including RCTs – on legitimate versions of our therapies. Among other things, the time is particularly ripe for research on:

- Person-centred therapies for depression
- Person-centred and emotion-focused therapies for specific anxiety problems such as social anxiety and generalized anxiety

- Pre-therapy for schizophrenia, dementia and other psychological contact impairments
- PCE therapies for chronic health problems such as cancer, MS, HIV, chronic pain and so on
- Emotion-focused therapies for eating difficulties (e.g., bulimia, anorexia)

Carl Rogers famously said, 'The facts are friendly'. However, we would add that it is up to us to collect facts in a fair and transparent manner and not to let others construct reality for us by presenting distorted, diluted versions of our therapies.

REFERENCES

Bergin, A. E., & Garfield, S. L. (Eds.). (1994). *Handbook of psychotherapy and behavior change* (4th ed.) (pp. 509–539). New York: Wiley.

Cain, D. J., & Seeman, J. (Eds.). (2001). *Humanistic psychotherapies: Handbook of research and practice*. Washington, DC: APA.

Chambless, D. L., & Hollon, S. D. (1998). Defining empirically supported therapies. *Journal of Consulting and Clinical Psychology, 66*, 7–18.

Elliott, R. (1996). Are client-centered/experiential therapies effective? A meta-analysis of outcome research. In U. Esser, H. Pabst, & G-W Speierer (Eds.), *The power of the person-centered-approach: New challenges-perspectives-answers* (pp. 125–138). Köln, Germany: GwG Verlag.

Elliott, R. (2001). Research on the effectiveness of humanistic therapies: A meta-analysis. In D. J. Cain & J. Seeman (Eds.), *Humanistic psychotherapies: Handbook of research and practice* (pp. 57–81). Washington, DC: APA.

Elliott, R. (2007). Person-centred approaches to research. In M. Cooper, P. F. Schmid, M. O'Hara, & G. Wyatt (Eds.), *The handbook of person-centred therapy* (pp. 327–340). Basingstoke, UK: Palgrave Macmillan.

Elliott, R., & Freire, B. (2008). Person-centred/experiential therapies are highly effective: Summary of the 2008 meta-analysis. *Person-Centred Quarterly, November, 1–3.*

Elliott, R., Greenberg, L. S., & Lietaer, G. (2004). Research on experiential psychotherapies. In M. J. Lambert (Ed.), *Bergin & Garfield's handbook of psychotherapy and behavior change* (5th ed.) (pp. 493–539), New York: Wiley.

Elliott, R., Stiles, W. B., & Shapiro, D. A. (1993). Are some psychotherapies more equivalent than others? In T. R. Giles (Ed.), *Handbook of effective psychotherapy* (pp. 455–479). New York: Plenum Press.

Greenberg, L. S., Elliott, R., & Lietaer, G. (1994). Research on humanistic and experiential psychotherapies. In A. E. Bergin & S. L. Garfield (Eds.), *Handbook of psychotherapy and behavior change* (4th ed., pp. 509–539). New York: Wiley.

Greenberg, L. S., & Johnson, S. M. (1988). *Emotionally focused therapy for couples*. New York: Guilford.

Greenberg, L. S., Rice, L. N., & Elliott, R. (1993). *Facilitating emotional change: The moment-by-moment process*. New York: Guilford.

Hunter, J. E., & Schmidt, F. L. (1990). *Methods of meta-analysis*. Newbury Park, CA: Sage.

Johnson, S. M., & Greenberg, L. S. (1985). The differential effects of experiential and problem-solving interventions in resolving marital conflict. *Journal of Consulting and Clinical Psychology, 53*, 313–317.

Lambert, M. J. (Ed.). (2004). *Bergin & Garfield's handbook of psychotherapy and behavior change* (5th ed.). New York: Wiley.

Lerner, M. S., & Clum, G. A. (1990). Treatment of suicide ideators: A problem-solving approach. *Behavior Therapy, 21*, 403–411.

Luborsky, L., Diguer, L., Seligman, D. A., Rosenthal, R., Krause, E. D., Johnson, S., et al. (1999). The researcher's own therapy allegiances: A 'wild card' in comparisons of treatment efficacy. *Clinical Psychology: Science and Practice, 6*, 95–106.

Rogers, C. R. (1951). *Client-centered therapy*. Boston: Houghton Mifflin.

Rogers, J. L., Howard, K. I., & Vessey, J. T. (1993). Using significance tests to evaluate equivalence between two experimental groups. *Psychological Bulletin, 113*, 553–565.

Smith, M. L., Glass, G. V., & Miller, T. I. (1980). *The benefits of psychotherapy*. Baltimore, MD: The Johns Hopkins University Press.

Stiles, W. B., Barkham, M., Mellor-Clark, J., & Connell, J. (2008). Effectiveness of cognitive-behavioural, person-centred, and psychodynamic therapies as practised in UK primary care routine practice: Replication in a larger sample. *Psychological Medicine, 38*, 677–688.

Stiles, W. B., Barkham, M., Twigg, E., Mellor-Clark, J., & Cooper, M. (2006). Effectiveness of cognitive-behavioural, person-centred and psychodynamic therapies as practised in UK National Health Service settings. *Psychological Medicine, 36*, 555–566.

Table 1. *Summary of Meta-analyses Reviewed*

Meta-analysis	Number of Studies	Pre–post Effect Size				Controlled Effect Size				Comparative Effect Size			
		N^a	Clients	Mean	SD	N^b	Clients	Mean	SD	N^b	Clients	Mean	SD
Smith, Glass, & Miller (1980)	-	-	-	-	-	150	-	.62	.87	-	-	-	-
Greenberg, Elliott & Lietaer (1994)	35	36	1,239	1.20	.75	15	695	1.24	.82	26	646	.04	.74
Elliott (1996)	63	66	2,066	1.21	.7	28	1,519	1.04	.74	38	823	.04	.6
Elliott (2001)[c]	86	99	5,030	.80	.45	36	1,096	.72	.53	48	993	.00	.44
Elliott, Greenberg & Lietaer (2004)[c]	112	127	6,569	.86	.42	42	1,149	.78	.57	74	1,375	.01	.44
Elliott & Freire (2008)[c]	186	203	14,235	1.01	.50	63	2,144	.78	.44	135	6,097	.00	.26

a Number of research samples/ therapy conditions
b N = Number of comparisons
c Mean ESs for these analyses weighted by sample size

EFFECTIVENESS OF PERSON-CENTERED AND EXPERIENTIAL PSYCHOTHERAPIES WITH CHILDREN AND YOUNG PEOPLE

A REVIEW OF OUTCOME STUDIES

DAGMAR HÖLLDAMPF, MICHAEL BEHR, & INA CRAWFORD

RATIONALE FOR PSYCHOTHERAPY WITH CHILDREN AND YOUNG PEOPLE

About five percent of all children are estimated to have chronic mental health problems. Another five percent are in need of psychotherapy because they suffer from psychological disorders (Lopez, 1996). Mental health issues with children and young people have received attention within the last decade and have led to the assumption that changes within governmental health departments are needed. As in the British Department of Health, which supports the use of interventions that focus on children and work with families (Wilson & Ryan, 2005), the US President's New Freedom Commission on Mental Health (2003) recommends the promotion of screening, assessing and providing services for young people's mental health. Also, the annual report of the Professional Association of Psychologists (bdp) in Germany, regarding families in Germany, points out that families and children need more professional support (Schneewind, 2009).

From a humanistic point of view, a child's need for psychotherapy can be understood in terms of the experiencing of incongruence – a dissonance between the child's developing self-concept and their organismic experiences. Reasons for this incongruence may be manifold: They could be rooted in physical or mental disabilities, or have their source in social and economic disadvantages. However, most often, dysfunctional families and difficult relationships among family members are the core of difficulties (Bratton, 1993; Costas, 1998; Harris, 1995; Lobaugh, 1991; Smith, 2000; Walker, 2002). Compensation for the resulting tensions may lead to dysfunctional behavior such as aggression and withdrawal, as well as speech or learning disabilities (Bratton, 1993; Kale, 1997; Yuen, 1997).

Behr, Hölldampf and Hüsson (2009b) describe the person-centered understanding of emerging disorders in children as follows: 'It might happen that parents will value only the sweet, adorable, playful character of a child. Over time this child will experience itself likewise as being sweet and adorable. However, not all of the child's organismic experiences will be sweet and adorable. As a result the child will experience incongruence, tension, dissatisfaction, inconsistencies, and unexplainable behavioral impulses' (p. 15).

PLAY IN PSYCHOTHERAPY

> Play therapy is based upon the fact that play is the child's natural medium of self-expression. It is an opportunity for the child to 'act out' his feelings and problems just as, in certain types of adult Psychotherapy, an individual 'acts out' his difficulties. (Axline, 1993, p. 9)

Especially for younger children the medium of 'language' is not sufficiently developed in order to symbolize experiences. A more natural and child-like manner of communication is playing. Axline (1993) describes play as the language of children, as children's means of enacting emotional issues. Axline views play as a child's natural manner of self-representation. As Bratton, Ray, Edwards, & Landreth (2009) state 'Through play therapy, the therapist is allowed the opportunity to enter into the child's experience as it is played out' (Bratton et al., 2009, p. 268). From Weinberger's point of view (2001) play is a fundamental factor in the development of social roles and therefore the core of building a child's unique identity. 'In play a child will express his unique experiences symbolically' (Goetze, 2002, p. 14). Goetze points out that this function of symbolization which is fundamental to play is used in play therapy to work through experiences the child has had, helping the child to find ways to symbolize, thus developing deeper understanding, promoting and/or expanding congruence. Child psychotherapy that relies solely on verbal interaction between child and therapist does not appropriately address the developmental needs of young children, who communicate their thoughts and feelings most effectively by playing them out.

Person-centered play therapy is based on the central humanistic hypothesis regarding personality structure, assuming that the individual has the potential to grow and develop himself (e.g. Dorfman, 2005). Axline (1947) posits the existence of an inert drive to mature, to expand one's range of experiences, and to grow. Through play a child symbolizes his or her experiences, establishing meanings in a more profound way, thus gaining maturity. Without this core function of symbolization inherent to playful activities of children, the child's development would not be possible. This is supported by Woltmann (1964) who asserts that play is both regressive, in which experiences are repeated and played out again, and progressive, displaying a tendency toward growth, in which a number of different outcomes to various situations/experiences are tested – thus a variety of alternating behaviors are learned.

Describing the use of play in therapy for children it also needs to be said that play is not therapeutic in itself, but the relationship that develops in a play therapy session based on faith, acceptance, and trust is therapeutic. Play on its own cannot substitute for a good therapeutic relationship, but it is a medium or therapeutic tool through which a good therapeutic relationship can be established, just as talking and self-disclosing is for adults.

HISTORY AND DEVELOPMENT OF PCE PSYCHOTHERAPIES FOR CHILDREN AND YOUNG PEOPLE

Based on Rogers' humanistic nondirective approach (1942, 1951) Virginia Axline (1947) developed a set of eight fundamental principles for child psychotherapy, which are still represented at the core of any nondirective play therapy approach today. Landreth (1991) revised and extended those eight principles as follows:

1. The therapist is genuinely interested in the child and develops a warm, caring relationship with the child, in which good rapport is established as soon as possible.

2. The therapist experiences unqualified acceptance of the child and does not wish the child were different in some way, accepts the child exactly as he/she is.

3. The therapist creates a feeling of safety and permissiveness in the relationship so the child feels free to explore and express him/herself completely.

4. The therapist is always sensitive to the child's feelings and gently reflects those feelings in such a manner that the child develops self-awareness.

5. The therapist believes deeply in the child's capacity to act responsibly, unwaveringly respects the child's ability to solve personal problems, and allows the child to do so. The responsibility to make choices and to institute change is the child's.

6. The therapist trusts the child's inner direction, allows the child to lead in all areas of the relationship, and resists any urge to direct the child's play or conversation. The child leads the way; the therapist follows.

7. The therapist appreciates the gradual nature of the therapeutic process and does not attempt to hurry therapy along.

8. The therapist establishes only those therapeutic limits that help the child accept personal and appropriate relationship responsibility.

In nondirective therapy there is no need for interpretations. The child is able to act freely throughout the therapeutic relationship which is completely nondirective yet empathic and built on unconditional positive regard without any distraction or disturbance. While interpretations are still used in psychoanalytic play therapy, all other play therapeutic approaches are based on Axline's (1947) work. They use play and an in-depth relationship experience to clarify self-experience and help the child become more congruent. In some other play therapy approaches more directive interventions are provided to guide children's play, nevertheless children's play experiences and the therapeutic relationship are seen as the main healing factors. Other approaches corresponding to person-centered play therapy are: *Release Play Therapy* (Levy, 1938), *Structured Play Therapy* (Hambidge, 1955), *Adlerian Play Therapy* (Adler, 1930; Dreikurs, 1966; Ackerknecht, 1982) and *Theraplay* (Des Lauriers, 1962; Jernberg, 1979).

In the United States, classical person-centered child and adolescent psychotherapy was further developed through the work of authors such as Norton and Norton (2002), Bernard and Louise Guerney (L. Guerney, 2001) and especially through the work of Garry Landreth (1982, 1991, 2002), who described specific nondirective therapeutic interventions for different issues, dynamics of the process, and special populations in detail. Bernard and Louise Guerney developed the so-called *Filial Therapy*, (B. G. Guerney, 1964, 1976; Guerney & Guerney, 1985) which is an empirically supported treatment (Bratton, Ray, Rhine, & Jones, 2005; Cornelius-White & Motschnig-Pitrik, Chapter 3, this volume). In this approach, parents are trained to play therapeutically using person-centered practices, while at the same time group supervision for the parents is provided. The work of Janet West (1996), and Kate Wilson and Virginia Ryan (2005) in Great Britain should also be mentioned.

In German-speaking countries the development of play therapy was slow after the war. Hans Zulliger (1952), a psychoanalyst and pedagogue from Switzerland, developed an approach similar to the person-centered approach in his work with children. Like Axline (1947) he did not provide interpretations for the child. The therapist only provided meanings for him or herself to gain an understanding of the play process. According to Zulliger the child is healed through the play process, which can be optimized by structuring interventions of the therapist. Classical person-centered child psychotherapy was spread through the work of Reinhard and Anne-Marie Tausch (1956) and the translation of Axline's publication in 1972. Stefan Schmidtchen (1973), Herbert Goetze and Wolfgang Jaede (1974) developed the approach further. In particular Schmidtchen's (1976, 1989, 1996, 2001) work focused on process evaluation.

Further developments following Schmidtchen's work based on the classic person-centered relationship and developmental theories were broadened with *experiential methods*, such as fairy tales, stories and creative media, to reach a deeper emotional experience (Behr, Hölldampf, & Hüsson, 2009a; Goetze, 1981, 2002; Weinberger, 2001). Behr (2003, 2009b) expanded the approach with the concept of *interactive resonance*; he states that a child's self-concept is the unique result of interpersonal experiences, similar to Stern's concept of the self being the actual set of interpersonal experiences (1986). Through interactive resonance and playing together with the child the therapist provides opportunities to experience a relationship with an authentic, self-disclosing genuine and present person. This interactive behavior of the therapist in the here and now is based on attachment theory (Bowlby, 1951), infant research (Stern, 1986) and the schema concept of Barlett (1932) and Piaget (1976) (Behr, 2009a). Other authors such as Goetze (2002), Weinberger (2001), Landreth (2001) focused on disorder specific person-centered treatments. Weinberg (2005) and Hüsson (2008, 2009) developed treatments for traumatized children based on person-centered psychotherapy.

As this article includes PCE studies conducted in school settings and as their core foundation is seen in talking therapies, we would like to give a brief history of the development of counseling services in schools. Worldwide, the various developments in this particular area display a wide range in differences and even at present considerable variation can be seen. Generally however, the roots of counseling in schools are seen in the ideology inherent of pastoral care in schools, dating back in Britain to the late eighteenth and early nineteenth century (King, 1999). The first school psychologist in Germany was Hans Lämmerstein, founder of the first psychological school counselling center in 1922. Since psychology at that time was generally linked to Sigmund Freud, and as Freud was Jewish, the school counseling center was closed again in 1933, after the takeover by the National Socialists. Up until the beginning of the 1950s psychologists were not working in any area linked to schools (Keller, 1997). Between the 1950s and the 1960s the concept of counseling in schools was introduced in Britain following practices in the United States (Baginsky, 2004). In Germany more and more school counseling services have been instituted since that time but their number and tasks, e.g., diagnosis or assessment and school career counseling or psychosocial counseling vary across regions.

Objectives of person-centered psychotherapy with children and young people
Since person-centered psychotherapy focuses on the client as a person rather than the child's problem, the emphasis is on facilitating the child's efforts to become more adequate, as a person, in coping with current and future problems that may impact the child's life. Thus, the objectives of person-centered psychotherapy for children are to help the child: (1) develop a more positive self-concept; (2) assume greater self-responsibility; (3) become more self-directing; (4) become more self-accepting; (5) become more self-reliant; (6) engage in self-determined decision making; (7) experience

a feeling of control; (8) become sensitive to the process of coping; (9) develop an internal source of evaluation; (10) become more trusting of self (Landreth, 1991).

Psychotherapeutic treatment for adolescents is seen often as more difficult than treating children or adults. In order to reach children therapeutically, play therapy was developed; to treat adults, therapy is usually based on talking. However for adolescents neither play nor verbal communication seems to be an adequate instrument to achieve therapeutic contact. Only recently, in the twentieth century, have modern societies started to understand adolescence as the time when a young person is trying to figure out who he is, trying to take on a role, no more that of a child and not yet the role of an adult, a difficult and stressful time which provides a lot of developmental tasks and opportunities. For the treatment of adolescents special methods were used and implemented. Zulliger, for example, used to go for walks with adolescents, while others used group work to provide a different setting.

RESEARCH ON EFFECTIVENESS OF CHILD AND ADOLESCENT PSYCHOTHERAPY

Hölldampf and Behr (2009) reviewed several meta-analyses on child and adolescent psychotherapy. They evaluated three meta-analyses as particularly clarifying for the person-centered approach:

Bratton, Ray, Rhine, and Jones (2005) published the most recent meta-analysis which predominantly covers play and filial therapy. The authors studied the effectiveness of play therapy analyzing 93 controlled outcome studies covering the years 1953–2000, with a total of 3,248 participants consisting of boys and girls with an average age of seven years who displayed various mental and behavioral problems. Of these 93 outcome studies, only 72 studies analyzed the effectiveness of the person-centered approach. The authors calculated an overall effect size of 0.80, implying that children treated with play therapy improved more than three-quarters of a standard deviation on average. On analyzing the results, the authors concluded that they were able to generate equally large effect sizes with a variety of disorders. Moreover, when classified in different treatment categories, they continued to calculate large effect sizes. Differences in effect size were seen only in different settings with inpatient settings outperforming outpatient settings. Nevertheless this difference was not significant. Another difference appeared when treatment providers were compared. Para-professionals such as trained parents, teachers, or peers seemed to be more effective than professional therapists, reaching significantly higher effect sizes. With respect to treatment format, the group interventions proved to be therapeutically more effective compared to individual psychotherapy (Bratton, Ray, Edwards, & Landreth, 2009).

LeBlanc and Ritchie (2001) published the first meta-analysis solely concerned with the effectiveness of different approaches using play as medium for therapy with children. The aim of their meta-analysis was to study the general effectiveness of play therapy, as well as to identify variables responsible for the degree of effectiveness. Studies from English-speaking countries were included; the age of test subjects ranged from one to twelve years. Among the inclusion criteria was an experimental design with an untreated control group, as well as statistics that allowed the calculation of effect sizes.

The meta-analysis of Beelmann and Schneider (2003) provided an inventory of research in the German language of controlled psychotherapy outcome studies on children and adolescents, consisting of 47 compared treatment groups, out of 37 research projects up to 2000. In studies of German-speaking countries clear evidence for the effectiveness of behavioral and person-centered treatments was found. A strength of this study is that the researchers were not themselves therapists and consequently had no allegiance to any therapeutic paradigm.

Five further major meta-analyses about child and adolescent psychotherapy have been conducted which basically confirm these findings. Table 1 provides a short overview; for further details see Behr and Cornelius-White (2008).

Based on related meta-analyses, it is hypothesized that the current review which is the base for a meta-analysis will yield positive effect sizes that support the overall effectiveness of person-centered and experiential (PCE) psychotherapies for children and adolescents.

METHOD

Objectives

This review was conducted to determine the effectiveness of PCE psychotherapies and counseling for children and adolescents with emotional distress. Nomenclature for this psychotherapy approach has changed over the decades and varies by region. Thus PCE psychotherapies with children and young people include nondirective therapy, client-centered (play) therapy, person-centered psychotherapy, emotion-focused therapy, experiential psychotherapy, child-centered therapy, and client- or person-centered school counseling. For those settings that included parents based on the approach client- or person-centered family therapy, filial therapy and parent–child relationship therapy are the terms used. Another chapter in this book will report on the latter two therapies.

Table 1. *Overview on 8 Major Meta-analyses on Child and Adolescent Psychotherapy*

	Casey & Berman (1985)	Weisz et al. (1987)	Kazdin et al. (1990)	Weisz et al. (1995)	Ray et al. (2001)	LeBlanc & Ritchie (2001)	Beelmann & Schneider (2003)	Bratton et al. (2005)
Psychodynamic Approaches								
Effect size	.21	.01	no info	.31	no info	no info	-	no info
No. of studies	5	3	5	9			0	
Person-Centered Approaches								
Effect size	.49	.56	no info	.15	.93	no info	.55	.92
No. of studies	12	20	10	2	55		5	73
Behavioral Approaches								
Effect size	.91	.88	no info	.76	.73	no info	.55	.71
No. of studies	37	126		197	12		33	12

Criteria for considering studies for this review

Types of studies

Published and unpublished randomized controlled trials, quasi-experimental trials and single group studies with at least a pre- and post-test design were included. We deliberately did not limit our review to the usual criteria of randomized control studies as advised by Division 12 of the American Psychological Association (Chambless et al., 1998; Chambless & Hollon, 1998; Chambless & Ollendick, 2001) and later by the German Scientific Council of Psychotherapy (Wissenschaftlicher Beirat Psychotherapie, 2004) as 'gold standard' or state of the art for scientific research, as the external validity of randomized control studies is questionable. In addition, a great number of high quality quasi-experimental studies including a notable number of PCE psychotherapies studies on the work with children and adolescents would not be reflected nor merited. Randomized controlled trials (RCTs, which are also called efficacy studies) explore psychotherapeutic effects achieved under experimental controlled conditions, with a randomized assignment of patients to the various treatments. While the internal validity is high, the external validity (application to everyday situations) is rather questionable. Researchers who criticize a preference for RCT studies include Leichsenring and Rüger, (2004), Revenstorf (2005), Seligman (1995), and Sexton, Leblov, Johnson and Gurman (2005). They claim that it is important to include different sorts of methodologically well-constructed effectiveness studies.

Types of participants
Children and adolescents who are enrolled in kindergarten through 12th grade (or the international equivalents) at public, private, parochial or alternative schools and who are between the ages of 3 and 18 years, were included. Persons identified as attending 'preschool' or 'college' were also included, as long as they met the age criteria.

Types of interventions
Types of interventions included in the review were person-centered and experiential interventions that were provided for children and adolescents in residential or outpatient settings. Rather than exploring isolated symptoms, PCE psychotherapies are based on a comprehensive and multi-dimensional exploration of the whole person and subordinate the role of symptoms in an individual functioning as an organism. The therapeutic relationship and the interaction between therapist and client allow and foster active reflection on existing patterns in the client's life, and exploration of experiential processes. The client explores, analyzes, and reflects on his or her existence, to ultimately reach a creative, co-constructed reappraisal of his or her life situation and to rework or revise problematic ways of being (Lietaer, 2002).

Types of outcome measures
Standardized measures of symptom reduction, coping behavior and other objectives of PCE psychotherapies and unstandardized measures with adequate face validity were considered to be acceptable forms to evaluate the effectiveness of the treatments. At least one quantitative measure needed to be reported in each study. Therefore both self-evaluation and external evaluation were considered as an acceptable outcome measure.

Search strategy for identification of studies

A multimodal search strategy was applied in order to maximize chances of capturing all relevant literature. Electronic databases were searched for published and unpublished studies. To avoid language bias no language restrictions were imposed on any results from any search attempts, although most databases were searched in English. Electronic searches were conducted in bibliographic databases, government policy databanks and Internet search engines including: Psychology: PsycINFO, Psyndex, PubMed (MEDLINE), A SAGE Full-Text Collection; Education: ERIC, British Education Index, Australian Education Index; Multidisciplinary: Academic Search Premier, ProQuest Dissertations and Theses, Social Sciences Index, Web of Science; Google and Yahoo. No filters based on methodology were applied because test searches indicated that such filters might eliminate relevant studies. As search terms the following key words were used: 'humanistic therapy, nondirective therapy, person-centered therapy, Rogerian therapy, play therapy, filial therapy, experiential therapy, effectiveness, efficacy, child therapy, adolescent therapy, counseling, counselling, intervention, gestalt therapy, outcome, emotion-focused therapy, focussed expressive, encounter, pre-therapy, emotive therapy, focussing, attention therapy, supportive therapy, Gesprächstherapie, client-centered, client-centred, evaluation'. Additionally, informal networks were used and experts in the field were contacted to reveal ongoing and unpublished studies. Relevant websites, journals, congress contributions and reference lists from previous reviews, as well as all included and excluded studies, were searched to identify relevant studies.

A total of 910 studies were identified. Studies mentioned more than once were singled out and after analyzing abstracts and titles for relevance 267 unique studies were identified. Finally two reviewers independently read the full study reports for inclusion. This left 94 research projects eligible for the review. Only the studies that met the above-mentioned criteria were included as part of the meta-analysis conducted by Hölldampf and Behr and only those are summarized in this article.

DESCRIPTION OF STUDIES

Person-centered and experiential psychotherapies and their range of application

PCE psychotherapies aim to alleviate the inconsistency of organismic experience and self-concept. This conceptualization may be seen to be the root of most disorders listed in the *ICD-10* and *DSM-IV* manuals and can be understood under this paradigm (Rogers, 1959). PCE psychotherapies should be effective for a wide range of disorders in childhood and adolescence. Axline (1947) points out that children who are referred to play therapy are usually labeled as 'problem children', children that attract their environment's attention with maladjusted behavior or even aggressiveness. Goetze (2002), who also claims a vast area of application for play therapy, reports positive treatment outcomes with cardinal disorders as well as with certain forms of speech, hearing, or mental disorders. In his first publication, *The Clinical Treatment of the Problem Child*, Rogers (1939) stated:

> There are children – boys and girls – with very different backgrounds and personalities, and some of these children steal, and some of them run away from schools, and others find satisfaction in sucking their thumbs, or in saying obscene words or in defying their parents; but in each instance it is the child with whom we must deal, not the generalization which we can make about his behaviour. (Rogers, 1939, p. 3)

At this point of the chapter the authors want to point out very clearly that we totally agree with Rogers' view of the child as a whole person. And in our clinical practice we refuse to reduce a client to symptoms, even though it is a requirement given the political climate, to examine the evidence of PCE therapies for ICD and DSM categories.

Thus the following section will present outcome studies, retrieved through systematic search on the effectiveness of PCE psychotherapies for children and young people, which are classified, according to ICD-10 diagnosis (WHO, 2004) and DSM-IV diagnosis (APA, 2000) and different application areas.

Mood [affective] disorders (F30–39 / 296.xx)
Four studies evaluating the effectiveness and efficacy of PCE psychotherapies on children with mood disorders were identified (Birmaher et al., 2000; Brent et al., 1997; Diamond, Reis, Diamond, Siqueland & Isaacs, 2002; Stice, Burton, Bearman, & Rohde, 2007). The studies conducted by Diamond and Stice evaluated the efficacy of applying randomized controlled trials while Brent and Birmaher used a quasi-experimental design. Key findings of the last-mentioned studies were that no significant difference between cognitive behavioral therapy (CBT), systemic behavior family therapy (SBFT), and individual nondirective supportive therapy (NST) was found, similar to the findings of Stice. Diamond et al. (2002) successfully proved the effectiveness of attachment-based family therapy which may be considered under the umbrella of emotion-focused therapy, an experiential treatment.

Neurotic, stress-related and somatoform disorders (F40–48 / 300.xx; 307.xx; 309.xx)
• Anxiety
Four individual studies explored treatments to reduce anxiety. Two of the studies were quasi-experimental (Andrews, 1971; Schmidtchen & Hobrücker, 1978), while

one was of a RTC design (Rae, Worchel, Upchurch, Sanner & Daniel, 1989) and one not-yet published single group study (Fröhlich-Gildhoff & Rönnau-Böse, 2010). Andrews (1971) compared the effectiveness of a behavioral group treatment to client-centered counseling and found significant anxiety reduction occurred in the behavioral group only, whereas Rae and colleagues (1989) concluded that hospitalized children receiving nondirective child-centered play therapy sessions showed a significant reduction in hospital fears when compared to a verbally oriented support condition, a diversionary play condition or a control group. Schmidtchen and Hobrücker (1978) found that children displayed a significant decrease in anxiety after client-centered play therapy when compared to two untreated control groups. Fröhlich-Gildhoff and Rönnau-Böse (2010) found a significant decrease on anxiety symptoms measured with four different standardized anxiety symptom measures. Thus three out of three studies found PCE treatments to be effective.

• Post-traumatic Stress Disorder (F43.1 / 309.81)

We found six studies dealing with post-traumatic stress disorder (PTSD). Of these, three followed the RCT design (Cohen & Mannarino, 1996; Cohen, Mannarino, & Knudsen, 2005; Deblinger, Mannarino, Cohen & Steer, 2006). Comparing cognitive-behavioral intervention (CBT) and nondirective supportive treatment (NST), the authors of these studies concluded that sexually abused children and their parents showed significantly better outcomes for the CBT-treatment group on symptom reduction. These studies used a nondirective supportive treatment as a control condition, typically a non-bona fide version of PCE therapies, commonly used by CBT researchers, especially in the USA. One study (Shen, 2002) was a randomized controlled trial investigating the effectiveness of short-term child-centered group play therapy in an elementary school setting. Children in the experimental group scored significantly lower on anxiety level and suicide risk after play therapy than did children in the control group, thus supporting person-centered experiential treatment with PTSD. This effect was also supported by studies comparing effects of individual and group settings employing PCE approaches (Perez, 1987; Scott, Burlingame, Starling, Porter & Lilly, 2003; Zion, 1999). Statistical analysis revealed mixed results. Perez concluded that client-centered play therapy benefited children regardless of age, gender, type of abuse, or current living arrangements. Plus, there were no significant differences in treatment effects between individual and group play therapy. However Scott et al.'s (2003) and Zion's (1999) overall findings indicate mixed support for the efficacy of play therapy.

• Adjustment Disorders (F43.2) / 309.xx

Another group of six studies dealt with adjustment disorders (Baggerly, 2004; Barrett, 1975; Brandt, 1999; Kot, 1995; McGuire, 2000; Tyndall-Lind, 1999). While Brandt (1999) demonstrated the effectiveness of client-centered play therapy as a viable intervention for adjustment disorders in a randomized controlled trial, Barrett (1975) and Kot (1995) reached mixed results in two quasi-experimental studies investigating the effects of person-centered play therapy, finding a significant difference for social adjustment yet no significant change in personal adjustment.

Tyndall-Lind (1999) and Baggerly (2004) each conducted a single group outcome study with children receiving child-centered group play therapy. Pre–post measures showed a significant improvement in self-esteem, anxiety, and depression. This is backed by a study performed by McGuire (2000) finding positive trends in the children's behavior, self-control, and self-concept after play therapy treatment.

Behavioural syndromes associated with physiological disturbances and physical factors (F50–59 / 307.51)

For this type of disorder we found only one study: Johnson, Maddeaux, and Blouin (1998) investigated the efficacy of an emotion-focused family therapy intervention for bulimic adolescents referred to an outpatient hospital clinic, using a randomized controlled trial. The results showed that emotion-focused family therapy significantly reduced bulimic symptoms, including the frequency and severity of purging or vomiting and reduced the drive for thinness.

Mental retardation[1] (F70–79 / 317–319)

Seven treatment evaluations were performed in the field of mental retardation. Only one used an RCT design (Morrison & Newcomer, 1975) comparing directive and nondirective play therapy to a control group. Mentally challenged children in both treatment groups improved in fine motor skills compared to a control group, but no evidence was found showing that one of the treatment groups was more effective than the other. Four studies (Calabro, 2003; Mehlmann, 1953; Mundy, 1957; Sokoloff, 1959) used a quasi-experimental setting. While Calabro (2003) compared the effectiveness of person-centered child therapy and rational-emotive play therapy for disabled preschool children and did not find any significant differences between the two approaches, Mundy (1957) assessing the impact of nondirective play therapy on levels of IQ and social adjustment of children who were mentally challenged, found relevant differences between treatment and control groups, indicating improvement after treatment. This was confirmed by Sokoloff's (1959) findings showing that the play therapy group improved significantly in the areas of attention, concentration, responsiveness to therapeutic techniques, social confidence, self-confidence, and appropriate expressions of nonverbal and verbal hostility. Furthermore

---

1. Although the term 'mental retardation' is used in diagnostic manuals, e.g., *ICD-10* and *DSM-IV*, in several countries it is an extremely pejorative and stigmatising term. Other, more acceptable terms are 'learning disability' (UK), 'developmental disability' or 'intellectual disability' (Australia). To avoid use of several terms, the authors use the, albeit problematic, current diagnostic term in the text.

a significant improvement on social maturity, communicative abilities and personality ratings occurred in the play therapy group. In an earlier study, Mehlman (1953) also examining the effectiveness of client-centered group play therapy for mentally retarded children by means of a quasi-experimental design, was likewise able to demonstrate positive behavioral and personality changes.

In two single-group studies, one by Axline (1949) and one by Leland, Walker and Taboada (1959), the researchers concluded that children receiving play therapy improved. Axline (1949) demonstrated higher IQ scores and concluded that the child being free from emotional constraint after therapy and was able to express capacities in a better way. Leland, Walker and Taboada (1959) confirmed that mildly retarded boys with behavioral problems participating in person-centered group play therapy displayed a significant improvement in speech. Thus, for this group of disorders, positive outcome was found for behavioral, emotional and cognitive abilities.

Disorders of psychological development (F80–89 / 299.xx)
In four randomized-controlled studies the effect of person-centered interventions was tested on disorders of psychological development all with positive results. DeGangi, Wietlisbach, Goodin and Scheiner (1993) compared the benefits of a child-centered therapy approach emphasizing child-initiated play interactions within a structured therapy environment to those of a therapist-directed, structured sensomotoric therapy approach. No differences between the two therapies were found regarding gains in play, attention, behavior, temperament, attentional abilities, or family stress, but the child-centered therapy did promote fine motor skills better. Even stronger support is provided by a study by Danger (2003) who found that child-centered group play therapy was an effective intervention for children with speech difficulties, improving expressive and receptive language skill development.

Packmann (2002) evaluated the effectiveness of group activity therapy as a school-based intervention with fourth and fifth graders with learning disabilities and behavior problems. Significant decreases in total behavior problems and internalizing problems were noted, as well as a decreasing trend for externalizing behavior. Jenny & Schär (2010) compared four intervention groups of participants diagnosed with Asperger's syndrome (F84.5) or atypical (high functioning) autism (F84.1) with a waitlist control group and confirmed that the person-centered intervention yielded significant increases in social competencies and social reactivity, and significant decreases in autistic symptoms.

Behavioral and emotional disorders with onset usually occurring in childhood and adolescence (F90–98 / 307.3–313.9)
Behavioral and emotional disorders were evaluated in twelve studies, seven of them in a randomized controlled trial (Dodge, 2003; Dogra & Veeraraghavan, 1994; Gaulden, 1975; House, 1970; Kaczmarek, 1983; Shashi, Kapur & Subbakrishna,

1999; Truax, Wargo, & Silber, 1966). Over a period of more than 40 years of evaluation the person-centered experiential approach has continuously displayed positive results.

In an early randomized controlled trial, Truax et al. (1966) studied the effects of group psychotherapy with high accurate empathy and nonpossessive warmth on female institutionalized delinquents. The obtained results indicated a significant improvement in the treated subjects, as compared with a control group. Just a few years later, House (1970) found that child-centered group play therapy had positive effects on self-concept of socially maladjusted children. Gaulden (1975) was able to confirm these positive effects in his study, comparing the effectiveness of two treatments, developmental play group and play group counselling (nondirective group play therapy) to a non-intervention control group. Children in the play therapy group scored significantly higher in reduction of classroom disturbance, maintaining these positive effects in a follow-up evaluation. In 1983 Kaczmarek found that individual play therapy produced positive results when a child needed to release anger and negative emotions.

These positive effects were consolidated in an RCT study in 1994, when Dogra and Veeraraghavan, comparing a psychological intervention including play therapy and parental counseling to a no-treatment control group, found that psychological intervention proved to be successful in bringing about changes in children suffering from an aggressive conduct disorder as compared to the control group. Shashi et al. (1999) evaluated the effects of client-centered play therapy on emotionally disturbed children. Again, quantitative analysis revealed statistically significant reduction of symptoms between pre- and post-therapy assessments in the study group but not in the control group. A qualitative analysis revealed consistent changes in the identified parameters.

Dodge (2003), evaluating two therapeutic approaches to oppositional defiant disorder (ODD) and a control group, did not show the person-centered approach to be superior to an integrated approach relying on mostly cognitive techniques. He did nevertheless demonstrate that the convergent approach outperformed the control group.

Four quasi-experimental designed studies (Döpfner, Schlüter, & Rey, 1981; Hume, 1967; Schumann, 2004; Seeman, Barry, & Ellinwood, 1964) described the benefits of PCE psychotherapies. Seeman, Barry and Ellinwood (1964) found that aggressive and withdrawn pupils participating in nondirective play therapy showed significant improvement on symptoms. These findings were backed by Hume (1967), who found that play therapy participants showed considerable improvement concerning their behavior in school, at home and in play therapy by the end of the school year and at a follow-up.

A somewhat different result was established in an evaluation of a social skills training program for unassertive or insecure children performed by Döpfner et al. (1981). The authors compared the effects of a group social skills training program to a no-treatment design and a competing treatment design, consisting of client-centered play therapy. Treatments were tested for reducing social anxiety, improving self-concept, frequency and ability of social interaction, and overall maladjustment. For all variables, except for social anxiety, the social skills training proved to be more effective than play therapy.

Last in the series of quasi-experimental studies, Schumann (2004) performed a study in order to determine the effectiveness of child-centered play therapy and curriculum-based small-group guidance on the behaviors of aggressive children in an elementary school as determined by reduction of aggressive and problem behavior of aggressive children. The data of this study tentatively support the effectiveness of both modalities in decreasing the aggressive and problem behaviors of aggressive children. However, parents and teachers experienced a more noticeable reduction of children's aggressive behavior in school-based child-centered play therapy settings.

Only one study followed the single group design. Jenny (Jenny, Goetschel, & Käppler, 2006; Jenny & Käppler, 2009) researched the effectiveness of person-centered group therapy for children with a lack of social competencies at the University of Zürich. Results of this study indicate the benefits of the group intervention. High effect sizes demonstrate a significant decline in anxiety-based and aggressive symptoms. Moreover, parents and teachers reported an increase in social competence and self-confidence.

Attention Deficit Hyperactivity Disorder (ADHD) (F90.1/314.xx)
Two studies investigated the person-centered experiential treatment of children diagnosed with ADHD, both performed by the same author. In a randomized controlled study, Ray (2007) compared three interventions, child-centered play therapy only, teacher consultation only, and the two combined for their effects on reducing teacher–child relationship stress as affected by student characteristics and ADHD behavior. All treatment groups were found to have statistically significant reduction in teacher and student problem characteristics displaying large effects for total stress. In a single group study just a year later, Ray et al. (2007) investigated play therapy again with children exhibiting symptoms of ADHD. Two treatment conditions, child-centered play therapy (CCPT) or reading mentoring (RM) were compared. Again the results indicated that children in both treatment groups demonstrated significant improvement, however children who participated in CCPT scored higher on the student characteristics domain and on the Emotional Lability and Anxiety/Withdrawal subscales of the Index of Teaching Stress than did the children of the RM treatment group.

Different issues
An additional 37 further studies were identified in which client groups that did not fit into the ICD or DSM categories were treated, because their problems were co-morbid in nature or they were selected according to psychosocial problem categories,

Table 2. *Outcome Studies on PCE Psychotherapies by Diagnosis*

Disorder (ICD-Classification/ DSM-Classification)	Number of publications investigating effectiveness of PCE Intervention	Randomized controlled trials	Quasi-experimental research	Uncontrolled single group studies	Authors and Publication Year of Studies
mood [affective] disorders (F3/296.xx)	4	2	2	0	Brent et al., 1997; Birmaher et al., 2000; Diamond et al., 2002; Stice et al., 2007
neurotic, stress-related and somatoform disorders (F4/300.xx;307.xx;309.xx)	4	1	2	1	Andrews, 1971; Fröhlich-Gildhoff & Rönnau-Böse, i.p.; Rae et al., 1989; Schmidtchen & Hobrücker, 1978
traumatic life events (F43.0-1/309.81)	7	4	3	0	Cohen & Mannarino, 1996; Cohen, Mannarino & Knudsen, 2005; Deblinger et al., 2006; Perez, 1987; Scott et al., 2003; Shen, 2002; Zion, 1999
special live events and adjustment difficulties (F43.2;309.xx)	6	1	2	3	Baggerly, 2004; Barrett, 1975; Brandt, 1999; Kot, 1995; McGuire, 2000; Tyndall-Lind, 1999
behavioural syndromes associated with physiological disturbances and physical factors (F5/307.51)	1	1	0	0	Johnson et al., 1998

					References
mental retardation (F7/317-319)	7	1	4	2	Axline, 1949; Calabro, 2003; Leland, Walker & Taboada, 1959; Mehlmann, 1953; Morrison & Newcomer, 1975; Mundy, 1957; Sokoloff, 1959
disorders of psychological development (F8/299.xx)	4	4	0	0	Danger, 2003; DeGangi, Wietlisbach, Goodin & Scheiner, 1993; Packmann, 2002; Jenny & Schär, 2010
behavioural and emotional disorders with onset usually occurring in childhood and adolescence (F.9/307.3-313.9)	12	7	4	1	Dodge, 2003; Dogra & Veeraraghavan, 1994; Döpfner et al., 1981; Gaulden, 1975; House, 1970; Hume, 1967; Jenny et al., 2006, 2009; Kaczmarek, 1983; Schumann, 2004; Seemann, Barry & Ellinwood, 1964; Shashi, Kapur & Subbakrishna, 1999; Truax et al., 1966
ADHD (F90.1/314.xx)	2	1	0	1	Ray, 2007; Ray, 2008
multiple issues	36	12	14	10	Brandt, 1999; Cooper, 2004, 2006; Cooper & Freire, 2007; Cooper et al., 2010; Dorfmann, 1958; Dougherty, 2006; Dulsky, 1942; English & Higgins, 1971; Fall et al., 1999, 2002; Felton & Davidson, 1973; Freire et al., 2008; Freire & Hough, 2009; Garza, 2004; Groome & Isaacson, 1999; Herd, 1969; Jones, 2000; Lopez, 2000; Muro et al., 2006; Ogawa, 2006; Oualline, 1975; Post, 1999; Quayle, 1991; Ray, 2008; Schmidtchen, 1973; Schmidtchen et al. 1993, 1995; Schmidtchen & Hennies, 1996; Shen, 2002; Tausch et al., 1973; Trostle, 1988; Vlerick, 2008; Wall, 1973; Weiss et al., 1999, 2000
Totals	83	34	31	18	

e.g., survivors of child abuse, or similar. Twelve RCTs (Brandt, 1999; Cooper, Rowland, Pattison, Cromarty, & Richards, 2010; English & Higgins, 1971; Fall, Balvanz, Johnson, & Nelson, 1999; Fall, Navelski, & Welch, 2002; Jones, 2000; Lopez, 2000; Quayle, 1991; Schmidtchen, 1973; Wall, 1973; Weiss et al., 1999; Weiss et al., 2000), fourteen studies with a quasi-experimental design (Dorfman, 1958; Dougherty, 2006; Felton & Davidson, 1973; Garza, 2004; Groome & Isaacson, 1999; Herd, 1969; Oualline, 1975; Post, 1999; Schmidtchen, Acke, & Hennies, 1995; Schmidtchen, Hennies, & Acke, 1993; Schmidtchen & Hennies, 1996; Shen, 2002; Tausch, Kettner, Steinbach, & Tönnies, 1973; Trostle, 1988), and ten uncontrolled studies (Cooper, 2004; Cooper, 2006; Cooper & Freire, 2007; Freire & Hough, 2009; Dulsky, 1942; Freire et al., 2008; Muro, Ray, Schottelekorb, Smith, & Blanko et al., 2006; Ogawa, 2006; Ray, 2007; Vlerick, 2008) were found in this area. These studies provide strong support that PCE psychotherapies are not only effective in regard to specific disorders according to the ICD-10 and DSM-IV classification systems but also with client groups which normally are found in health care and similar settings.

CONCLUSION

A review of all the studies conducted to assess the effectiveness of PCE therapies with children and adolescents provides strong evidence for the effectiveness of person-centered and experiential psychotherapies (Table 2). Across disorders it is proven that PCE treatment is always better than no treatment. Support is given in all studies for all diagnoses using a PCE treatment group compared to an untreated control or waiting group. The most benefit of PCE treatment can be seen in the treatment of children with anxiety symptoms occurring as a result of adjustment problems to specific live events, traumatic stress or anxiety disorders. It is also beneficial for depressive children and adolescents or children suffering from co-morbid diagnoses.

The very strength of this body of research can be seen in both the firm link to the reality of psychotherapy in practice and in providing evidence from randomized clinical trials according to the criteria required to demonstrate effectiveness by various regulatory bodies and policy makers. A large number of the studies focus on clients' special situations and problem constellations while another large number focus on client groups diagnosed with a specific disorder. As co-morbidity may be regarded as a common phenomenon at the beginning of child or adolescent psychotherapy, in a vast number of studies the process of diagnosis and intake of data has focused chiefly on the combination of problems and complex situation of the clients. For this reason, a good part of the outcome research consistent with the focus of PCE psychotherapies enlists clients' views of their problems and their everyday life difficulties, and gives evidence about what works practically in treatment.

Many of the studies use outcome measures above and beyond psychopathological symptoms. Symptom reduction is generally included as one of the outcome indicators; yet, in addition, most studies also focus on parameters such as increasing social competency and emotional adjustment, improving the parent–child relationship, and many similar items with close reference to everyday life and experience. It is noteworthy that, for a good deal of improvement in these areas, a majority of the studies underline the special value of PCE psychotherapies. Almost all existing institutional settings of psychotherapy are covered.

The present body of research reviewed a large number of randomized controlled trials, as well as studies in naturalistic settings, both of which provided evidence of the effectiveness of PCE psychotherapies in practice. While RCTs attempt to isolate most sources of variance, at the same time it is difficult to verify operational capacities in a real-life setting.

Future investigations should feature designs including more than one treatment group, a randomized no-treatment control group if ethically possible, a view of clients' problems from their perspective as well as a diagnosis based on established categories for symptoms, including provisions for a follow-up assessment. A meta-analysis processing outcome scores on the basis on this body of research will be presented at the next stage of our research.

REFERENCES

Ackerknecht, L. K. (1982). *Individualpsychologische Kinder- und Jugendpsychotherapie.* [Adlerian child- and adolescent psychotherapy]. München: Reinhardt.

Adler, A. (1930). *The education of children.* New York: Greenberg.

American Psychiatric Association (APA). (2000). *Diagnostic and statistical manual of mental disorders – DSM-IV-TR* (4th ed., text revision). Washington, DC: Author.

Andrews, W. R. (1971). Behavioral and client-centered counseling of high school underachievers. *Journal of Counseling Psychology, 18*(2), 93–96.

Axline, V. M. (1947). *Play therapy: The inner dynamics of childhood.* Boston: Houghton Mifflin.

Axline, V. M. (1949). Mental deficiency: Symptom or disease? *Journal of Consulting Psychology, 13*(5), 313–327.

Axline, V. M. (1972). *Kinder-Spieltherapie im nichtdirektiven Verfahren* [Non-directive play therapy]. München: Reinhardt.

Axline, V. M. (1993). *Kinder-Spieltherapie im nicht-direktiven Verfahren* [Non-directive play therapy] (10th ed.). München: Reinhardt.

Barlett, F. C. (1932). *Remembering.* Cambridge: Cambridge University Press.

Baggerly, J. (2004). The effects of child-centered group play therapy on self-concept, depression and anxiety of children who are homeless. *International Journal of Play Therapy, 13*(2), 31–51.

Baginsky, W. (2004). *School counselling in England, Wales and Northern Ireland: A review.* London:

National Society for Prevention of Cruelty to Children (NSPCC).

Barrett, D. (1975). *The effects of play therapy on the social and psychological adjustment of five- to nine-year old children.* Unpublished doctoral dissertation, University of North Texas, Denton.

Beelmann, A., & Schneider, N. (2003). Wirksamkeit von Psychotherapie bei Kindern und Jugendlichen. Eine Übersicht und Meta-Analyse zum Bestand und zu Ergebnissen der deutschsprachigen Effektivitätsforschung [Effectiveness of psychotherapy with children and adolescents. A review and meta-analysis on the content and on results of the German effectiveness research]. *Zeitschrift für Klinische Psychologie und Psychotherapie, 32*(2), 129–143.

Behr, M. (2003). Interactive resonance in work with children and adolescents: A theory-based concept of interpersonal relationship through play and the use of toys. *Person-Centered and Experiential Psychotherapies, 2*, 89–103.

Behr, M. (2009a). Constructing emotions and accommodating schemas: A model of self-exploration, symbolization, and development. *Person-Centered and Experiential Psychotherapies, 8*, 44–62.

Behr, M. (2009b). Interaktionsresonanz: Antworten auf das Klientenverhalten durch Handlung und im Spiel. [Interactive resonance: Responses on client behavior through play actions]. In M. Behr, D. Hölldampf, & D. Hüsson (Eds.), *Psychotherapie mit Kindern und Jugendlichen: Personzentrierte Methoden und interaktionelle Behandlungskonzepte* [Psychotherapy with children and adolescents: Person-centered methods and interactive treatment concepts] (pp. 37–58). Göttingen: Hogrefe.

Behr, M., & Cornelius-White, J. H. D. (2008). Relationship and development: Concepts, practice and research in person-centred work with children, adolescents and parents. In M. Behr & J. Cornelius-White (Eds.), *Facilitating young people's development: International perspectives on person-centred theory and practice.* (pp. 1–24). Ross-on-Wye: PCCS Books.

Behr, M., Hölldampf, D., & Hüsson, D. (Eds.). (2009a). *Psychotherapie mit Kindern und Jugendlichen. Personzentrierte Methoden und interaktionelle Behandlungskonzepte.* [Psychotherapy with children and adolescents. Person-centered methods and interactive treatment concepts]. Göttingen: Hogrefe.

Behr, M., Hölldampf, D., & Hüsson, D. (2009b). Beziehung und Methode – Theorien und personzentriert-interaktionelle Behandlungskonzepte bei Kindern, Jugendlichen, Eltern und Familien. [Relationship and method: Theories and person-centered interactive treatment concepts with children, adolescents, parents and families] In M. Behr, D. Hölldampf, & D. Hüsson, (Eds.), *Psychotherapie mit Kindern und Jugendlichen: Personzentrierte Methoden und interaktionelle Behandlungskonzepte* [Psychotherapy with children and adolescents. Person-centered methods and interactive treatment concepts] (pp. 13–33). Göttingen: Hogrefe.

Bowlby, J. (1951). *Attachment and loss. Vol. I: Attachment.* London: Hogarth.

Brandt, M. (1999). *An investigation of the efficacy of play therapy with young children.* Unpublished doctoral Dissertation, University of North Texas, Denton.

Bratton, S. C. (1993). *Filial therapy with single parents.* Unpublished doctoral Dissertation, University of North Texas, Denton.

Bratton, S. C., Ray, D. C., Edwards, N. A., & Landreth, G. (2009). Child-centered play therapy (CCPT): Theory, research, and practice. *Person-Centered and Experiential Psychotherapies, 8*, 266–281.

Bratton, S., Ray, D. C., Rhine, T., & Jones, L. (2005). The efficacy of play therapy with children: A meta-analytic review of treatment outcomes. *Professional Psychology: Research and Practice,*

36(4), 376–390.

Brent, D. A., Holder, D., Kolko, D., Birmaher, B., Baugher, M., Roth, C., et al. (1997). A clinical psychotherapy trial for adolescent depression comparing cognitive, family, and supportive therapy. *Archives of General Psychiatry, 54*, 877–885.

Birmaher, B., Brent, D. A., Kolko, D., Baugher, M., Bridge, J., Holder, D., et al. (2000). Clinical outcome after short-term psychotherapy for adolescenys with major depressive disorders. *Archives of General Psychiatry, 57*, 29–36.

Calabro, E. (2003). *Rational emotive behavior play therapy vs. client-centered therapy.* Unpublished doctoral dissertation, St. John's University, New York.

Casey, R. J., & Berman, J. S. (1985). The outcome of psychotherapy with children. *Psychological Bulletin, 98*, 388–400.

Chambless, D. L., & Hollon, S. D. (1998). Defining empirically supported therapies. *Journal of Consulting and Clinical Psychology, 66*(1), 7–18.

Chambless, D. L., Baker, M. J., Baucom, D. H., Beutler, L. E., Calhoun, K. S., Chrits-Christoph, P. et al. (1998). Update on empirically validated therapies II. *Clinical Psychologist, 51*(1), 3–15.

Chambless, D. L., & Ollendick, T. H. (2001). Empirically supported psychological interventions: Controversies and evidence. *Annual Review of Psychology, 52*, 685–716.

Cohen, J. A., & Mannarino, A. P. (1996). A treatment outcome study for sexually abused preschool children: Initial findings. *Journal of the American Academy of Child & Adolescent Psychiatry, 35*(1), 42–50.

Cohen, J. A., Mannarino, A. P., & Knudsen, K. (2005). Treating sexually abused children: One year follow-up of randomized controlled trial. *Child Abuse and Neglect, 29*(2), 135–145.

Cooper, M. (2004). *Counselling in Schools Project: Evaluation report.* Glasgow, UK: Counselling Unit, University of Strathclyde.

Cooper, M. (2006). *Counselling in Schools Project, Phase II: Evaluation report.* Glasgow: Counselling Unit, University of Strathclyde.

Cooper, M., & Freire, E. (2007). *'Audit and evaluation', in East Renfrewshire Youth Counselling Service (ERYCS): Review of the service including Phase II evaluation.* East Renfrewshire, UK: East Renfrewshire Council.

Cooper, M., Rowland, N., McArthur, K., Pattison, S., Cromarty, K., & Richards, K. (2010). Randomised controlled trial of school-based humanistic counselling for emotional distress in young people: Feasibility study and preliminary indications of efficacy. *Child and Adolescent Psychiatry and Mental Health, 4*, 12.

Costas, M. B. (1998). *Filial therapy with non-offending parents of children who have been sexually abused.* Unpublished doctoral dissertation, University of North Texas, Denton.

Danger, S. E. (2003). *Child-centered group play therapy with children with speech difficulties.* Unpublished doctoral dissertation, University of North Texas, Denton.

Deblinger, E., Mannarino, A. P., Cohen, J. A., & Steer, R. A. (2006). A follow-up study of a multisite, randomized controlled trial for children with sexual abuse-related PTSD symptoms. *Journal of the American Academy of Child and Adolescent Psychiatry, 45*(12), 1474–1484.

DeGangi, G., Wietlisbach, S., Goodin, M., & Scheiner, N. (1993). A comparison of structured sensorimotor therapy and child-centered activity in the treatment of preschool children with sensorimotor problems. *The American Journal of Occupational Therapy, 47*, 777–786.

Des Lauriers, A. (1962). *The experience of reality in childhood schizophrenia.* New York: International University Press.

Diamond, G. S., Reis, B. F., Diamond, G. M., Siqueland, L., & Isaacs, L. (2002). Attachment-based family therapy for depressed adolescents: A treatment development study. *Journal of the American Academy of Child & Adolescent Psychiatry, 41,* 1190–1196.

Dodge, W. (2003). *A comparison between a convergent and an integrated approach to the treatment of oppositionally defiant adolescents with family therapy.* Unpublished doctoral dissertation, Saybrook Graduate School, San Francisco.

Dogra, A., & Veeraraghavan, V. (1994). A study of psychological intervention of children with aggressive conduct disorder. *Individual Journal of Clinical Psychology, 21,* 28–32.

Döpfner, M., Schlüter, S., & Rey, E. R. (1981). Evaluation eines sozialen Kompetenztrainings für selbstunsichere Kinder im Alter von 9–12 Jahren – Ein Therapievergleich [Evaluation of a social competence training program for insecure children in the age of 9–12 years: A comparison of therapies]. *Zeitschrift für Kinder-Jugendpsychiatrie, 9,* 233–252.

Dorfman, E. (1958). Personality outcomes of client-centered child therapy. *Psychological Monographs: General and Applied, 72*(3), Whole No. 456.

Dorfman, E. (2005). Spieltherapie. In C. R. Rogers (Ed.), *Die klientzentrierte Gesprächspsychotherapie* [Client-centered therapy], (pp. 219–254). Frankfurt: Fischer.

Dougherty J. L. (2006). *Impact of child-centered play therapy on children of different developmental stages.* Unpublished doctoral dissertation, University of North Texas, Denton.

Dreikurs, R. (1966). Kinder fordern uns heraus [Children are challenging us]. Stuttgart: Klett.

Dulsky, S. (1942). Affect and intellect: An experimental study. *The Journal of General Psychology, 27,* 199–220.

English, R. W., & Higgins, T. E. (1971). Client centered group counselling with pre-adolescents. *Journal of School and Health. 41*(9), 507–510.

Fall, M., Balvanz, J., Johnson, L., & Nelson, L. (1999). A play therapy intervention and its relationship to self-efficacy and learning behaviors. *Professional School Counseling, 2,* 194–204.

Fall, M., Navelski, L. F., & Welch, K. K. (2002). Outcomes of a play intervention for children identified for special education services. *International Journal of Play Therapy, 11*(2), 91–106.

Felton, G. S., & Davidson, H. R. (1973). Group counseling can work in the classroom. *Academic Therapy, 8,* 461–468.

Freire, E., & Hough, M. (2009). *School-based person-centred counselling: An evaluation.* Paper presented at the 15th BACP Research Conference 2009 'Research Relationships' in Portsmouth.

Freire, E., Koller, E., Piatson, A., Goncales, G., Freund, B., Wagner, M., et al. (2008). *Client-centered play therapy with disadvantages children in Brazil: A naturalistic effectiveness study.* Congress Contribution at PCE 2008.

Fröhlich-Gildhoff, K., & Rönnau-Böse, M. (2010). *Effectiveness of person-centred child and adolescent therapy on anxiety.* Manuscript in preparation.

Garza, Y. (2004). *Effects of culturally responsive child-centered play therapy compared to curriculum-based small group counseling with elementary-age Hispanic children experiencing externalizing and internalizing behavior problems: A preliminary study.* Unpublished doctoral dissertation University of North Texas, Denton.

Gaulden, G. (1975). *Developmental-play group counseling with early primary grade students exhibiting behavioral problems.* Unpublished doctoral dsertation, University of North Texas, Denton.

Goetze, H. (Hrsg.). (1981). *Personenzentrierte Spieltherapie. Grundlagen, Erfahrungen und Perspektiven einer Kindertherapie nach Carl Rogers* [Person-centered play therapy. Basics, experiences and perspectives of child psychotherapy according to Carl Rogers]. Göttingen: Hogrefe.

Goetze, H. (2002). *Handbuch personzentrierter Spieltherapie* [Handbook of person-centered play therapy]. Göttingen: Hogrefe.

Goetze, H., & Jaede, W. (1974). *Die nichtdirektive Spieltherapie. Eine wirksame Methode zur Behandlung kindlicher Verhaltensstörungen.* [Nondirective play therapy. An effective method to treat conduct disorders in childhood]. München: Kindler.

Groome, K., & Isaacson, E. (1999). *Play therapy outcome research.* Psychology 402: Directed Readings in Play Therapy, Summer 1999. James Madison University, Harrisburg, VA.

Guerney, B. G., Jr. (1964). Filial therapy: Description and rationale. *Journal of Consulting Psychology, 28*(4), 303–313.

Guerney, B. G., Jr. (1976). Filial therapy used as a treatment method for disturbed children. *Evaluation, 3,* 34–35.

Guerney, L. (2001). Child-centered play therapy. *International Journal of Play Therapy, 10*(2), 13–31.

Guerney, L., & Guerney, B. G., Jr. (1985). The relationship enhancement family of family therapies. In L. L'Abate & M. Milan (Eds.), *Handbook of social skills training and research* (pp. 506–524). New York: Wiley.

Hambidge, G. (1955). Structured play therapy. *American Journal of Orthopsychiatry, 25,* 601–617.

Harris, Z. L. (1995). *Filial therapy with incarcerated mothers.* Unpublished doctoral dissertation, University of North Texas, Denton.

Herd, R. H. (1969). *Behavioral outcomes of client-centered play therapy.* Unpublished doctoral dissertation, North Texas State University.

Hölldampf, D., & Behr, M. (2009). Wirksamkeit beziehungsorientierter Kinder- und Jugendlichenpsychotherapie [Effectiveness of relation-orientated child and adolescent psychotherapy]. In M. Behr, D. Hölldampf, & D. Hüsson (Hrsg.), *Psychotherapie mit Kindern und Jugendlichen – Personzentrierte Methoden und interaktionelle Behandlungskonzepte* [Psychotherapy with children and adolescents. Person-centered methods and interactive treatment concepts] (pp. 319–339). Göttingen: Hogrefe.

House, R. (1970). *The effects of nondirective group play therapy upon the sociometric status and self-concept of selected second grade children.* Unpublished doctoral dissertation, Oregon State University.

Hume, K. (1967). A counseling service project for grades one through four. *Dissertation Abstracts, 27A,* 4130.

Hüsson, D. (2008). Sexually abused children and adolescents: A person-centred play therapy protocol. In M. Behr & J. Cornelius-White (Eds.), *Facilitating young people's development: International perspectives on person-centred theory and practice.* (pp. 52–64). Ross-on-Wye: PCCS Books.

Hüsson, D. (2009). Sexuell missbrauchte Kinder und Jugendliche: Differentielles und therapeutisches Vorgehen in der Personzentrierten Psychotherapie [Sexually abused children and adolescents: Differential and therapeutic treatment in person-centered psychotherapy]. In M. Behr, D. Hölldampf, & D. Hüsson (Eds.), *Psychotherapie mit Kindern und Jugendlichen: Personzentrierte Methoden und interaktionelle Behandlungskonzepte.* [Psychotherapy with children and adolescents: Person-centered methods and interactive treatment concepts] (pp. 243–264). Göttingen: Hogrefe.

Jenny, B., Goetschel, P., & Käppler, C. (2006). Personzentrierte Gruppentherapie mit Kindern: Konzept, Vorgehen, Evaluation. [Person-centered group therapy with children: Concept, treatment protocol and evaluation]. *PERSON, 2,* 93–107

Jenny, B., & Käppler, C. (2009). Gruppentherapie – Konzept, Vorgehen, und Evaluation einer Gruppenbehandlung bei Kindern mit sozialen und emotionalen Problemen [Group therapy – Concept, treatment and evaluation of a group therapy for children with social and emotional problems]. In M. Behr, D. Hölldampf, & D. Hüsson (Hrsg.), *Psychotherapie mit Kindern und Jugendlichen: Personzentrierte Methoden und interaktionelle Behandlungskonzepte.* [Psychotherapy with children and adolescents: Person-centered methods and interactive treatment concepts] (pp. 101–120). Göttingen: Hogrefe.

Jenny, B., & Schär, C. (2010). Personzentrierte Gruppenpsychotherapie für Jugendliche mit Autismus-Spektrum-Störungen – das KOMPASS-Training [Person-centered group therapy for adolescents with pervasive developmental disorders]. *PERSON, 14*(1).

Jernberg, A. M. (1979). *Theraplay: A new treatment using structured play for children and their families.* San Francisco: Jossey-Bass.

Johnson, S.M., Maddeaux, C., & Blouin, J. (1998). Emotionally focussed family therapy for bulima: Changing attachment patterns. *Psychotherapy, 35,* 238–247.

Jones, E. M. (2000). *The efficacy of intensive individual play therapy for children diagnosed with insulin-dependent diabetes mellitus.* Unpublished doctoral dissertation, University of North Texas, Denton.

Kaczmarek, M. G. (1983). *A comparison of individual play therapy and play technology in modifying targeted inappropriate behavioral excesses of children.* Unpublished doctoral dissertation, New Mexico State University.

Kale, A. (1997). *Filial therapy with parents of children experiencing learning difficulties.* Unpublished doctoral dissertation, University of North Texas, Denton.

Kazdin, A. E., Bass, D., Ayres, W. A., & Rodgers, A. (1990). Empirical and clinical focus of child and adolescent psychotherapy research. *Journal of Consulting and Clinical Psychology, 58,* 729–740.

Keller, G. (1997). Die deutsche Schulpsychologie wird 75 Jahre alt [German school psychology is 75 years old]. *Report Psychologie, 22*(8), 573–575.

King, G. (1999). *Counselling skills for teachers: Talking matters.* Buckingham: Open University Press.

Kot, S. (1995). *Intensive play therapy with child witnesses of domestic violence.* Unpublished doctoral dissertation, University of North Texas, Denton.

Landreth, G. L. (Ed.), (1982). *Play therapy: Dynamics of the process of counseling with children.* Springfield, IL: Charles C. Thomas.

Landreth, G. L. (1991). *Play therapy: The art of the relationship.* Muncie, IN: Accelerated Development Press.

Landreth, G. L. (Ed.), (2001). *Innovations in play therapy: Issues, process, and special populations.* Philadelphia, PA: Brunner-Routledge.

Landreth, G. L. (2002). *Play therapy: The art of the relationship* (2nd ed.). New York: Brunner-Routledge.

LeBlanc, M., & Ritchie, M. (2001). A meta-analysis of play therapy outcomes. *Counseling Psychology Quarterly, 14*(2), 140–163.

Leichsenring, F., & Rüger, U. (2004). Psychotherapeutische Behandlungsverfahren auf dem Prüfstand der Evidence Based Medicine [Psychotherapeutic treatments proven by criteria of evidence-based medicine]. *Zeitschrift für Psychosomatische Medizin & Psychotherapie, 50,* 203–217.

Leland, H., Walker, J., & Taboada, A. (1959). Group play therapy with a group of post-nursery male retardates. *American Journal of Mental Deficiency, 63,* 848–851.

Levy, D. (1938). Release therapy in young children. *Psychiatry, 1,* 387–389.

Lietaer, G. (2002). The client-centered/experiential paradigm in psychotherapy: Development and identity. In J. C. Watson, R. N. Goldman, & M. S. Warner (Eds.), *Client-centered and expeiential psychotherapy in the 21st century: Advances in theory, research and practice* (pp. 1–15). Ross-on-Wye: PCCS Books.

Lobaugh, F. A. (1991). *Filial therapy with incarcerated parents.* Unpublished doctoral dissertation, University of North Texas, Denton.

Lopez, A. D., Mathers, C. D., Ezzati, M., Jamison, D. T., & Murray, C. J. (Eds.). (2006). Global burden of disease and risk factors [Disease Control Priorities Project]. New York: The World Bank and Oxford University Press.

Lopez, H. T. (2000). *The effects of play intervention on Hispanic children's reading achievment, self concept and behavior.* Unpublished doctorial dissertation, University of North Texas, Denton.

McGuire, M. (2000). *Child-centered group play therapy with children experiencing adjustment difficulties.* Unpublished doctoral dissertation, University of North Texas, Denton.

Mehlmann, B. (1953). Group play therapy with mentally retarded children. *Journal of Abnormal and Social Psychology, 48,* 53–60.

Morrison, T., & Newcomer, B. (1975). Effects of directive vs. nondirective play therapy with institutionalized mentally retarded children. *American Journal of Mental Deficiency, 79,* 666–669.

Mundy, L. (1957). Therapy with physically and mentally handicapped children in a mental deficiency hospital. *Journal of Clinical Psychology, 13,* 3–9.

Muro, J., Ray, D., Schottelkorb, A., Smith, M. R., & Blanco, P. J. (2006). Quantitative analysis of long-term child-centered play therapy. *International Journal of Play Therapy, 15*(2), 35–58.

New Freedom Commission on Mental Health. (2003). *The President's New Freedom Commission on Mental Health.* Available at: www.mentalhealthcommission.gov/reports/finalreport/downloads/finalreport.pdf

Norton, C. C., & Norton, B. E. (2002). Reaching children through play therapy: An experiential approach. Denver, CO: White Apple Press.

Ogawa, Y. (2006). *Effectiveness of child-centered play therapy with Japanese children in the United States.* Unpublished doctoral dissertation, University of North Texas, Denton.

Oualline, V. (1975). *Behavioral outcomes of short-term nondirective play therapy with preschool deaf children.* Unpublished doctoral dissertation, North Texas State University.

Packmann, J. (2002). *Group activity therapy with learning disabled preadolescents exhibiting behavior problems.* Unpublished doctoral dissertation, University of North Texas, Denton.

Perez, C. L. (1987). *A comparison of group play therapy and individual play therapy for sexually abused children.* Unpublished doctoral dissertation, University of Northern Colorado.

Piaget, J. (1976). *Die Äquilibration der kognitiven Strukturen* [The equilibrium of cognitive structures]. Stuttgart: Klett-Cotta.

Post, P. (1999). Impact of child-centered play therapy on the self-esteem, locus of control, and anxiety of at-risk 4th, 5th, and 6th grade students. *International Journal of Play Therapy, 8*(2), 1–18.

Quayle, R. (1991). *The primary mental health project as a school-based approach for prevention of adjustment problems: An evaluation*. Unpublished doctoral dissertation, Pennsylvania State University.

Rae, W., Worchel, F. F., Upchurch, J., Sanner, J., & Daniel, C. A. (1989). The psychosocial impact of play on hospitalized children. *Journal of Pediatric Psychology, 14*, 617–627.

Ray, D. C. (2007). Two counseling interventions to reduce teacher–child relationship stress. *Professional School Counseling, 10*(4), 428–440.

Ray, D. C. (2008). Impact of play therapy on parent–child relationship stress at mental health training setting. *British Journal of Guidance & Counselling, 36*(2), 165–187.

Ray, D. C., Bratton, S. C., Rhine, T., & Jones, L. (2001). The effectiveness of play therapy: Responding to the critics. *International Journal of Play Therapy, 10*(1), 85–08.

Ray, D. C., Schottelkorb, A., & Mei-Hsiang, T. (2007). Play therapy with children exhibiting symptoms of Attention Deficit Hyperactivity Disorder. *International Journal of Play Therapy, 16*(2), 95–111.

Revenstorf, D. (2005). Das Kuckucksei. Über das pharmakologische Modell in der Psychotherapieforschung [The cuckoo's egg: About the pharmacological model in psychotherapy research]. *Psychotherapie in Psychiatrie, Psychotherapeutischer Medizin & Klinischer Psychologie, 10*(1), 22–31.

Rogers, C. R. (1939). *The clinical treatment of the problem child*. Boston: Houghton Mifflin.

Rogers, C. R. (1942). *Counseling and psychotherapy*. Boston: Houghton Mifflin.

Rogers, C. R. (1951). *Client-centered therapy*. London: Constable.

Rogers, C. R. (1959). A theory of therapy, personality, and interpersonal relationships, as developed in the client-centered framework. In S. Koch (Ed.), *Psychology: A study of a science: Vol. 3. Formulations of the person and the social context* (pp. 184–256). New York: McGraw-Hill.

Schmidtchen, S. (1973). Effekte von klientenzentrierter Spieltherapie. [Effects of client-centered play therapy]. *Zeitschrift für. Klinische Psychologie, 2*, 49–63.

Schmidtchen, S. (1976). *Handbuch der klientenzentrierten Kindertherapie* [Handbook client-centered child therapy]. Kiel: Selbstverlag.

Schmidtchen, S. (1989). *Kinderpsychotherapie* [Child psychotherapy]. Stuttgart: Kohlhammer.

Schmidtchen, S. (1996). *Klientenzentrierte Spiel- und Familientherapie* [Client-centered play and family therapy] (4. Auflage). Weinheim: Beltz.

Schmidtchen, S. (2001). *Allgemeine Psychotherapie für Kinder, Jugendliche und Familien: ein Lehrbuch* [General psychotherapy for children, adolescents and families: A textbook]. Stuttgart: Kohlhammer.

Schmidtchen, S., Acke, H., & Hennies, S. (1995). Heilende Kräfte im kindlichen Spiel. Prozessanalyse des Klientenverhaltens in der Kinderspieltherapie. [Healing power in children's play. Process analysis of client behavior in play therapy]. *GwG Zeitschrift. 99*, 15–23.

Schmidtchen, S., & Hennies, S. (1996). Wider den Non-Direktivitätsmythos. Hin zu einer differentiellen Psychotherapie! Empirische Analyse des Therapeutenverhaltens in erfolgreichen Kinderspieltherapien. [Against the nondirectivity myth. Towards a differential psychotherapy! Empirical analysis of therapists' behavior in successful child play therapies]. *GwG Zeitschrift 104*, 14–24.

Schmidtchen, S., Hennies, S., & Acke, H. (1993). Zwei Fliegen mit einer Klappe? Evaluation der Hypothese eines zweifachen Wirksamkeitsanspruches der klientenzentrierten Spieltherapie. [Two Birds with one stone? Evaluation of the hypothesis with a double effectiveness expectation of client-centered play therapy.] *Psychologie in Erziehung und*

Unterricht, (40), 34–42.

Schmidtchen, S., & Hobrücker, B. (1978). Effektivitätsüberprüfung der klientenzentrierten Spieltherapie bei Kindern aus Erziehungsberatungsstellen [Effectiveness evaluation of client-centered play therapy with children in counseling centers]. *Praxis der Kinderpsychologie und Kinderpsychiatrie, 27*, 117–125.

Schneewind, K. A. (2009). *Familien in Deutschland. Beiträge aus familienpsychologischer Sicht* [Families in Germany. Contributions from a familiy psychological perspective]. Berlin: Deutscher Psychologen Verlag.

Schumann, B. R. (2004). *Effects of child-centered play therapy and curriculum-based small-group guidance on the behaviors of children referred for aggression in an elementary school setting.* Unpublished doctoral dissertation, University of North Texas, Denton.

Scott, T. A., Burlingame, G., Starling, M., Porter, C., & Lilly, J. P. (2003). Effects of individual client-centered play therapy on sexually abused children's mood, self-concept, and social competence. *International Journal of Play Therapy, 12*(1), 7–30.

Seemann, J., Barry, E., & Ellinwood, C. (1964). Interpersonal assessment of play therapy outcome. *Psychotherapy: Theory, Research, and Practice, 1*(2), 64–66.

Seligman, M. E. P. (1995). The effectiveness of psychotherapy. The consumer report study. *American Psychologist, 50,* 965–974.

Sexton, T., Lebov, J., Johnson, S. M., & Gurman, A. (2005, June). *Report on the APA Division 43 Taskforce 'Evidence-based treatments in Family Psychology.'* Presentation at the international conference 'Politics, Community and Clinical Practice' of the American Family Therapy Academy and the International Family Therapy Association, Washington, DC.

Shashi, K., Kapur, M., & Subbakrishna, D. K. (1999). Evaluation of play therapy in emotionally disturbed children. *NIMHANS Journal, 17*(2), 99–111

Shen, Y-J. (2002). Short-term group play therapy with Chinese earthquake victims: Effects on anxiety, depression and adjustment. *International Journal of Play Therapy, 11*(1), 43–63.

Smith, N. R. (2000). *A comparative analysis of intensive filial therapy with intensive individual play therapy and intensive sibling group play therapy with children witnesses of domestic violence.* Unpublished doctoral dissertation, University of North Texas.

Sokoloff, M. (1959). *A comparison of gains in communicative skills, resulting from group play therapy and individual speech therapy, among a group of non-severely dysarthric, speech-handicapped cerebral-palsied children.* Unpublished doctoral dissertation, New York University.

Stern, D. (1986). *The interpersonal world of the infant.* New York: Basic Books.

Stice, E., Burton, E., Bearman, S. K., & Rohde, P. (2007). Randomized trial of brief depression prevention program: An elusive search for a psychosocial placebo control condition. *Behaviour Research and Therapy, 45*(5), 863–876.

Tausch, R., & Tausch, A-M. (1956). *Kinderpsychotherapie in nicht-directivem Verfahren* [Child psychotherapy in nondirective approach]. Göttingen: Hogrefe.

Tausch, A-M., Kettner, U., Steinbach, I., & Tönnies, S. E. (1973). Effekte kindzentrierter Einzel- und Gruppengespräche mit unterprivilegierten Kindergarten- und Grundschulkindern [Effects of child-centered single and group counseling with underprivileged kindergarten and elementary school children]. *Psychologie in Erziehung und Unterricht, 20*, 77–88.

Trostle, S. (1988). The effects of child-centered group play sessions on social-emotional growth of three- to six-year-old bilingual Puerto Rican children. *Journal of Research in Childhood Education, 3*, 93–106.

Truax, C. B., Wargo, D. G., & Silber, L. D. (1966). Effects of group psychotherapy with high accurate empathy and nonpossessive warmth upon female institutionalized delinquents. *Journal of Abnormal Psychology, 71*(4), 267–274.

Tyndall-Lind, A. (1999). *A comparative analysis of intensive individual play therapy and intensive sibling group play therapy with child witnesses of domestic violence.* Unpublished doctoral dissertation, University of North Texas, Denton.

Vlerick, E. (2008). Focusing training for adolescents with low self-confidence and a negative self-image. In M. Behr & J. H. D. Cornelius-White (Eds.), *Facilitating young people's development: International perspectives on person-centred theory and practice* (pp. 80–95). Ross-on-Wye: PCCS Books.

Walker, K. F. (2002). *Filial therapy with parents court-referred for child maltreatment.* Unpublished doctoral dissertation, University of North Texas, Denton.

Wall, M. (1973). *The effectiveness of therapeutic self-directed play in self-concept of educationally handicapped children in Saratoga, California elementary schools.* Unpublished doctoral dissertation, Oregon State University.

Weinberg, D. (2005). *Traumatherapie mit Kindern* [Trauma therapy with children]. Stuttgart: Pfeiffer.

Weinberger, S. (2001). *Kindern spielend helfen. Eine personzentrierte Lern- und Praxisanleitung* [Helping children in a playful way. A person-centered learning and practice guide]. Weinheim: Juventa.

Weiss, B., Carton, T., Harris, V. et al. (1999). The effectiveness of traditional child psychotherapy. *Journal of Consulting and Clinical Psychology, 67,* 82–94.

Weiss, B., Carton, T., & Harris, V. (2000). A 2-year follow-up of the effectiveness of traditional child psychotherapy. *Journal of Consulting and Clinical Psychology, 68,* 1094–1101.

Weisz, J. R., Weiss, B., Alicke, M. D., & Klotz, M. L. (1987). Effectiveness of psychotherapy with children and adolescents: A meta-analysis for clinicians. *Journal of Consulting and Clinical Psychology, 55,* 542–549.

Weisz, J. R., Weiss, B., Han, S., Granger, D. A., & Morton, T. (1995). Effects of psychotherapy with children and adolescents: A meta-analysis of treatment outcome studies. *Psycholgical Bulletin, 117,* 450–468.

West, J. (1996). *Client-centred therapy* (2nd ed.). London: Jessica Kingsley.

Wilson, K., & Ryan, V. (2005). *Play therapy: A non-directive approach for children and adolescents* (2nd ed.). Oxford: Elsevier.

Wissenschaftlicher Beirat Psychotherapie. (2004). Mindestanforderungen für die Begutachtung von Wirksamkeitsstudien im Bereich der Psychotherapie (geänderte Fassung nach dem Beschluss des Beirates vom 15.9.2003). *Deutsches Ärzteblatt PP, 3,* 81. www.aerzteblatt.de/v4/archiv/artikel.asp?id=40485

Woltmann, A. G. (1964). Varieties of play techniques. In M. R. Haworth (Ed.), *Child psychotherapy* (pp. 20–32). New York: Basic Books.

World Health Organization (2004). International statistical classification of diseases and related health problems. Geneva: Author.

Yuen, T. (1997). *Filial therapy with immigrant Chinese parents in Canada.* Unpublished doctoral dissertation, University of North Texas, Denton.

Zion, T. A. (1999). *Effects of individual client-centered play therapy on sexually abused children's mood, self-concept, and social competence.* Unpublished doctoral dissertation, Brigham Young University.

Zulliger, H. (1952). *Heilende Kräfte im kindlichen Spiel* [Healing power in children's play]. Frankfurt: Fischer.

CHAPTER 3

EFFECTIVENESS BEYOND PSYCHOTHERAPY
THE PERSON-CENTERED AND EXPERIENTIAL PARADIGM IN EDUCATION, PARENTING, AND MANAGEMENT

JEFFREY H.D. CORNELIUS-WHITE &
RENATE MOTSCHNIG-PITRIK

INTRODUCTION

There is a significant literature of empirical studies concerned with the application of the person-centered and experiential paradigm beyond psychotherapy and counseling, particularly in education, parent training, and management (approximately 500 studies). Effectiveness rates are similar to those found in psychotherapy research. Educational, parenting, and management studies show superior effects for the person-centered paradigm as compared to alternative interventions, in particular for self-efficacy, emotional, and interpersonal outcomes. In addition, the nonviolent communication/mediation model has exerted a strong international influence in training and practice, though it has limited empirical support. Limited empirical information exists regarding the effectiveness of the person-centered and experiential paradigm in fields such as encounter and community group work, supervision, health promotion, self-help, forensics, and peace studies.

EFFECTIVENESS BEYOND PSYCHOTHERAPY

The empirical basis for the person-centered and experiential (PCE) paradigm began in the 1940s, not only with investigations of what was called nondirective individual, group, and play therapy (See Chapters 1 and 2), but also nondirective education. Increasingly, across the subsequent decades, interest grew in the application of the person-centered approach to additional areas. The approach has generated a large body of quantitative studies in the areas of student or learner-centered education, parenting, especially with the parent effectiveness training (PET) and filial therapy, also more recently known as child–parent relationship therapy (CPRT), and human relations management.

45

METHODOLOGY: INCLUSION AND STATISTICS

Because of the breadth of the task, it was difficult to decide the parameters for what non-therapeutic applications to include as sufficiently PCE. This review took a generous approach, stemming from the principles of the World Association for Person-Centered and Experiential Psychotherapy and Counseling (WAPCEPC), which included the importance of facilitative relationships, persons' actualization and phenomenology in a rich, diverse context, and openness to development in light of ongoing research and practice (http://pce-world.org/). The authors read and considered research from a variety of areas and related theoretical perspectives. Ultimately, from all the models or approaches that resonated with the underlying principles of PCE (as defined by WAPCEPC) and that had the capability of producing effects that could be shown by means of scientific inquiry, those that were selected for inclusion had a considerable body of empirical studies as found through PsycINFO or other sources like personal contacts.[1]

Three areas of research fit: learner-centered education, humanistic parenting interventions, and human relations management and systemic planning. All three of these broad areas have associated meta-analyses that encompass studies adhering to the PCE paradigm. For the purposes of this chapter, these meta-analyses were supplemented with readings of some original studies and related studies not included in the meta-analyses.

The first author utilized Cohen's d as the statistic for comparing the relative levels of effectiveness as this was the most commonly used in the relevant meta-analyses and may be most familiar to readers. For those not familiar with Cohen's d, it is a standardized expression of effect size which can be computed or transformed from many other statistics. In simple terms, a d of 1.0 means that the average outcome of an experimental group is one standard deviation above the average outcome of the control (or comparison) group. Table 1 provides a set of comparison points for effect sizes often termed 'small', 'medium', or 'large' (Cohen, 1988). As further point of reference, the psychotherapy literature generally finds effect sizes near the 'large' benchmark for various treatments overall. Specific interventions, outcomes, or components in psychotherapy are more often in the 'small' or 'medium' ranges.

---

1. For future publications, we would also be very keen to hear from readers who have published, or know about, empirical studies that are not addressed in this article.

Table 1. *Interpretive guide for understanding effect sizes*

Size	*d*	*r²*	Intuitive Description
Small	0.20	0.01	Significant but invisible to naked eye
Medium	0.50	0.06	Noticeable
Large	0.80	0.14	Obvious

EDUCATION

Core elements

Cornelius-White (2007) found approximately 1,000 manuscripts related to person-centered education and synthesized results from 119 studies with 1,450 findings, involving approximately 355,325 students, 14,851 teachers, and 2,439 schools across six countries and multiple regions with publications in English and German. A majority of manuscripts in English stem from David Aspy and Flora Roebuck while most German studies originate from research done by Anne-Marie and Reinhard Tausch. Studies included pre-school and kindergarten through further and higher education though the majority of studies concerned primary and secondary education. Intellectual aptitude, economic class and ethnicity of the samples were relatively diverse.

Person-centered education aims to provide a facilitative climate, similar to that found in psychotherapy, which is characterized by empathic understanding, warmth and realness, but also integrates within the educational system with its specific curriculum and goal requirements. The goal of person-centered education is *significant learning* which, in Rogers' words (1983, p. 20) 'combines the logical and the intuitive, the intellect and the feelings, the concept and the experience, the idea and the meaning. When we learn in that way, we are whole.' Rogers defines the elements that are involved in such significant or experiential learning in the following way:

- *It has a quality of personal involvement* – the whole person in both feeling and cognitive aspects being in the learning event.
- *It is self-initiated.* Even when the impetus or stimulus comes from the outside, the sense of discovery, the reaching out, of grasping and comprehending, comes from within.
- *It is pervasive.* It makes a difference in the behavior, the attitudes, perhaps even the personality of the learner.
- *It is evaluated by the learner.* She knows whether it is meeting her need, whether it leads toward what she *wants* to know, whether it illuminates the dark area of ignorance she is experiencing. The locus of evaluation, we might say, resides definitely within the learner.

- *Its essence is meaning.* When such learning takes place, the element of meaning to the learner is built into the whole experience. (Rogers, 1983, p. 20)

Readers who wish to learn more about person-centered education may want to consult one or more of the following texts: Aspy, 1972; Barrett-Lennard, 1998; Cornelius-White & Harbaugh, 2010; Patterson, 1973; Rogers, 1969, 1983; Rogers & Freiberg, 1994; Tausch & Tausch, 1963/1998.

Cornelius-White, Renate Motschnig-Pitrik and colleagues rated the studies' findings using the Scientific Method Score (Sherman et al., 1997), showing that 919 of 1,450 individual findings were from studies with quasi-experimental or experimental designs. The overall study level effect size was $d = 0.65$. This effect size represents a combination of the 919 comparison findings, which included comparisons between classrooms high or low in the facilitative conditions (e.g., empathy, realness, warmth, or other dimensions) or between person-centered approaches and traditional classrooms, and 531 simple correlation findings that showed a relationship between the person-centered element(s) and beneficial student behavioral, affective, and cognitive outcomes (e.g., motivation to learn, attendance at school, self-efficacy, critical thinking scores, grades, etc.). When comparing the 284 findings at the lowest level of comparison designs characterized by correlation methods ($d = 0.49$) with the 279 in the top category characterized by large sample, controlled comparisons ($d = 0.80$), one finds that the best designed studies showed a larger effect size. Of significance, 531 of the 1,450 findings did not involve comparison groups. In other words, causality cannot be inferred from the specific results presented below that rely on the entire sample of findings.

Table 2 provides effect sizes for selected variables for the PCE paradigm in education. Facilitative relationships ($d = 0.77$), empathy ($d = 0.68$), warmth ($d = 0.68$), and nondirectivity ($d = 0.75$) (Cornelius-White & Cornelius-White, 2005) all showed medium to large effect sizes on positive student outcomes like achievement or motivation (Cornelius-White, 2007). Congruence of the educator showed a small association with student outcomes ($d = 0.28$), suggesting that its role is less important, harder to measure and/or mediated by other variables (Cornelius-White & Harbaugh, 2010). Additional components of person-centered teaching explored included challenge for higher order thinking ($d = 0.61$), encouragement of learning ($d = 0.47$), adaptation to differences ($d = 0.41$), and learner-centered beliefs ($d = 0.10$).

Learner-centered instruction showed differential relationships with student success dimensions. In general, outcomes for affective and behavioral dimensions ($d = 0.75$) were slightly higher than outcomes for cognitive dimensions ($d = 0.65$). Within the affective and behavioral domain, correlations varied from a negligible effect on reducing negative motivation (e.g., effort avoidance) of $d = 0.12$ to a large effect on students willingness to initiate and participate in discussions ($d = 1.32$).

Table 2. *Effect sizes of selected variables (interventions, components, outcomes) in PCE education*

Intervention, Component, or Outcome	Effect Size (Cohen's *d*)	Source	Number of Findings
Overall	0.65	Cornelius-White, 2007	1,450 (119 studies)
Quality of study			
Poorer designed comparison studies	0.49	Cornelius-White, 2007	284
Best designed comparison studies	0.80	Cornelius-White, 2007	279
Components			
Facilitative relationships	0.77	Cornelius-White, 2007	605
Empathy	0.68	Cornelius-White, 2007	146
Warmth	0.68	Cornelius-White, 2007	138
Nondirectivity	0.75	Cornelius-White, 2007	131
Congruence	0.28	Cornelius-White, 2007	34
Challenge	0.61	Cornelius-White, 2007	75
Encouragement	0.47	Cornelius-White, 2007	53
Outcomes			
Adaptation	0.41	Cornelius-White, 2007	98
Learner-centered beliefs	0.10	Cornelius-White, 2007	N/A
Affective/behavioral outcomes	0.68	Cornelius-White & Harbaugh, 2010	956
Cognitive outcomes	0.61	Cornelius-White & Harbaugh, 2010	490
Participation	1.32	Cornelius-White, 2007	86
Reducing negative motivation	0.12	Cornelius-White, 2007	N/A
Critical thinking	1.00	Cornelius-White, 2007	55
Achievement tests	0.32	Cornelius-White, 2007	59
Cooperative vs. competitive learning	0.67	Johnson & Johnson, 1989	Near 100 studies
Cooperative vs. individualistic learning	0.64	Johnson & Johnson, 1989	Near 100 studies

Within the cognitive domain, correlations varied from a small effect on achievement test scores (*d* = 0.32) to a large effect (*d* = 1.00) for critical and creative thinking measures (Cornelius-White, 2007).

Moderator analysis showed that when students' IQ or prior achievement standing was controlled for, the effect size of the relationship between person-centered educational components and positive student outcomes rose to $d = 1.04$, suggesting that, on average, 21% of the remaining variance in outcomes was due to person-centered educational variables like empathy or warmth. Likewise, moderator analysis concerned with the perspective of the measurement of the learner-centered variables suggests that students' perspectives on the relationship ($d = 0.87$) are more valid than teachers' own perspectives ($d = 0.35$). This is consistent with the sixth core condition (Rogers, 1957, 1959) concerned with the perception (or successful communication) of the attitudes and the psychotherapy research showing stronger effects for client-perceived rather than therapist-reported empathy, regard, and congruence (Cornelius-White, 2002).

Investigation into sample characteristics showed that learner-centered environments are useful for student success with a range of populations. Effect sizes for teacher samples that were all female ($d = 1.29$) or all persons of color ($d = 1.12$) showed larger effect sizes than for non-specified samples ($d = 0.82$ and $d = 0.77$), respectively). Ethnicity of student and other potential moderators (e.g., teacher experience, grade level, location, publication year, etc.) did not show different effect sizes.

Cornelius-White and Harbaugh (2010) reviewed additional research, including the American Psychological Association's (1997) *Learner-Centered Psychological Principles* and research on guided discovery and cooperative learning, triangulating the findings from about 130 additional studies from other perspectives.

Related research

The Learner-Centered Psychological Principles (APA Work Group, 1997) bring together information about how students learn and develop. In 1991, the APA Work Group reviewed decades of research to identify the principles and then met again a few times during the next decade to revise them. The principles support the agentic, meta-cognitive, developmental, affective and social aspects of learning with a knowledge base of principles that can guide instruction. Examples include: '8. The learner's creativity, higher order thinking, and natural curiosity all contribute to motivation to learn. Intrinsic motivation is stimulated by tasks of optimal novelty and difficulty, relevant to personal interests, and providing for personal choice and control' and '11. Learning is influenced by social interactions, interpersonal relations, and communication with others' (http://www.apa.org/ed/governance/bea/learner-centered.pdf). Interestingly, while the APA Learner-Centered Psychological Principles clearly acknowledge the importance of interpersonal relationships in learning, they do not go as far as proposing which interpersonal attitudes are most facilitative of significant learning.

Mayer (2004) reviewed four decades of research on discovery (i.e., active, constructivist) teaching methods, finding that teaching is more effective when it includes not only an appreciation of students' agency in making meaning, but also an appreciation of the knowledge about learning. For example, much has been learned about how learning to read is related to the phonics or 'sounding out' of words. More specifically, he reviewed how underlying problem-solving, conservation, and programming rules can be shared with students through guidance (or selective direct instruction) to help people more efficiently learn curricular-defined content. Situating Mayer's findings in relation to person-centered education, Cornelius-White and Cornelius-White (2005) suggested that the more 'right and wrong' a content field is (e.g., spelling, computation), the more guidance is needed, whereas the more expansive, emotional, or holistic a task (such as typically occurs in psychotherapy), the more indirect and nondirective methods of instruction are supported. Cornelius-White and Harbaugh (2010) suggest that nondirectivity and other facilitation of student development forms the principled center of the learner-centered enterprise, but exists in dialectic with the instrumental use of pedagogical knowledge and direct, and other (e.g., cooperative) instructional methods.

In their review of over 100 studies, Johnson and Johnson (1989) showed that cooperative teaching methods have larger effect sizes than the individual and competitive methods that more typically occur in schools ($d = 0.67$ for cooperative compared to competitive and $d = 0.64$ compared to individualistic teaching methods). They suggest that all three methods are necessary and useful for balance but that cooperative methods should comprise 60–70% of all the methods employed. Specifically, Johnson and Johnson's review found that student cooperation in small heterogeneous groups, characterized by reciprocal communication, individual accountability, and positive interdependence, is vital for cooperative climates, such as that advocated for by person-centered education.

Technology-enhanced person-centered learning

During the last decade, the Research Lab for Educational Technologies at the University of Vienna, Austria, has produced approximately 100 internationally published manuscripts. These are mostly concerned with how person-centered education with a clear primacy on providing the person-centered core conditions is fostered in the age of the Internet through technology and encounter-group-enhanced learning environments in university settings (Motschnig-Pitrik, 2009). Most of these studies were not available during the data collection phase of the meta-analysis reviewed above. These studies have generally used mixed quantitative–qualitative designs with small samples. Some studies explored features of individual person-centered, technology enhanced courses, such as their effects on interpersonal relationships of students, the development of students' communication/team skills, and aspects of community building within courses. The majority of studies, however, compared traditional courses with person-centered courses employing educational technologies.

These studies employed pre–post surveys, action research, case studies and interviews with individuals and groups. Typical application areas were communication, management, organizational development, and technology-enhanced learning. Furthermore, three PhD theses (published as books) were written in which the person-centered value base served as the foundation for:

- deriving design patterns for person-centered e-learning and empirically studying their effects on various features of students' learning (Derntl, 2006),

- team development, skills and attitudes in academic, person-centered courses (Figl, 2009),

- case studies investigating facilitative activities in technology-enhanced environments (Bauer, 2009).

The following conclusions regarding various beneficial effects of person-centered, technology-enhanced learning on motivation, whole-person learning, self-initiation and active engagement, feeling of community, and improved interpersonal relationships can be drawn from this literature (Motschnig-Pitrik, 2009):

- In the case that computer support can take over significant parts of the transfer of intellectual information, more time will be left for significant learning (i.e., actualizing, whole-person learning that emphasizes the integration of cognitions, intuitions/feelings, and skills) and face-to-face interactions in a facilitative climate. There is initial qualitative evidence that person-centered technology-enhanced learning (PCeL) based on communicating person-centered attitudes while integrating face-to-face with online sessions is perceived as more motivating and promoting of significant learning than traditional course designs.

- Students indicate that in person-centered, technology-enhanced courses they learn similarly at the level of intellect, but significantly more ($p = 0.001$) at the level of skills and the level of attitudes, feelings, and personality than in traditional courses, confirming the findings of Cornelius-White (2007).

- Profitable motivational elements which students rated to be present in person-centered technology-enhanced classrooms significantly more strongly than in traditional courses included active participation in the course, exchange with peers and instructor, opportunity of bringing in personal interests and contributions, and support via an accompanying web-based platform.

- In terms of creating a feeling of community (Barrett-Lennard, 2005), the most significant increases in person-centered technology-enhanced environments were improvements in 'attentive listening to others', 'climate of respect, caring, trust', and 'experience of connectedness and community', across all courses. Some other features like 'experiencing being heard' and 'communication of owned feelings and meanings' were evaluated particularly highly in those courses that included encounter-group-like phases.

• Although students experience a significant rise in team skills, their team orientation and team attitudes do not change significantly as the result of attending one person-centered course. Still, semi-structured interviews indicate that students feel they have improved their teamwork competencies as a result of person-centered-technology enhanced courses more than when attending traditional courses that included teamwork (Figl, 2009).

• Interpersonal relationships improved as a result of attending person-centered technology-enhanced courses for at least one semester. This was not only the case for relationships with classmates but also with family, partners, and work colleagues.

Conclusions on the effectiveness of the PCE paradigm in education
There is strong evidence of the effectiveness of the PCE paradigm in education for a range of affective, behavioral and intellectual outcomes, especially for the core variables of empathy, unconditional positive regard, and nondirectivity. Likewise, there is evidence of education-specific variables such as focusing on learning over lecturing and small cooperative learning groups (typically medium to large effect sizes). Person-centered technology-enhanced learning (PCeL) is associated with improvements in skills, attitudes and feelings, particularly concerned with interpersonal relationships, team skills, feeling of community, motivation, and communication.

PARENTING

Like education, research on the person-centered paradigm in parenting is large and strong, with definitive evidence of effectiveness. There are two main applications that have been researched extensively: parent effectiveness training (PET) (Gordon, 1970); and filial therapy (Guerney, 1969), more recently described as child–parent relationship therapy (CPRT) (Landreth & Bratton, 2006). A meta-analytic review of components of approaches to parenting from a variety of theoretical perspectives shows support for the underlying concepts of the person-centered approach (Kaminski, Valle, Filene, & Boyle, 2008).

Parent effectiveness training

First developed in the early 1960s by Thomas Gordon, a colleague of Rogers, PET prioritizes parent empathy, positive regard, congruence, and democratic interactions with an emphasis on skills such as active listening, I-Messages, and No-Lose conflict resolution.

In addition to earlier reviews that were smaller in scope and less sophisticated, Cedar and Levant (1990) found 60 relevant studies and meta-analyzed 26 of these that included comparison of at least two groups, pre- and post-treatment quantitative measures, and included parents. Table 3 provides effect sizes for selected variables for the PCE paradigm in parenting. Cedar and Levant (1990) found a small overall effect size of $d = 0.33$, which improved to a medium effect size, $d = 0.45$ for the more methodologically sound studies, and to large, $d = 0.81$ for the published study subset. Parent outcomes were generally higher than child outcomes. In terms of outcomes, parent knowledge of the parent effectiveness methods showed the highest effect size ($d = 1.1$), followed by attitudes ($d = 0.41$), and behavior ($d = 0.37$). Parent self-esteem ($d = 0$) appeared unaffected by PET. Child outcomes were less favorable. Small effects were found for child self-esteem ($d = 0.38$), but child attitudes ($d = 0.12$) and child behavior ($d = 0.03$) seemed mostly unaffected, at least at the conclusion of the training. Studies with follow-up measurements were not significantly lower or higher than those at post-treatment, with one exception. Child behavior significantly improved at follow-up (3–6 months typically) to a medium effect size ($d = 0.53$), suggesting that as parents utilized the knowledge gained, children's behaviors improved. Also, older children benefited statistically significantly more than younger children.

Müller, Hager, and Heise (2001) also meta-analyzed studies on PET, including 15 studies published in German and English with few overlapping studies in Cedar and Levant's (1990) review. They included nine studies comparing PET with a waitlist (control) group and six that compared PET with alternative treatments or used a mixed methodology. Their findings corroborated the earlier meta-analyses in some respects and not in others. Overall, they found very large effects post-treatment ($d = 1.47$, 15 studies) and at follow-up ($d = 2.06$, 4 studies) for PET. They found a very large effect size from four studies concerning parents' learning and use of the communication skills ($d = 2.63$), similar to Cedar and Levant's finding. From two studies, Müller et al. (2001) found a large effect size on the change of attitude and the self-concepts of parents ($d = 1.15$). This contrasts with the no significant effect with respect to parents' self-esteem reported by Cedar and Levant. According to the Müller et al's. (2001) meta-analysis, the change of parent behavior ($d = 0.75$) and improvement in parent–child communication patterns and skill learning ($d = 1.60$) was also much larger (three studies for each finding). Two studies that focused on child self-concept showed large effects ($d = 0.77$), which were larger than those reported by Cedar and Levant. With women-only parenting groups, the effects were very large ($d = 1.50$, seven studies), but also large with mixed sex groups ($d = 1.16$, eight studies).

Table 3. *Effect sizes of selected variables (interventions, components, outcomes) in PCE parenting*

Intervention, Component, or Outcome	Effect Size (Cohen's *d*)	Source	Number of Studies[a] or Findings[b]
PET: Parenting Effectiveness Training			
Overall effect	0.33	Cedar & Levant, 1990	290[b] (26 Studies)
Study Attributes			
Post-test (immediate)	0.35	Cedar & Levant, 1990	232[b]
Follow-up (3–6 months)	0.24	Cedar & Levant, 1990	58[b]
Methodologically sound	0.45	Cedar & Levant, 1990	104[b]
Published studies	0.81	Cedar & Levant, 1990	19[b]
Women-only parenting groups	1.50	Müller et al., 2001	7[a]
Mixed-sex parenting groups	1.16	Müller et al., 2001	8[a]
Parents of older children (ages 7–12)	1.30	Müller et al., 2001	10[a]
Parents of younger children (ages 3–7)	0.92	Müller et al., 2001	3[a]
Post-test overall	1.47	Müller et al., 2001	15[a]
Follow-up	2.06	Müller et al., 2001	4[a]
Learning and using communication skills compared to control	2.63	Müller et al., 2001	4[a]
Outcomes			
Parent knowledge	1.10	Cedar & Levant, 1990	7[b]
Parent attitudes	0.41	Cedar & Levant, 1990	122[b]
Parent behavior	0.37	Cedar & Levant, 1990	83[b]
Parent self-esteem	0.00	Cedar & Levant, 1990	6[b]
Child self-esteem	0.38	Cedar & Levant, 1990	10[b]
Child attitudes	0.12	Cedar & Levant, 1990	13[b]
Child behavior	0.03	Cedar & Levant, 1990	49[b]
Child behavior (follow-up)	0.53	Cedar & Levant, 1990	N/A
Self-concept and attitude-change in parents	1.15	Müller et al., 2001	7[a]
Parent-behavior and improvement of parent–child communication	1.18	Müller et al., 2001	6[a]
Parent behavior change	0.75	Müller et al., 2001	3[a]

Table 3. *Effect sizes of selected variables (interventions, components, outcomes) in PCE Parenting ... cont'd*

Intervention, Component, or Outcome	Effect Size (Cohen's *d*)	Source	Number of Studies[a] or Findings[b]
Improved parent–child interactions	1.6	Müller et al., 2001	3[a]
Child self-concept	0.77	Müller et al., 2001	2[a]
Filial Therapy (Overall)	1.15	Bratton et al., 2005	22[a]
Parent Trainings across Orientations		Kaminski et al., 2008	77[a]
Emotional communication			
Parent behavior	1.47	Kaminski et al., 2008	N/A
Child behavior	0.03	Kaminski et al., 2008	N/A
Positive interaction			
Parent behavior	0.39	Kaminski et al., 2008	N/A
Child behavior	0.04	Kaminski et al., 2008	N/A
Practice with own child			
Parent behavior	0.91	Kaminski et al., 2008	N/A
Child behavior	0.69	Kaminski et al., 2008	N/A
Consistent Responding			
Parent behavior	0.59	Kaminski et al., 2008	N/A
Child behavior	0.22	Kaminski et al., 2008	N/A

Similar to Cedar and Levant's finding, PET seems to work better with families with older children (ages 7–12, d = 1.3, ten studies) as compared with younger children (ages 3–7, d = 0.92, three studies). Some of the difference in the strength of the findings between Cedar and Levant's and Müller et al.'s reviews may be due to the larger proportional number of families with older children in the Müller et al. review. Although Müller et al. still found larger effects for families with younger children than did Cedar and Levant. Perhaps most noteworthy was Müller et al.'s finding that follow-up effects show stronger effects than immediate ones.

Filial therapy

Bernard and Louise Guerney developed filial therapy in the early 1960s (Guerney, 1969) and it was further developed and popularized by Garry Landreth and colleagues as CPRT (Landreth & Bratton, 2006). Filial therapy is an intervention that teaches parents basic child-centered play therapy skills. The training is for parents with children near ages 2–12. Unlike PET, work proceeds specifically between identified parent and child rather than with the entire family level. Originally the training involved several months, but more recently this has been reduced to 10 weeks using the CPRT model.

Bratton, Ray, Rhine, and Jones (2005), in their meta-analysis of play therapy studies, found that those treatments that employed filial therapy (n = 22) had a large effect size (d = 1.15). All 22 studies employed comparisons with controls and/or alternative treatments and many of these studies were dissertations, which generally had smaller effect sizes than published studies. Teaching parents to conduct special playtimes with their children had significantly greater effect sizes than professionally provided play therapy (d = 1.15 vs. d = 0.72). Likewise, faster results were obtained from filial as compared to professional play therapy. Filial therapy appears to help children at all tested ages and genders with internalizing and externalizing problems and parenting/family functioning variables at similar levels.

Program component support

A recent meta-analysis of components associated with parent training effectiveness from a variety of approaches (not just humanistic paradigms) (Kaminski et. al., 2008) shows that the components most supported are those postulated by person-centered theory.

The review involved 77 published studies with parents of children ages 0–7. This meta-analysis provides empirical support for the validity of person-centered principles in the parenting of infants (> 2 years of age). Filial therapy and PET are not applicable for infants. Four of the 18 components that were assessed met the authors' most conservative test to significantly predict effect sizes. All four of these components are stressed in person-centered approaches. The components and their relationship to a person-centered approach include: (1) requiring in vivo practice (parents have to apply it as in filial therapy); (2) teaching skills related to emotional communication (e.g., active listening, identifying children's emotions, reducing judgmental communications as in PET); (3) facilitating positive parent–child interactions (e.g., how to offer positive attention, interact on level of play, and follow children's leads in play as in filial therapy); and (4) consistency in responding, as in Freiberg's (Rogers & Freiberg, 1994) consistency management educational model.

Emotional communication (e.g., identifying children's emotions and paraphrasing their emotional expressions) showed large effects on parents' behaviors

(d = 1.47) but negligible effects on child (externalizing) behavior (d = 0.03). Positive interactions with child showed small to medium effects on both parent (d = 0.39) and child (d = 0.036) behaviors. Practice with one's own child showed medium to large effects for both parent (d = 0.91) and child (d = 0.69) behaviors. Consistent responding showed medium effect on parents (d = 0.59) and small effects on child (d = 0.22) behavior. This component meta-analysis offers broad support for predicting the effectiveness of the person-centered paradigm in parent training, but does not represent tests of causality of person-centered models.

Conclusions on the effectiveness of the PCE paradigm in parenting

The present review includes evidence from approximately 135 studies concerned with PCE applications to parent training. Filial therapy (with large effect sizes), PET (with medium to large effect sizes) and humanistic components of a variety of parenting approaches (with small to large effect sizes) all have evidence to support their use. For children between ages 2–11, filial therapy and PET appear most effective. PET appears to be a better approach for helping families with older children and adolescents (medium to large effect sizes) as compared to younger children (small to large effect sizes). PET's effects appear more pronounced on parents than on their children though the effects on children rise at follow-up. Parenting approaches with humanistic components appear most effective with parents with infants as compared to approaches that are behavioral or do not have techniques or methods emphasized in humanistic approaches (medium effect sizes).

MANAGEMENT

The human relations approach to management is an approach that emphasizes 'interpersonal attitude and skills training … Such training includes positive regard for democratic leadership, consideration for the contribution of others, and … self awareness training' (Brannick, 1987, p. 1). As it began prior and ran parallel to client-centered therapy, it is distinct from the other person-centered and experiential approaches reviewed in this chapter. However, its core ingredients show its obvious relationship and its empirical basis is large. Likewise, Rogers and Roethlisherger wrote a highly influential article in 1952 that helped connect this movement from a relatively early time within the development of the person-centered paradigm. Person-centered planning, an influential approach emerging in the last two decades for helping persons with developmental delays in milieu settings is treated here as a subset of the PCE paradigm in management due to its focus on training staff leaders to change systems.

Human relations management

There have been at least three meta-analyses that examined studies concerned with managerial training emphasizing human relations approaches. Brannick's (1987) meta-analysis was the only one that focused exclusively on human relation studies while Burke and Day (1986) separated studies on human relations approaches from others for easy comparisons. Many of the studies in these two meta-analyses overlapped. More recently, Collins and Holton (2004) meta-analyzed managerial leadership development studies in broader terms (involving 62 comparison studies), but what was 'measured most were the interpersonal skills' (p. 220). Hence, findings from the Collins and Holton (2004) meta-analysis provide support from more recent research, but, because of its broader focus, the reader must use caution in interpreting the minimal information provided here on overall effects as studies are included that are clearly outside the PCE paradigm. The results discussed from these meta-analyses only included comparison designs.

Table 4 provides effect sizes for selected variables for the PCE paradigm in management. Brannick (1987) reported an overall study level effect size of $d = 0.47$ (46 studies) and a finding level effect size of $d = 0.39$ (263 findings). Burke and Day (1986) included 45 studies concerned with human relationships management.

Both Brannick (1987) and Burke and Day (1986) separated the interpersonal from the self-awareness aspects in the human relationships management studies. Subjective learning refers to changes in attitudes, whereby the trainees learned to value the facilitative dimensions of management. The objective indicators related how the trainings affected short-term and long-term performance, for instance in the efficiency of the workforce or meeting of external goals. Burke and Day (1986) reported a mean effect size of $d = 0.76$ and Brannick (1987), $d = 0.23$ – a significant discrepancy. Brannick suggested that this and other differences in results may have been due more to differences in meta-analytic methodologies rather than other factors.

Person-centered planning

Person-centered planning is a milieu management approach to improving quality of life of persons in residential programming with developmental delays (e.g., learning or intellectual disabilities) by reducing social isolation, promoting friendships, and increasing autonomy, competence, social contribution, and respect for persons with such developmental difficulties and disabilities through consumer empowerment (O'Brien & Lovett, 1992). Person-centered planning ideas have been influential in recent reforms within institutions serving persons with developmental delays (e.g., New York state institutions) (O'Brien & Lovett, 1992). There are few studies of the effectiveness of person-centered planning, but the few that were found show statistically significantly better outcomes as compared with conventional individual service planning rooted in behavioral methods. For example, in an alternative treatment

Table 4. *Effect sizes of selected variables (interventions, components, outcomes) in PCE management*

Intervention, Component, or Outcome	Effect Size (Cohen's *d*)	Source	Number of Studies[a] or Findings[b]
Overall Effect from Study Level Analysis	0.47	Brannick, 1987	46[a]
Overall Effect from Findings Level Analysis	0.39	Brannick, 1987	263[b]
Interpersonal Training			
Short-term effects			
Subjective learning	0.76	Burke & Day, 1986	8[a]; 21[b]
Subjective learning	0.23	Brannick, 1987	6[a]; 34[b]
Objective performance	0.41	Burke & Day, 1986	8[a]; 33[b]
Objective performance	0.36	Brannick, 1987	7[a]; 12
Objective performance	0.96	Collins & Holton, 2002	18[a]
Long-term effects			
Subjective behavior or attitudes	0.44	Burke & Day, 1986	17[a]; 118[b]
Subjective behavior or attitudes	0.47	Brannick, 1987	9[a]; 45[b]
Subjective behavior or attitudes	0.41	Collins & Holton, 2002	11[a]
Objective performance	1.04	Brannick, 1987	3[a]; 3[b]
Objective performance	0.56	Burke & Day, 1986	17[a]; 93[b]
Self-Awareness Training			
Short-term effects			
Subjective learning	0.86	Burke & Day, 1986	7[a]; 15[b]
Subjective learning	0.33	Brannick, 1987	5[a]; 12[b]
Long-term effects			
Subjective behavior or attitudes	0.65	Burke & Day, 1986	7[a]; 52[b]
Subjective behavior or attitudes	0.74	Brannick, 1987 Brannick, 1987	5[a]; 15[b]
Objective performance	0.46		4[a]; 21[b]
Person-Centered Planning			
Processes	1.78	Holburn et. al., 2004	1[a]
Outcomes	1.31	Holburn et. al., 2004	1[a]
Community placement	0.73	Holburn et. al., 2004	1[a]

experimental design with 38 participants, Holburn, Jacobson, Schwartz, Flory, and Vietze (2004) showed an effect size of d = 1.71 for process variables (i.e., strategy, relationship, motivation, vision, commitment, flexibility), d = 1.38 for outcome (i.e., autonomy, activities, respect, competence, satisfaction), and d = 0.73 for movement from institutional to community placement. Holburn and Vietze's (2002) collection of studies from various authors include qualitative studies and quantitative multiple base-line and mixed methods designs using mostly small samples with very positive results but did not provide information for easily computing effect sizes.

Conclusions on the effectiveness of the PCE paradigm in management
This review includes evidence from approximately 150 studies concerned with PCE applications to management. The results generally show medium effect sizes for human relations management training that focus on interpersonal and/or self-awareness components. Long-term attitudinal or performance outcomes were generally higher than short-term outcomes, often in the large effect range, suggesting that the positive effects of human relations training may take some time before they are fully realized.

ADDITIONAL AREAS OF APPLICATION WITH THE PCE PARADIGM

Rogers and his colleagues also paved the way for applications of the person-centered approach to fields like group work, interpersonal relationships and cross-cultural communication (Barrett-Lennard, 1998; Lago & McMillan, 1999; Rogers, 1970), business and leadership (Rogers, 1978; Ryback, 1998), creativity, intergroup conflict resolution, and international peacekeeping (Rogers, 1978). They demonstrated how the facilitative conditions of positive regard, empathic understanding, and congruence could promote growth, creativity, better understanding, learning, and healing. Furthermore, although its empirical basis is nearly nonexistent in PsycINFO searches and is not explicitly reviewed in this chapter, any review of PCE applications needs to mention the enormous influence of nonviolent (or compassionate) communication (e.g., Rosenberg, http://cnvc.org), given its presence in 59 countries and more than a million practitioners in mediation and related fields. Likewise, the person-centered approach has been applied in nursing, medicine, dentistry, law, self-help, communication (Rogers, 1983), rhetoric (Brent, 1991) and other settings, though the authors did not find evidence of effectiveness or studies that evaluated effectiveness.

CONCLUSIONS ON THE PCE PARADIGM BEYOND THERAPY

The PCE paradigm is supported by research involving more than 500 diverse studies in education, parenting and management. Other applications do not appear to have as strong or clear empirical foundation. Some findings are robustly confirmed (e.g., teacher–student facilitative relationships, filial therapy for improvements in child behavior, long-term attitudinal change in managers) while other are more tenuous (e.g., teacher congruence, PET effect on parent self-esteem, person-centered planning). PCE education appears effective for all ages of formal schooling, in a variety of countries and settings, including technology-enhanced learning environments that have proliferated in the last decade. PCE parenting appears effective for all ages of children with different applications showing greater effects for some ages than others. The management studies the authors reviewed have less explicit relationship to the PCE paradigm than the educational and parenting studies, but still provide evidence of the importance of person-centered principles within leadership training in organizations. This review has confirmed the effectiveness of the PCE paradigm for vast areas beyond therapy. However more research is needed to keep the approach alive in the competitive scientific world of today and tomorrow.

REFERENCES

APA Work Group of the Board of Educational Affairs. (1997, November). *Learner-centered psychological principles: A framework for school reform and redesign*. Washington, DC: American Psychological Association.

Aspy, D. N. (1972). *Toward a technology for humanizing education*. Champaign, IL: Research Press.

Barrett-Lennard, G. T. (1998). *Carl Rogers' helping system, journey and substance*. London: Sage.

Barrett-Lennard, G. T. (2005). *Relationship at the centre: Healing in a troubled world*. Philadelphia, PA: Whurr.

Bauer, C. (2009). *Promotive activities in technology-enhanced cooperative whole person learning*. PhD thesis, University of Vienna, Research Lab Educational Technologies, in press.

Brannick, J. P. (1987). A meta-analytic study of human relations training research. (Doctoral Dissertation, Bowling Green University, 2005). *Dissertation Abstracts International, 48*, 3439B. (UMI No. 88004290)

Bratton, S. C., Ray, D. C., Rhine, T., & Jones, L. (2005). The efficacy of play therapy with children: A meta-analytic review of treatment outcomes. *Professional Psychology: Research and Practice, 36*, 376–390.

Brent, B. (1991). Young, Becker and Pike's 'Rogerian' rhetoric: A twenty-year reassessment. *College English, 53*(4), 452–466.

Burke, M. J., & Day, R. R. (1986). A cumulative study of the effectiveness of managerial training. *Journal of Applied Psychology, 71*, 232–245.

Cedar, B., & Levant, R. F. (1990). A meta-analysis of the effects of parent effectiveness training.

The American Journal of Family Therapy, 18, 373-384.

Cohen, J. (1988). *Statistical power analysis for the behavioral sciences* (2nd ed.). Hillsdale, NJ: Lawrence Erlbaum Associates.

Collins, D., & Holton, E. (2004). The effectiveness of managerial leadership development programs: A meta-analysis of studies from 1982–2001. *Human Resource Development Quarterly, 15*(2), 217–248.

Cornelius-White, J. H. D. (2002). The phoenix of empirically supported therapy relationships: The overlooked person-centered foundation. *Psychotherapy: Theory, Research, Practice, Training, 39,* 219–222.

Cornelius-White, J. H. D. (2007). Learner-centered teacher-student relationships are effective: A meta-analysis. *Review of Educational Research, 77,* 113–143.

Cornelius-White, J. H. D., & Cornelius-White, C. F. (2005). Trust builds learning: Context and effectiveness of nondirectivity in education. In B. Levitt (Ed.), *Embracing nondirectivity: Reassessing theory and practice in the 21st century* (pp. 314–323). Ross-on-Wye: PCCS Books.

Cornelius-White, J. H. D., & Harbaugh, A. P. (2010). *Learner-centered instruction: Building relationships for student success.* Thousand Oaks, CA: Sage.

Derntl, M. (2006). *Patterns for person-centered e-learning.* Akademische Verlagsgesellschaft Aka GmbH, Berlin. (PhD thesis, University of Vienna, Research Lab Educational Technologies.)

Figl, K. (2009). *Team and media competencies in information systems.* Oldenbourg Wissenschaftsverlag, DE. (PhD thesis, University of Vienna, Research Lab Educational Technologies.)

Gordon, T. (1970). *P. E. T.: Parent effectiveness training.* New York: Peter H. Wyden.

Guerney, B. G. (1969). Filial therapy: Description and rationale. In B. G. Guerney, (Ed.), *Psychotherapeutic agents: New roles for nonprofessionals, parents and teachers* (pp. 450–460). New York: Holt, Rinehart, and Winston.

Johnson, D. W., & Johnson, R. T. (1989). *Cooperation and competition: Theory and research.* Edina, MN: Interaction Book Co.

Holburn, S. H., & Vietze, P. M. (Eds.). (2002). *Person-centered planning: Research, practice, and future directions.* Baltimore, MD: Brookes.

Holburn, S., Jacobson, J. W., Schwartz, A. A., Flory, M. J., & Vietze, P. M. (2004). The Willowbrook Futures Project: A longitudinal analysis of person-centered planning. *American Journal of Mental Retardation, 109,* 63–74.

Kaminski, J. W., Valle, L. A., Filene, J. H., & Boyle, C. L. (2008). A meta-analytic review of components associated with parent training program effectiveness. *Journal of Abnormal Child Psychology, 36,* 567–589.

Lago, C., & McMillan, M. (1999). *Experiences in relatedness: Groupwork in the person-centred approach.* Ross-on-Wye: PCCS Books.

Landreth, G. L., & Bratton, S. C. (2006). *Child parent relationship therapy: A 10-session filial therapy model.* New York: Routledge.

Mayer, R. (2004). Should there be a three-strike rule against pure discovery learning? The case for guided methods of instruction. *American Psychologist, 59,* 14–19.

Motschnig-Pitrik, R. (2009). The person-centered educational paradigm in the age of the Internet: A synthesis of studies conducted through the Research Lab for Educational Technologies at the University of Vienna, Austria. Manuscript in preparation. See also http://www.cs.univie.ac.at/publications.php for a listing of relevant publications and downloads.

Muller, C. T., Hager, W., & Heise, E. (2001). Zur Effektivitat des Gordon-Eltern-Trainings

(PET) – eine Meta-Evluation [The effectiveness of the Gordon parent trainings (PET): A meta-analysis]. *Guppendynamik and Organisationsberatung, 32,* 339–364.

O'Brien, J., & Lovett, H. (1992). *Finding a way toward everyday lives: The contribution of person-centered planning.* Harrisburg: Pennsylvania Office of Mental Retardation.

Patterson, C. H. (1973). *Humanistic education.* Englewood Cliffs, NJ: Prentice Hall.

Rogers, C. R. (1957). The necessary and sufficient conditions of personality change. *Journal of Consulting Psychology, 21*(2), 95–103. (Reprinted as Rogers, C. R. (2007). The necessary and sufficient conditions of personality change. *Psychotherapy: Theory, Research, Practice, Training, 44,* 240–248.)

Rogers, C. R. (1959). A theory of therapy, personality, and interpersonal relationship as developed in the client-centered framework. In S. Koch (Ed.), *Psychology: A study of a science. Vol 3: Formulations of the person and the social context* (pp. 184–256). New York: McGraw-Hill.

Rogers, C. R. (1961). *On becoming a person: A psychotherapist's view of psychotherapy.* London: Constable.

Rogers, C. R. (1969). *Freedom to learn: A view of what education might become.* Columbus, OH: Charles E. Merrill.

Rogers, C. R. (1970). *Carl Rogers on encounter groups.* New York: Harper & Row.

Rogers, C. R. (1978). *On personal power.* London: Constable.

Rogers, C. R. (1983). *Freedom to learn for the 80s.* Columbus, OH: Charles E. Merrill.

Rogers, C. R., & Freiberg. H. J. (1994). *Freedom to learn.* (3rd ed.). Columbus, OH: Charles E. Merrill.

Rogers, C. R., & Roethlisherger, F. J. (1952). Barriers and gateways to communication. *Harvard Business Review, 30*(4), 46–52.

Ryback, D. (1998). *Putting emotional intelligence to work,* Boston: Butterworth-Heinemann.

Sherman, L. W., Gottfredon, D., MacKenzie, D., Eck, J., Reuter, P., & Bushway, S. (1997). *Preventing crime: What works, what doesn't, what's promising* (NCJ No.165366). College Park: University of Maryland.

Tausch, R., & Tausch, A.-M. (1998). *Erziehungs-Psychologie* [Educational psychology] (11th ed.). Göttingen: Hogrefe. (Original work published 1963)

CHAPTER 4

QUALITATIVE META-ANALYSIS OF OUTCOMES OF PERSON-CENTRED AND EXPERIENTIAL PSYCHOTHERAPIES[1]

LADISLAV TIMULAK & MARY CREANER

Psychotherapy outcome research is traditionally understood in terms of quantitative pre–post outcomes. It is especially dominated by the experimental methodology of randomized controlled trials (RCTs) (see Elliott & Freire, this volume). However, with the greater use of qualitative methodology in the field of psychotherapy and counselling, outcome studies utilising qualitative methodology have started to appear (see review in McLeod, 2001). The appearance of such studies reflects both the ever-increasing availability and accessibility of qualitative methodology and certain dissatisfaction with the dominant quantitative outcome culture, and especially the RCT culture (see Elliott, 1998).

McLeod (2001) proposed the argument for the potential enrichment that qualitative methods can bring in conceptualising outcomes of therapy. The main advantage he sees is that clients may comment more directly on the link between an intervention and an outcome. McLeod stresses that the key benefit of qualitative outcome research is in facilitating clients to 'narrativize' their experience more freely. Furthermore, he suggests that qualitative outcome research may allow for a more balanced and complex view of outcome, as it stimulates the client's reflection on what therapy actually brought to their life, rather than quantifying how much they changed in the domain that the researcher considers to be important.

We are assuming that the endeavour of looking at qualitative outcome studies on humanistic/person-centred/experiential therapies may be quite welcomed by therapists of this orientation, for the following reasons. Firstly, we assume that qualitative methodologies may be quite popular among humanistic therapists. This may stem from the phenomenological nature of such methods, which tend to be more holistic and tentative in approach and more commensurate with the values

---

1. While the term 'person-centred/experiential therapies' is used in the title and while the 'person-centred/experiential approach' is the main focus of this paper, the term 'humanistic' is also used throughout. The main reason for this was our expectation that this developing area of research would only have a limited number of studies from which to draw. As we wanted to look at the bigger picture of similar therapies, our research focus included 'humanistic therapies' in a broad sense. However, despite this broader focus, the study refers almost solely to person-centred/experiential therapies.

endorsed by humanistic practitioners. Secondly, humanistic/person-centred/experiential therapists may believe that RCTs are limiting (see Bohart, O'Hara, & Leitner, 1998) and may not capture the effects of psychotherapies related to personal growth, as compared with symptom removal.

Although we could see the potential benefits of using qualitative outcome studies to evaluate person-centred and experiential (PCE) therapies, we were cautious about what could be found. Since McLeod's review of qualitative outcome studies covered only four studies, three of which were clearly not humanistic therapies, we were unsure if sufficient studies existed for review. This was compounded by the fact that currently, there is no consensus on what constitutes a qualitative outcome study. This was one of the reasons why we extended our search for qualitative outcome studies beyond PCE therapies to broadly defined humanistic therapies.

The endeavour to review qualitative outcome studies on humanistic therapies was intriguing. The enthusiasm also stemmed from the interest of the first author in the methodology of qualitative meta-analysis (Timulak, 2009) that seemed to be an appropriate method to use in reviewing any such studies. Qualitative meta-analysis is characterized by '*the aggregating of a group of studies for the purposes of discovering the essential elements and translating the results into an end product that transforms the original results into a new conceptualization*' (Schreiber et al., 1997, p. 314; italics in original). In qualitative meta-analysis, the results of the original studies' categories, abstracted descriptions, and vivid narrative paradigmatic examples [serve] as data for further analysis (Timulak, 2007, pp. 305–306). Recently, a similar method was also employed as an approach for accumulating findings across case studies (Iwakabe & Gazzola, 2009). We were, therefore, hopeful that if we found any qualitative outcome studies on humanistic therapies that we would have a tool of analyzing and synthesizing them.

After these initial thoughts, we started our investigation of qualitative outcome studies on humanistic therapies. The main research question that led this investigation was, '*What outcomes/effects are reported in qualitative studies investigating outcome of humanistic therapies?*'

METHOD

Procedure

The qualitative meta-analysis of qualitative outcome studies of humanistic therapies took several steps. The first step consisted of searching for and identifying appropriate studies that would fulfil the criterion, (i.e., studied outcomes of a humanistic therapy by qualitative means). Secondly, selected studies were evaluated to determine the impact of the methodology employed on the reported findings, which were pertinent for our research question. Thirdly, selected studies were inspected for relevant findings that constituted data for this meta-analysis. Fourthly, analysis of data (i.e., findings of primary studies) was conducted by the first author using a descriptive-interpretative framework (Timulak, 2009; Elliott & Timulak, 2005; see Data analysis section below). Finally, credibility checks were employed, specifically by the use of an auditor, who was also the second author.

Selecting primary studies

When starting the search for studies investigating outcomes of humanistic therapy, we assumed that we would find studies that would match the research question, (i.e., studies that wanted to investigate qualitative outcomes of some humanistic therapy) or that we would find studies that focused on some other research questions (e.g., quantitative outcomes) but at least partially report also on qualitative outcomes of a humanistic therapy. A qualitative outcome study we understood to be a study that referred to post-therapy or outside the therapy session changes (positive or negative) in the client functioning as reported by the client. The search consisted of using PsycINFO database. The following search terms were entered into the database: (1) humanistic, therapy, qualitative, outcome; (2) experiential, therapy, qualitative, outcome; (3) client-centred, therapy, qualitative, outcome; (4) emotion-focused, therapy, qualitative, outcome. The abstracts of all papers thus selected were read and pertinent studies shortlisted (10 studies). We then tried to localize these studies and investigate them further. One study (a research dissertation) was not accessible. At this stage, it was also apparent that not all of the selected studies, either fully or partially, were qualitative outcome studies. However, inspection of references of the selected studies brought two other studies that were then accessed and proved to be relevant for the meta-analysis. As this process also showed that one of the included studies was a case study, we also included another two case studies that we were aware of which were either just published or submitted for publication.

One problem transpired at this stage. In the case of two studies, it was apparent that they did not focus solely on humanistic therapy, but partially on other forms of therapy. In the interim, we decided to keep them as a part of the overall selection that was being inspected and analyzed further. However, we excluded one study (Gallegos, 2005) as it was not clear whether any of the therapies provided were humanistic given the context of the study (mostly unspecified, provided by psychiatrists). We were particularly interested in whether further analysis would show that findings of those studies differed from the studies focusing solely on humanistic therapy. Finally, during the process of refining the write-up of this chapter, one more published qualitative outcome study on an experiential therapy was detected through communication with Robert Elliott, who, as was found, conducted a similar meta-analysis on four unpublished experiential therapy studies and one psychodynamic study in 2002 (see Elliott, 2002b – see also Discussion section below).

This process ended in selecting nine studies that were then further appraised and analyzed. The studies and their main characteristics are presented in Table 1. Though we used the broad category of 'humanistic therapies', as can be seen we identified almost solely person-centred/experiential therapies. Of the nine studies selected, seven specifically covered outcome of some person-centred/experiential therapy. Two studies covered various therapies (including or most likely including person-centred therapy – in Dale et al. (1998) no therapy was specified but given the sample and the fact that it referred to 'counselling' in the UK context, we assumed that it also contained humanistic and specifically person-centred therapy).

Appraisal of primary studies

Once the studies were selected, they were assessed and relevant information was identified. Each study was double-checked to ensure that it addressed the research question of the performed qualitative meta-analysis, (i.e., it had to include qualitative outcome findings of a humanistic therapy or at this stage *also* of a humanistic therapy). Further information was identified in each study: namely, the number of clients, the presenting issues of the clients, the type of therapy provided, the data collection method and data analysis method. In addition, important methodological aspects of the study that might be influencing results were identified and included: (1) the theoretical basis of interpretative framework used in analysis; (2) the data collection method influence on the analysis; (3) the potential sampling and study location issues influencing analysis; (4) the study focus influence on reported qualitative outcomes; and (5) the credibility of analysis performed (e.g., the use of credibility checks).

The potential influence of methodological features on the findings presented in the primary studies was deliberated. Consideration was also given to how it may impact the current meta-analysis. Specifically, the primary studies were assessed to determine convergence or divergence in their reported findings. This written reflection was then audited by the second author and is presented in the results section of this chapter. However, here we have to offer a caveat regarding one important factor present in some of the studies. Some studies (three) did not differentiate between attributions of what clients saw as helpful in therapy and a qualitative account of their current state of functioning. This would not be unexpected, as McLeod (2001) stated, this may be an important advantage of qualitative outcome research. Indeed, for instance, in the case of interpretative case studies (Elliott, 2002a), this is the main goal of such methodology. For the purpose of this qualitative meta-analysis, it presented difficulties as it was clear that in some cases (e.g., Rodgers, 2002), the difference between what was helpful in therapy and how the client changed after therapy was not conceptually discriminated. Therefore, we distilled only accounts of how the client changed post-therapy (even though it may have started earlier than after the last session) from their accounts of what was helpful or unhelpful in therapy.

Table 1. *Studies included in qualitative meta-analysis and their main characteristics*

Study	N of clients	Clients' Presenting Issues	Therapy Type	Data Collection Method	Data analysis Method	Important Methodological Factors Influencing Results
Dale, Allen, & Measor (1998)	40	Adult survivors of sexual, emotional, physical abuse and neglect	Various	Interview and questionnaire focused on biographical details, experience of abuse and perception of outcomes of counselling	Grounded theory method; no explicit description of the procedure	No explicit description of the analysis procedure; authors do not provide the interview or questionnaire schedule; attributional study; no theoretical framework underlying the analysis; therapy not solely humanistic
Davis & Piercy (2007)	2 couples	Couple difficulties	Emotion-focused couple therapy	Research interview with several questions. Among them also questions: In what ways are you different now? In what ways is your partner different?	Grounded theory performed by one researcher (well-described)	Analysis atheoretical though findings contrasted with theory; the study attributional; analysis well-described but performed by one researcher; findings contrasted with the perspectives of therapists – model developers who were also interviewed
Elliott (2002a)	1	Financial worries, general negativity and cynicism, problem communicating with his son, unresolved grief	Emotion-focused	Client change interviews mid, end, follow-up	Qualitative outcomes are stated as raw data in the paper	Analysis atheoretical, phenomenological; less inferential; a good control of the data by having a lot of corroboration and triangulation; good causal links to therapy sessions

Table 1. *Studies included in qualitative meta-analysis and their main characteristics*
... cont'd

Study	N	Problem	Therapy	Data	Analysis	Notes
Elliott et al., (1990)	10	Depression	Emotion-focused	Post-therapy interviews	Grounded theory analysis by four researchers	'Atheoretical' open-coding though one researcher emotion-focused; descriptive, not many inferences offered; good saturation
Elliott et al., (2009)	1	Disorder with agoraphobia; major depression and alcohol abuse in remission; panic attacks, bridge phobia, interpersonal difficulties (abrasive personality)	Emotion-focused	Client change interviews, mid-therapy, end of therapy and a follow-up	Qualitative outcomes are stated as raw data in the paper	Analysis atheoretical, phenomenological; less inferential; a good control of the data by having a lot of corroboration and triangulation; good causal links to therapy sessions
Klein & Elliott (2006)	40	Depression, anxiety, trauma or other personal or interpersonal difficulties	Emotion-focused	Client change interviews, mid-therapy, end of therapy and a follow-up	Open-coding analysis derived from grounded theory method performed by two psychologists; analysis first done independently and consensus was reached; the consensus was audited by an auditor (RE) and discussed	'Atheoretical' open-coding though researchers emotion-focused; descriptive, not many inferences offered; the findings are part of 'attribution' study; good saturation

**Table 1. *Studies included in qualitative meta-analysis and their main characteristics*
… cont'd**

Lipkin (1954)	2	Veterans, vocational problems, neurosis, marital problems, withdrawal into self	Client-centred	Interviews after every session also focused on the current perception of self, insight into self and planning and working on solutions	For the purpose of meta-analysis only raw descriptions of self after therapy were used	Raw data provided in the text (not analysed); interviews done after every session (confusion of outcome and process?); two questions could be leading (insight and solutions).
Rodgers (2002)	9	Relationship difficulties, depression, anxiety and stress	A counselling centre offering a variety of counselling (psychodynamic, person-centred, solution-focused, and gestalt)	Open-ended interview of experiences of counselling, a part of it was a reflection on their life now (still included how counselling played role in it)	Grounded theory performed by one researcher	Researcher was inferential, however, the study was attributional, so the outcomes had to be distilled from an overall narrative of clients' experiences of counselling; no theoretical leaning declared in interpretation, but the researcher is person-centred; caveat – the therapy not only humanistic but also psychodynamic and solution-focused
Timulak et al., (2009)	1	Depression	Person-centred	Client-change interview	Qualitative outcomes are stated as raw data in the paper	Raw data provided in the text (not analysed); interviews done twice including follow-up

Data preparation

After the selected studies were appraised as to how the findings therein could be influenced by methodological aspects, they were then used for data preparation. The findings from selected (primary) studies serve as data in qualitative meta-analysis (Timulak, 2009). Therefore, the results sections of all selected studies were inspected and all text providing categories, descriptions, or quotes relevant for the research question of this meta-analysis (*What outcomes/effects are reported in qualitative studies investigating outcome of humanistic therapies?*) were underlined. The discussion sections were also inspected as they sometimes offer further refinement of findings or quotes. All relevant findings were thus prepared to be used as data for further meta-analysis.

Data analysis

The data analysis procedure followed the framework outlined in Timulak (2009). It is a descriptive-interpretative framework (see Elliott & Timulak, 2005), that is, atheoretical, and attempts to generate findings (categories) from the participants' accounts by observing similarities in common-sense meanings present in the participants' responses (in this case, findings in the original studies). Though the analysts do not use a particular theoretical framework (e.g., emotion-focused theory) and try to stay truthful to the common-sense meaning of the data, generated categories may be implicitly informed by their theoretical persuasions. In that regard, we (the analysts) both are of a broadly defined humanistic theoretical orientation.

Firstly, the conceptual framework that structures the analysis and that the researcher brings to analysis was formulated (domain development). Only one domain was created – *Effects/outcomes of therapy*. It was clear that the majority of studies also focused on helpful/nonhelpful aspects of therapy that contributed to outcome in a positive or negative way. However, the current meta-analysis focused solely on the effects/outcomes as this was the main remit of the research question posed.

Secondly, all available data was divided into meaning units so it was more manageable to analyze further. Meaning units structured the data in units that conveyed a coherent meaning (see Rennie, Philips, & Quartaro, 1988). An example from Rodgers' (2002) study: *'Permission: C has permission for the first time to say what is really going on instead of holding it all inside 'once I started coming to therapy I was able to open up and tell that things were not OK'; person giving themselves permission; only the person themselves could give permission for their own hurt, anger or other inner turmoil to come out; the person permitted themselves to stay with it, to not avoid things, and to do what needed to be done.'*

This example shows results from a study mixing attributions of what was good in therapy ('able to open up') with outcomes ('permission for own hurt to come up').

Thirdly, different meaning units and descriptions within them were compared to each other and an abbreviated description (categorization) that captured the essence of all available data was prepared. The authors ensured that no data was lost or not represented in the final description and conceptualization of the phenomenon of the clients' reported outcomes/effects of humanistic therapy. It was also established that the two studies which also referred to therapies other than humanistic therapies (Dale et al., 1998; Rodgers, 2002) did not yield qualitatively different results and seem to merge neatly into the overall description. Therefore, they were retained in the study.

Fourthly, the final description and conceptualization was inspected and methodological influences from the primary studies, as well as from the conducted meta-analysis, were reflected and an interpretation was provided as to how they were shaping the meta-analysis.

RESULTS

Methodological features of primary studies

The primary studies in general did not use any explicit theoretical framework (e.g., person-centred theory of a fully functioning person) that would lead to inferences from the analysts of the qualitative accounts. The only study that attempted to link the participant accounts with a theoretical framework was the Davis and Piercy (2007) study on couple therapy that interpreted findings from the perspective of emotion-focused and other couple therapies perspectives. Nonetheless, the majority of researchers were humanistic (it is not clear in the case of the Dale et al. (1998) study). This would suggest that the participants' accounts were analyzed using a common-sense understanding framework (often using the participants' own language). However, as noted, reading and perception of the participants' accounts was most likely informed by the preferred (PCE therapy) view as was also in the case with the researchers conducting the meta-analysis.

In general, the reported qualitative findings were rather more descriptive than interpretative (see Elliott & Timulak, 2005; McLeod, 2001). Several studies presented simple categorisation based on the most obvious content in the data (Dale et al., 1998; Elliott et al., 1990; Klein & Elliott, 2006), case studies in general produced raw data, i.e., direct quotes from clients (see Elliott, 2002a; Elliott et al., 2009; Lipkin, 1954; Timulak et al., 2009), an inferential work was present in Rodgers (2002) and to a certain extent in Davis and Piercy (2007).

Two studies (Dale et al., 1998; Rodgers, 2002) also contained non-humanistic therapy. We were particularly interested in whether the findings differ from or fit coherently with the rest of the studies. As will be seen below, these studies yielded results which fit readily into the main meta-categories. Interestingly, one study (Klein

& Elliott, 2006) specifically looked at whether there is a difference in qualitative outcomes/effects reported in quantitatively successful vs. unsuccessful cases and found no difference.

With the exception of case studies, primary studies did not use a follow-up perspective, which is often used in quantitative studies. Several studies were primarily attributional (which is probably embedded in the use of qualitative methodology – see McLeod, 2001), looking at aspects of therapy that clients found helpful or unhelpful including their link to any potential change. Some studies (Dale et al., 1998; Davis & Piercy, 2007) provided a very limited description of the method (data collection and data analysis), thus effectively preventing assessment of their impact on the findings.

In the primary studies, the clients' presenting issues covered depression, anxiety, child abuse, veterans' problems, problems in interpersonal relationships as well as social/vocational problems (see Table 1). It seems that the studies did not cover more serious problems (e.g., psychosis) but rather referred to outpatient settings only.

Qualitative outcomes/effects of humanistic therapies

Qualitative outcomes/effects found in the primary studies can be categorized in several meta-categories capturing changed experiencing or view of self and others (see Table 2). Clients in primary studies reported most typically new *Appreciating Experiences of Self*. The first meta-category among 'Appreciating Experiences of Self' is *Smoother and healthier emotional experiencing* (e.g., Dale et al., 1998; Elliott, 2002a; Elliott et al., 1990; Klien & Elliott, 2006; Lipkin, 1954). This category, which covers primary studies' findings reporting healthier emotional functioning was characterized by the ability to be open to, contain and express emotions, experience hopefulness (optimism) and calmness, and more peaceful, stable and improved general functioning. An example would be a short expression of a client cited in Klein and Elliott (2006, p. 98): *'I have achieved a better emotional balance.'* Similarly, a client in Elliott et al. (1990, p. 563) recounted: *'I have not been thinking about death. I used to feel like it took too much energy to live, but now I have lots of energy.'* Another example provided by a client in Lipkin (1954, p. 19) illustrates this point: *'... one of the most surprising, most amazing things that would ever happen to a man ... I believe ... in the way I was feeling ... to ah suddenly come about and feel this way ... more free and easy, more lively, more light ... and to shake off this whole heaviness that seemed to be surrounding me and gripping.'*

The second meta-category *Appreciating vulnerability* refers to findings reporting on the client's defencelessness, honesty with self (openness to change) and permission to feel the pain (Rodgers, 2002) as well as awareness of sadness, grief (Elliott, 2002a) and self-acceptance of existential isolation (Dale et al., 1998). As the client in Elliott (2002a, p. 5) expresses it: *'I do not think I would have looked at those [feelings] on my*

Table 2. *Qualitative outcomes/effects found in the primary studies*

Main Meta-category	Meta-categories	Primary Studies Findings
Appreciating experiences of self	Smoother and healthier emotional experiencing	Hopefulness (Klein & Elliott, 2006), peace and stability (Klein & Elliott, 2006), emotional well-being, greater sense of energy (Klein & Elliott, 2006); calmer, at peace (Elliott, 2002a; Lipkin, 1954); improved mood, optimism (Elliott et al., 1990); general openness to own feelings (Elliott et al., 1990); ability to express and contain feelings (Dale et al., 1998); feeling more free and easy, more light and lively (Lipkin, 1954) (4/8; 4 out of 8 studies on individual therapy contributed to this meta-category)
	Appreciating vulnerability	Permission to feel the pain (Rodgers, 2002); transparency (dropping barriers and defences) (Rodgers, 2002); honest with self (Rodgers, 2002; Elliott, 2002a); open to change (Elliott, 2002a); awareness of being old, process of grieving, grieving is undoing problematic anger/anxiety (Elliott, 2002a); self-acceptance of existential isolation (Dale et al., 1998); more tolerant of difficulties and setbacks (Elliott et al., 2009) (4/8)
	Experience of self-compassion	Self-esteem, self-care (Klein & Elliott, 2006); improved self-esteem (Elliott et al., 1990); engagement with self (experiencing support from within) (Rodgers, 2002); valuing self (Dale et al., 1998) (4/8)
	Experience of resilience	Restructuring (recycling the bad things) (Rodgers, 2002); insight first painful then feeling better (Lipkin, 1954) (2/8)
	Feeling empowered	Self-confident, strength within (Rodgers, 2002; Klein & Elliott, 2006; Lipkin, 1954); general sense of well-being: health, energy, activities (Klein & Elliott, 2006), newfound or improved abilities to act (Klein & Elliott, 2006); improved general day-to-day coping (Dale et al., 1998); giving self credit for accomplishments, try new things, reading (Elliott, 2002a); improved ability to cope (Elliott et al., 1990); preparing to take action to deal with problems (Elliott et al., 1990); specific wishes/attitudes strengthened (Elliott et al., 1990); being able to make decision, gaining control over life (Timulak et al., 2009; Lipkin, 1954; Rodgers, 2002); able

Table 2. *Qualitative outcomes/effects found in the primary studies ... cont'd*

Main Meta-category	Meta-categories	Primary Studies Findings
		to stand up for himself, more initiative instead of fear of doing things (Lipkin, 1954) (7/8)
	Mastering symptoms	Can cross bridges, can fly (Elliott et al., 2009); symptoms went one by one, sudden relief (Lipkin, 1954) (2/8)
	Enjoying change in circumstances	Improved non-relationship aspects of life independent of therapy (Elliott et al., 1990; Elliott, 2002a) (2/8)
Appreciating experience of self in relationship with others	Feeling supported	Feeling respected by own children, seeking support group (Klein & Elliott, 2006) reported changes in others' view of self (Elliott et al., 1990); people tell me I am a nicer person (Elliott et al., 2009); in many studies attributions to therapy/therapist as providers of support (3/8)
	Enjoying interpersonal encounters	Better interpersonal functioning (all, romantic, family) (Klein & Elliott, 2006); reordering relationships (Dale et al., 1998); being able to cope with reactions of others (Timulak at al., 2009); increased independence/assertion (Elliott et al., 1990); increased positive openness (Elliott et al., 1990); improved relationships (Elliott et al., 1990); better relationship with my wife, more tolerant (Elliott at al., 2009) (5/8)
Changed view of self/others	Self-insight and/or self-awareness	Development of meaning and understanding of abuse, learning from therapy (Dale et al., 1998; Lipkin, 1954); more aware and true to myself (Klein & Elliott, 2006); realizations about self (Elliott et al., 1990); enlightened (problem fitting in like a glove), better understanding of self (I am not in the dark, I can do something about it), seeing patterns (Lipkin, 1954) (4/8)
	Changed view of others	See other viewpoints (Klein & Elliott, 2006); being more interested in others (Timulak at al., 2009); changes in C's views and attitudes towards others (Elliott et al., 1990); accepting parent faults (Timulak at al., 2009) (3/9)

own … I think the therapy actually in some way … gave me a process of grieving.'

The third meta-category *Experience of self-compassion* refers to newly reported experiences of self-esteem (Klein & Elliott, 2006; Elliott et al., 1990), experiences of self-care (Klein & Elliott, 2006) as well as experienced engagement with self (experiencing support from self) (Rodgers, 2002) or valuing of self (Dale et al., 1998). As a client in Rodgers (2002, p. 189) put it: *'You might find friendship or support from other people, but the real you is inside.'* Or as a client in Elliott et al. (1990, p. 563) expressed: *'I don't beat myself over the head over mistakes. I see myself as more human.'*

The fourth meta-category covers *Experiences of resilience.* Findings in primary studies were reporting on participants' experiences of 'restructuring as recycling the bad things' (Rodgers, 2002) or by first having painful insight then feeling better and have 'buttressed confidence' (Lipkin, 1954). This meta-category captures the client's sense of being able to overcome adversity and stay firm. An example may be found in a citation from Rodgers (2002, p. 190): *'It was like recycling the bad things, which is upsetting. You really want to put it behind you, but it's difficult to discard it. With the counselling, again we were recycling it. But in order to recycle, I mean when you recycle rubbish, eventually it's thrown out.'*

The fifth meta-category covers experiences of *Feeling empowered.* The primary studies that we built this category on talked about experiences of feeling strong, more self-confident (Klein & Elliott, 2006; Rodgers, 2002). They also referred to experiences of a general sense of well-being, health, energy, involvement in activities (Klein & Elliott, 2006). They covered reports of being ready and able to deal with problems (Dale et al., 1998; Elliott et al., 1990) as well as being stronger in pursuing their own values (Elliott et al., 1990). Furthermore, they covered experiences of giving self credit for accomplishments and having courage to try new things (Elliott, 2002a). One client also declared being able to make decisions and gaining control over her life (Lipkin, 1954; Rodgers, 2002; Timulak at al., 2009). While another talked about being able to stand up for himself and take more initiative instead of fearing doing things (Lipkin, 1954). A good example of experienced empowerment is the client's expression in Rodgers (2002, p. 190): *'I've got all my confidence back now, my self belief … I feel that it's not other people that have control of me, I've got control of myself.'* Another good example is provided by a client in Elliott et al., (1990) *'Deepening and clarifying the realisation that I want to give something back to the world'* (p. 564).

The sixth meta-category captures experiences of *Mastering symptoms.* The clients recounted different types of overcoming symptoms such as being able to cross bridges or being able to fly, activities that the client was not able to do before therapy (Elliott et al., 2009) or just referred to a more general change in symptoms that went away *'little by little, one by one'* (Lipkin, 1954, p. 21).

The seventh meta-category that was found only in two studies (Elliott et al., 1990; Elliott, 2002) referred to experiences of changes in the client's circumstances. These could be changes not directly connected to therapy (e.g., '*I am financially better*', Elliott et al., 1990, p. 564).

Alongside the new *Appreciating experiences of self,* some studies also reported new *Appreciating experiences of others*. In the studies reviewed two meta-categories falling in this scope were formulated: that of *Feeling supported/respected* and *Enjoying interpersonal encounters*. While feeling supported was present in many studies that also included helpful aspects of therapy attributed to the therapeutic relationship, here we refer to experienced support in the relationships outside of therapy, such as support from close ones ('*I feel more respected by my children*') or from going to a support group (Klein & Elliott, 2006). In some instances, clients referred to others noticing positive changes in clients and appreciating them (Elliott et al., 1990, 2009).

The second relational meta-category that we distilled from the findings of the primary studies refers to experiences of *Enjoying interpersonal encounters*. Some studies captured the clients' experiences of improved relationships in general and/or in close relationships (Elliott et al., 1990; Elliott et al., 2009; Klein & Elliott, 2006). Some studies reported on re-ordering of the importance of relationships (Dale et al., 1998). One client in a case study talked of being able to cope with reactions of others (Timulak at al., 2009). A nice example is an excerpt from Klein and Elliott (2006, p. 98): '*But, one time I was here, and [the therapist] said, 'Well, pretend your children are sitting in that seat there, and tell them what you want.' So I did, and I talked to each one of them, sitting in that seat right there. That was weird … that gave me the permission … So I went home and I called up my kids and talked to most of them. And I even e-mailed with my oldest son; we sent some e-mail back and forth. So that opened up that line of my life that I was really confused and worried about.*'

Apart from the experienced/experiential change, clients in the primary studies also reported cognitive change in their view of self or others. We saw it as a distinct main meta-category 'Changed View of Self/Others'. This cognitive change consisted of two meta-categories: *Self-insight and/or self-awareness* and *Changed view of others*.

Self-insight and/or self-awareness referred to the findings that spoke of: development of meaning and understanding of abuse (Dale et al., 1998); experiences of being enlightened ('*problem fitting in like a glove*', Lipkin, 1954, p. 21) and having better understanding of self ('*I am not in the dark, I can do something about it*', Lipkin, 1954, p. 22) or being more aware (Elliott et al., 1990; Klein & Elliott, 2006) and true to self (Klein & Elliott, 2006). In two studies clients also referred to understanding in terms of learning (Dale et al., 1998; Lipkin, 1954). One of the clients in Lipkin (1954, p. 22) puts it nicely: '*If it's something that you know, then there's something you can do about it. I can do something about it now. I don't have to be in the dark any more ….*'

The meta-category *Changed view of others* covered findings in the primary studies that showed that the client sees other viewpoints (Elliott et al., 1990; Klein & Elliott, 2006) or changed their attitude to others (Elliott et al., 1990; Timulak et al., 2009). This was presented, for example, in '*being more interested in others*' or specifically '*being more accepting of parents' faults*' (Timulak at al., 2009).

The study on couple therapy (Davis & Piercy, 2007) was not included in the meta-analysis, as its findings seemed to be somewhat distinct – the goal of therapy being primarily change in the relationship. The conceptualization of the generated findings of that study was also more theoretically informed by couple therapy (mainly emotion-focused) theory. The reported findings in this study suggested following relational effects: softening of the couple towards each other through awareness, in attitude, emotions, and behaviour (being kinder). Partners also reported support of the partner's autonomy (making a space for the other). In addition, controlling partners eased-up and the submissive re-engaged, while both parties reported an increased sense of self-confidence. The partners also reported 'slowing down' and having a more curious stance in relation to each other. Finally, the partners reported being able to take personal responsibility for their experience in the relationship.

Interestingly, few studies reported negative qualitative outcomes/effects of person-centred/experiential. The negative outcomes/effects are summarized in Table 3. They included reports of still having the same problems that brought clients to therapy, (e.g., in the Dale et al., 1998 study, the majority of clients continued to experience problems stemming from abuse). While the problems may be less severe, the clients still did not have a sense of resolution (Dale et al., 1998). Some clients felt overwhelmed by abuse-related cognition and affect. Many clients also felt harmed by the therapist, referring to power struggles, being forced to fake being better, as they could not otherwise leave counselling (Dale et al., 1998). One client put it: '*Oh, I'd politely sit there and nod and agree and, you know – the way I was brought up ...* ' (Dale et al., 1998, p. 10).

Table 3. *Negative qualitative outcomes/effects found in the primary studies*

- Still the same problems: majority of clients continued to experience problems stemming from abuse (major problems moved into some problems), not having sense of resolution (Dale et al., 1998)
- Being overwhelmed (Dale et al., 1998)
- Feeling harmed by T (power struggles, forced to fake being better, C could not leave counselling, etc.) (Dale et al., 1998)
- Afraid of changing (too big), emotional restriction and fear of overcoming it (Lipkin, 1954)
- Disappointment of not having feelings understood (Lipkin, 1954)

An interesting negative outcome/effect was reported in Lipkin's (1954) study. The client in the study reported being afraid of changing (the change was too big). The client reported emotional restriction and fear of overcoming it. Lipkin (1954, pp. 22– 23) provides poignant citations capturing it: '*I was little afraid of changing. I felt maybe it would be too big. I felt maybe it would be a big change and I wouldn't be able to handle it. And I was little frightened of changing because I'd more or less gotten used to the idea of taking everything and keeping it within myself. I … ah … never lost my temper or anything. I just kept everything within myself and it was … well, that grew up with me, I think, that fear, that inward feeling. And ah I just … I didn't think … well, at first, I didn't think that I could get those feelings out. And then, a lot of times, I rely on those feelings … they're something like memories .. not good or bad memories … but ah a lot of times, they're something to think about. And I figured if I got rid of those feelings or those … well, those feelings that I had about certain things, ah what would I do? What would I go back on? … think about?'* And also '*I've kept myself ah under emotionally so long that it would be hard to bring any of that out.*' We present it here as a part of negative outcomes, however, one must note that it is rather an increased awareness of actively avoiding change, which may be an important and useful awareness. It may be also an important step in first being aware of the need for protection against change, which may be reassessed in the future. On the other hand, the same client also stated '*Until I feel that someone will understand how I feel, I will probably always keep it under*', which may be read as disappointment with the therapist and/or other people and a missed opportunity in therapy.

Interpretation of methodological influences reflected in the presented outcomes/effects

Similar to the primary studies (with the exception of the Davis and Piercy, 2007, couple study) our meta-analysis did not utilize any particular theoretical framework. Therefore, the meta-categories are attempting to capture a common-sense essence of what the clients in the primary studies disclosed and what the primary researchers captured in their categories or brief narrative accounts. The fact that we do not use any particular theoretical framework also limits potential inferences that could be achieved in reviewing the data. Thus, our categories and descriptions as in the original studies are more descriptive than interpretative (see Elliott & Timulak, 2005).

On the other hand, we share a humanistic leaning, as was the case with the majority of researchers/analysts in the primary studies, which may mean that we saw the findings in a manner that paid particular attention to relational, emotional, and empowering qualities of human functioning. However, we were surprised by some of the findings, which may counterbalance any potential biases. For instance, we did not expect experienced vulnerability as a positive outcome; we also did not expect a number of negative effects, such as fear of change, that were evoked by therapy.

Another aspect of our approach, again similar to that evident in the primary studies, was an attempt to look for similarities across the findings (participants' accounts) rather than differences. This may bring 'narrative smoothing' (Spence, 1994) to the final viewpoint of this meta-analysis. It was especially interesting that primary studies that also included non-humanistic therapies did not reveal anything specific just for these studies. Again, the fact that we also discovered negative outcomes in two studies with credible face validity somewhat compensates for the potential limitations of our looking for similarities.

As an interesting observation, one of the studies that utilized quantitative measurement (Klein & Elliott, 2006) did not find differences in qualitative accounts of quantitatively differentially effective cases. This raises a new question concerning the relationship between quantitative and qualitative outcome. Namely, is it possible to distinguish between qualitatively successful and qualitatively unsuccessful cases given that in both cases the picture may be complex and mixed (i.e., a 'successful' client may report negative impacts and an 'unsuccessful' client may report positive impacts)?

With regard to the data collection method, it does not seem to have a bearing on the meta-analytic findings, as all of the studies used interviews as the main method. However, the fact that negative outcomes were reported only in two studies may be a result of these not being specifically asked about in other studies.

The presented results of the meta-analysis appear to be quite coherent with primary studies bringing, in general, similar and overlapping, convergent findings. The studies that had the largest number of participants (40) appear most frequently among the 10 meta-categories, with the Klein and Elliott (2006) study contributing to 7 out of 10 positive meta-categories and the Dale et al., (1998) study feeding into 6 out of 10 positive categories and considerably into the negative outcomes findings. Similarly, the Elliott et al. (1990) study on 10 participants contributed significantly to 7 meta-categories. The Rodgers (2002) study on 9 participants contributed to the overall findings as well by being present in 4 meta-categories. As visible in Table 3, the meta-categories were typically based on findings from 2 to 5 primary studies with the exception of categories *Feeling supported, Enjoying change in circumstances* and *Negative outcomes* that were based on one or two studies.

Finally, one must bear in mind that our meta-analysis yielded mutually exclusive meta-categories, meaning that each meaning unit (a unit of data taken from a primary study) was assigned only in one meta-category. This was not explicitly required and we expected that in the case of longer meaning units it may be somewhat arbitrary to assign a meaning unit to one category only as one can find multiple meanings in a longer account taken from a primary study. However, we ended up having meta-categories each using different meaning units. Still, it is possible that other analysts would have difficulty in some cases of being exactly sure where to put a given excerpt (e.g., *Experience of resilience* vs. *Feeling empowered* meta-categories). This, however, should not cause any problem, as the final outline of the meta-categories should be used as a conceptual framework of the types of effects/impacts reported by the clients as a consequence of participating in humanistic therapy, rather than a clear-cut difference-seeking description of such effects/impacts.

DISCUSSION

The qualitative meta-analysis of qualitative outcome studies on predominantly PCE therapies brought some expected and some surprising findings. For instance, *Changed view of others and self* is often reported as a positive impact in psychotherapy (Elliott & Wexler, 1994; Timulak, 2007). It is also postulated by many therapeutic approaches such as psychodynamic and cognitive (e.g., Grosse Holtforth et al., 2007; Messer & McWilliams, 2007). In its 'new awareness' form, it is also recognized by humanistic approaches (e.g., Elliott, 2007; Pascual-Leone & Greenberg, 2007). Similarly, *Mastering of symptoms* is expected across the board for different theoretical approaches and it is probably a common presentation and expectation of clients in therapy.

Many of the other reported positive experiences (under the meta-category *Appreciating experiences of self*) are not surprising from the perspective of PCE therapies theory. Healthier emotional experiencing, experienced resilience, experienced self-compassion and feelings of empowerment are explicitly seen as the goals of emotion-focused therapy (see Greenberg et al., 1993; Greenberg & Watson, 2006) and definitely can be recognized as being in line with the original conceptualisation of outcome in client-centred therapy (see Rogers, 1961). Some of those outcomes (e.g., smoother emotional processing (relief), empowerment) are also reported as helpful therapy process in-session impacts in PCE therapies, but also other forms of therapy (see Timulak, 2007; Timulak & Elliott, 2003; Timulak & Lietaer, 2001). It is, therefore, good to see it distinctly recognized as post-therapy outcome by the client, though we have to be mindful that their therapists were typically PCE and may 'prompt' clients in valuing and recognising it. Again, the primary researchers, while conducting the meta-analysis, could have been more attuned to recognizing this in the clients' accounts, as were we as well.

Similarly, with empowerment or relief, the experiences of feeling supported were previously reported as in-session helpful impacts (Timulak, 2007). These experiences, however, meant experiencing support from the therapist. The current meta-analysis extended that to experiences of support from people outside of the therapy session, probably achieved by the client actively seeking it. Interestingly, the clients in the primary studies also reported enjoyment of interpersonal interaction with other people as an important outcome of therapy. Therefore, it was not only their self–self relation and experience that shifted but also their experience of interacting with others. This interpersonal functioning domain, though implicitly making sense and definitely present in the writings of PCE therapists (e.g., Rogers, 1959), was often under-emphasized by PCE theorists who placed greater emphasis on self-acceptance and fluid experiencing.

Definitely surprising for us was the finding that the clients can see and appreciate vulnerability as an important outcome of therapy. Though emotional pain (Bolger, 1999) and vulnerability (Rogers, 1961) is seen by PCE theorists as an important part of a healing process in therapy, it is not typically construed as a desired outcome of therapy. This finding definitely contradicts the current (evidence-based) climate of expecting symptom relief and change very early in therapy. Indeed, it is hard to imagine how the evidence-based movement would see the appreciation of vulnerability and emotional pain as a desired outcome of psychological therapy. However, seeing it as a more genuine way of being, when there is a real suffering in life, and contrasting it with unauthentic and avoidant ways of being, makes it perfectly clear why it is reported by the clients as a 'positive' outcome. It seems that this, together with a change in self-experiencing (such as empowerment, self-compassion, etc.), is an area of outcome that could be uniquely conceptualized by PCE theorists. Person-centred/experiential therapists could do a good service to mainstream psychotherapy and mental health if they highlighted that a good outcome may superficially or initially appear as a 'defeat'.

Our study also revealed some negative effects reported by clients. They focused on the lack of resolution, and also on experiences, for example, being overwhelmed by the experience of problems (in the session) or being scared of facing the emotionally difficult 'issues' in the session. Although in the case of being scared of facing difficult feelings, it may also be an important awareness that may not be the last step in addressing the difficulty. Nevertheless, this accentuates the fact that although improved emotional functioning is reported by some clients, it may not be the case for all clients. The study would also suggest that it actually might not be always two distinct groups of clients, as it may be difficult to find a typical positive vs. negative outcome (more see below). Thus, there may be a fine line between experiencing the emotional impact of therapy as building an emotional resilience or, on the contrary, making the client emotionally more vulnerable.

It is possible that therapists will have to become more sophisticated in working with emotions and distinguishing 'productive' and 'unproductive' emotional experience (Greenberg, Auszra, & Herrmann, 2007). While unproductive emotions are typical for feeling overwhelmed, stuck in unpleasant emotion and being the victim of emotion (Greenberg et al., 2007), productive emotions are characterized by a specific manner of processing. This involves attention to the emotion, symbolization of it, congruence between verbal and nonverbal aspects of experiencing emotion, acceptance of emotion, optimal regulation of emotion, experienced agency in emotional experiencing, and differentiation of different aspects of emotional experiencing (Greenberg et al., 2007). It is possible that positive outcomes reported by clients in the primary studies reflected productive emotional experiencing, while negative outcomes were describing what can be seen as unproductive emotional experiencing. To differentiate between the two and develop alternative ways of working with them may be an important task for the future of PCE therapies. Emotion-focused therapy (Greenberg, 2002; Greenberg et al., 1993) is a good example of attempting to do so.

Another type of negative outcome reported in one of the primary studies was harm caused by the therapist through exercising power over the client. Conflicts in the therapeutic relationship (Safran & Muran, 2000) are not that atypical. Several studies reported (e.g., Piper et al., 1999; Rhodes et al., 1994) that unresolved conflicts end up with the client dropping out of therapy. Dale et al.'s (1998) study shows that the client can go to great lengths in order to 'escape' from therapy and can be negatively impacted and feel hurt as a consequence of therapy. The type of studies included in the analysis does not look at this phenomenon from an interactional perspective nor does it include the therapist's perspective on it. However, while we do not understand this phenomenon fully, this finding can still alert us to the fact that this is how clients can experience the effects of therapy.

One methodological issue stems from an interesting finding on negative outcomes/effects of therapy. These were only reported in two studies. It is not clear whether it reflects the reality of participants in different studies (good vs. bad outcomes) or whether it can be attributed to differences in the data collection, where in some cases interviewers actively prompted for negative experiences and in some cases did not. It seems to be an important area where qualitative methodology could gather valuable information. Therefore, future qualitative outcome studies could routinely include prompts on any negative or hindering outcomes.

Several other methodological issues transpired in the process of our meta-analysis. Firstly, some studies were attributional (i.e., looking at what the clients found helpful in therapy, often not distinguishing it from the outside-sessions effects of therapy on clients). It is logical, as predicted by McLeod (2001), that this may be an important feature of qualitative outcomes studies and their advantage as they directly allow for asking the client to interpret causal links between the therapy and outcome. Since helpful aspects of the therapy process were not a remit of our task, we had to cogently distinguish between in-session helpful aspects and impacts and outside-session effects and outcomes. This distinction is somewhat artificial and as a result, some of the richness and information in the primary studies is not reported here. On the other hand, we noticed that several studies (see Table 1) did not differentiate conceptually between in-session helpful processes and outside-therapy effects and outcomes. This is problematic if not reflected, particularly when qualitative outcomes are compared to quantitative, as quantitative studies strictly distinguish between the process and outcome aspects of therapy.

Another methodological caution is that the primary studies, as well as the meta-analysis, used an atheoretical framework for analyzing data, which could lead to losing some of the potential richness present in the data. The researchers/analysts were trying to be faithful to the exact words of the clients, which often happens when there is no firm theoretical framework used for interpreting data (for an alternative approach, see Elliott, 2008). Though the majority of researchers have a person-centred/experiential background, which most likely shaped the wording of final categories, the presented categories are still more descriptive than inferential (see Elliott & Timulak, 2005). If we (or the primary researchers) used a specific theory (e.g., emotion-focused), we could infer more theoretically laden conclusions/interpretations that may be more informative (e.g., if we were actively looking for it, we could identify as a positive outcome, a better access to primary emotions in the clients). Elliott (2008) presented an excellent example of a theoretically laden qualitative analysis from the perspective of emotion theory.

An interesting finding was that we could not discover any difference between qualitative outcomes of the studies of purely humanistic (PCE) therapies and the studies that also involved other forms of therapy. This may be due to methodological factors such as the use of open-ended questions that may not actively ask for differences in the clients' accounts. On the other hand, in the case of the two studies that reported on outcomes of other than humanistic therapies, it was not possible to determine from the primary studies whether the data belonged to a particular therapy, so we could not check whether there was a specific pattern in the data for humanistic versus non-humanistic therapy. Thus, it may be possible that all potential differences had already been missed at the primary studies level. Interestingly, the Davis and Piercy (2007) study on couple therapy which directly compared several theoretical frameworks, found convergence in the reported outcomes across different approaches.

It is not clear whether the outcomes we found are unique to humanistic (PCE) therapies. There are only very few qualitative outcomes studies on therapies other than PCE. One of them, a qualitative study by Clarke, Rees, and Hardy (2004) on the impacts of cognitive therapy of five clients, showed a different pattern of results (the study combines helpful therapy processes and outside-therapy outcomes). While it showed the importance of insight and self-understanding, mastery of symptoms, ease in functioning and recognition of changes in the self by others – all found in our analysis – it also ascertained that clients in cognitive therapy internalized the cognitive model and were actively using it to combat their problematic thinking. They were also challenging it by applying behavioural experiments similar to the ones used in therapy. The authors also report (though do not provide examples), similar to our study, that the clients were more self-compassionate, confident, reflective, etc. What seems to differ is this appreciation of vulnerability that some of our studies reported, although one of the cited client in Clarke et al.'s study acknowledged being different after 'going through the pains'. Moreover, appreciation of interpersonal encounters is not that visible in the cognitive therapy study, although interpersonal assertiveness is mentioned. Although self-confidence is mentioned, it is difficult to say whether it central as it is not elaborated upon in the reported findings. Interestingly, the change in the view of the client by others that appears in our study, is not mentioned in Clarke et al. All these differences have to be taken with caution as Clarke et al.'s study is based on five clients, while ours is based on nine studies involving more than 100 clients. Furthermore, the theoretical background of the analysts (cognitive vs. humanistic) may be responsible for the differences, too.

Also of interest may be a finding reported in Klein and Elliott (2006) that there was not much discrepancy in the reported qualitative outcomes of quantitatively differentially effective therapies. This raises an issue of whether qualitative methodology allows for making a distinction between a good and a bad therapy case. As seen in Lipkin (1954), who presented an example of a successful and an unsuccessful case, it is possible, but it may be more visible in the extremes (very successful vs. very unsuccessful) rather than as a general rule.

A separate issue, pertinent for any qualitative meta-analysis, is whether other researchers would come to a similar conceptualization. Interestingly, only after finishing our meta-analysis, we discovered that Robert Elliott (2002b) reported on a meta-analysis that he conducted with his students on four unpublished experiential therapy qualitative outcomes studies combined with one semi-qualitative outcomes study of psychodynamic therapy (Connolly & Strupp, 1996). Though he does not describe the methodology of this study at length, it seems that it roughly followed similar principles of analysis as our meta-analysis. All seven second-order meta-categories presented by him were found in our study (see Table 4). For instance, *Leaving distress behind* in Elliott (2002b) corresponds with *Healthier emotional experiencing* and *Mastery of symptoms* in our study; *Increased contact with emotional self* (including *Increased self-understanding*) from their study corresponds with the *Healthier emotional experiencing* and *Self-insight and self-awareness* categories that we found. *Improved self-esteem* in Elliott corresponds with *Experience of self-compassion* in our study. *Increased sense of personal power* corresponds with *Feeling empowered*; *Defining self with others* and *Engaging with others*, correspond with *Enjoying interpersonal encounters*, and finally *Experiencing world more/mobilising self to act* corresponds again with what we conceptualized as *Feeling empowered*. Interestingly, Elliott also reports unspecific negative changes. Although the data from one of the studies in our meta-analysis – Elliott et al., 1990 – is included in one of the unpublished papers in the meta-analysis reported in Elliott's paper (Elliott, 2010; email communication), there are several independent studies (although one is on non-humanistic therapy) in the meta-analysis that Elliott

Table 4. *Meta-categories of the qualitative meta-analysis presented in Elliott (2002b) and corresponding meta-categories in our qualitative meta-analysis*

Elliott (2002b)	Our study
Leaving distress behind	Healthier emotional experiencing mastery of symptoms
Increased contact with emotional self (incl. increased self-understanding)	Healthier emotional experiencing self-insight and self-awareness
Improved self-esteem	Experience of self-compassion
Increased sense of personal power	Feeling empowered
Defining self with others	Enjoying interpersonal encounters
Engaging with others	Enjoying interpersonal encounters
Experiencing world more/mobilising self to act	Feeling empowered
n/a	Appreciating vulnerability category
n/a	Enjoying change in circumstances
n/a	Feeling supported

conducted with his students. Still, with the exception of *Appreciating vulnerability* category, *Enjoying change in circumstances,* and *Feeling supported* the findings are converging, speaking in favour (triangulating) of the usefulness and value of the conceptualization captured in our meta-categories.

Finally, we would like to caution the reader about the methodological problems inherent in the methodology of qualitative meta-analysis (see Timulak, 2009). These may vary from favouring converging results (by looking at similarities), providing findings in an abstract form without a direct contact with participants, over-representation of some studies over others and collating studies of different methodological quality. Nonetheless, we believe that the conceptualization that transpired from our meta-analysis is a practically relevant and empirically based view of what sorts of outcomes can be expected from people participating in PCE therapies. From what we have presented, it is obvious that impacts are broad, differentiated and go well beyond what is probably understood as a successful outcome of psychological or other mental health intervention in mainstream mental health care. It seems clear that symptom reduction is only one part of it. We hope that this study will contribute to the debate regarding what therapy may provide to people whose suffering brings them to seek help.

REFERENCES

Bohart, A., O'Hara, M., & Leitner, L. (1998). Empirically violated treatments: Disenfranchisement of humanistic and other psychotherapies. *Psychotherapy Research 8*, 141–157.

Bolger, E. (1999). Grounded theory analysis of emotional pain. *Psychotherapy Research, 9*, 342–362.

Clarke, H., Rees, A., & Hardy, G. (2004). The big idea: Clients' perspectives of change processes in cognitive therapy. *Psychology and Psychotherapy: Theory, Research and Practice, 77*, 67–89.

Connolly, M., & Strupp, H. (1996). Cluster analysis of patient reported psychotherapy outcomes. *Psychotherapy Research, 6*, 30–42.

Dale, P., Allen, J., & Measor, L. (1998). Counselling adults who were abused as children: Clients' perceptions of efficacy, client-counsellor communication, and dissatisfaction. *British Journal of Guidance and Counselling, 26*, 141–157.

Davis, S. D., & Piercy, F. P. (2007). What clients of couple therapy model developers and their former students say about change. Part I: Model-dependent common factors across three models. *Journal of Marital and Family Therapy, 33*, 318–343.

Elliott, R. (1998). Editor's introduction: A guide to the empirically-supported treatments controversy. *Psychotherapy Research, 8*, 115–125.

Elliott, R. (2002a). Hermeneutic single case efficacy design. *Psychotherapy Research, 12*, 1–20.

Elliott, R. (2002b). Render unto Caesar: Quantitative and qualitative knowing in research on humanistic therapies. *Person-Centered and Experiential Psychotherapies, 1*, 102–117.

Elliott, R. (2007). Decoding insight talk. In L. G. Castonguay & C. E. Hill (Eds.), *Insight in psychotherapy* (pp. 167–186). Washington, DC: American Psychological Association.

Elliott, R. (April, 2008). *Emotion processes in first sessions of process-experiential therapy: An interpretive discourse analysis of clients' accounts of significant events.* Paper presented at conference of the British Psychological Society, Dublin, Ireland.

Elliott, R., Clark, C., Kemeny, V., Wexler, M. M., Mack, C., & Brinkerhoff, J. (1990). The impact of experiential therapy on depression: The first ten cases. In G. Lietaer, J. Rombauts, & R. Van Balen (Eds.), *Client-centered and experiential psychotherapy in the nineties* (pp. 549–578). Leuven, Belgium: Katholieke Universiteit Leuven.

Elliott, R., Partyka, R., Wagner, J., Alperin, R., Dobrenski. R., Messer, S.B., et al. (2009). An adjudicated hermeneutic single-case efficacy design of experiential therapy for panic/phobia. *Psychotherapy Research, 19*, 543–557.

Elliott, R., & Timulak, L. (2005). Descriptive and interpretive approaches to qualitative research. In J. Miles & P. Gilbert (Eds.), *A handbook of research methods in clinical and health psychology* (pp. 174–160). Oxford: Oxford University Press.

Elliott, R., & Wexler, M. M. (1994). Measuring the impact of treatment sessions: The Session Impacts Scale. *Journal of Counseling Psychology, 41*, 166–174.

Gallegos, N. (2005) Client perspectives on what contributes to symptom relief in psychotherapy:

A qualitative outcome study. *Journal of Humanistic Psychology, 45*(3), 355–382 .

Greenberg, L. S. (2002). *Emotion-focused therapy*. Washington, DC: American Psychological Association.

Greenberg, L. S., Auszra, L., & Herrmann, I. R. (2007). The relationship among emotional productivity, emotional arousal and outcome in experiential therapy of depression. *Psychotherapy Research, 17*(4), 482–493.

Greenberg, L. S., Rice, L. N., & Elliott, R. (1993). *Facilitating emotional change: The moment-by-moment process*. New York: Guilford.

Greenberg, L. S., & Watson, J. C. (2006). *Emotion-focused therapy for depression*. Washington, DC: American Psychological Association.

Grosse Holtforth, M., et al. (2007). Insight in cognitive-behavioral therapy. In L. G. Castonguay & C. E. Hill (Eds.), *Insight in psychotherapy* (pp. 57–80). Washington, DC: American Psychological Association.

Iwakabe, S., & Gazzola, N. (2009). From single case studies to practice-based knowledge: Aggregating and synthesizing case studies. *Psychotherapy Research, 19*, 601–611.

Klein, M. J., & Elliott, R. (2006). Client accounts of personal change in process-experiential psychotherapy: A methodologically pluralistic approach. *Psychotherapy Research, 16*, 91–105.

Lipkin, S. (1954). Clients' feelings and attitudes in relation to the outcome of client-centered therapy. *Psychological Monographs, 68*, 1–30.

McLeod, J. (2001) *Qualitative research in counselling and psychotherapy*. London. Sage.

Messer, S. B., & McWilliams, N. (2007). Insight in psychodynamic therapy. In L. G. Castonguay & C. E. Hill (Eds.), *Insight in psychotherapy* (pp. 9–30). Washington, DC: American Psychological Association.

Pascual-Leone, A., & Greenberg, L. S. (2007). Insight and awareness in experiential therapy. In L. G. Castonguay & C. E. Hill (Eds.), *Insight in psychotherapy* (pp. 31–56). Washington, DC: American Psychological Association.

Piper, W. E., Ogrodniczuk, J. S., Joyce, A. S., McCallum, M., Rosie, J. S., O'Kelly, J. G., & Steinberg, P. I. (1999). Prediction of dropping out in time-limited, interpretive individual psychotherapy. *Psychotherapy, 36*, 114–122.

Rennie, D. L., Phillips, J. R., & Quartaro, G. K. (1988). Grounded theory: A promising approach to conceptualization in psychology? *Canadian Psychology, 29*, 139–150.

Rhodes, R. H., Hill, C. E., Thompson, B. J., & Elliott, R. (1994). Client retrospective recall of resolved and unresolved misunderstanding events. *Journal of Counseling Psychology, 41*, 473–483.

Rodgers, B. (2002). Investigation into the client at the heart of therapy. *Counselling and Psychotherapy Research, 2*, 185–193.

Rogers, C. R. (1959). A theory of therapy, personality and interpersonal relationships as developed in the client-centered framework. In S. Koch, (Ed.), *Psychology: A study of a science. Vol. 3: Formulations of the person and the social context*. New York: McGraw-Hill.

Rogers, C. R. (1961) *On becoming a person: A therapist's view of psychotherapy*. London: Constable.

Safran, J. D., & Muran, C. J. (2000) *Negotiating the therapeutic alliance: A relational treatment guide*. New York: Guilford.

Schreiber, R., Crooks, D., & Stern, P. N. (1997). Qualitative meta-analysis. In J. M. Morse (Ed.), *Completing a qualitative project: Details and dialogue* (pp. 311–316). Thousand Oak, CA: Sage.

Spence, D. P. (1994). The failure to ask hard questions. In P. F. Talley, H. H. Strupp, & S. F.

Butler (Eds.), *Psychotherapy research and practice: Bridging the gap* (pp. 19–38). New York: Basic Books.

Timulak, L. (2007). Identifying core categories of client identified impact of helpful events in psychotherapy: A qualitative meta-analysis, *Psychotherapy Research, 17*, 305–314.

Timulak, L. (2009). Qualitative meta-analysis: A tool for reviewing qualitative research findings in psychotherapy. *Psychotherapy Research, 19*, 591–600.

Timulak, L., Belicova, A., & Miler, M. (2009). *Client identified significant events in a successful therapy case: The link between the significant events and outcome.* Paper under review.

Timulak, L., & Elliott, R. (2003). Empowerment events in process-experiential psychotherapy of depression: A qualitative analysis. *Psychotherapy Research, 13*, 443–460.

Timulak, L., & Lietaer, G. (2001). Moments of empowerment: A qualitative analysis of positively experienced episodes in brief person-centred counseling. *Counselling & Psychotherapy Research, 1*, 62–73.

CHAPTER 5

CLIENTS AS ACTIVE SELF-HEALERS
IMPLICATIONS FOR
THE PERSON-CENTERED APPROACH

ARTHUR C. BOHART & KAREN TALLMAN

INTRODUCTION

In 1961, Carl Rogers wrote:

> I had been working with a highly intelligent mother whose boy was something of a hellion. The problem was clearly her early rejection of the boy, but over many interviews I could not help her to this insight ... Finally, I gave up. I told her that it seemed we had both tried, but we had failed, and that we might as well give up our contacts ... We concluded the interview ... and she walked to the door of the office. Then she turned and asked, 'Do you ever take adults for counseling here?' When I replied in the affirmative, she said, 'Well then, I would like some help.' She ... began to pour out her despair about her marriage, her troubled relationship with her husband ... Real therapy began then, and *ultimately* it was very successful.
>
> This incident was one of a number which helped me to experience the fact ... that it is the client who knows what hurts, what directions to go, what problems are crucial, what experiences have been deeply buried. It began to occur to me that unless I had a need to demonstrate my own cleverness and learning, I would do better to rely upon the client for the direction of movement ... (Rogers, 1961, pp. 11-12)

Rogers also said:

> The central hypothesis of this approach can be briefly stated. It is that the individual has within himself or herself vast resources for self-understanding, for altering his or her self-concept, attitudes, and self-directed behavior – and that these resources can be tapped if only a definable climate of facilitative psychological attitudes can be provided. (Rogers, 1990/1986, p. 135)

It is clear from these quotations, as well as from others over his career, that Carl Rogers saw the client as the primary source of productive movement in therapy. It is clients who know what hurts, it is clients who know what directions to go in, and it is clients who have vast resources of self-understanding and potential for self-change. Therapists, therefore, are not instigators of change. They are interactive support systems, or environments, which provide the space or the arena within which clients' naturally occurring growth processes can operate. The key implication of these quotes is that ultimately it is clients who create personality change, or, as Bohart and Tallman (1999) have argued, it is clients who make therapy work. Put differently, Wood (2008) has argued that the essence of the person-centered approach is to rely upon clients' capacities for *self-organizing wisdom* to facilitate change.

Experiential therapists such as those who utilize focusing-oriented therapy (Gendlin, 1996) or emotion-focused therapy (Greenberg & Watson, 2006) hold this assumption only a little less radically than do classical person-centered therapists. Although they do 'process-guiding', they still do not see themselves as having the answers for clients. They view themselves as sharpening the process of helping clients focus on needed internal information in order that clients can engage with these self-reorganization processes.

Person-centered therapy therefore starts with the client (Schmid, 2004). Everything else is secondary, even the facilitative conditions of unconditional positive regard, empathic understanding, and congruence. They are helpful because they support or 'release' clients' growth potential, not because they are active interventions that 'fix' this or that aspect of client functioning. Despite Rogers' postulating that these conditions (along with three others) are 'necessary and sufficient', theoretically they are 'not necessarily necessary' (Bozarth, 1993). Clients' capacities for actualization may sometimes operate without their presence (a position that is supported by research).

The hypothesis that it is clients who make therapy work implies each of the following things. First, the active efforts of clients are important to make therapy work. Therapy does not 'operate on' the organism to change it, as the descriptions from some other therapy approaches imply (e.g., cognitive therapists sometimes talk about 'restructuring' the client's cognitions, or using exposure to reprogram their 'fear structures'). This implies that their involvement will be a crucial or key element in how therapy works. Rogerian theory would predict that client involvement is important, not only because of the fundamental postulate that it is clients that make therapy work, but also because the importance of involvement is related to Rogers' (1957) necessary and sufficient conditions of *incongruence* and *contact*. For Rogers, client incongruence is the motivating factor that leads clients to want to make therapy work. If they are not motivated to change, they will be less likely to involve themselves. Being in contact could be thought of as a necessary component of involvement. If one is not involved it is unlikely one will be in contact, although there is more to contact than being involved.

Second, the hypothesis that it is clients who make therapy work implies that clients ought to be able to make widely different approaches to therapy work as long as the therapy provides enough facilitative support. Clients could utilize psychodynamic approaches and explore their childhoods, or cognitive behavioral approaches and work with their dysfunctional cognitions, to create personal change.

Third, the hypothesis of the client as active self-healer implies that it is not *merely* active client involvement and motivation that makes therapy work, but client *generativity* and *creativity*. Clients actively and generatively transform what they learn in therapy. They do not merely ingest what they have been given. They creatively operate on it to create change.

Clarification of concepts

In this paper we at various times use the terms 'self-healing' and 'self-righting.' We also use the term 'self-organizing wisdom'. We need to clarify them. First, 'self-healing' is a metaphor. Psychological problems are not literally the equivalent of wounds that heal. Self-healing needs to be understood as meaning that persons experiencing psychological dysfunction have the capacity to find ways of reorganizing themselves such that psychological dysfunction is either resolved or presents less of a problem. 'Self-righting' is another metaphor. The image is of something, such as a ship, which 'rights' itself by bouncing back up when knocked off-center. Self-righting, then, is the organismic capacity to bounce back from adversity, to get things back in order, and to find ways to move forward productively with life. Self-organizing wisdom could be thought of as the process that makes self-healing and self-righting happen. It is the organism's capacity for coming to know what it needs to do to change, for creating new and more adaptive person–situation relationships, and for generating new and creative solutions to life problems.

The core Rogerian concept that underlies the capacity for self-healing and self-righting is the actualizing tendency. For Rogers, the actualizing tendency is a tendency to preserve the organism and to promote its ongoing development and growth in order to cope more and more adaptively with the world. The belief in an actualizing tendency implies capacities for self-healing and self-righting. However, the concept of the actualizing tendency is broader. It includes, for instance, all motivational tendencies of the organism. Nonetheless, many examples of the actualizing tendency are examples of self-righting, such as, for instance, the example of potatoes growing towards the light in a cellar.

We also need to clarify what it means to talk about *self*-healing and *self*-righting. In order to understand these concepts we must understand what they are meant to be in contrast to. They are in contrast to the idea that it is another entity, such as the therapist or the therapy, who fixes the person. It does not literally mean that all self-healing and self-righting is entirely self-generated. In fact, much self-healing and self-righting involves others, both inside and outside of therapy. In informal surveys where we have asked students in classes to describe instances where they have 'self-healed' from some kind of problem without the aid of a professional therapist, individuals often describe having utilized interpersonal resources in their environments, such as friends, ministers, or relatives. At the same time, though, people do often self-right without the explicit help of others. Many individuals report self-healing through activities such as prayer. One student who was in a serious automobile accident reported overcoming her fear of driving by using the behavioral technique of exposure, without ever having learned about that from a professional or from any book. There is empirical evidence that journaling is a potent form of self-healing.

Finally we need to clarify the idea that it is the persons themselves who know what needs to be changed and how to change it. What this means is that, as complex organisms, only persons themselves know 'how all the parts fit together' of their experience, values, and lived-in environments. Therefore, ultimately only they know how to reorganize themselves in relationship to their environments in more adaptive and functional ways. This is why, from a Rogerian point of view, therapists are support systems rather than expert guides or interventionists.

However, when we say that it is clients who 'know how' to reorganize themselves, we do not mean to imply that this process is under complete conscious control. From the person-centered perspective, the person is a holistic organism. It is the whole organism that engages in these productive self-reorganizing processes. They are not necessarily consciously generated or controlled. Rogers, for instance, was fond of talking about things just 'bubbling up' – new insights, new perspectives appearing unbidden in consciousness. Gendlin has said:

> Roger's method brought it home that the decisions a person must make are inherently that person's own. No book knowledge enables another person to decide for anyone. That goes for life decisions and life-style as well as, moment by moment, what to talk about, feel into, struggle with. Another person might make a guess, but ultimately personal growth is from the inside outward. *A process of change begins and moves in ways even the person's own mind cannot direct, let alone another person's mind.* (Gendlin, 1984, p. 297, italics ours)

Therefore, while it is clients who take therapists' input and work on it in their own personal, meaningful, and idiosyncratically productive ways to generate therapeutic change, the process is a complex organismic one, involving both conscious and unconscious processes. The whole organism, in ways not entirely known to the organism itself consciously, or to an observer such as the therapist, or even to theoretical psychologists, generates productive growth.

Goal of this paper

The goal of this paper is to explore the research base for the hypothesis that clients (and persons in general) have capacities for self-healing and self-righting, and that it is they who play the most important role in generating change in psychotherapy. In so doing we will consider relevant evidence from all approaches to psychotherapy.

HUMAN POTENTIAL FOR CHANGE

If Rogers is right that clients have considerable potential for self-healing, then there should also be evidence of this in everyday life. We therefore first consider evidence on human potential for self-righting and resilience in general.

Once upon a time, in the heyday of classical psychoanalysis, it was believed that personality structure was so fixed that people could not easily self-heal without the aid of a professional psychotherapist. Although most approaches to psychotherapy still emphasize the power of the therapist, there has been a growing recognition that human beings actually have much more potential for self-healing than originally supposed (e.g., Miller & Rollnick, 1991; Orlinsky, Grawe, & Parks, 1994). Evidence regarding the human capacity for self-healing is substantial and comes from several sources, including but not limited to: (1) spontaneous recovery, (2) placebo effects, (3) resilience, (4) post-traumatic growth, and (5) corrective effects of self-expression/disclosure.

Self-generated change and spontaneous recovery

People often overcome personal problems without the benefit of professional help. In one survey of a sample of the general population it was found that 90% reported having overcome a significant health, emotional, addiction, or lifestyle problem in the prior year (Gurin, 1990). Many individuals recover from substance abuse problems without professional help. Miller and Carroll (2006) have noted, 'Most people who recover from drug problems do so on their own, without formal treatment' (p. 295). Antisocial, aggressive behavior is thought to be one of the more chronic and enduring forms of problem behavior. Yet many individuals outgrow it. Pulkkinen (2001) found that after age 26 the number of arrests of men with histories of aggressive or criminal behavior declined markedly. Men interviewed at age 36 attributed this to maturation, environmental changes, the negative consequences of offending, and the influence of another person (often a wife).

Many individuals diagnosed with personality disorders show improvement over time (e.g., Skodol et al., 2007), although others continue to exhibit problems. Zanarini,

Frankenburg, Hennen, Reich, and Silk (2006) found that over a 10-year period, 88% of those diagnosed with borderline personality disorder achieved remission. Zanarini et al. found that there were seven predictors of remission: younger age, absence of childhood sexual abuse, no family history of substance use disorder, good vocational record, absence of an anxious cluster personality disorder, low neuroticism, and high agreeableness. This study is confounded because in many cases the individuals studied had received some kind of treatment. Nonetheless, the concept of a personality disorder implies the existence of a stable and enduring structure which ought to be difficult to alter. Indeed, the general belief has been that personality disorders are difficult to change. Hence these research results are encouraging. Supporting these results, Fonagy and Bateman (2006) have pointed out that the natural course of borderline personality disorder is more benign than previously believed. They suggest that the treatment resistance of people with this diagnosis may have more to do with the iatrogenic effects of therapy than with the condition itself.

There is now evidence that even schizophrenia does not necessarily have to have the negative course that many have attributed to it. Several studies have shown that many schizophrenics recover or significantly improve without the use of medication (Harding et al., 1987a, 1987b). The International Pilot Study of Schizophrenia (Leff, 1992) found that recovery rates in undeveloped countries, where schizophrenics were less likely to be hospitalized or treated with drugs, were considerably higher than in more developed countries. Mosher, Hendrix, and Fort (2004), in their study of Soteria House, found that many schizophrenics were able to recover without the use of drugs, with nothing but empathic support from staff who simply kept them company as they went through their psychotic experiences. Cohen (2005) did a qualitative study of 36 'psychiatric survivors' and found that most had managed to self-right using a variety of self-help strategies, many doing it without the use of medication.

Research on spontaneous recovery rates also provides support for the capacity of human beings to self-right and self-heal without professional assistance. Although varying across diagnoses, Lambert, Shapiro, and Bergin (1986) have estimated the overall rate of spontaneous recovery to be approximately 40%. Spontaneous recovery occurs, in part, through individuals accessing resources in their natural environments. For example, Gurin, Veroff, and Feld (1960) found that the majority of individuals faced with problems contacted persons other than mental-health professionals (such as priests).

Yet another source of evidence for human self-change potential comes from studies of pretreatment change. Weiner-Davis, de Shazer, and Gingerich (1987) and Lawson (1994) found that 60% or more of clients coming to their first session report improvement in the presenting problem since the appointment was made. Simply scheduling an appointment may help clients mobilize their self-healing capacities.

Finally, there is 'quantum change' (Miller & C'de Baca, 2001). Quantum changes are significant personal transformations that occur relatively suddenly and without the specific aid of psychotherapeutic intervention (although the individual may have had therapy or counseling at some time in his or her life). Miller and C'de Baca advertised in the Alburquerque, New Mexico area for people who had undergone such major transformations and interviewed 55 individuals. They are of the opinion that there are many more, suggesting that such major personal changes are hardly rare. One example is an individual who experienced panic episodes while in college. He was a loner, had a poor self-image, and drank. One New Year's Eve, after drinking, he saw himself in a mirror and realized what he was doing to himself. He started walking, eating healthier, and drinking less. However he still had a negative self-image. A year later he went to the town where he grew up and went to his parents' graves. He talked to them, cried, and had the experience of a cloud lifting. From then on he felt like he knew who he was and came to like himself. He subsequently did well in college and eventually graduated.

Placebo effects

Placebos are inert treatments that clients are led to believe are real treatments (for instance, they may be given sugar pills instead of real medication). Therefore, if a placebo works, it must be through the client's own capacity for self-healing. In a study of antidepressant drugs (Bridge et al., 2007), 50% of depressed patients improved on placebo, as did 32% of those diagnosed with obsessive-compulsive disorder, and 39% with anxiety disorders. These rates were less than the recovery rates for those taking medication. Nonetheless, they are substantial.

The power of placebos has repeatedly been observed in psychotherapy research. Grissom (1996) studied the effects of placebos over 46 meta-analytic reviews. Overall, the effect size of placebos versus control groups was .44. Honos-Webb (2005) has pointed out that in two major studies, the National Institute of Mental Health Treatment of Depression Collaborative Research Program (Elkin, 1994), and a study for cocaine dependency (Crits-Christoph et al., 1997, 1999), placebos and minimal clinical management did as well as psychotherapy. Honos-Webb concluded that placebo control and minimal clinical management met the criteria for being an empirically supported treatment!

It is even possible that the effects of specific psychotherapeutic procedures could primarily be due to what is called the 'active placebo' effect. In medical research active placebos are substances that are not relatively inert like sugar pills. Instead, they produce physiological changes and bodily sensations so that the person taking the active placebo will experience something actually happening from the pill. However active placebos do not do actual healing. Change occurs through the patients' self-healing activated by the perceived bodily changes (see Greenberg, 1999, for more on active placebos).

It is possible that the various procedures in psychotherapy, to the extent that they lead the client to believe that something is happening, operate as active placebos. It is even conceivable that therapy itself is primarily an active placebo activating the natural healing propensity of the client. For instance, procedures that arouse emotion can have powerful bodily effects. Emotional arousal may lead clients to believe that something important is happening, which in turn may mobilize hope, energy, and creativity. We are not suggesting that there is nothing to therapy but active placebos, but the possibility exists that the active placebo effect plays a role in therapy outcome and may be one reason why, as we discuss below, different approaches to therapy all work about equally well – because they all activate clients' capacities for self-healing.

Resilience

It is commonly held that childhood trauma can cause psychological damage and there is evidence to support this contention. But what researchers have been discovering for the last 40 years is how many children actually manage to grow and thrive despite major threats to adaptation or development (Masten, 2001). This is known as *resilience*. Masten, Best and Garmazy (1990) have concluded that '… studies of psychosocial resilience support the view that human psychological development is highly buffered and self-righting' (p. 438). In one of the first demonstrations of resilience, Werner and Smith (1982) studied disadvantaged institutionalized children who were later adopted into homes. Werner and Smith (1982) concluded, 'As we watched these children grow from babyhood to adulthood we could not help but respect the self-righting tendencies within them that produced normal development under all but the most persistently adverse circumstances' (p. 159). Werner and Smith estimated that about 10% of their sample were highly resilient and most of the rest were resilient in varying degrees.

Vaillant (1993) studied 456 men from age 15 into their 60s. Eleven men had been rated as being at the highest risk for poor outcomes due to a variety of factors. All were rated as 'broken beyond repair' at age 25, However, by their 60s, seven of the eleven were rated in the top 25% of mental health, and eight of the eleven as having 'self-righted.' Some of these individuals utilized psychotherapy to help them self-right, but the important point is that, 'broken beyond repair,' by their 60s, so many of them were doing so well.

Elder (1986) studied men who had joined the military service who had various negative prognistic signs such as below-average grades or not having completed high school, being less assertive and less self-confident. Military service helped many of these individuals restructure their lives. Many subsequently went on to college and by their forties had shown significant gains in psychological competence.

Masten (2001) notes that resilience '… appears to be a common phenomenon that results in most cases from the operation of basic human adaptational systems. If those systems are protected and in good working order, development is robust even in the face of severe adversity' (p. 227). However, not everyone exhibits resilience. Many children continue to have serious and chronic problems (Masten, 2001).

Resilience is a product of both individuals and environment. Personal factors play a role, such as the child's temperament and disposition, IQ, and level of self-esteem. People who are more self-disclosing and more trusting of others are also more likely to be resilient (Lepore & Revenson, 2006). Situational factors also play a role. Lepore and Revenson (2006) have used the metaphor of a tree. It is not only the strength of the tree which is important, but availability of water, nutrients, the composition of soil, and the presence of other trees to buffer the wind. For humans, having a good social support network is important, particularly finding someone who can be a good mentor. Other factors include: finding spiritual faith, marriage to psychologically healthy partners, leaving or staying away from deviant peer groups, having opportunities present themselves at opportune times, making good choices at crucial moments, socio-economic status, and having someone who can provide support, such as a parent, minister, or teacher. Yet, children even without good environmental buffering show some degree of resilience (Masten, 2001).

With regard to trauma, being exposed does not necessarily cause post-traumatic stress disorder. Ozer, Best, Lipsey, and Weiss (2003) have noted that 'roughly 50%–60% of the US population is exposed to traumatic stress but only 5%–10% develop PTSD [post-traumatic stress disorder]' (p. 54). Similar results have been found in the literature on recovery from traumatic life events. Tedeschi, Park, and Calhoun (1998) reported that 40%–60% of people who suffer a trauma recover on their own or report personal growth following the experience. Such changes include positive self-perception, improved sense of personal strengths, and perception of new possibilities (Calhoun & Tedeschi, 2006). Also there may be changes in how the individual relates to others, such as feeling more of a sense of connection, experiencing more intimacy, and feeling more free to be oneself. Changes in philosophy of life may also occur. These may include coming to value relationships over achievement, and finding more meaning in life.

As is the case with resilience, not all human beings are equally likely to respond to trauma by growing. Those who do have already developed some useful coping devices from earlier experience. Environmental factors also matter. For instance, having someone who one can talk to in a productive way helps promote post-traumatic growth (Calhoun & Tedeschi, 2006).

Corrective effects of self-expression or disclosure
Added support for human resilience comes from research that has shown that writing or discussing a troubling or traumatic event facilitates healing. Pennebaker (1990, 1997) and others have demonstrated that self-expression and self-disclosure are both

psychologically and physically beneficial, even if they are not done with another person. In one study, college students wrote about a traumatic experience for 15 minutes a day for four consecutive days. At a six-month follow-up, it was found that these students, compared with a control group, reduced their visits to the student health center by 50%. Harvey, Orbuch, Chwalisz, and Garwood (1991) found that giving traumatized individuals a chance to 'tell their story' and engage in 'account making' is a pathway to healing. In a related finding, Segal and Murray (1994) found that talking into a tape recorder worked about as well as cognitive therapy in helping individuals resolve feelings about traumatic experiences. An early study by Schwitzgebel (1961) showed that paying juvenile delinquents to talk into a tape recorder about their experiences led to meaningful improvements in their behavior, including fewer arrests. Hemenover (2003) had participants write about a traumatic life event or plans for next day. They completed measures of resilience and distress three months later. Trauma participants increased in positive self-perceptions and decreased in distress compared to controls. These data again show that humans have a good deal of capacity for self-righting.

Self-healing techniques in everyday life
Prochaska and his colleagues (Prochaska, Norcross, & DiClemente, 1994) have studied how individuals self-right in everyday life. Consistent with the above evidence, they have found that many individuals are able to overcome problems without the aid of professional therapists. Moreover, they found that individuals utilize the same procedures outside of therapy that therapists use in therapy. For instance, a central procedure used by behavior therapists is exposure. Yet exposure is a part of everyday wisdom (Efran & Blumberg, 1994). In other words, what therapists do in therapy is built upon naturally occurring human change processes.

Summary
The research on spontaneous recovery, self-change without psychotherapy, placebo effects, resilience, post-traumatic growth, self-expression, and quantum change show that humans are more robust than once supposed. They have considerable potential for self-healing and self-righting, although they may need supportive environments for that potential to manifest itself.

These data raise the question of why, if people have potential for self-righting, they sometimes need psychotherapy. This topic is too complex to consider in this chapter in the depth it deserves (but see Bohart & Tallman, 1999). Let us briefly note the following. First, the empirical fact is that while many people self-right without psychotherapy, the research also demonstrates that many do not. Second, the research cited suggests a complex combination of factors that may be responsible for why a given individual is able to self-right without professional psychotherapy, while someone else may not be able to: temperamental (genetic) factors, childhood experiences, belief system, marriage to psychologically healthy partners, situational factors such as being in the army or getting a good job, and, most of all, social support. In addition, some individuals may run into the naturally occurring equivalent of a placebo, or may spontaneously engage in a self-help activity such as journaling. In contrast, individuals who need to come to therapy may face an inopportune confluence of personal and/or situational factors that make it less likely that they are able to self-right on their own.

HUMAN POTENTIAL FOR CHANGE IN PSYCHOTHERAPY: CLIENT CONTRIBUTIONS TO THE THERAPY PROCESS

We now turn to the question of how clients make therapy work.

Evaluating the traditional model of psychotherapy: Implications for the client's role

Bohart and Tallman (1996, 1999) originally developed the hypothesis that it was clients who made therapy work empirically by evaluating the evidence for the dominant model of psychotherapy. We briefly review this. The current dominant model of psychotherapy is the 'medical' model. In this model psychological problems are thought of as analogous to medical problems. In order to 'treat' them, expert therapists must first diagnose the 'condition' that the patient has. Then a specific treatment designed to treat that disorder is chosen by the therapist and applied to the client and to the disorder. The therapist must be a professional who has expertise in diagnosing client problems, in picking the appropriate treatment for the problem, and then in applying the treatment. Although it is valuable for the therapist to 'provide' a good relationship for the client, the real 'gold' of treatment lies in the set of procedures and interventions chosen to treat the problem. The person of the therapist, as well as the relationship, are secondary, as in medicine where, while a good 'bedside' manner is desirable for a physician, it is not the bedside manner that fixes a problem, but rather the medication or the surgery. Similarly, in psychotherapy, the treatment does the work.

This approach can be modeled as follows:

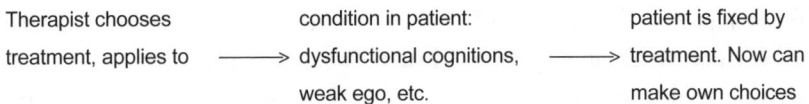

Therapist chooses treatment, applies to	$\longrightarrow$	condition in patient: dysfunctional cognitions, weak ego, etc.	$\longrightarrow$	patient is fixed by treatment. Now can make own choices

By and large, the evidence does not support this model. First, research has found that all bona fide approaches to psychotherapy appear to be approximately equally effective for most if not all disorders (the Dodo bird verdict; see Wampold, 2001, 2007; Wampold, Imel, & Miller, 2009). For instance, Stiles, Barkham, Twigg, Mellor-Clark, and Cooper (2006) studied the outcomes of more than 1,300 clients in the United Kingdom National Health Service. No differences were obtained in effectiveness among cognitive-behavioral, person-centered, and psychodynamic therapies.

The fact that widely different approaches, using different theories and strategies, work about equally well for most disorders suggests that the idea that specific interventions are needed for specific disorders is not true. Supporting this, techniques have been found to be relatively unimportant (Wampold, 2001). For instance, Asay and Lambert's (1999) estimates of the contributors to therapeutic outcome assign 40% to the client and to extra-therapeutic factors in the client's life such as his or her social support network; 30% to common therapeutic factors, particularly the therapeutic relationship; 15% to placebo; and 15% to techniques. Wampold's (2001) estimate is even less: Techniques account for at most about 1%. In contrast, 87% of the variance is not accounted for by therapy and is most likely due to the client and to extra-therapeutic factors in the client's life. Beutler et al. (2004) have reported correlations between specific techniques and outcome ranging from 0 to .11. In accord with this, Bergin and Garfield (1994), based on a review of evidence to that date, concluded that 'With some exceptions … there is massive evidence that psychotherapeutic techniques do not have specific effects; yet there is tremendous resistance to accepting this finding as a legitimate one …' (p. 822).

A further challenge to the medical model is data that suggests that the professional expertise of the therapist, as defined by experience and training, makes relatively little difference in outcome (Beutler et al., 2004; Christensen & Jacobson, 1994) or to the therapeutic alliance (Horvath & Bedi, 2002). This is in contrast to research that shows that therapists as persons are important (Wampold, 2006; Najavits & Strupp, 1994). Supporting these data, studies by Strupp and Hadley (1979) and Anderson (1999) have shown that therapists' interpersonal skills predict outcome in therapy while professional training does not. Consider how shocking it would be if the same thing were true in medicine: having medical training was irrelevant to being an effective physician while all that mattered were the physician's interpersonal skills.

These data can be taken to support both Rogers' hypothesis about the importance of the therapeutic relationship and the hypothesis that it is clients who make therapy work. It supports this latter hypothesis in that if no specific professional interventional expertise is needed, and all that is needed is interpersonal relationship skill, this implies that the generation of personal changes comes from clients themselves, supported by the relationship with the therapist.

However, there is evidence that questions even the idea that the therapist is required. Studies of self-help procedures, such as self-help books and self-help groups, have found that self-help frequently works as well as, or almost as well as, professionally provided psychotherapy. Earlier meta-analyses by Scogin, Bynum, Stephens, and Calhoun (1990) and by Gould and Clum (1993) found that self-help treatments, such as self-help books, were as effective for a wide range of problems as treatments involving therapists. More recently Norcross (2006) has summarized the evidence and suggested that self-help procedures typically work as well or almost as well as professionally provided therapy. Mean effect sizes are around .70–.80, which compares favorably to the overall effect size of psychotherapy. Self-help procedures have been shown to be effective for a wide range of problems, from depression to anxiety disorders to substance abuse disorders.

For instance, Gregory, Canning, Lee, & Wise (2004) did a meta-analysis of cognitive bibliotherapy compared to psychotherapy. Cognitive bibliotherapy did almost as well as psychotherapy (effect size of .77 to .83). Jacobs et al. (2001) found that computer-assisted therapy worked as well as therapist-provided therapy for a variety of problems on standardized measures of outcome, although clients' ratings of helpfulness were slightly higher in the therapy condition (it appears that clients like to talk to therapists). The computer program primarily prompted clients to think about their goals each week and then prompted them to think about specific ways of accomplishing them.

On the other hand, while Clum's (2008) summary concludes that self-help treatments are in general reasonably effective with results comparable to those of therapist-provided treatments, he also concludes that self-help is not equivalent to therapist-delivered treatments for every disorder. Arkowitz and Lilienfeld (2006) have argued that many studies of self-help have not been pure. Participants have talked with therapists for the average of 36 minutes. Arkowitz and Lilienfeld have also argued that some of the studies were not on serious problems. Menchola, Arkowitz, and Burke (2007) did a meta-analysis of studies for depression and anxiety disorders in which self-help was compared to professionally provided psychotherapy and to controls. The studies were screened so that only studies where therapist–participant contact was minimal (primarily to assess things like suicidality) were included. They found that, compared to control groups, self-help had an effect size of 1.0. This is a large effect size and comparable to the effect sizes found for psychotherapy in other studies. For the research studies included in this meta-analysis, however, the effect size for professionally provided psychotherapy was 1.31. This suggests that therapy does provide something over and above self-help. However it is important to note that the .31 difference between the self-help effect size and the psychotherapy effect size is small compared to the large effect of self-help. Furthermore, according to Elliott, Greenberg, and Lietaer (2004), an effect size difference needs to be at least .4 to be of clinical significance, meaning that, by their criteria, the .31 difference is clinically not significant. Thus, this study too, although indicating that therapists do make a contribution, supports the importance of the client as the primary source of change.

Implications of these research findings

- all therapies work about the same for virtually all disorders
- techniques and treatment account for little of therapy's effectiveness
- therapist professional expertise is not important
- what is important is the therapist as a person
- self-help treatments work as well or almost as well as professionally provided therapy

The findings pose a serious challenge to the dominant model of psychotherapy. That model places the locus for change primarily in the hands of the expert therapist and in the therapist's techniques. These findings contradict that model. Furthermore, the findings on the potency of self-help procedures contradict even the Rogerian hypothesis that the presence of therapists providing the facilitative conditions is necessary. How can we explain these findings?

Bohart and Tallman (1999) have argued that the most parsimonious explanation is that it is clients who ultimately make therapy work. The reason widely different approaches to therapy all work about the same for most disorders is that it is clients who are able to take interventions and experiences from different approaches and utilize them to resolve their problems. Therapy works to the degree that clients actively utilize the available resources in psychotherapy. Clients take what is offered, invest their effort, intelligence and creativity, and transform what has been offered into positive change. Clients can operate on widely different techniques from different approaches to produce change.

This suggests an alternative model of how therapy works, compatible with the Rogerian view. It can be diagrammed as follows:

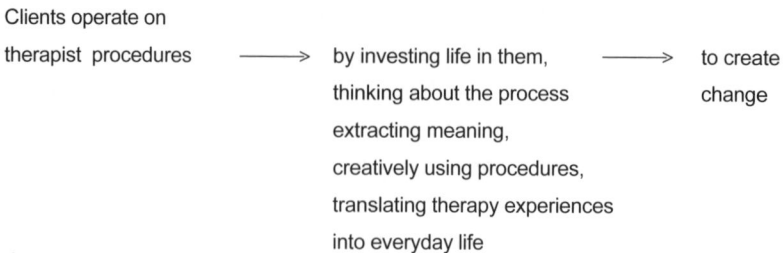

Clients operate on
therapist procedures   ⟶   by investing life in them,   ⟶   to create
                                        thinking about the process   change
                                          extracting meaning,
                                          creatively using procedures,
                                          translating therapy experiences
                                          into everyday life

Factors involved in how clients make therapy work

In the sections that follow we consider evidence on how clients actively contribute to the therapy process. We start with client involvement and participation.

Client involvement and participation

The active involvement of the client in the therapeutic process is the most important factor in determining whether therapy succeeds or not. Orlinsky, Grawe, and Parks (1994) conclude, based on a comprehensive review of 50 years of research, that 'the quality of the patient's [sic] participation ... emerges as the *most* important determinant of outcome' (p. 324; emphasis added) – more than therapist attitudes, behaviors, or techniques. In a later review, Orlinsky, Rønnestad, and Willutzki (2004) identified 11 additional variables linked to improvement:

- reciprocal affirmation
- therapeutic realizations (i.e., in-session impacts of therapy events)
- treatment duration
- *client* suitability
- *client* cooperation
- *client* experience of the therapeutic bond
- *client* contribution to the bond
- *client* interactive collaboration
- *client* expressiveness
- *client* affirmation of the therapist
- *client* openness

Therefore, 8 of 11 are client factors.

In particular, Orlinsky and his colleagues have tabulated results of studies on factors that contribute to client involvement and participation in psychotherapy. In their latest review, Orlinsky et al. (2004) note that in 36 of 45 findings, client openness (versus defensiveness) relates to positive outcome. Clients' willingness and ability to engage in the tasks of psychotherapy was found to significantly relate to outcome in 35 of 54 findings. In 34 of 49 findings client cooperative involvement versus resistance related positively to outcome. Clients who collaborated versus acting dependently or controlling also were more likely to benefit from psychotherapy in 27 of 42 findings. One example of the importance of client involvement and participation is a study by Sachse (1992), who found that clients who at the third session were rated as actively endeavoring to clarify their own problems had better outcomes.

Clients' perceptions of psychotherapy

Clients also contribute to psychotherapy by actively shaping the therapy process.

They do this in part by constructing it through selective attention to aspects that are important to them, and by interpreting what happens. In the past, clients' selective perceptions and interpretations were typically attributed to transference and treated as symptoms of their pathology. However research suggests that clients' perceptions are more trustworthy than once thought. Findings abound that the client's perceptions of the relationship or alliance, more so than the therapist's, correlate highly with therapeutic outcome (Bachelor & Horvath, 1999; Busseri & Tyler, 2004; Marcus, Kashy, & Baldwin, 2009; Orlinsky et al., 1994; Zuroff et al., 2000). Clients' ratings of empathy, for instance, correlate more highly with outcome than do those of the therapist (Bohart, Elliott, Greenberg, & Watson, 2002). Client ratings of empathy also correlate as highly, or more highly, with outcome as do the ratings of objective observers (Bohart et al., 2002). The client's ratings of the collaborative nature of the relationship also correlate with outcome more so than the therapist's (Orlinsky et al., 2004).

Yet, clients' perceptions of therapy typically show only a modest relationship with the perceptions of therapists. Elliott and Shapiro (1992) and Elliott et al. (1994) found that some of the events clients perceive as significant are ones that therapists and observers see as minor occurrences. This may be because clients see them as embodying important themes. Helmeke and Sprenkle (2000) asked therapists and members of couples in couples therapy to identify pivotal moments. They found that the identification of pivotal moments was highly individualized, with little overlap between members of the couples themselves, and little overlap with what therapists identified as pivotal moments. Marcus, Kashy, & Baldwin (2009) found that clients' perceptions of the therapeutic alliance were idiosyncratic to the client (and not primarily a function of the nature of the therapist). Levitt and Rennie (2004) report that when therapists and clients look at tapes of their interactions, the perspectives of the therapists and clients only partially overlapped in their interpretations of what each was doing and the usefulness of what each was doing. They note 'Three stories may be occurring at once: the story of the dialogue between the client and the therapist, the client's inner story, and the therapist's inner story' (p. 308).

Putting these data together, clients' perceptions of the nature of the alliance, and of what is going on in therapy, are relatively idiosyncratic to clients. Yet it is clients' perceptions (at least of the therapeutic alliance) that correlate most highly with outcome. This suggests that it is clients' constructions of what is happening in therapy that correlate with outcome.

Corsini (1989) gives an example. The case was one of an inmate he tested while working at a prison. Two years after the psychological testing, when the inmate was being released on parole, he came in to see Corsini. He told Corsini he wanted to thank him for what he had done for him. After meeting with Corsini once, the man had decided to turn his life around.

This greatly surprised Corsini, as he was not the prisoner's psychotherapist. He asked for elaboration. The man said he had stopped hanging out with the 'bad prisoners,' and had started going to the prison high school and church. Now he was planning to go to college. He thanked Corsini for changing his life.

The problem was that Corsini could not remember ever talking to the inmate. Corsini looked up his folder and discovered that he had given the man an IQ test two years before. He still could not remember having said or done anything to help this man, and so asked him what he had said that was so helpful. The man replied the event that had turned his life around was that Corsini had told him that he had a high IQ.

This story is a clear example of the active, creative, self-changing efforts of the client. Corsini was not even the client's psychotherapist. Yet his 'intervention' was creatively interpreted by the client in a growth-producing way.

There are other examples of how clients actively interpret the therapy environment in ways that meet their needs. In a qualitative analysis of clients' responses to three sessions of therapy, Bohart and Boyd (1997) found that a client might perceive an empathy response as offering support if what she believed she needed was support, while perceiving it as offering insight if what she believed she needed was insight. Talmon (1990) interviewed ex-clients. He discovered that '… I had taken my interventions and my words much too seriously. Patients reported following suggestions that I could not remember having made. They created their own interpretations, which were sometimes quite different from what I recollected and sometimes more creative and suitable versions of my suggestions …' (p. 60).

Dreier (2000) studied families at home as they discussed a recent family therapy session. Different family members had different interpretations of what had gone on. The discussion, however, led to the family's opening up of new possibilities for productive behavior. In other words, what helped from the family therapy was not what the therapist had in mind, but that it got clients thinking productively again. Kühnlein (1999) found from interviews with 49 inpatients who had cognitive-behavior therapy that participants did not blindly adopt what was presented in therapy. They took what they found useful and combined it with their own previously existing schemas.

In recent research we were interested in exploring the various possibilities in how clients might interpret and use therapy responses. We had graduate students imagine themselves into the role of clients in published psychotherapy films. Their instructions were to go response-by-response and try to imagine their thoughts and feelings and how they were utilizing what the therapist was saying. We found that they continuously interpreted what was going on as they went. They did not only focus on individual therapist responses, but rather continually tried to 'sniff out' underlying regularities. For instance, they tried to figure out the therapist's agenda. In a particularly striking example, one vicarious client, from a traditional sociocentric culture, found herself privately disagreeing on a response-by-response basis with what cognitive therapist Aaron Beck was doing. She perceived him as emphasizing not needing to depend on people for one's happiness, when her cultural background made relationships paramount. Towards the end, when Beck suggested to the client to handle depression by naming names of friends, she was able to accept this advice because she now saw Beck as coming around to a sociocentric way of thinking (Bohart, Bekele, & Byock, 2007)! While this research was not on 'real' clients in therapy, it does provide a model of how clients might interpret therapy responses, and the findings converge with what Rennie (1990, 1992, 1994, 2000) has found in his tape-assisted recall with real clients.

Finally, clients enter therapy with their own ideas about what they need (e.g., Philips, Werbart, Wennberg, & Schubert, 2007). Their ideas may influence how they construe and use what therapists offer. For instance, Mackrill (2008) had clients keep diaries on their experiences both inside and outside of therapy. He found that clients' pre-existing ideas about what they needed to do influenced ongoing therapy. One client entered therapy with the belief that what he had to achieve in order to alter his life was to learn to think positively. He later interpreted what happened in therapy in terms of that belief, including why therapy had helped. The therapist did not refer to a gain in positive thinking as one of her goals.

In conclusion, there is evidence that clients are active interpreters of the therapy environment. They focus on aspects that are important to them and assimilate what is happening to their plans, beliefs, and goals. This is compatible with Carl Rogers' (1957) assertion that a necessary and sufficient condition for therapeutic change was that clients perceive helpful aspects of the therapeutic relationship (and by implication, perceive, or are able to interpret, other aspects as helpful).

Client agency, activity, and reflexivity

Clients also actively work on the therapy environment. A particularly striking demonstration of the potential humans have for actively working with and interpreting the therapy environment, as if it were clay, to mold it into the shapes they need, is given in a study by Garfinkel (1967). Garfinkel had participants interact with a therapist who was behind a screen. The participants posed problems to the therapist. They then asked questions to which the therapist responded only with a 'yes' or a 'no.' Unbeknownst to the participants, however, the therapist responded *randomly* with yes or no. Nonetheless the participants were able to piece together coherent accounts and derive solutions for their problems.

In an intriguing series of studies, Rennie (1990, 1992, 1994, 2000) conducted qualitative analyses on tape-assisted recall data (Elliott, 1984) on 14 therapy sessions from 12 therapist–client pairs. Therapy sessions were taped. Soon after, clients met with Rennie, listened to the tape, and stopped it whenever they wanted to comment.

Rennie discovered that clients were highly active at a covert level during the sessions. They steered sessions in directions they wanted, deferred to therapists overtly, but then covertly thought about experiences in the way they wanted. They also did not share their covert processing and actively tried to redirect the therapists if they went off course. Clients were anything but passive recipients of therapeutic wisdom.

Levitt and Rennie (2004) review evidence that suggests that most clients enter therapy with a plan. They give an example from Rennie (1994): a client who starts a session by telling a humiliating experience at work, knowing there is more beneath the story, but she didn't want to launch directly into that. After the therapist shows understanding, she then goes deeper. But in addition, through this process of narration she has several realizations which she keeps to herself because she is not yet ready to share with the therapist. She also gets rid of some disturbing feelings around the humiliating event through this storytelling.

A second example is as follows:

> ... one client entered a series of interactional pauses when her cognitive therapist asked her to imagine what a friend might tell her to help her raise her self-esteem. The client sat silently, thinking about her friends who in fact had abandoned her in her depression but knowing that a disgruntled reply would not meet the task demands ... She replied '... I don't know.' Trying another approach, the therapist then asked her to consider what she might tell a friend. But being placed in the position of supporting the friends who had hurt her was even more difficult. In an attempt to provide the therapist with the expected answer, the client gave a disingenuous response, while doubting the purpose of the entire exercise.
>
> (Levitt & Rennie, 2004, p. 303)

Levitt (2004) did a qualitative research analysis of interviews with 26 clients who had recently completed psychotherapy. She found that the same interventions were reacted to by clients in sharply different ways at different times. She also found that participants reported managing the therapist's style so that their own needs could be met within the session. She concluded that using blanket 'manualized' interventions was not sensitive to clients' experience.

Hoerner (2007) did a qualitative study of 11 clients with various problems who experienced a variety of different therapy approaches. She found that most clients reported that change resulted from their agentic efforts. They highly valued their own contributions to therapy. Different clients saw different approaches as best facilitating their agency. Some felt, for instance, that more directive therapies facilitated their agency by placing responsibility on them to do homework. Others reported that more exploratory approaches facilitated agency.

In a therapy analogue study, Tallman, Robinson, Kay, Harvey, and Bohart (1994) compared the effects of 'bad' (vapid, superficial) empathy responses with 'good' (more richly detailed and deep) empathy responses. Tallman et al. noticed that despite the vapid nature of many bad empathy responses, some clients found a creative way to make lemonade out of the lemon of the response. In some cases, the client would give a nod to the therapist, as though trying to protect her feelings, by saying something like, 'Yes, that is really close ...' before going off in a different direction. The client would use what the therapist said, but in an innovative way to pursue what he or she wanted to pursue, conduct the analysis he or she wanted to conduct, or achieve the insight for which he or she was searching. Similarly, Elliott (1984) reported finding much sloppiness and slippage in interpretation/insight processes in therapy–therapists made mistakes, but clients ignored mistakes and used what was beneficial to them.

Newfield, Kuehl, Joanning, and Quinn (1991) demonstrated how teenagers in family therapy for drug abuse actively manipulated therapy to their ends. Often in such therapy situations, adolescents are nonresponsive, and are typically labeled as *defensive* and *resistant*. Newfield et al. found that the teens were actually highly active. They were quiet, not because they were being defensive and resistant, but rather because they were actively trying to figure out what was going on so they could get what they wanted out of the situation. Their aim was to use the information they gathered to placate and maneuver their therapists and parents later. The teens also reported saying what their parents wanted to hear, and trying to talk their parents out of the therapist's interventions during the week.

The lesson of this study is that what may look like a passive or a resistant client is often a highly proactive one, probably pursuing an agenda other than that of the therapist. It is probably better to view clients as active agents, pursuing agendas that make sense within their frame of reference, rather than simply label them as resistant or passive because they are not conforming with the therapist's agenda.

McKenna and Todd (1997) did a qualitative study of nine adults. Participants evaluated the effectiveness of therapy episodes depending on what they were looking for at various stages in their life. Participants were aware that they used therapy at different times in their life in different ways. Similarly, Gold (1994) documented cases where clients spontaneously and creatively generated their own forms of psychotherapy integration.

Brinegar (2007) found in a qualitative study, based on Stiles' (2002) assimilation of problematic experiences model, that clients have different 'voices' which represent different parts of their problem. These voices can even sound different. The different voices can even show up in the same sentence, as the client shifts back and forth among them. Clients construct dialogues among the voices. Continued dialogue leads to the voices tending to slow down and listen to one another. They develop shared understandings.

We conclude this section by citing a study by Greaves (2006). Greaves conducted a qualitative study of 13 clients and found a pattern of results to support many of the findings I have previously cited indicating that clients are overall, active, agentic self-healers in therapy. She found four themes of client activities, based on 21 categories and 65 subcategories. To quote her:

> The clients exhibited initiative and engaged in meaning-making processes to make sense of their difficulties, redefine and remoralize themselves, and try out new ways of being. Not only did they act in planning and management capacities, they also played the role of truth-seeker, motivator, advocator, and negotiator to further the pursuit and attainment of their goals. They blended their own wisdom with their therapist's expertise in idiosyncratic ways, after having prepared their therapist to potentially offer the most appropriate assistance. These clients also nurtured a strong therapeutic relationship and utilized learning and healing opportunities within the context of that relationship. (p. vii)

In summary, there is evidence to support the hypothesis of client agency in psychotherapy. Clients monitor what is going on, reflect on it, evaluate it, and try to arrange events to suit their perceived purposes, both overtly and covertly.

Client creativity

We have suggested that clients contribute to therapy through their capacities for generative and creative thinking (Bohart & Tallman, 1999). Virtually no theory of psychotherapy grants clients the capacity for generative thinking. In psychoanalysis, insight comes from without in the form of the analyst's interpretation. In cognitive therapy, client thinking is described in dysfunctional terms, which is corrected by the therapist. Humanistic therapy has traditionally focused on the process of attending to feelings and emotions and putting them into words. Although creativity is implied by humanistic approaches, there is little in the way of descriptions of how humans actually engage in generative thinking.

Yet, Cantor (2003, p. 53), a personality psychologist, has argued that the human capacity for adaptive creativity is important:

> One of the signature features of individuals' proclivity for constructive cognition is its creativity, as contrasted with two attributes – accuracy and straightforwardness – that one might instead expect to characterize the strengths of social cognition. In fact, a great deal of what people think about themselves and others is adaptive precisely to the extent that it plays creatively with 'reality.'

Much of the evidence we have cited previously supports this capacity in clients. We mentioned Talmon's (1990) interview study where clients reported making creative modifications on suggestions that he had given. In addition, Selby (2004) did a qualitative study of 20 clients in therapy. She tape recorded 97 sessions and interviewed both clients and therapists. She found that 10 of the 20 exhibited creativity. Creativity was a joint product of therapist and client contributions. In the cases of the noncreative clients, some of the lack of creativity could be attributed to clients' unwillingness to enter into the therapy process, and some to the inability of therapists to meet clients who were ready to be creative.

Relying on client resources
In 1994 Bergin and Garfield, based on their review of the evidence, argued that,

> Clients are not inert objects upon which techniques are administered ... [Therefore] it is important to rethink the terminology that assumes that 'effects' are like Aristotelian impetus causality. *As therapists have depended more upon the client's resources, more change seems to occur.* (pp. 825–826, italics added)

Bergin and Garfield's call for a focus on client resources is increasingly being heeded. Baker and Neimeyer (2003) have noted that for depression, 'contrary to traditional belief, treatments appear to capitalize on client strengths rather than compensate for their deficiencies' (p. 136). Rude and Rehm (1991) have pointed out that cognitive therapy does not correct cognitive weaknesses but rather builds on the strengths people already have. Activating and working with patients' resources has also generally been found to relate to positive outcome in a series of studies (reviewed in Orlinsky et al., 2004). As one example, Willutzki, Neumann, Haas, Koban, & Schulte (2004) found that resource activation is generally related to positive outcome. Gassman and Grawe (2006) conducted minute-by-minute analyses of 120 sessions involving 30 clients treated for a range of psychological problems. They found that unsuccessful therapists focused on problems but neglected client strengths. When the unsuccessful therapists did focus on clients' strengths, they did so more at the end of a therapy session. Successful therapists focused on their clients' strengths from the very start of an appointment. Gassman and Grawe (2006) concluded that successful therapists 'created an environment in which the patient felt he was perceived as a well functioning person. As soon as this was established, productive work on the patient's problems was more likely' (p. 10).

The fact that therapists of other orientations are learning that a focus on clients' strengths and resources facilitates therapy supports the person-centered hypothesis that clients have important resources for personal change and that the proper supportive conditions can mobilize them.

How clients relate therapy to their lived-in environments

As Mackrill (2008) has observed, there is relatively little evidence on how clients actually integrate their therapy experiences with everyday life. The traditional models assume that therapy 'fixes' things inside the patient, such as ego strength or dysfunctional cognitions, so that the client can go out into everyday life and function better. Such models do not grant the client much agency in the work of integrating therapy with life.

Although there is relatively little evidence, what evidence there is shows that clients actively work to bring therapy and life together. First, clients engage in efforts to change outside of therapy. Clients may show improvement even before their first therapy session (McKeel, 1996). Clients may also increase utilization of resources outside of therapy. For instance, clients in therapy increase their use of other people to talk to (Cross, Sheehan, & Kahn, 1980). Levitt, Butler, and Hill (2006) found that some clients engage in activities outside of therapy such as reading self-help books, engaging in self-questioning, thinking about dialogues with the therapist, or allowing time before or after the session to prepare. Clients also consciously decided to bridge therapy and their life situation by becoming less emotional towards the end of a therapy session in order to be able to compose themselves sufficiently to go home.

Second, Dreier's (2000) observations of how families utilized experiences in family therapy led him to conclude that therapy does not take place primarily in the therapist's office. Clients actively transform what they have learned in therapy and apply it to their life situations. They do not merely transfer what they have experienced to their life situations. 'Clients configure the meaning of therapy within the structure of their ongoing social practice' (Dreier, 2000, p. 253).

Along these lines, Mackrill (2008) did a qualitative study where he had four clients keep intensive diaries of their out-of-therapy experience. He found that clients used their own ideas of what is helpful to structure their experience of therapy, leading to a kind of 'seamless' translation of therapy into the natural environment. Clients also compared what others in their natural environments had told them about what could be helpful to what therapists say. For instance, the client might compare what a girlfriend told him to what the therapist is telling him. Clients then were more likely to use what the therapist said if it reinforced what someone else had told them.

Mörtl & Von Wietersheim (2008) studied clients in a day clinic and found that they took day clinic experiences home. They tried to apply structures useful in the clinic in everyday life. They talked over their experiences in the clinic with people in their everyday life, and they reflected on their experiences in the clinic while at home. They also got people at home to help them confront everyday problems. Conversely, Mörtl & Von Wietersheim found that clients also transferred experiences from everyday life into the day clinic. For instance, they compared experiences at home with feedback they were receiving in the day clinic. They compared their relationships at home with relationships at the day clinic and learned from that.

In conclusion, clients are active information processors in sifting and sorting through experiences in therapy, in order to compare and contrast them to experiences in their everyday life. They find ways to integrate the two together. Furthermore they actively engage in helping processes outside of psychotherapy to coordinate with and facilitate what is happening in therapy.

Summary
Overall, the evidence shows that clients play an active role in shaping the therapy process. Clients are not merely dependent variables upon which the independent variables of therapy operate. Instead they are thinkers who attempt to generate solutions to problems. They modify old concepts and use them, create new concepts, think of alternatives, and derive rules and implications. They are active agents, creatively working to get from the therapist what they want and need, protecting themselves when necessary, and supporting the therapist when they think the therapist needs it. In particular, it is *when* clients are active agents that therapy seems to work best, no matter what the therapeutic approach. Finally, it is when therapy utilizes clients' strengths and resources that it is most likely to be effective.

Client factors in psychotherapy
The previously reviewed research suggests that clients have the potential to actively and generatively contribute to outcome in therapy. Yet it is apparent that not all clients benefit equally from psychotherapy, including person-centered psychotherapy. Is this because, for whatever reasons, they are unable to actively and creatively operate on the therapy process to make it work for them? Is it because, for whatever reasons, they do not commit to the process and get involved? At present we do not know the answers. The research suggests that not all individuals are the same in their capacity for resilience, although the degree of resilience is partially dependent on resources available in the person's natural environment. Perhaps not all clients will be the same in their likelihood to engage in the kinds of active processes we have described above to make therapy work either. Indeed, there is research showing that clients are not equally likely to benefit from psychotherapy. Next we review factors associated with clients that may interact with the probability of productively utilizing psychotherapy.

Client characteristics and beliefs
Studies have found that clients who are rated as more functionally impaired do more poorly in psychotherapy (Castonguay & Beutler, 2006; Clarkin & Levy, 2004). Similarly, clients diagnosed with personality disorders are less likely to benefit from therapy and to have greater difficulty in establishing good working therapeutic alliances

(Castonguay & Beutler, 2006; Clarkin & Levy, 2004). Clients who have poor object relations or attachment problems, i.e., who have experienced significant interpersonal problems during childhood may benefit less from psychotherapy (Castonguay & Beutler, 2006; Clarkin & Levy, 2004).

There is evidence that some client characteristics interact with different approaches to therapy. For instance, clients high in reactance or resistance (clients who are highly motivated to preserve their autonomy) have been found to benefit more from nondirective or self-help approaches to therapy, while clients low in reactance did better with directive approaches (Beutler et al., 2004; Castonguay & Beutler, 2006). Externalizing clients (clients who externalize blame and are undercontrolled) have been found to do better with behavioral approaches, while internalizing/introspective clients did better with approaches that are interpersonal and insight-oriented (Castonguay & Beutler, 2006; Clarkin & Levy, 2004). Clients who were focused more on relationships do better in supportive expressive psychotherapy, while clients who were focused more on developing a positive sense of self do better in long-term psychoanalysis (Blatt, Shahar, & Zuroff, 2002).

Clients' beliefs about their problems also matter. Hester, Miller, Delaney, and Meyers (1990) found that clients who believed alcohol problems were caused by a disease did better in traditional treatment. Those who believed they were a bad habit did better in a learning-based approach. Crane, Griffin, & Hill (1986) found that how well family therapy treatment seemed to fit clients' views accounted for 35% of outcome variance. Crits-Christoph et al. (2003) found that endorsement of 12-step beliefs was related to outcome in a study of cocaine-dependent patients.

Early responders and client trajectories of change in psychotherapy
There is evidence that clients exhibit different patterns of change and that these relate to their chances for positive outcomes (Barkham et al., 2006; Barkham, Stiles, & Shapiro, 1993; Krause, Howard, & Lutz, 1998). For instance, some clients show a great deal of discontinuity from one session to the next, showing sudden gains, then losses, then gains (Stiles et al., 2003; Thompson, Thompson, & Gallagher-Thompson, 1995; Tang & DeRubeis, 1999). Others are more likely to show steady trajectories. Thompson et al. (1995) found that older clients who had up and down shifts in depression during treatment had higher recovery rates but also had a greater risk of relapse later on.

Two factors best predict the degree of change in therapy (Brown, Burlingame, Lambert, Jones, & Vaccaro, 2001). Higher levels of distress at the start of therapy is the best predictor of outcome, more so than the client's diagnosis, chronicity of his or her problem, or the treatment population. The other predictor is the degree of early change. As Brown et al. (2001) note, this suggests that clients and their degree of change potential (which may be a complex combination of individual personality variables and extra-therapeutic environmental factors) is itself a major factor in whether therapy is effective. They note, 'The most tenable hypothesis is that the patients themselves are the primary determinant of duration of treatment ...' (p. 929).

Of particular interest has been the identification of those who exhibit early change, or *early responders*. These are individuals who show dramatic positive changes early in psychotherapy. They are also highly likely to have positive outcomes from psychotherapy. Lambert (2007) estimates that about 25% of clients are early responders. Howard, Kopta, Krause, and Orlinsky (1986) found that about 30% of their sample showed significant improvement after two sessions. Rosenbaum (1994) has studied the phenomenon of 'single session therapy,' which is that many clients improve after only a single session. Rapid change in substance abuse has also been noted (Miller, 2000).

Early responders tend to have better outcomes and to maintain their changes. The effect has been found for depression, panic disorders, and addictive disorders (Lambert, 2007). It is unclear what is occurring with early responders. One of the possibilities is that this is a 'transference cure.' However the fact that gains are maintained over treatment and seem to persist suggests that there is more to it than that. Lambert (2007) mentions some possibilities, clients:

> may be more resilient, better prepared, more motivated, and thus more receptive to therapeutic influences of any kind. Early responders may be more likely to proceed from one problem to the next in therapy (a sequential pattern), whereas delayed responders continue to revisit the same therapy topic across sessions (Fennel & Teasdale, 1987). Early response may also indicate a better fit between client and therapist and reflect the positive effects of the working alliance. (p. 7)

Stage models of client change

There are two models of 'where clients are at' in their relationship to the process of change that have been shown to predict to how well clients do in therapy. These two models suggest that change is a process and that how clients do in therapy depends on where they are in the process. The first is Prochaska's (1999) *stages of change* model. This model breaks therapy into five stages of change depending upon client readiness to take action. Prochaska has argued that different therapeutic approaches and different therapeutic interventions are differentially appropriate at different stages of change. For instance, during the early stages of change, when clients are either unaware of their problems, or are still contemplating the nature of their problems, clients are more likely to benefit with interventions associated with approaches such as psychodynamic and client-centered therapy. On the other hand, clients who are in the 'action' stage – ready to work, will be more likely to benefit from action-oriented strategies, such as those of behavioral approaches. Prochaska (1999) cites research that shows that matching interventions to clients' stage of change can improve both retention in psychotherapy and outcome.

Stiles' (2002) assimilation of problematic experience model is based on the underlying process of change in therapy. Early in the model clients have warded off problems or are actively avoiding them. Later they are vaguely aware of having problems. Still later on they have clarified the problem and gained insight. Finally they work on problem solutions. Stiles cites some evidence that psychodynamic/interpersonal approaches, such as person-centered therapy, fit better with clients who are at early stages of assimilation, while cognitive-behavioral interventions fit better with clients at later stages. A series of carefully done case studies have supplied support for this model.

Summary
Putting the literature reviewed in this section together, clients themselves play an important role in how they participate in therapy and how likely change is to occur. Factors include:

- How they see their problems
- How upset they are
- How quickly they are able to utilize therapy to change
- How able they are to participate effectively in the therapy relationship
- How their personalities interact with the therapy environment
- How difficult their problems are

In conclusion, some clients manifest an ability to use the therapy environment more effectively than others. That does not mean that clients who are less able to utilize it lack the ability to self-right and self-heal. If all humans have a capacity for resilience to at least some degree, it is possible that they may need something different than what current therapy environments provide for that capacity to manifest itself. Further research is needed to clarify this issue.

EVALUATION

The evidence is strong that human beings, on average, have, in varying degrees, the potential for resilience, self-healing and self-righting. This supports Carl Rogers' view of the person. The evidence on psychotherapy suggests that client involvement is crucial for therapy to work. It also suggests that clients often play an active role in interpreting the therapy environment, incorporating what is learned into their own perspectives, actively and creatively operating on the therapy environment in order to make change happen, actively and creatively operating outside of therapy to facilitate change, and actively blending what happens in therapy with what happens outside. These findings also support Rogers' views.

The question is raised as to how true this is of all clients who come to therapy. While these studies can be said to demonstrate what clients can do, and what many clients do do, it is not clear that they demonstrate that this is what all clients are capable of, or how all clients act. In fact, as we have seen, not all clients benefit equally from currently provided therapy environments. Further research will be needed to clarify this.

Finally, it needs to be pointed out that the evidence that supports the idea that it is clients who ultimately make therapy work does not imply that therapists or therapy is not needed. Although self-help procedures work as well or almost as well for many disorders, clients come to therapy because whatever resources are available in their natural environments have not served to help them right the ship. We have to remember that clients do want some structure to help them. Why cannot clients just use self-help procedures in their everyday life? Using self-help procedures in a research study is different than using them on your own. There is more structure. One thing therapy provides is systematic, ongoing structure. This would seem to be one thing that clients want that they may not be able to get or provide for themselves in their everyday life. Furthermore, although clients can do well without therapists, in one study it was found that clients felt better if they had therapists, in contrast to just using self-help materials (Jacobs et al., 2001).

Thus, although it is clients who ultimately make therapy work, the evidence suggests that therapist and techniques do make a contribution. They should be thought of as support structures that help clients mobilize and utilize their capacities for self-healing, but nonetheless important and useful support structures.

IMPLICATIONS FOR THE PRACTICE OF PERSON-CENTERED THERAPY

Before we draw out implications for the practice of person-centered psychotherapy, in a chapter that is based on the idea that clients are active self-healers in therapy, it becomes important to hear their voice about what is important. What do they see as the kinds of changes that are valuable to them, and what are their views of what is helpful in psychotherapy? We will then take that data and put it together with the research we have previously considered to draw out implications for therapy practice.

Clients' views of psychotherapy
Benefits to clients

First, across therapy approaches, clients value attaining insight (Levitt, 2004; Marcus, Westra, Angus, Stala, & Kagan, 2007; Timulak, 2007; Westra, Angus, & Stala, 2007). For instance, Lilliengren and Werbart (2005), and Werbart and Johansson (2007) found that an increase in self-knowledge was seen as a positive change. Some of the positive understandings that came out of group therapy in the Webert and Johansson study included learning that others also have problems, and understanding oneself in relationship to others. Mörtl and Von Wietersheim (2008) found that becoming aware of patterns in behavior was useful.

Second, learning how to deal with emotions was also valued. Westra, Angus, and Stala (2007) found that it was helpful to express painful emotions. Kagan, Angus, and Pos (2007) found that accessing, accepting, understanding, and experiencing emotion was helpful. This was also found by Werbart and Johansson (2007). Conversely, if clients cannot reach their feelings or have trouble expressing them they rate that as a hindering event in therapy (Von Below & Werbart, 2007).

Other positive benefits mentioned by clients include the opportunity to take risks and try out new behaviors (Mörtl & Von Wietersheim, 2008), sharing with others in group psychotherapy and day clinic situations (Mörtl & Von Wietersheim, 2008); Werbart & Johannson (2007), gaining a sense of empowerment (Timulak, 2007), and gaining a new strategy to attain goals (Timulak, 2007).

What are the helpful things therapists do? Studies of what clients say about what is helpful in therapy find over and over that general therapist activities and ways of being rather than specific interventions are emphasized. For instance, Levitt (2004) did a grounded theory analysis of client interviews and found that clients did not focus upon or recall specific interventions, but rather upon the tenor of the therapeutic relationship and new insights they achieved. Clients consistently emphasize variables such as being understood, accepted, and listened to; having a safe space to explore in; support for dealing with current crises; support for trying out new behaviors; and advice (e.g., Cullari, 2001; Elliott & James, 1989; Howe, 1993; Kagan et al., 2007; Levitt, 2004; Marcus et al., 2007; Mörtl & Von Wietersheim, 2008; Phillips, 1984; Rodgers, 2003; Timulak, 2007; Westra et al., 2007). Specific activities such as confrontation (Mörtl & Von Wietersheim, 2008); Werbart & Johannson, 2007), practical exercises (Levitt, Butler, & Hill, 2006; Von Below & Werbart, 2007), and getting tools and strategies from their therapists (Carey et al., 2007; Timulak, 2007) are sometimes mentioned, but they are not emphasized as often as factors like feeling understood.

For instance, Howe (1993) found that for clients the following was important: accept me, understand me, and talk to me. Levitt, Butler, and Hill (2006) did a qualitative analysis of 26 clients. They found that 21 reported that the relationship was a central part of therapy. Acceptance, genuineness, empathy, and attentiveness were listed by 25 of 26 as important. Clients also liked a variety of general therapist activities, particularly ones that encouraged their own self-reflection, such as by challenging them, identifying patterns, encouraging self-reflection, offering new perspectives, and questioning and probing. Clients also liked therapist activities such as teaching and allowing emotional experiences. Although interventions were rarely mentioned as leading to outcome, clients reported enjoying structured tasks. However they wanted therapeutic structure to be neither too loose nor too tight.

Having a safe space in which to talk and explore is particularly valued. Phillips (1984) interviewed clients who were in a variety of therapy approaches, including cognitive-behavioral therapy, and found that the most helpful factor was having a time and a place to focus on themselves and talk. They use therapy as a place where they feel safe to talk out their problems (Phillips, 1984), reflect on them (Rennie, 1992; Watson & Rennie, 1994), and explore them and gain perspective on them (Phillips, 1984). They feel more free to talk because the therapist is a stranger who is not involved in their lives (Dreier, 2000).

Conversely, clients report that such therapist activities as saying hurtful things, being too authoritative, not listening, being silent, distant, or unresponsive, refusing to give advice, ideas, or practical exercises, or where there is too little closeness and trust, or unbridgeable personality differences, get in the way of positive outcomes (Conrad & Auckenthaler, 2007; Von Below & Werbart, 2007).

Finally, clients value collaboration with their therapists. Orlinsky et al. (2004) report that collaboration, as rated from the patient's point of view, correlates with positive therapeutic outcome. Bachelor, Laverdière, Gamache, and Bordeleau (2007) found that 26.7% of clients were active collaborators who placed primary emphasis on their own activities. Another 36.7% were mutual collaborators who placed emphasis on joint involvement, while 33.3% were classified as dependent on the therapist to provide direction. However even they were not necessarily passive. Genuine collaboration means that therapists should be willing to listen to clients, respect their frame of reference, utilize clients' wisdom, establish common ground, and work together to forge solutions.

In summation, from the client's perspective, the most frequently emphasized aspects of therapy typically are the 'nonspecific' factors. In contrast to a matter of diagnosis and application of specific interventions to specific disorders, therapy is primarily a matter of talking with someone who will listen to you, support you, provide a space for you in which to think, share ideas with you that might help you gain insight, encourage you to take risks, and empower you. However, clients do want therapists to suggest things, give feedback, and provide challenges.

We next put this together with research we have previously considered to suggest implications for therapy practice, and implications for models of psychotherapy.

Implications for therapy practice

The results provide support for the value of the original, traditional person-centered manner of conducting therapy, which relies upon client resources for the generation of change in psychotherapy. In this model the therapist proceeds by providing the facilitative conditions and by responding primarily with empathic understanding directed at the client's frame of reference. Based on the findings we have reviewed, this model should work for many clients.

However, the findings also challenge the *necessity* of sticking to a traditional modality of responding almost exclusively with empathic understanding.

First, the original nondirective philosophy was based on the idea that therapists needed to stay out of the way of clients. Only by staying within the client's frame of reference would clients be freed up to get in touch with their own resources. However, the general picture that emerges from the research findings is that many clients are active, resilient constructors of the therapy process. They operate to shape it to get what they need, sometimes in spite of the therapist. The idea of them as fragile creatures whose autonomy will be crushed if the therapist responds from his or her frame of reference, or offers advice or suggestions, does not appear to hold true, at least for many clients. If clients are more robust and resilient than one might expect, then one does not necessarily have to be worried that one will automatically derail the client by saying something from the therapist's frame of reference, or by suggesting a technique.

To the contrary, many clients actively prefer therapists to give their thoughts, advice, to challenge them, and to suggest useful exercises. Many clients prefer active collaboration with therapists. Some clients say that their agency is mobilized by getting homework assignments. The research shows that although clients want understanding more than anything, they are not shy about wanting advice, or the provision of some structure.

In fact, offering thoughts, ideas, advice, or techniques may, for some clients, be a way of mobilizing self-organizing wisdom. A colleague of ours, for instance, does not particularly like to receive empathic understanding responses, at least not all the time. She prefers to hear what the therapist thinks. She feels capable of evaluating for herself what she gets from the therapist, to see if it fits or does not fit. Furthermore, the therapist's thoughts and ideas, even if she rejects them, often stimulate her own generative thinking and feeling processes.

Similarly, the research on client differences suggests that different folks may want or need different strokes. Valuing different strokes for different folks ought to be compatible with person-centered philosophy, having as it does at the core a valuing and respecting of each individual client's experience, as well as having faith in the client and in what the client wants and needs. This suggests a more integrative approach to person-centered practice within which therapists at times may suggest techniques and procedures that might be differentially useful to clients, as long as that is done in collaborative consultation with clients rather than in the form of the expert therapist telling the client what to do.

Wood (2008) has argued that the core of the person-centered approach is to *trust the self-organizing wisdom of the person one is working with.* Wood shows how, if one really does this in groups, one does not always behave as traditional client-centered therapists do in therapy, because that does not always work in group settings. To really trust the self-organizing wisdom of the client therefore means that the person working with the client or group must really listen, and respond in ways appropriate to that person or group. This means they may not always respond with empathic understanding responses. Instead, they might differentially respond uniquely to that person in the moment. That would really honor the person's capacity for self-organizing wisdom. This means to take seriously, for instance, that the client may want guidance, ideas, or structure from time to time, and to possibly respond in kind.

The trick becomes how to respond with guidance, ideas, and techniques in a person-centered fashion. Here again the idea of trusting self-organizing wisdom comes into play. It suggests that it is not so much *what* therapists say, but *how* they say it that is important. In whatever they say or do, do they do it in a way that honors, respects, and supports clients' capacities for self-judgment, self-management, and self-direction? It could be argued that to give advice in an honoring and respectful way is a way of showing unconditional positive regard for the client's capabilities and judgment. To do it sensitively and in tune with the client is a way of showing empathic understanding. And to do it at all is a way of being congruent in the relationship.

Some traditional person-centered therapists will object. One objection has to do with the nature of therapist power. They will point out that clients may defer to therapists because therapists are seen as the experts. This is indeed a danger and there is evidence that clients do defer to therapists (Rennie, 2000). However, although they publicly defer, they do not necessarily privately defer (Levitt & Rennie, 2004). This suggests that with many clients therapists should be able to trust that clients will often utilize their own capacities for judgment and understanding to evaluate what therapists offer. If the person-centered therapist is demonstrating, over and over, his or her unconditional positive regard for the client and empathic understanding, and respect for the client's self-organizing wisdom, we suspect that clients will feel freer to disagree publicly if they do not want to use what the therapist has suggested, particularly if suggestions are not made frequently but instead as an occasional supplement to a primarily empathic listening relationship.

A bigger concern may be clients who are more 'fragile,' who do not trust themselves. They may defer both publicly and privately. Here too the fundamental person-centered emphasis on the primacy of listening to and respecting clients and their self-organizing wisdom should help therapists be sensitive to when they can suggest something without interfering with clients' self-organizing processes.

The kind of potential for integrative person-centered practice we are suggesting here is not new. It is compatible with Carl Rogers' own position. In an interview in 1975, he said, 'One thing about the client-centered approach is that I think it can utilize many modes from other points of view and keep a basically person-centered philosophy' (Francis, 2009, p. 16). In the 1970s and 1980s there was a trend among some person-centered practitioners to emphasize integrative practice (e.g., Hart & Tomlinson, 1970; Tausch, 1990). This trend has continued (e.g., Tausch, 2006). What we are suggesting here that is different is that this integrative way of proceeding can be based on what we now know about clients and how they make therapy work.

REFERENCES

Anderson, T. (1999). *Specifying non-'specifics' in therapists: The effect of facilitative interpersonal skills in outcome and alliance formation.* Paper presented at the 30th annual meeting of the International Society for Psychotherapy Research, Braga, Portugal.

Arkowitz, H., & Lilienfeld, S. O. (2006, October/November). *Do self-help books help?* Scientific American Mind Digital Magazine. Retrieved from http://www.sciamdigital.com

Asay, T. P., & Lambert, M. J. (1999). The empirical case for the common factors in therapy: Quantitative findings. In M. A. Hubble, B. L. Duncan, & S. D. Miller (Eds.), *The heart and soul of change: What works in therapy* (pp. 33–56). Washington, DC: American Psychological Association.

Bachelor, A., & Horvath, A. O. (1999). In M. A. Hubble, B. L. Duncan & S. D. Miller (Eds.), *The heart and soul of change: What works in therapy* (pp. 133–178). Washington, DC: American Psychological Association.

Bachelor, A., Laverdière, O., Gamache, D., & Bordeleau, V. (2007). Clients' collaboration in therapy: Self-perceptions and relationships with client psychological functioning, interpersonal relations, and motivation. *Psychotherapy: Theory, Research, Practice, Training, 44,* 175–192.

Baker, K. D., & Neimeyer, R. A. (2003). Therapist training and client characteristics as predictors of treatment response to group therapy for depression. *Psychotherapy Research, 13,* 135–151.

Barkham, M., Connell, J., Miles, J. N. V., Evans, C., Stiles, W. B., Marginson, F., et al. (2006). Dose-effect relations and responsive regulation of treatment duration: The good enough level. *Journal of Consulting and Clinical Psychology, 74,* 160–167.

Barkham, M., Stiles, W. B., & Shapiro, D. A. (1993). The shape of change in psychotherapy: Longitudinal assessment of personal problems. *Journal of Consulting and Clinical Psychology, 61,* 667–677.

Bergin, A. E., & Garfield, S. L. (1994). Overview, trends, and future issues. In A. E. Bergin & S. L. Garfield (Eds.), *Handbook of psychotherapy and behavior change* (4th ed., pp. 821–830). New York: Wiley.

Beutler, L. E., Malik, M., Alimohamed, S., Harwood, T. M., Talebi, H., Noble, S., et al. (2004). Therapist variables. In M. J. Lambert (Ed.), *Bergin and Garfield's handbook of psychotherapy and behavior change* (5th ed., pp. 227–306). New York: Wiley.

Blatt, S. J. , Shahar, G., & Zuroff, D. C. (2002). Anaclitic/sociotropic and introjective/autonomous dimensions. In J. C. Norcross (Ed.), *Psychotherapy relationships that work* (pp. 315–334). New York: Oxford University Press.

Bohart, A. C., Bekele, A., & Byock, G. (2007, June). *How one client productively constructs a therapy interaction from within her world view: A vicarious-ethnographic examination of one client's experience.* Paper presented at the conference of the Society for Psychotherapy Research, Madison, WI.

Bohart, A. C., & Boyd, G. (1997, December). *Clients' construction of the therapy process: A qualitative analysis.* Paper presented at the meeting of the North American Association of the Society for Psychotherapy Research, Tucson, AZ.

Bohart, A. C., Elliott, R., Greenberg, L. S., & Watson, J. C. (2002). Empathy. In J. C. Norcross (Ed.), *Psychotherapy relationships that work* (pp. 89–108). New York: Oxford University Press.

Bohart, A., & Tallman, K. (1996). The active client: Therapy as self-help. *Journal of Humanistic Psychology, 36*(3), 7–30.

Bohart, A., & Tallman, K. (1999). *How clients make therapy work: The process of active self-healing.* Washington, DC: American Psychological Association.

Bozarth, J. D. (1993). Not necessarily necessary but always sufficient. In D. Brazier (Ed.), *Beyond Carl Rogers.* (pp. 92–105). London: Constable.

Bridge, J. A., Iyengar, S., Salary, C. B., Barbe, R. P., Birmaher, B., Pincus, H. A., et al. (2007). Clinical response and risk for reported suicidal ideation and suicide attempts in pediatric antidepressant treatment: A meta-analysis of randomized controlled trials. *Journal of the American Medical Association, 297,* 1683–1696.

Brinegar, M. G. (2007, June). *The experience of intrapersonal dialogue from the client's perspective: Implications for the assimilation model.* Paper presented at the conference of the Society for Psychotherapy Research, Madison, WI.

Brown, G. S., Burlingame, G. M., Lambert, M. J., Jones, E., & Vaccaro, J. (2001). Pushing the quality envelope: A new outcomes management system. *Psychiatric Services, 52,* 925–934.

Busseri, M. A., & Tyler, J. D. (2004). Client-therapist agreement on target problems, working alliance, and counseling outcome. *Psychotherapy Research, 14,* 77–88.

Calhoun, L. G., & Tedeschi, R. G. (2006). The foundations of posttraumatic growth: An expanded framework. In L. G. Calhoun & R. G. Tedeschi (Eds.), *Handbook of posttraumatic growth: Research and practice* (pp. 1–23). Mahwah, NJ: Erlbaum.

Cantor, N. (2003). Constructive cognition, personal goals, and the social embedding of personality. In L. G. Aspinwall & U. M. Staudinger (Eds.), *A psychology of human strengths* (pp. 49–60). Washington, DC: American Psychological Association.

Carey, T. A., Carey, M., Stalker, K., Mullan, R. J., Murray, L. K., & Spratt, M. B. (2007). Psychological change from the inside looking out: A qualitative investigation. *Counselling & Psychotherapy Research, 7*(3), 178–187.

Castonguay, L. G., & Beutler, L. E. (2006). Common and unique principles of therapeutic change: What do we know and what do we need to know? In L. G. Castonguay & L. E. Beutler (Eds.), *Principles of therapeutic change that work* (pp. 353–370). New York: Oxford University Press.

Christensen, A., & Jacobson, N. S. (1994). Who (or what) can do psychotherapy: The status and challenge of nonprofessional therapies. *Psychological Science, 5,* 8–14.

Clarkin, J. F., & Levy, K. N. (2004). The influence of client variables on psychotherapy. In M. J. Lambert (Ed.), *Bergin and Garfield's handbook of psychotherapy and behavior change* (5th ed., pp. 194–226). New York: Wiley.

Clum, G. A. (2008). Self-help interventions: Mapping the role of self-administered treatments in health care. In P. L. Watkins & G. A. Clum (Eds.), *Handbook of self-help therapies* (pp. 41–58). New York: Routledge.

Cohen, O. (2005). How do we recover? An analysis of psychiatric survivor oral histories. *Journal of Humanistic Psychology, 45,* 333–354.

Conrad, A., & Auckenthaler, A. (2007, June). *Client reports on failure in psychotherapy-further support for the contextual model of psychotherapy?* Paper presented at the conference of the Society for Psychotherapy Research, Madison, WI.

Corsini, R. J. (1989). Introduction. In R. J. Corsini & D. Wedding (Eds.), *Current psychotherapies* (4th ed., pp. 1–18). Itasca, IL: F. E. Peacock.

Crane, R. D., Griffin, W., & Hill, R. D. (1986). Influence of therapist skills on client perceptions of marriage and family therapy outcome: Implications for supervision. *Journal of Marital and Family Therapy, 12,* 91–96.

Crits-Christoph, P., Connolly Gibbons, M. B., Barber, J. P., Gallop, R., Beck, A. T., Mercer, D., et al. (2003). Mediators of outcome in psychosocial treatments for cocaine dependence. *Journal of Consulting and Clinical Psychology, 71,* 918–925.

Crits-Christoph, P., Siqueland, L., Blaine, J., Frank, A., Luborsky, L., Onken, L. S. (1997). The National Institute on Drug Abuse Collaborative Cocaine Treatment Study: Rationale and methods. *Archives of General Psychiatry, 54,* 721–726.

Crits-Christoph, P., Siqueland, L., Blaine, J., Frank, A., et al. (1999). Psychosocial treatments for cocaine dependence: National Institute on Drug Abuse Collaborative Cocaine Treatment Study. *Archives of General Psychiatry, 56,* 493–502.

Cross, D. G., Sheehan, P. W., & Kahn, J. A. (1980). Alternative advice and counseling psychotherapy. *Journal of Consulting and Clinical Psychology, 48,* 615–625.

Cullari, S. (2000). *Counseling and psychotherapy.* New York: Allyn & Bacon.

Dreier, O. (2000). Psychotherapy in clients' trajectories across contexts. In C. Mattingly & L. Garro (Eds.), *Narrative and the cultural construction of illness and healing* (pp. 237–258). Berkeley, CA: University of California Press.

Efran, J. S., & Blumberg, M. J. (1994). Emotion and family living: The perspective of structure determinism. In S. M. Johnson & L. S. Greenberg (Eds.), *The heart of the matter* (pp. 172–206). New York: Brunner/Mazel.

Elder, G., Jr. (1986). Military times and turning points in men's lives. *Developmental Psychology, 22,* 233–245.

Elkin, I. (1994). The NIMH treatment of depression collaborative research program: Where we began and where we are. In A. E. Bergin & S. L. Garfield (Eds.), *Handbook of psychotherapy and behavior change* (4th ed., pp. 114–142). New York: Wiley.

Elliott, R. (1984). A discovery-oriented approach to significant change events in psychotherapy: Interpersonal process recall and comprehensive process analysis. In L. S. Greenberg &. L. N. Rice (Eds.), *Patterns of change* (pp. 249–286). New York: Guilford.

Elliott, R., Greenberg, L. S., & Lietaer, G. (2004). Research on experiential psychotherapies. In M. J. Lambert (Ed.), *Bergin & Garfield's handbook of psychotherapy and behavior change* (pp. 493–540). New York: Wiley.

Elliott, R., & James, E. (1989). Varieties of client experience in psychotherapy: An analysis of the literature. *Clinical Psychology Review, 9,* 443–467.

Elliott, R., & Shapiro, D. A. (1992). Clients and therapists as analysts of significant events. In S. G. Toukmanian & D. L. Rennie (Eds.), *Psychotherapy process research: Pragmatic and narrative approaches* (pp. 163–186). Thousand Oaks, CA: Sage.

Elliott, R., Shapiro, D. A., Firth-Cozens, J., Stiles, W. B., Hardy, G. E., Llewelyn, S. P., & Margison, F. R. (1994). Comprehensive process analysis of insight events in cognitive-behavioral and psychodynamic-interpersonal psychotherapies. *Journal of Counseling Psychology, 41,* 449–463.

Fennel, M. J. V., & Teasdale, J. D. (1987). Cognitive therapy for depression: Individual differences and the process of change. *Cognitive Therapy and Research, 11,* 253–271.

Francis, K. C. (2009). Questions and answers: Two hours with Carl Rogers. *The Person-Centered Journal, 16*(1–2), 4–35.

Fonagy, P., & Bateman, M. (2006). Progress in the treatment of borderline personality disorder. *British Journal of Psychiatry, 188,* 1–3.

Garfinkel, H. (1967). *Studies in ethnomethodology.* New York: Prentice-Hall.

Gassman, D. & Grawe, K. (2006). General change mechanisms: The relation between problem activation and resource activation in successful and unsuccessful therapeutic interactions. *Clinical Psychology and Psychotherapy, 13,* 1–11.

Gendlin, E. T. (1984). The politics of giving therapy away: Listening and focusing. In D. Larson (Ed.), *Teaching psychological skills: Models for giving psychology away* (pp. 287–305). Monterey, CA: Brooks/Cole.

Gendlin, E. T. (1996) *Focusing-oriented psychotherapy: A manual of the experiential method.* New York: Guilford.

Gold, J. R. (1994). When the patient does the integrating: Lessons for theory and practice. *Journal of Psychotherapy Integration, 4,* 133–158.

Gould, R. A., & Clum, G. A. (1993). A meta-analysis of self-help treatment approaches. *Clinical Psychology Review, 13,* 169–186.

Greaves, A. L. (2006). *The active client: A qualitative analysis of thirteen clients' contribution to the psychotherapeutic process.* Unpublished doctoral dissertation, University of Southern California, Los Angeles.

Greenberg, L. S., & Watson, J. C. (2006). *Emotion-focused therapy of depression.* Washington, DC: American Psychological Association.

Greenberg, R. P. (1999). Common psychosocial factors in psychiatric drug therapy. In M. A. Hubble, B. L. Duncan, & S. D. Miller (Eds.), *The heart and soul of change: What works in therapy* (pp. 297–328). Washington, DC: American Psychological Association.

Gregory, R. J., Canning, S. S., Lee, T. W., & Wise, J. C. (2004). Cognitive bibliotherapy for depression: A meta-analysis. *Professional Psychology: Research and Practice, 35,* 275–280.

Grissom, R. J. (1996). The magical number .7 ± .2. Meta-meta-analysis of the probability of superior outcome in comparisons involving therapy, placebo, and control. *Journal of Consulting and Clinical Psychology, 64,* 973–982.

Gurin, J. (1990, March). Remaking our lives. *American Health,* 50–52.

Gurin, G., Veroff, J., & Feld, S. (1960). *Americans view their mental health.* New York: Basic Books.

Harding, C. M., Brooks, G. W., Ashikaga, T., Strauss, J. S., & Breier, A. (1987a). The Vermont longitudinal study of persons with severe mental illness: I. Methodology, study sample, and overall status 32 years later. *American Journal of Psychiatry, 144,* 718–726.

Harding, C. M., Brooks, G. W., Ashikaga, T., Strauss, J. S., & Breier, A. (1987b). The Vermont longitudinal study: II. Long-term outcome for subjects who retrospectively met DSM-III criteria for schizophrenia. *American Journal of Psychiatry, 144,* 727–735.

Hart, J. T., & Tomlinson, T. M. (Eds.). (1970). *New directions in client-centered therapy*. Boston: Houghton Mifflin.

Harvey, J. H., Orbuch, T. L., Chwalisz, K. D., & Garwood, G. (1991). Coping with sexual assault: The roles of account-making and confiding. *Journal of Traumatic Stress, 4,* 515–531.

Helmeke, K. B., & Sprenkle, D. H. (2000). Clients' perceptions of pivotal moments in couples therapy: A qualitative study of change in therapy. *Journal of Marital & Family Therapy, 26*(4), 469–483.

Hemenover, S. H. (2003). The good, the bad, and the healthy: Impacts of emotional disclosure of trauma on resilient self-concept and psychological distress. *Personality and Social Psychology Bulletin, 29,* 1236–1244.

Hester, R., Miller, W., Delaney, H., & Meyers, R. (1990, November). *Effectiveness of the Community Reinforcement Approach.* Paper presented at the 24th annual meeting of the Association for the Advancement of Behavior Therapy, San Francisco.

Hoerner, C. (2007, June). *Client experiences in psychotherapy: The importance of being active.* Paper presented at the conference of the Society for Psychotherapy Research, Madison, WI.

Honos-Webb, L. (2005). The meaning vs. the medical model in the empirically supported treatments program: A consideration of the empirical evidence. *Journal of Contemporary Psychotherapy, 35,* 55–66.

Horvath, A. O., & Bedi, B. P. (2002). The alliance. In J. C. Norcross (Ed.), *Psychotherapy relationships that work* (pp. 37–70). New York: Oxford University Press.

Howard, K. I., Kopta, S. M., Krause, M. S., & Orlinsky, D. E. (1986). The dose-effect relationship in psychotherapy. *American Psychologist, 41,* 159–164.

Howe, D. (1993). *On being a client: Understanding the process of counseling and psychotherapy.* London: Sage.

Jacobs, M. K., Christensen, A., Snibbe, J. R., Dolezal-Wood, S., Huber, A., & Polterok, A. (2001). A comparison of computer-based versus traditional individual psychotherapy. *Professional Psychology: Research and Practice, 32,* 92–96.

Kagan, F., Angus, L., & Pos, A. (2007, June). *Client experiences in emotion-focused and client-centered brief therapy for depression: A qualitative analysis.* Paper presented at the conference of the Society for Psychotherapy Research, Madison, WI.

Krause, M. S., Howard, K. I., & Lutz, W. (1998). Exploring individual change. *Journal of Consulting and Clinical Psychology, 66,* 838–845.

Kühnlein, I. (1999). Psychotherapy as a process of transformation: Analysis of post-therapeutic autobiographical narrations. *Psychotherapy Research, 9,* 274–288.

Lambert, M. (2007). Presidential address: What we have learned from a decade of research aimed at improving psychotherapy outcome in routine care. *Psychotherapy Research, 17,* 1–14.

Lambert, M. J., Shapiro, D. A., & Bergin, A. E. (1986). The effectiveness of psychotherapy. In S. L. Garfield & A. E. Bergin (Eds.), *Handbook of psychotherapy and behavior change* (3rd ed., pp. 157–212). New York: Wiley.

Lawson, D. (1994). Identifying pretreatment change. *Journal of Counseling and Development, 72,* 244–248.

Leff, J. (1992). The International Pilot Study of Schizophrenia: Five-year follow-up findings. *Psychological Medicine, 22,* 131–145.

Lepore, S., & Revenson, T. (2006). Relationships between posttraumatic growth and resilience: Recovery, resistance, and reconfiguration. In L. G. Calhoun & R. G. Tedeschi (Eds.),

Handbook of posttraumatic growth: Research and practice (pp. 24–46). Mahwah, NJ: Erlbaum.

Levitt, H. M. (2004, November). *What client interviews reveal about psychotherapy process: Principles for the facilitation of change in psychotherapy.* Paper presented at the meeting of the North American Society for Psychotherapy Research, Springdale, UT.

Levitt, H. M., Butler, M., & Hill, T. (2006). What clients find helpful in psychotherapy: Developing principles for facilitating moment-to-moment change. *Journal of Counseling Psychology, 53,* 314–324.

Levitt, H. M., & Rennie, D. L. (2004). Narrative activity: Clients' and therapists' intentions in the process of narration. In L. E. Angus & J. McLeod (Eds.), *The handbook of narrative and psychotherapy* (pp. 299–314). Thousand Oaks, CA: Sage.

Lilliengren, P., & Werbart, A. (2005). A model of therapeutic action grounded in the patients' view of curative and hindering factors in psychoanalytic psychotherapy. *Psychotherapy: Theory, Research, Practice, Training, 42,* 324–339.

Mackrill, T. (2008). *The therapy journal project: A cross-contextual qualitative diary study of psychotherapy with adult children of alcoholics.* Unpublished doctoral dissertation, Copenhagen University, Denmark.

Marcus, D. K., Kashy, D. A., & Baldwin, S. A. (2009). Studying psychotherapy using the one-with-many design: The therapeutic alliance as an exemplar. *Journal of Counseling Psychology, 56*(4), 537–548.

Marcus, M., Westra, H., Angus, L., Stala, D., & Kagan, F. (2007, June). *Client experiences of cognitive behavioral therapy for generalized anxiety disorder: A qualitative analysis.* Paper presented at the conference of the Society for Psychotherapy Research, Madison, WI.

Masten, A. S. (2001). Ordinary magic: Resilience processes in development. *American Psychologist, 56,* 227–238.

Masten, A. S., Best, K. M., & Garmazy, N. (1990). Resilience and development: Contributions from the study of children who overcome adversity. *Development and Psychopathology, 2,* 425–444.

McKeel, A. J. (1996). A clinician's guide to research on solution-focused brief therapy. In S. D. Miller, M. A. Hubble, & B. L. Duncan (Eds.), *Handbook of solution-focused brief therapy* (pp. 251–271). San Francisco: Jossey-Bass.

McKenna, P. A., & Todd, D. M. (1997). Longitudinal utilization of mental health services: A time line method, nine retrospective accounts, and a preliminary conceptualization. *Psychotherapy Research, 7,* 383–396.

Menchola, M., Arkowitz, H. S., & Burke, B. L. (2007). Efficacy of self-administered treatments for depression and anxiety. *Professional Psychology: Research and Practice, 38*(4), 421–429.

Miller, W. R. (2000). Rediscovering fire: Small interventions, large effects. *Psychology of Addictive Behaviors, 14,* 6–18.

Miller, W. R., & C'de Baca, J. (2001). *Quantum change.* New York: Guilford.

Miller, W. R., & Carroll, K. M. (2006). Drawing the scene together: Ten principles, ten recommendations. In W. R. Miller & K. M. Carroll (Eds.), *Rethinking substance abuse: What the science shows, and what we should do about it* (pp. 293–312). New York: Guilford.

Miller, W. R., & Rollnick, S. (1991). *Motivational interviewing: Preparing people to change addictive behavior.* New York: Guilford.

Mörtl, K., & Von Wietersheim, J. (2008). Client experiences of helpful factors in a day treatment program: A qualitative approach. *Psychotherapy Research, 18*(3), 281–293.

Mosher, L. R., Hendrix, V., & Fort, D. C. (2004). *Soteria.* Philadelphia, PA: Xlibris Corporation.

Najavits, L. M., & Strupp, H. (1994). Differences in the effectiveness of psychodynamic therapists: A process-outcome study. *Psychotherapy, 31,* 114–123.

Newfield, N. A., Kuehl, B. P., Joanning, H. P., & Quinn, W. H. (1991). We can tell you about 'psychos' and 'shrinks': An ethnography of the family therapy of adolescent drug abuse. In T. C. Todd & J. M. N. Selekman (Eds.), *Family therapy approaches with adolescent substance abusers* (pp. 277–310). Boston: Allyn & Bacon.

Norcross, J. C. (2006). Integrating self-help into psychotherapy: 16 practical suggestions. *Professional Psychology: Research and Practice, 37,* 683–693.

Orlinsky, D. E., Grawe, K., & Parks, B. K. (1994). Process and outcome in psychotherapy – Noch einmal. In A. E. Bergin & S. L. Garfield (Eds.), *Handbook of psychotherapy and behavior change* (4th ed., pp. 270–378). New York: Wiley.

Orlinsky, D. E., Rønnestad, M. H., & Willutzki, U. (2004). Fifty years of psychotherapy process-outcome research: Continuity and change. In M. J. Lambert (Ed.), *Bergin & Garfield's handbook of psychotherapy and behavior change* (5th ed., pp. 307–390). New York: Wiley.

Ozer, E. J., Best, S. R., Lipsey, T. L., & Weiss, D. S. (2003). Predictors of posttraumatic stress disorder and symptoms in adults: A meta-analysis. *Psychological Bulletin, 129*(1), 52–73.

Pennebaker, J. W. (1990). *Opening up: The healing power of confiding in others.* New York: Morrow.

Pennebaker, J. W. (1997). Writing about emotional experiences as a therapeutic process. *Psychological Science, 8,* 162–166.

Philips, B., Werbart, A., Wennberg, P., & Schubert, J. (2007). Young adults' ideas of cure prior to psychoanalytic psychotherapy. *Journal of Clinical Psychology, 63,* 213–232.

Phillips, J. R. (1984). Influences on personal growth as viewed by former psychotherapy patients. *Dissertation Abstracts International, 44,* 441A.

Prochaska, J. O. (1999). How do people change, and how can we change to help many more people? In M. A. Hubble, B. L. Duncan, & S. D. Miller (Eds.), *The heart and soul of change: What works in therapy* (pp. 227–258). Washington, DC: American Psychological Association.

Prochaska, J. O., Norcross, J. C., & DiClemente, C. C. (1994). *Changing for good.* New York: Morrow.

Pulkkinen, L. (2001). Reveller or striver? How childhood self-control predicts adult behavior. In A. C. Bohart & D. J. Stipek (Eds.), *Constructive and destructive behavior: Implications for family, school, and society* (pp. 167–186). Washington, DC: American Psychological Association.

Rennie, D. L. (1990). Toward a representation of the client's experience of the psychotherapy hour. In G. Lietaer, J. Rombauts, & R. Van Balen (Eds.), *Client-centered and experiential psychotherapy in the nineties* (pp. 155–172). Leuven, Belgium: Leuven University Press.

Rennie, D. L. (1992). Qualitative analysis of the client's experience of psychotherapy: The unfolding of reflexivity. In S. G. Toukmanian & D. L. Rennie (Eds.), *Psychotherapy process research: Paradigmatic and narrative approaches* (pp. 211–233). Newbury Park, CA: Sage.

Rennie, D. L. (1994). Storytelling in psychotherapy: The client's subjective experience. *Psychotherapy, 31,* 234–243.

Rennie, D. L. (2000). Aspects of the client's conscious control of the psychotherapeutic process. *Journal of Psychotherapy Integration, 10,* 151–168.

Rodgers, B. (2003). An exploration into the client at the heart of therapy: A qualitative perspective. *Person-Centered & Experiential Psychotherapies, 2,* 19–30.

Rogers, C. R. (1957). The necessary and sufficient conditions of therapeutic personality change. *Journal of Consulting Psychology. 21*(2), 95–103.

Rogers, C. R. (1961). *On becoming a person.* Boston: Houghton Mifflin.

Rogers, C. R. (1990). A client-centred/person-centred approach to therapy. In H. Kirschenbaum & V. L. Henderson (Eds.), *The Carl Rogers reader* (pp. 135–152). London: Constable. (Original work published 1986)

Rosenbaum, R. (1994). Single-session therapies: Intrinsic integration? *Journal of Psychotherapy Integration, 4,* 229–252.

Rude, S. S., & Rehm, L. P. (1991). Response to treatments for depression: The role of initial status on targeted cognitive and behavioral skills. *Clinical Psychology Review, 11,* 493–514.

Sachse, R. (1992). Differential effects of processing proposals and content references on the explication process of clients with different starting conditions. *Psychotherapy Research, 2,* 235–251.

Schmid, P. F. (2004). Back to the client: A phenomenological approach to the process of understanding. *Person-Centered and Experiential Psychotherapies, 3*(1), 36–51.

Schwitzgebel, R. (1961). *Streetcorner research: An experimental approach to the juvenile delinquent.* Cambridge, MA: Harvard University Press.

Scogin, F., Bynum, J., Stephens, G., & Calhoon, S. (1990). Efficacy of self-administered treatment programs: Meta-analytic review. *Professional Psychology: Research and Practice, 21,* 42–47,

Segal, D. L., & Murray, E. J. (1994). Emotional processing in cognitive therapy and vocal expression of feeling. *Journal of Social and Clinical Psychology, 13,* 189–206.

Selby, C. E. (2004). *Psychotherapy as creative process: A grounded theory exploration.* Unpublished doctoral dissertation, Saybrook Graduate School, San Francisco, CA.

Skodol, A. E., Bender, D. S., Pagano, M. E., Shea, M. T., Yen, S., Sanislow, C. A., et al. (2007). Positive childhood experiences: Resilience and recovery from personality disorder in early adulthood. *Journal of Clinical Psychiatry, 68,* 1102–1108.

Stiles, W. B. (2002). Assimilation of problematic experience. In J. C. Norcross (Ed.), *Psychotherapy relationships that work* (pp. 357–366). New York: Oxford University Press.

Stiles, W. B., Barkham, M., Twigg, E., Mellor-Clark, J., & Cooper, M. (2006). Effectiveness of cognitive-behavioural, person-centred, and psychodynamic therapies as practised in UK National Health Service Settings. *Psychological Medicine, 36,* 555–566.

Stiles, W. B., Leach, C., Barkham, M., Lucock, M., Iveson, S., Iveson, M., et al. (2003). Early sudden gains in psychotherapy under routine clinic conditions: Practice-based evidence. *Journal of Clinical Psychology, 71,* 14–21.

Strupp, H. H., & Hadley, S. W. (1979). Specific versus nonspecific factors in psychotherapy: A controlled study of outcome. *Archives of General Psychiatry, 36,* 1125–1136.

Tallman, K., Robinson, E., Kay, D., Harvey, S., & Bohart, A. (1994, August). *Experiential and non-experiential Rogerian therapy: An analogue study.* Paper presented at the 102nd annual convention of the American Psychological Association, Los Angeles.

Talmon, M. (1990). *Single session therapy.* San Francisco: Jossey-Bass.

Tang, T. Z., & Derubeis, R. J. (1999). Sudden gains and critical sessions in cognitive-behavioral therapy for depression. *Journal of Consulting and Clinical Psychology, 67,* 894–904.

Tausch, R. (1990). The supplementation of client-centered communication therapy with other valid therapeutic methods: A client-centered necessity. In G. Lietaer, J. Rombauts & R. Van Balen (Eds.), *Client-centered and experiential psychotherapy in the nineties* (pp. 447–456). Leuven, Belgium: Leuven University Press.

Tausch, R. (2006, July). *Promoting health: Challenges for person-centered communication and behavior in psychotherapy, counseling and daily life.* Opening speech at the 7th World Conference for

Person-Centered and Experiential Psychotherapy and Counseling, Potsdam, Germany.

Tedeschi, R. G., Park, C. L., & Calhoun, L. G. (Eds.). (1998). *Posttraumatic growth*. Mahwah, NJ: Erlbaum.

Thompson, M. G., Thompson, L., & Gallagher-Thompson, D. (1995). Linear and nonlinear changes in mood between psychotherapy sessions: Implications for treatment outcome and relapse risk. *Psychotherapy Research, 5,* 327–336.

Timulak, L. (2007). Identifying core categories of client-identified impact of helpful events in psychotherapy: A qualitative meta-analysis. *Psychotherapy Research, 17,* 305–314.

Vaillant, G. E. (1993). *The wisdom of the ego*. Cambridge, MA: Harvard University Press.

Von Below, C., & Werbart, A. (2007, June). *Dissatisfied psychotherapy patients: What went wrong?* Paper presented at the conference of the Society for Psychotherapy Research, Madison, WI.

Wampold, B. E. (2001). *The great psychotherapy debate: Models, methods, and findings*. Mahwah, NJ: Erlbaum.

Wampold, B. E. (2006). The therapist. In J. C. Norcross, L. E. Beutler, & R. F. Levant (Eds.), *Evidence-based practices in mental health: Debate and dialogue on the fundamental questions* (pp. 200–207). Washington, DC: American Psychological Association.

Wampold, B. E., Imel, Z. E., & Miller, S. D. (2009). Barriers to the dissemination of empirically supported treatments: Matching messages to the evidence. *The Behavior Therapist, 32*(7), 8–19.

Watson, J. C., & Rennie, D. L. (1994). Qualitative analysis of clients' subjective experience of significant moments during the exploration of problematic reactions. *Journal of Counseling Psychology, 41,* 500–509.

Weiner-Davis, M., de Shazer, S., & Gingerich, W. (1987). Building on pretreatment change to construct the therapeutic solution: An exploratory study. *Journal of Marital and Family Therapy, 13,* 359–364.

Werbart, A., & Johansson, L. (2007, June). *Patients' view of therapeutic action in group psychotherapy*. Paper presented at the conference of the Society for Psychotherapy Research, Madison, WI.

Werner, E. E., & Smith, R. S. (1982). *Vulnerable but invincible: A study of resilient children*. New York: McGraw-Hill.

Westra, H., Angus, L., & Stala, D. (2007, June). *Client experiences of motivational interviewing for generalized anxiety disorder: A qualitative analysis*. Paper presented at the conference of the Society for Psychotherapy Research, Madison, WI.

Willutzki, U., Neumann, B., Haas, H., Koban, C., & Schulte, D. (2004). Zur Psychotherapie sozialer Ängste: Kognitive Verhaltenstherapie im Vergleich zu einem kombiniert ressourcenorientierten Vorgehen: Eine randomisierte kontrollierte Interventionsstudie. [Psychotherapy for social phobia: Cognitive behavioral therapy in comparison to a combined resource-oriented approach. A randomized controlled intervention trial]. *Zeitschrift für Klinische Psychologie unde Psychotherapie: Forschung und Praxis, 33,* 42–50.

Wood, J. K. (2008). *Carl Rogers' person-centered approach: Toward an understanding of its implications*. Ross-on-Wye: PCCS Books.

Zanarini, M. C., Frankenburg, F. R., Hennen, J., Reich, D. B., & Silk, K. R. (2006). Prediction of the 10-year course of borderline personality disorder. *The American Journal of Psychiatry, 163*(5), 827–832.

Zuroff, D. C., Blatt, S. J., Sotsky, S. M., Krupnick, J. L., Martin, D. J., Sanislow, C. A., et al. (2000). Relation of therapeutic alliance and perfectionism to outcome in brief outpatient treatment of depression. *Journal of Consulting and Clinical Psychology, 68,* 114–124.

CHAPTER 6

RELATING PROCESS TO OUTCOME IN PERSON-CENTRED AND EXPERIENTIAL PSYCHOTHERAPIES

THE ROLE OF THE RELATIONSHIP CONDITIONS AND CLIENTS' EXPERIENCING

JEANNE C. WATSON, LESLIE S. GREENBERG,
& GERMAIN LIETAER

The two traditional pillars of person-centred and experiential (PCE) psychotherapies are the quality of the therapeutic relationship, and clients' experiencing (Watson, Greenberg, & Lietaer, 1998). The first pillar rests on Rogers' view of the importance of the relationship conditions in facilitating clients' change in psychotherapy. The second is concerned with the role of clients' experiencing in the change process. More recently a third pillar that is concerned with the role of clients' agency has emerged, however research pertinent to this focus is presented in a separate chapter. In this chapter we will review the research that pertains to the therapeutic relationship and clients' experiencing in relation to psychotherapy outcome.

THE THERAPEUTIC RELATIONSHIP AND OUTCOME

Initially Rogers advocated that therapists be nondirective with their clients in order to facilitate growth and change (Rogers, 1942). In this phase of his development he encouraged therapists to be open and receptive to clients' feelings. He was focused on redirecting therapists away from analyzing and interpreting their clients' behaviour. However, as his thinking about therapy developed and he studied the process of psychotherapy more intensively he came to recognize that it was the quality of the relationship that mattered (Rogers, 1959). This led him to emphasize the three therapist conditions of empathy, unconditional positive regard, and congruence as essential to the change process. In order to spur research on the role of the therapeutic relationship in effecting change he formulated his famous hypothesis consisting of six conditions: If two people are in psychological contact, and one, the client, is incongruent, being anxious or vulnerable, then if the therapist is congruent or integrated in the relationship and experiences unconditional positive regard for the client and empathic understanding of the client's internal frame of reference and tries to communicate that to the client, and this is received, then there is likely to be constructive personality change in the client (Rogers, 1959).

His hypothesis also stated that the more the conditions were present the more marked the change would be.

This hypothesis has led to much research and controversy since Rogers formulated it in 1959. Since then there have been numerous studies conducted to test his hypothesis (Cain & Seeman, 2002; Farber & Lane, 2002; Klein, Kolden, Michels, & Chisholm-Stockard, 2002; Lambert & Barley, 2002; Lambert, De Julio, & Stein, 1978; Orlinsky, Grawe, & Parks, 1994; Patterson, 1984), however the conclusion of N. Watson (1984) after his incisive review of the studies that had been conducted prior to 1980 still resonates some 30 years later. There are few if any studies that have rigorously and adequately addressed Rogers' hypothesis with respect to the therapist relationship conditions. In his review of the research N. Watson (1984) evaluated the research strictly on the basis of Rogers' initial hypothesis. He reviewed only those studies that: (1) included clients who suffered from incongruence, that is, were either anxious or vulnerable; (2) used clients' evaluations of the relationship; and (3) causally related clients' perceptions of the relationship conditions to outcome. This resulted in the exclusion of analogue studies, those that used external sources to evaluate the relationship, and those using correlational designs. As a consequence, all the studies that had been conducted until that time were eliminated leaving the author to conclude that the conditions had not been adequately tested and that the research that had been conducted was inadequate to either support or reject Rogers' hypothesis about the relationship conditions. N. Watson's (1984) review of the literature has been followed by numerous other reviews (Cain & Seeman, 2002; Norcross, 2002). While the conclusions of these later reviewers were generally positive, many of the studies cited in support of or as refuting Rogers' hypothesis have suffered from similar weaknesses to those identified by N. Watson (1984) in his review.

Since then a few studies have examined clients' perceptions of the therapeutic relationship, using the Barrett-Lennard Relationship Inventory (BLRI) (Barrett-Lennard, 1973), and their relationship to outcome with different client populations. Kolb, Beutler, Davis, Crago, and Shanfield (1985) sought to examine the relationship of psychotherapy process variables including the therapeutic relationship to change and premature drop-out in psychotherapy with adult outpatients. While client involvement was the best predictor of outcome the authors found that clients' ratings of the facilitative conditions were correlated with outcome, with low levels predicting premature drop-out. Another interesting finding was that clients' perceptions of the facilitative conditions were negatively associated with improvement in those clients who were more suspicious and distrustful. The results of this study suggest that the relationship between the facilitative conditions and outcome might be moderated by different client variables.

Further support for the role of client factors in moderating the impact of the facilitative conditions was provided in a study by Zuroff et al. (2000), who found that the facilitative conditions as measured by clients using the BLRI were predictive of outcome for clients with depression and who suffered from moderate levels of perfectionism as measured by the Dysfunctional Attitudes Scale (Weissman & Beck, 1978). However, the conditions were not predictive for those clients who suffered from lower or higher levels of perfectionism. The authors suggested that in short-term therapy the presence or absence of the relationship conditions may not be as crucial for clients with low levels of perfectionism and that clients with higher levels of perfectionism may require longer-term treatments before the impact of the relationship conditions becomes apparent. Sachse and Elliott (2002) made a similar observation in their review of studies looking at empathy alone; they noted that empathy did not yield identical results with all clients and client problems, as some clients seem to benefit and others not. These findings suggest that the relationship of the facilitative conditions to outcome is not strictly linear and somewhat more complex than initially thought.

With the advent of treatment guidelines based on lists of empirically supported treatments, there was the potential for the important role of the therapeutic relationship in effecting change to languish in favour of specific techniques or therapeutic approaches. This prompted Norcross (2002) to develop alternative guidelines based on data that empirically supported the role of relationship factors in promoting change in psychotherapy as opposed to specific treatments. As he observed in his opening chapter, specific techniques account for only 5% to 15% of the variance in outcome (Norcross, 2002). Most of the variance with respect to outcome is accounted for by client factors including motivation, with the second-largest proportion of variance in outcome being attributable to therapist factors. Based on comprehensive reviews by Lambert and Barley (2002) on the therapeutic relationship; Bohart, Elliott, Greenberg, and Watson (2002) on empathy; Klein, Kolden, Michels, and Chisholm-Stockard (2002) on congruence; and Farber and Lane (2002) on positive regard; it was concluded that the quality of the therapeutic relationship made 'substantial and consistent contributions to psychotherapy outcome' (p. 441). Empathy was considered to be demonstrably effective, and congruence and positive regard were deemed promising and probably effective. It is important to note that these findings do not pertain to PCE treatments only but represent a variety of different approaches.

In their meta-analysis, Bohart et al. (2002) reported effect sizes ranging from .26 to .32 for the role of empathy on outcome. According to these authors the amount of variance in outcome accounted for by empathy ranges from 7% to 10%, which is of the same order of magnitude as found in studies of the impact of the working alliance on outcome. This represents a moderate effect and suggests that empathy accounts for more of the outcome variance than specific techniques. Similarly Farber and Lane (2002), in their review of the research on positive regard, concluded that it showed a positive but moderate relationship to therapeutic outcome. However,

Klein et al. (2002), in their review of the research on congruence, found only a weak though positive relationship between therapist genuineness and therapy outcome. Hill and Knox (2002) reported similar evidence for the effects of therapist self-disclosure on outcome.

Klein et al. (2002) noted that much of the research on the relationship conditions had been conducted during the 1960s and 1970s and that there were no studies after 1989. Lambert and Barley (2002) attributed the decline of research on the relationship conditions to the ascendancy of the construct of the therapeutic alliance in psychotherapy research. The latter emphasizes the contribution of both participants in terms of the quality of the bond that develops between them, as well as their capacity to forge common goals and engage in common tasks to achieve clients' goals in psychotherapy. The reviewers who contributed to the APA Division 32 Task Force echoed the critiques of previous reviewers by identifying the methodological flaws of those studies that had investigated the impact of the relationship conditions on outcome. In particular they emphasized that researchers had used clients who were not incongruent, used poor sampling methods, small sample sizes and different rating perspectives, did not ensure adequate levels of the therapeutic conditions, and paid little attention to the restricted range of measurement of the relationship conditions, the low reliability in terms of measuring the conditions, and variability in terms of outcome with respect to the experience of the therapists (Klein et al., 2002). Notwithstanding these problems, the reviewers concur with the conclusions of Orlinsky and Howard (1978, 1986) and Patterson (1984) that the accumulation of evidence from these flawed studies points to a much stronger relationship between the therapeutic conditions and outcome than was being revealed by the data or was recognized by previous reviewers. In fact Patterson (1984) argued that the flaws should have militated against finding positive relationships.

The links between outcome, therapists' empathy, and the working alliance are some of the most highly evidence-based findings in the psychotherapy research literature (Bohart et al., 2002; Horvath & Bedi, 2002; Horvath & Greenberg, 1994; Lambert, 2005). In another study, Weerasekera, Linder, Greenberg, and Watson (2001) examined the development of the working alliance in emotion-focused therapy (EFT) and client-centred (CC) therapy for depression. Results revealed that the alliance–outcome relation varied with alliance dimension (goal, task, or bond), outcome measure (symptom improvement vs. self-esteem, relational problems), and the point at which the alliance was measured. Analyses revealed that early alliance scores predicted outcome independently of early mood changes. Although no treatment group differences were found for bond and goal alliance, the EFT group displayed higher task alliance scores in the mid-phase of therapy. This supports the view that therapists who are empathic, accepting, congruent and prizing of their clients, irrespective of the specific techniques they use, are able to negotiate agreement about the tasks and goals of therapy and develop a positive therapeutic bond. It is likely that therapists who are more empathic, accepting, nonjudgemental, and congruent will be able to implement specific tasks and interventions that fit with their clients' goals, thus increasing the likelihood of good outcome.

More recently, Watson and Geller (2005) investigated the relationships among clients' ratings of the relationship conditions, using the BLRI, psychotherapy outcome, and the working alliance in cognitive-behavioural therapy (CBT) and process-experiential therapy (PET). The relationship conditions as measured by the BLRI were found to correlate quite highly with client self-report measures of the working alliance. Clients' ratings of the relationship conditions were predictive of treatment outcome on four different measures, including the Beck Depression Inventory (Beck, Ward, Mendelson, Mock, & Erbaugh, 1961), Rosenberg Self-Esteem Scale (Rosenberg, 1965), the Inventory of Interpersonal Problems (Horowitz, Rosenberg, Baer, Ureno, & Villasenor, 1988), and the Dysfunctional Attitudes Scale (Weissman & Beck, 1978). Furthermore the impact of the relationship conditions was mediated through the therapeutic alliance on three out of four measures of outcome. An examination of clients' mean ratings of the facilitative conditions showed that there were no significant differences between the two psychotherapies in terms of clients' ratings of therapists' empathy, acceptance, and congruence in either CBT or PET. However, process-experiential therapists were rated as more highly regarding of their clients than cognitive-behavioural therapists.

The finding that the facilitative conditions are as important in other therapeutic approaches is supported by other studies such as that by Burns and Nolen-Hoeksma (1991) who found that therapist empathy was significantly predictive of improvement in cognitive behavioural psychotherapy. A meta-analytic study showed that empathy might be more important in CBT than in humanistic psychotherapy (Bohart, Elliott, Greenberg, & Watson, 2002). These authors reported a medium effect size of .30 for the relationship between empathy and outcome based on studies from different therapeutic approaches. However this was reduced to 0.25 in those studies that involved experiential psychotherapies only. One explanation for the reduction may be the likelihood of restricted range in a sample of PCE practitioners with most of them being rated highly on the therapist facilitative conditions.

Spurred by Norcross's (2002) observation that not enough attention had been paid to understanding what changes in psychotherapy as a function of the relationship conditions, Watson and her students have been investigating the role of the facilitative conditions and specifically empathy in the change process. Building on Barrett-Lennard's (1997) suggestion that therapist empathy leads to increased self-empathy, Steckley and Watson (2000, 2005) examined this hypothesis in clients who were treated for major depression with either CBT or process-experiential emotion-focused therapy (PE-EFT). Using path analysis they found that clients' ratings of therapists' empathy predicted changes in clients' attachment styles such that they were less insecure and were more self-accepting and protective of themselves at the termination of psychotherapy, and that these changes were associated with positive outcome, with the model accounting for moderate to large amounts of variance (42–70%) in outcome. In a further examination of the complex relationship between therapist empathy and outcome, Prosser and Watson (2007) investigated the relationship between empathy, affect regulation, and outcome as posited by Watson (2001, 2007) using path analysis. In this study it was found that the effect of therapist empathy on outcome was mediated by changes in clients' affect regulation (Prosser & Watson, 2007; Watson & Prosser, 2007).

Overall these more recent studies provide more convincing evidence of the role of the clients' experience of the therapeutic relationship in promoting positive outcomes in psychotherapy. Moreover there is converging evidence from a variety of sources about the importance of the quality of the relationship in positive and healing interpersonal encounters. A number of studies in which clients have been interviewed about their experience of psychotherapy have found that they value speaking to someone who is warm, understanding, and involved (Henry & Strupp, 1994; Lietaer, 1992). In an earlier study Bent, Putnam and Kiesler (1976) found that satisfied clients saw their therapists as warmer than did dissatisfied clients. Studies from different psychotherapy approaches that have looked at therapist interpersonal process using external raters to identify therapist behaviours associated with good outcome show that therapists in good outcome cases are supportive, affirming, openly receptive, involved, nurturing, and stimulating in their interactions with clients, whereas therapists in poor outcome cases were controlling, critical, and hostile (Henry, Schacht, & Strupp, 1990; Lorr, 1965; Najavits & Strupp, 1994; Watson, Enright, & Kalogerakos, 1998). The important role of being transparent and responding in a nondefensive way to alliance difficulties has been supported by the growing research literature on resolving ruptures in the therapeutic alliance (Safran, Muran, & Samstag, 1994). While studies on motivational interviewing show that empathic listening works better than confrontation with people who have alcohol problems (Miller & Rollnick, 2002).

Additional support for the importance of the facilitative conditions in promoting psychological health and well-being can be found in other areas of psychology. For example, empathy, acceptance, understanding, openness, and transparency are qualities that contribute positively to individual's psychological, social, emotional, and moral development (Benjamin, 1974; Bohart & Greenberg, 1997; Gottman, 1993; Siegel, 1999), whereas more negative behaviours including criticism, control, oppression, annihilation, neglect and withdrawal are inimical to psychological health, well-being, and physical survival (Strachan, Leff, Goldstein, Doane, & Burtt, 1986). Notwithstanding these converging trends more research is necessary to demonstrate the importance of the relationship conditions in promoting change in psychotherapy. Person-centred and experiential psychotherapies researchers need to continue to develop more rigorous studies in order to test Rogers' hypothesis and demonstrate effectively the role of the therapeutic relationship in promoting change in order that its importance continues to be recognized by training institutions, public health regulators, granting agencies, and the public at large, in order for us to maintain support for this way of being with our clients to promote growth and healing.

CLIENTS' EXPERIENCING

In the PCE theories of personality change (Gendlin, 1970; Greenberg & Van Balen, 1998; Rogers, 1959), depth of experiential self-exploration is seen as one of the pillars of psychotherapy process and change. During the past 50 years much research has been done on the relationship between experiential depth and outcome. Within this context several instruments have been constructed to measure levels of experiential depth, the first ones being Rogers' 'Process Scale' (Rogers, Walker, & Rablen, 1960) and Truax's 'Tentative Scale for the Measurement of Depth of Intrapersonal Exploration' (Truax, 1962; Truax & Carkhuff, 1967). Later came 'The Experiencing Scale' (Klein, Mathieu, Gendlin, & Kiesler, 1969; Klein, Mathieu-Coughlan, & Kiesler, 1986), still later Toukmanian's 'Levels of Client Perceptual Processing Scale' (1986, 1992, 1996; Toukmanian & Gordon, 2004) and Sachse's 'Processing Scales' (Sachse, 1992a; Sachse & Maus, 1991). Although there are some differences between these scales, they all refer in their upper scale steps to a high level of being involved in an experiential process of self-exploration. Since the Experiencing Scale has been the most widely used (see Chapter 7), a short description of the scale steps is presented here, as summarized by Elliott, Greenberg, and Lietaer (2004):

> The [client and therapist] Experiencing Scales ... measure the degree to which clients or therapists are fully engaged in their experience. Scores range from a 1, in which individuals narrate their experience in a detached manner and do not represent themselves as agents in their own narratives, to a 3, representing a simple, reactive emotional response to a specific situation, through a score of 4 in which a person focuses on feelings. At level 6, ready accessible feelings and meanings are synthesized to solve problems, and at level 7, clients are fully engaged in their momentary experience in a free-flowing, open, focused manner. (p. 518)

Depth of experiencing and outcome

Research on depth of experiencing in therapy has found a consistent relationship between the *average level* of experiencing of client self-exploration during therapy and outcome: the higher the experiencing level, the better therapy outcome (Bohart et al., 1996; Elliott, Greenberg, & Lietaer, 2004; Greenberg, Elliott, & Lietaer, 1994; Hendricks, 2002; Klein et al., 1986; Orlinsky, Grawe, & Parks, 1994; Purton, 2004). Part of Rogers' process view (1961), however, is not confirmed in most studies: namely an *increase* of experiencing level throughout the course of successful therapy. Methodological issues probably account for these findings. For example, it is simplistic to measure experiencing levels at the beginning, middle and end phase of therapy, and *at random* across sessions and within the therapy hour as has usually been the case in previous studies. Greenberg and collaborators (Rice & Greenberg, 1984) suggest that by sampling in this manner key events of the process are not being investigated. Therefore in their research they selected segments that were linked to clients' problematic core themes. Using this method they found a clear correlation between changes in experiencing level across therapy and a range of outcome measures; moreover an increase in clients' levels of experiencing from early to late in therapy was a stronger predictor of outcome than the working alliance (Goldman, Greenberg, & Pos, 2005).

Although the association between experiencing level and outcome is clear, it is never 'very high'. This suggests, among other things, that other factors likely play a role in a fruitful therapy process. Besides, it is simplistic to hold a linear view on the stages of the Experiencing Scale, in the sense of 'the higher the score, the better the process quality of the exploration process'. Especially as investigators of psychotherapy change process (Angus & McLeod, 2004; Watson, Goldman & Greenberg, 2007) emphasize that *all* narrative modalities are important and serve a function for clients in exploring their problems.

Experiencing and emotional arousal

Ratings of clients' depth of experiencing have been related to good outcome consistently in PCE psychotherapies (Bohart et al., 1996; Elliott, Greenberg, & Lietaer, 2004; Hendricks, 2002; Klein et al., 1986; Orlinsky & Howard, 1978; Watson & Greenberg, 1996). Moreover clients' emotional processing in the session has been found to be beneficial across a range of therapeutic approaches, other than PCE, including CBT, and psychodynamic (Castonguay, Goldfried, Wiser, Raue, & Hayes, 1996; Giyaur et al., 2005; Godfrey et al., 2007; Stanton et al., 2000). Like the early observations of Rogers and Gendlin, a number of studies have revealed significant differences in the manner in which good and poor outcome cases refer to their emotional experience during the session across different therapeutic approaches (Pos, Greenberg, Goldman, & Korman, 2003; Watson & Bedard, 2006). For example,

Watson and Bedard (2006) found that good outcome clients in both process-experiential, an emotion-focused approach (PE-EFT) and cognitive-behavioural therapy (CBT) for depression, began, continued, and ended therapy at higher modal and peak experiencing levels during the session than did clients with poor outcome. Good outcome clients engaged in deeper exploration, referred to their emotions more frequently, were more internally focused, and examined and reflected upon their experience to create new meaning and resolve their problems in personally meaningful ways than poor outcome clients. In contrast, clients with poorer outcomes were not as engaged in processing their emotional experience, nor did they reflect on or pose questions about their experience during the session to examine it and try to understand the origins and implications of their experience more fully. As a result poor outcome clients did not report important shifts in perspective or feeling during the session. These findings suggest that processing one's bodily felt experience and deepening this in therapy may well be a core ingredient of change in psychotherapy regardless of approach.

Depth of experiencing, emotional arousal and productivity in EFT

Much of the research that has been done to investigate the role of clients' experiencing and outcome has been conducted by experiential practitioners. Greenberg and Watson (1998) examined the relationship between theme-related depth of experiencing (EXP) and outcome in a group of clients who sought treatment for depression. The sample consisted of 35 clients, each of whom received 16–20 weeks of either PE-EFT or CC therapy. Analyses revealed that EXP on core themes in the last half of therapy was a significant predictor of a reduction in symptom distress and increases in self-esteem but did not correlate significantly with changes in interpersonal problems. Depth of experiencing on core themes also accounted for outcome variance over and above that accounted for by early EXP and the alliance. EXP therefore mediated between any client individual capacity for early experiencing and positive outcome. The early working alliance was also shown to predict outcome. However an increase in depth of emotional experiencing across therapy was shown to contribute 8% to 16% of the outcome variance over and above the alliance. This suggests that deepening experiencing over therapy is a specific change process, integral to the alleviation of depression through emotion-focused psychotherapies.

Subsequently Adams and Greenberg (1996) tracked moment-by-moment client–therapist interactions and found that therapist statements that were high in experiencing influenced client experiencing and that depth of therapist experiential focus predicted outcome. More specifically, if the client was externally focused, and the therapist made an intervention that was targeted towards internal experience, the client was more likely to move to a deeper level of experiencing. Adams and Greenberg's study highlights the importance of the therapist's role in deepening emotional processes.

Given that client experiencing predicts outcome, and that therapist depth of experiential focus influences client experiencing and predicted outcome, a path to outcome was established that suggests that therapists' depth of experiential focus influences clients' depth of experiencing and this relates to outcome.

A subsequent study by Pos et al. (2003) suggested that the effect of early emotional processing on outcome was mediated by late emotional processing. Here emotional processing was defined as Depth of Experiencing on emotion episodes. Emotion episodes (EEs) (Greenberg & Korman, 1993) are in-session segments in which clients express or talk about having experienced an emotion in relation to a real or imagined situation. The EXP variable was used to rate only on those in-session episodes that were emotionally laden. It was found that clients' early capacity for emotional processing did not guarantee good outcome; nor did entering therapy without this capacity guarantee poor outcome. Therefore, while likely an advantage, early emotional processing skill appeared not as critical as the ability to acquire and/or increase depth of emotional processing throughout therapy. In this study late emotional processing independently added 21% to the explained variance in reduction in symptoms, over and above early alliance and emotional processing.

A recent study by Pos, Greenberg, and Warwar (2009) measured emotional processing and the alliance across three phases of therapy (beginning, working, and termination) for 74 clients who each received PE-EFT for depression. Using path analysis, a model of these two processes across phases of therapy and how these processes relate to and predict improvement in depression and other symptoms, self-esteem, and interpersonal problems at the end of treatment, was proposed and tested. Both therapy processes significantly increased across phases of therapy. Controlling for both client processes at the beginning of therapy and clients' level of experiencing during the working phase was found to directly and best predict reductions in depressive and general symptoms, as well as gains in self-esteem. Within working and termination phases of therapy, the alliance significantly contributed to emotional processing and indirectly contributed to outcome. Surprisingly, the alliance (measured after session one) also directly predicted outcome. Furthermore, only clients' beginning therapy process predicted reductions in interpersonal problems. Therefore while PE-EFT theory of change was supported, clients' beginning therapy processes may constrain clients' success in an experiential treatment and in particular their reports of resolution of interpersonal problems.

Process-outcome research on PE-EFT for depression has shown that both higher emotional arousal at mid-treatment, coupled with reflection on the aroused emotion (Warwar & Greenberg, 2000) and deeper emotional processing late in therapy (Pos, Greenberg, Goldman, & Korman, 2003), predicted good treatment outcomes. High emotional arousal plus high reflection on aroused emotion distinguished good and poor outcome cases indicating the importance of combining arousal and meaning

141

construction (Missirlian, Toukmanian, Warwar, & Greenberg, 2005; Warwar, 2003). PE-EFT thus appears to work by enhancing the type of emotional processing that involves helping people experience, and accept their emotions and make sense of them.

Warwar (2003) examined mid-therapy emotional arousal (EA) as well as experiencing in the early, middle, and late phases of therapy. In this study clients who had higher EA mid-therapy were found to have more change at the end of treatment. In addition, not only did mid-therapy arousal predict outcome, but also a client's ability to use internal experience to make meaning and solve problems as measured by EXP, particularly in the late phase of treatment, added to the outcome variance over and above middle phase EA. This study thus showed that a combination of emotional arousal and experiencing was a better predictor of outcome than either index alone.

It is important to note this study measured *expressed* as opposed to *experienced* emotion. In a study examining in-session client reports of *experienced* emotional intensity Warwar, Greenberg, and Perepeluk (2003) found that clients' reports of in-session experienced emotion were not related to positive therapeutic change. A discrepancy was observed between clients' reports of in-session *experienced* emotions and the emotions that were actually *expressed* based on arousal ratings of videotaped therapy segments. For example, one client reported that she had experienced intense emotional pain in a session. Her level of expressed emotional arousal however was judged to be very low based on observer ratings of emotional arousal from videotaped therapy segments.

In a final study, the relationships between the alliance, frequency of aroused emotional expression and outcome were examined in PE-EFT for the treatment of depression (Carryer & Greenberg, 2010). The frequency of expression data showed that expression of high emotional arousal and expression of low emotional arousal had different correlations with the different types of outcome variable. Moderate frequency of heightened emotional arousal was found to add significantly to the outcome variance predicted by the working alliance. Up to this point our process research studies focused on a direct linear relationship between process and outcome. This study however showed that a frequency of 25% of moderately to highly aroused emotional expression was found to best predict outcome. Deviation toward lower frequencies, indicating lack of emotional involvement, represented an extension of the generally accepted relationship between low levels of expressed emotional arousal and poor outcome, while deviation toward higher frequencies showed that excessive amounts of highly aroused emotion was negatively related to good therapeutic outcome. This suggests that having the client achieve an intense and full level of emotional expression is predictive of good outcome, as long as the client doesn't maintain this level of emotional expression for too long a time or too often. In addition, frequency of reaching only minimal or marginal level of arousal was found to predict poor outcome. Thus expression that is on the way to the goal of heightened expression of emotional arousal but does not attain it, or that reflects an inability to express full arousal and possibly indicates interruption of arousal, appears undesirable, rather than a lesser but still desirable goal.

Another study further discriminated between productive and unproductive emotional arousal in the session. In an intensive examination of four poor and four good outcome cases, Greenberg, Auszra, and Herrmann (2007) did not find a significant relationship between the frequency of higher levels of expressed emotional arousal measured over the whole course of treatment and outcome. They measured both aroused emotional expression and productivity of the expressed emotion, and concluded that productivity of aroused emotional expression was more important to therapeutic outcome than arousal alone.

The measure of productive emotional arousal used in the above study was further developed and its predictive validity was tested on a sample of 74 clients from the York depression studies (Auszra, Greenberg & Herman, 2006). Emotional productivity was defined as a person being contactfully aware of a presently activated emotion, where contactfully aware was defined as involving the following six necessary features: attending symbolization, congruence, acceptance, agency, regulation, and differentiation. Emotional productivity was found to increase from the beginning to the working and the termination phases of treatment. Working phase emotional productivity was found to predict 66% of treatment outcome, over and above the variance accounted for by beginning phase emotional productivity, session four working alliance, and high expressed emotional arousal in the working phase. These results indicated that the productive processing of emotion was the best predictor of outcome of all variables studied thus far.

In addition to the above studies on arousal and experiencing, Greenberg and Pedersen (2001) found that in-session resolution of two core emotion-focused therapeutic tasks predicted outcome at termination and 18 month follow-up and, most importantly, the likelihood of non-relapse over the follow-up period. Both of these core tasks, resolving splits and unfinished business, involve facilitation of the restructuring of people's core emotion schematic memories and responses. These results thus support the hypothesis that deeper emotional processing and emotion schematic restructuring during therapy lead to more enduring change.

In studies of emotion-focused trauma therapy (EFTT) (Paivio & Pascual-Leone, 2010) good client process, early in trauma therapy, has been found to be particularly important because it sets the course for therapy and allows maximum time to explore and process emotion related to traumatic memories (Paivio, Hall, Holowaty, Jellis, & Tran, 2001). One practical implication of this research is the importance of facilitating clients' emotional engagement with painful memories early in therapy.

Emotional arousal during imaginal exposure appears thus to be, at least, a partial mechanism of change. Overall, the findings suggest a chain of influence on the degree to which a client processes emotion in trauma. First, the severity of trauma symptoms sets a limiting factor in the facilitation of emotional arousal and processing, then, early engagement in imaginal exposure tasks and finally, the repetition of exposure tasks, over the course of therapy all have a successively cumulative impact on functioning at outcome (Paivio et al., 2001).

Another study of EFTT found that a therapist's competence in facilitating imaginal confrontations, by way of an empty-chair dialogue, predicted better client processing. Moreover, when adult survivors of child abuse engaged in an empty-chair dialogue, it contributed to the reduction of interpersonal problems and that this contribution was independent from the therapeutic alliance (Paivio, Holowaty, & Hall, 2004). These important findings are consistent with those found in research on PE-EFT for depression, which showed deeper levels of emotional experiencing had a curative effect over and above the alliance (Pos et al., 2003). Emotional processes also have been studied in the two controlled studies on resolving emotional injuries and interpersonal difficulties. Emotional arousal during imagined contact with a significant other was a process factor that distinguished PE-EFT from a psychoeducational treatment and was related to outcome (Greenberg & Malcolm, 2002; Greenberg, Warwar, & Malcolm, 2003; Paivio & Greenberg, 1995).

Qualitative studies of clients' experience during the session

Besides the process-outcome research there is also a more direct method to study therapeutic processes, namely asking the involved parties (client and therapist) what they have experienced as helping and hindering during a therapeutic session or a series of sessions. In 1994, Elliott conducted a survey of 10 studies in which the helping-factors methodology was used and summarized the identified helping factors (Greenberg, Elliott, & Lietaer, 1994, pp. 520–521). From this survey and some more recent studies (Dierick & Lietaer, 2008; Timulak, 2007; Vanaerschot & Lietaer, 2010) it is shown that processes referring to depth of experiential self-exploration take a central place among the therapeutic ingredients mentioned by clients and therapists as helpful and that these processes discriminate between 'very good' and 'rather poor' sessions. In a content analysis, studies done by Lietaer and co-workers (Lietaer, 1992; Vanaerschot & Lietaer, 2007, 2010) show that about 20 to 40% of all meaning units mentioned by clients and therapists belong to the following three categories:

> *Stimulation and deepening of self-exploration.* The therapist helps and urges the client to reflect upon, find more exact words, and go deeper into his or her own experiences. The therapist tries to help the client express him- or herself

in a concrete and deeply felt manner by asking exploratory questions; the therapist's reformulations and reflections enable the client to correct him- or herself or explain things more thoroughly.

Focusing on and exploring more deeply. The client is able to focus on and explore more thoroughly his or her experience; he or she verbalizes it and makes it more explicit. The client is able to delve more deeply into certain perceptual and relational patterns. The therapist appreciates the manner of the client's self-exploration: The client is able to create space for him- or herself, is open, and can attend to his or her experience (sometimes more effectively than in previous sessions). The client is in touch with his or her bodily felt sense and assumes responsibility for his or her self-exploration.

Intensively living through, experiencing fully. The client experiences and expresses certain feelings and emotions in the moment. The client becomes more aware of his or her own needs and problems, experiences and emotions. He or she dares to look his or her grief, loneliness, fear, and so on, in the eyes. He or she becomes aware of the emotional impact of his or her narrative, often as a result of the therapist bringing him or her more in touch with personal feelings. This is very often described as an experiential shift: suddenly coming in touch with new or changed experiences.

In a study on hindering processes (Lietaer, 1992), clients identified therapist responses that are 'non-experiential' – like giving inadequate advice or interpretations, which clients find inaccurate – and their own 'resistance', e.g., talking about superficial issues as hindering. Therapists in their turn referred to interventions that were off the client's experiential track (e.g., too rational, badly timed); forms of client self-exploration that would score low on the Experiencing Scale, e.g., being blocked, talking too much about non-self topics, and being too chaotic or too abstract in their narrative.

Sequential analyses of clients' and therapists' processing levels

While the Experience Scale (Klein, Mathieu-Coughlan, & Kiesler, 1986) has mainly been used to investigate client's process in psychotherapy, Sachse has focused on the *interaction* between therapist and client. To do so he constructed two parallel scales, respectively for 'the processing modes' (PM) of the client and the 'processing proposals' (PP) of the therapist. The scales contain eight stages, as shown in the client form of the scale (Sachse, 1990, 1992b; Sachse & Elliott, 2002; Takens, 2008):

1. No processing of relevant contents discernible
2. Intellectualizing (using 'knowledge' without reference to personal data)
3. Report (without explicit reference to opinions, evaluations and feelings)

4. Assessment/evaluation (seen as a characteristic of the content)
5. Personal assessment (with recognition that it is part of C's own frame of reference)
6. Personal meaning (C senses a felt meaning about the content and says so explicitly)
7. Explication of relevant structures of meaning (C verbalizes aspects of meaning which the content has in relation to her/his own frame of reference)
8. Integration (making connections between the verbalized meanings and other meanings; finding similarities and contradictions)

In this type of research so-called 'triples' are examined. A triple is a sequence of client–therapist–client (C-T-C) speaking turns. Client statements are rated on the Processing Mode Scale (PM) and therapist statements on the Processing Proposal (PP) Scale. Using these ratings, it can be determined whether a therapist offers to the client (within a triple) a *deepening* PP (e.g., C Level 3; T Level 5), a *level-maintaining* PP (e.g., C Level 3; T Level 3), or a *flattening* PP (e.g., C Level 3; T Level 2). The analysis thus determines whether the client's processing mode (from the first to the second statement in a triple) deepens (e.g., C response 1: Level 3; C response 2: Level 5), whether the level is maintained, or flattens. The relation between the therapist's relative PPs and the client's response defines the process-directive effect a therapist has on the quality of the client's explicating work.

A series of empirical studies (described and summarized in Sachse, 1992a; Sachse & Elliott, 2002; Sachse & Maus, 1991; Sachse & Takens, 2004) showed the impact of therapist proposals on the depth of clients' exploration process. The findings are summarized below (Sachse & Elliott, 2002, pp. 95–99):

- Therapist responses influenced client processing strongly and consistently. On average, 50%–60% of clients reacted to therapist deepening PPs by intensifying their processing efforts. With respect to level-maintaining PPs, 50%–70% of clients stayed at the same level of processing, whereas 60%–80% responded to therapists' flattening PPs by allowing their processing work to become less thorough, resulting in a relative impairment of their explication processes.

- Clients had difficulty maintaining constructive explication work on their own without purposeful assistance by the therapist. It was found that if therapists made level-maintaining PPs, clients deepened the explication process in only 6%–10% of all cases. Furthermore clients accepted flattening PPs from therapists to a much higher degree than deepening ones.

- Experienced therapists worked at higher processing levels than less experienced therapists; and they usually offered relatively more PPs at levels 6 and 7.

146

- The better the therapist understood the client empathically, the greater the effect of her/his deepening PPs. On average, the more trusting the therapist–client relationship, the better the client's performance in the explication process.

- Deepening of the explication process improved from the beginning to the middle of therapy.

- Formal characteristics of the therapist's PPs also influenced the client's explication process. They were most influential when they were short, unambiguous, not too complex, and given one at a time.

- The client's processing performance depended on the nature of the disorder. E.g., clients suffering from psychosomatic disorders were less influenced by therapist interventions, used deepening PPs less effectively, and operated, on the average, at a lower explication level. For these clients, 'metaprocessing work' (processing their processing) in the initial phase of the therapy was seen as being more effective (Sachse, 1998).

Similar to Rogers' and Gendlin's early observations about variations in clients' process, Sachse emphasized that the results of these microanalytic studies suggest that the manner in which therapists respond to their clients can exert a significant influence on clients' exploration processes. As some clients may find it quite difficult to clarify, check, and modify their own feelings, needs, goals, and convictions, therapists can offer active assistance to support clients' processing efforts.

Research on specific therapeutic tasks
In addition to the general therapeutic processes reviewed above, research has been done on several key PE-EFT tasks, each characterized by a particular sign from the client of readiness to work on a specific issue (marker), a sequence of therapist actions and client in-session micro-processes, and successful resolution (Greenberg, Rice, & Elliott, 1993).

Two-chair dialogue for conflict splits
Intensive analyses of clients' change process in the two-chair dialogue led to the development of a model of the essential components of the resolution of splits (Greenberg, 1979, 1993). Further research on this task has provided support for and elaboration of models of resolution, while also placing more focus on understanding self-critical processes. Greenberg and Webster (1982) showed that softening of the harsh critic in two-chair dialogue predicted resolution of decreased conflict. Sicoli and Hallberg (1998) investigated novice client performance using the Gestalt two-chair technique. The presence of 'wants and needs' was found to be significantly greater overall for sessions in which the critic softened, compared to sessions with no softening while Whelton and Greenberg (2000) found that high contempt and low resilience in response to the critic related to depression proneness.

Empty-chair dialogue for unfinished business

In two preliminary studies empty-chair dialogue was shown to be more effective in resolving unfinished business than empathy on both in-session process and session outcome measures (Greenberg & Foerster, 1996). In a controlled trial of the efficacy of empty-chair dialogue for the resolution of unfinished business, Paivio and Greenberg (1995) found that using an empty-chair intervention in therapy was significantly more effective than a psychoeducational group intervention in reducing symptom and interpersonal distress, reducing discomfort in target complaints, and in achieving resolution of unfinished business. Beutler and his colleagues (Beutler, Daldrup, Engle, Guest, & Corbishley, 1988, Beutler et al., 1991) also demonstrated that an expressive form of this dialogue can be effective in working with pain and depression, especially when working with people with over-controlled anger.

Intensive analyses of the client's change process in the empty-chair dialogue led to the development of a model of the essential components of resolution of unfinished business (Greenberg, 1991; Greenberg & Foerster, 1996). This model specified a number of components of resolution (Greenberg, Rice, & Elliott, 1993). In the process of resolution the person moves through expressing blame, complaint and hurt, to the arousal and expression of the unresolved emotion, to the mobilization of a previously unmet interpersonal need. In more successful dialogues the view of the other shifts and the other is enacted in a new way. Resolution finally occurs by means of the person adopting a more self-affirming stance and understanding and possibly forgiving the imagined other, or by holding the other accountable.

A refined model of the micro-processes involved in change was validated by comparing successful and unsuccessful resolution of unfinished business (Greenberg & Foerster, 1996). Four performance components – intense expression of feeling, expression of need, shift in representation of other, and self-validation or understanding of the other – were found to discriminate between resolution and non-resolution performances. McMain (1995) related changes in self–other schemas to psychotherapy outcome in the treatment of unfinished business. The results indicated that successful outcome was predicted by change in the representation of the self. Specifically, an increase in self-autonomy, self-affiliation, and positive responses of self in relation to the significant other were each predictive of treatment outcome at post-therapy and four-month follow-up. Change in the representation of the other failed to predict treatment outcome. In addition McMain (McMain 1995; McMain, Goldman, & Greenberg, 1996) found that assertion of needs was a better predictor of therapy outcome than new view of other, due in part to the fact that in abuse cases, resolution can occur without changing the view of the other. Using the same sample, Paivio and Bahr (1998) found that interpersonal problems at the beginning of treatment predicted alliance.

Greenberg and Malcolm (2002) demonstrated that clients who resolved their unfinished business with a significant other in a manner consistent with the model enjoyed significantly greater improvement in symptom distress, interpersonal problems, affiliation toward self, degree of unfinished business, and change in target complaints. This suggests that the components of resolution capture a clinically important process that relates to outcome. More specifically, a significantly greater number of clients in the resolved group were found to express intense emotions. In addition, almost all clients in the resolution group experienced the mobilization of an interpersonal need and a shift in their view of the other, while no clients in the unresolved group experienced a shift in their view of the other. These results provide evidence of the importance of emotional arousal in this task and that those clients who identified and expressed previously unmet interpersonal needs, and experienced a shift in their view of the other, changed more than those who did not engage in these processes.

Finally, in a study of childhood maltreatment, Paivio, Hall, Jellis and Tran (2001) found that high and low engagers in imaginal confrontations in empty-chair dialogue differed significantly in their outcomes. High engagers achieved significantly greater resolution of issues with abusive and neglectful others, and reduced discomfort on current abuse-related target complaints. The preceding studies, in combination, provide substantial evidence that degree of client engagement in expression of emotions and unmet needs during empty-chair work predicts successful resolution of unfinished issues with significant others.

Evocative unfolding of problematic reactions

Watson and Rennie (1994) used tape-assisted process recall to obtain clients' reports of their subjective experiences during the exploration of problematic reactions, and found that clients alternated between two primary activities: symbolic representation of their experience and reflexive self-examination. In addition, Watson (1996) found that resolution sessions, in contrast to non-resolution sessions, were characterized by high levels of referential activity defined as vivid, concrete and specific descriptions of situations and events (Bucci, 1985), when clients described problematic situations during systematic evocative unfolding. These descriptions were often followed by clients experiencing a change in mood immediately following vivid descriptions of the problematic situation which then led to further differentiation of their feelings. These two studies highlight both the role that vivid description can play in promoting clients' access to their episodic memories, which in turn helps clients access their feelings and reactions to particular situations, and highlights the role of self-reflection in the change process. These findings suggest that vividly re-evoking the situation, and clients' subsequent differentiation of their subjective experience, are both necessary but different aspects of productive therapy process, and in particular are important steps in resolving problematic reactions (Rice & Saperia, 1984; Watson & Greenberg, 1996).

Focusing

Empirical research on focusing (Gendlin, 1981, 1996) is closely interwoven with research on the experiential process in the broad sense: indeed the focusing process is situated within the levels 4 to 7 of the Experience Scale (Mathieu-Coughlan & Klein, 1984). We limit our survey to the research on aspects of the focusing procedure in the strict sense (Gendlin, 1981), with special attention to the publications since 1990. Our main sources are the survey publications of Greenberg, Elliott, and Lietaer (1994), Jaison and Lawlor (1996–1997), Hendricks (2002), Elliott, Greenberg, and Lietaer (2004), Purton (2004), and Coffeng and Vlerick (2008).

Elliott, Greenberg, and Lietaer (2004) noted that a number of studies (Clark, 1990; Durak, Bernstein, & Gendlin, 1996, 1997; Leijssen, 1997; Sachse, Atrops, Wilke, & Maus, 1992) show that there are more focusing characteristics in successful therapies and therapy sessions than in those which are non-successful. Leijssen found that 75% of positive sessions contained focusing steps, while only 33% of negative sessions contained them. Iberg (1991, 1996a, 2002) has developed scales to measure the degree to which focusing processes have taken place in a session. In a study of successful therapies Leijssen (1997, 2000) observed that nearly every session acquired an intense experience-oriented character in which the client discovered aspects of the problem which had remained hitherto out of awareness. In this process the clients achieved contact with their bodily felt experience without being flooded by it. However focusing is only one of the important processes in psychotherapy, as research suggests that not all clients need to engage in focusing to resolve their problems and some that do engage in focusing do not always make progress (Elliott et al., 2004). In her review Hendricks (2002) noted that focusing – either alone or as an additional procedure – correlated with successful outcome for prison inmates, patients with psychoses, the elderly, cancer patients in remission, and clients with obesity problems, stress, and intrapsychic conflicts.

A number of studies have been conducted to identify the factors that enhance the effectiveness of focusing. Clients can be taught to focus with separate training sessions, however some clients have difficulty maintaining their level of focusing in therapy; for these clients it might be helpful for their therapists to remind them of what they have learned and assist them with specific focusing-oriented interventions. Morikaya (1997) found three activities to be useful in helping clients to focus on their inner experience. These included 'clearing a space', 'finding a right distance', and having a listener refer to their experiencing (Elliott et al., 2004). In another study, Iberg (1996b) found that clients reported increased impact in sessions in which therapists used focusing-type questions. Some of the factors that interfere with focusing include clients' experiencing level and the working alliance. Leijssen, Lietaer, Stevens, and Wels (2000) found that focusing was difficult for clients with low levels of experiencing, and suggested that for these clients to maintain and sustain their levels of focusing activity, continued process direction by their therapists may be necessary. Similarly, problems in the working alliance may interfere with clients' engaging in the focusing process (Leijssen, 1996, 2000).

Further research on emotional change processes

A task analysis on the emotional processing steps involved in clients' resolution of global distress, defined as an unprocessed emotion with high arousal and low meaningfulness, produced a rational/empirical model. The model showed that clients moved from global distress through fear, shame, and aggressive anger as undifferentiated and insufficiently processed emotions, to the articulation of needs and negative self-evaluations as a pivotal step in change, and finally to assertive anger, self-soothing, hurt, and grief as states of advanced processing (Pascual-Leone & Greenberg, 2007). The model was tested using a sample of 34 clients. Results show that the model of emotional processing predicted in-session outcomes and that distinct emotions emerged moment by moment in predicted sequential patterns.

Intermediate model components that represent the level of personal evaluation and re-evaluation proved to be a point of critical distinction between in-session outcomes. Statements of Negative Evaluation about the self were shown to be present in virtually the same number of cases across event outcome. Thus, painful and heartfelt statements about feeling worthless, frail, or unlovable could not be predicted by in-session outcome – just as the experience of Fear/Shame did not distinguish between event outcomes. However, a heartfelt statement expressing an existential need to feel valuable, lovable, safe, or alive was predictive of in-session outcome – and occurred more often in emotional processing that preceded good in-session outcome (i.e. high experiencing levels).

This finding is consistent with EFT's model of theoretically articulated change steps (Greenberg & Paivio, 1997) and supports the view held in emotion-focused therapy that the expression of a need – a wish for attachment, validation, personal agency, or survival – is the 'gateway' to deeper adaptive emotional experiencing (Greenberg, 2002; Greenberg & Paivio, 1997; Greenberg, Rice, & Elliott, 1993). A further study (Pascual-Leone & Greenberg, 2007) examined observable moment-by-moment steps in emotional processing as they occurred within productive sessions of experiential therapy. It further tested the model of emotional processing (Greenberg, 2007) using a sample of 34 global distress events, 17 that ended in poor and 17 that ended in good in-session events. Univariate and bootstrapping statistical methods to examine how dynamic emotional shifts accumulate moment by moment to produce in-session gains in emotional processing showed that effective emotional processing was simultaneously associated with steady improvement and increased emotional range. Consequentially, good events were shown to occur in a 'two-steps-forward, one-step-backward' fashion. Finally, good events were also shown to have increasingly shortened emotional collapses backwards whereas the opposite was true for poor in-session events.

Narrative sequences

Angus and colleagues, in their studies of narrative sequences in EFT, have revealed interesting patterns associated with good outcomes (Angus, Levitt, & Hardtke, 1999; Lewin, 2001). Using log-linear narrative-sequence analyses, Angus et al. (1999) found that perceptual process client-centred (Toukmanian, 1992), EFT and psychodynamic therapy dyads differed significantly from one another in terms of both the number of identified narrative sequences and the type of narrative sequences (External, Internal, Reflexive). More specifically, in the psychodynamic therapy sessions a pattern of Reflexive (40%) and External (54%) narrative sequences predominated, with therapist and client engaged in a process of meaning construction (Reflexive) linked to the client's descriptions of past and current episodic memories (External). In contrast, the EFT dyad evidenced a pattern of Internal (29%) and Reflexive (46%) narrative sequences, in which the client and therapist engaged in a process of identifying and differentiating emotional experiences (Internal) and then generating new understandings of those experiences (Reflexive) during the therapy hour. As compared to the other two dyads, the proportion of Internal narrative sequences were three times higher in EFT sessions than in the client-centred (CC) sessions and five times higher than in the psychodynamic sessions. The primary goal of EFT is to assist clients in developing more differentiated and functional emotion schemes, and the evidence from these analyses indicates that this goal is achieved by an alternating focus on client exploration of experiential states (Internal narrative modes/sequences), followed by meaning-making inquiries (Reflexive narrative modes/sequences) in which new feelings, beliefs, and attitudes are contextualized and understood.

For its part, the CC therapy dyad revealed a pattern of consecutive reflexive narrative sequences (54%) occurring across topic segments in which client and therapist engaged in extended reflexive analyses of both life events (External, 36%), and to a lesser extent emotional experiences (Internal, 19%). The chaining of the Reflective narrative sequences with other types of narrative sequences appeared to facilitate an extended client inquiry into core self-related issues in which automatic processing patterns were identified and challenged.

In a further study (Lewin, 2001) good outcome EFT therapists were found to be twice as likely to shift clients to emotion-focused and reflexive narrative modes than poor outcome EFT therapists. Additionally, good outcome depressed clients initiated more shifts to emotion-focused and reflexive discourse than poor outcome clients. Depressed clients, who achieved good outcomes in brief experiential therapy, were found to spend significantly more time engaged in reflexive and emotion-focused discourse than were poor outcome clients. These findings provide empirical support for the importance of emotion and reflexive processes in the treatment of depression.

Honos-Webb, Stiles, Greenberg, and Goldman (1998) applied the Assimilation of Problematic Experience Scale (APES), in which degree of assimilation of a particular problematic experience, from Level 0, Warded Off, through Level 7, Mastery, is measured, to two cases of EFT, one with good outcome and one with relatively poor outcome. Qualitative analysis of the successful client's transcripts suggested that in good cases assimilation occurred over time in at least three areas of problematic experiences. Analysis of three themes in the less successful therapy suggested that assimilation was blocked. In a further qualitative assimilation analysis of the successful case, the researchers excerpted 43 relevant passages tracking two major themes, and rated each passage on the APES (Honos-Webb, Surko, Stiles, & Greenberg, 1999). APES ratings tended to increase across sessions, as expected in successful therapy. In this study, the client's dominant 'superwoman' voice was shown to assimilate a voice of need and weakness while her dominant 'good-girl' voice assimilated a voice of rebellion and assertiveness, yielding a more complex and flexible community of voices within the self. This was interpreted as supporting an emerging formulation of the self as a 'community of voices', leading to a reformulation of the goal of therapy as facilitating diversity and tolerance among the different self-aspects or voices.

CONCLUSION

PCE psychotherapies have more research than any other treatment approach on the process of change (Elliott, Greenberg, & Lietaer, 2004). The two central tasks in person-centred and experiential psychotherapies are the provision of a therapeutic relationship and the deepening of clients' experiencing. Our survey of studies – spread over half a century – confirms the important role that these two factors play in clients' change process in psychotherapy, thereby providing support for PCE psychotherapies' macro-theory of personality change. Further, more recent studies in PE-EFT suggest that emotional awareness and arousal, when expressed in supportive relational contexts, in conjunction with some sort of conscious cognitive processing of the emotional experience, is important for therapeutic change, for certain classes of people and problems. As emotion has been shown to be both adaptive and maladaptive, at times it may need to be accessed and used as a guide and at other times regulated and modified. The role of the cognitive processing of emotion in therapy is twofold; either to make sense of the emotion, or to help regulate it.

However, emotional arousal and expression, although helpful, are not always useful in therapy or life (Greenberg, Korman, & Pavio, 2002; Kennedy-Moore & Watson, 1999). Factors that need to be considered are whether a client's emotion is over- or under-regulated and whether the emotion is a sign of distress or of working through the distress (Greenberg, 2002; Kennedy-Moore & Watson, 1999). The role of arousal and the degree to which it could be useful in therapy also depend on how and what emotion is expressed, by whom, to whom and when, and under what conditions, as well as whether emotional expression is followed by other experiences of emotion and meaning making (Greenberg, 2002; Kennedy-Moore & Watson, 1999; Whelton, 2004). Finally, it is not arousal alone but the manner of processing the aroused emotion that is most predictive of outcome. When clients are moderately aware (mindful) of their emotions they fare best, as the evidence suggests that emotional processing is mediated by arousal. This means that for effective emotional processing to occur the distressing affective experience must be activated and viscerally experienced by the client. Arousal appears to be essential but is not necessarily sufficient for therapeutic progress. In addition to these generic processes, specific therapeutic micro-processes, such as the softening of a previously harsh critic, a new view of the other, and letting go and forgiving, have been shown to be effective in resolving specific emotional problems.

Given the strong support for the role of clients' experiencing in the change process it no longer seems necessary to investigate this process-outcome association in its general and linear form. We think that in future it would be more fruitful to investigate specific change processes related to specific process stagnations on a meso-level. This asks for more fine-grained hypotheses, in which the change path of the client is specified as a function of the process phase and in which the interventions of the therapist are also part of the change model under study. The empirical studies on process tasks in process-experiential therapy are an illustration of this more finely tuned approach to research (Rice & Greenberg, 1984).

REFERENCES

Adams, K. E., & Greenberg, L. S. (1996, June). *Therapists' influence of depressed clients' therapeutic experiencing and outcome*. Paper presented at the 43rd annual convention of the Society for Psychotherapeutic Research, St. Amelia, FL.

Angus, L., Levitt, H., & Hardtke, K. (1999). The narrative processes coding system: Research applications and implications for psychotherapeutic practice. *Journal of Clinical Psychology, 55*, 1255–1270.

Angus, L., & McLeod, J. (2004). *The handbook of narrative and psychotherapy*. London: Sage.

Auszra, L., Greenberg, L. S., & Herrmann, I. (2007, July). Emotional productivity in experiential therapy for depression. Symposium in Lisbon, Portugal.

Barrett-Lennard, G. T. (1973). *Relationship inventory*. Unpublished manuscript, University of Waterloo, Ontario, Canada.

Barrett-Lennard, G. T. (1997). The recovery of empathy: Towards others and self. In A. Bohart & L. Greenberg (Eds.), *Empathy reconsidered: New directions in psychotherapy* (pp. 103–

121). Washington, DC: American Psychological Association.

Baucom, D. H., Shoham, V., Stickle, T. R., Mueser, K. T., & Daiuto, A. D. (1998). Empirically supported couple and family interventions for marital distress and adult mental health problems. *Journal of Consulting and Clinical Psychology, 66*(1), 53–88.

Beck, A. T., Ward, C. H., Mendelson, M., Mock, J., & Erbaugh, J. (1961). An inventory for measuring depression. *Archives of General Psychiatry, 4,* 561–571.

Benjamin, L. S. (1974). Structural analysis of social behavior. *Psychological Review, 81,* 392–425.

Bent, R. J., Putnam, D. G., & Kiesler, D. J. (1976). Correlates of successful and unsuccessful psychotherapy. *Journal of Consulting and Clinical Psychology, 44,* 149–154.

Beutler, L. E., Daldrup, R., Engle, D., Guest, P. D., & Corbishley, A. (1988). Family dynamics and emotional expression among patients with chronic pain and depression. *Pain, 32*(1), 65–72.

Beutler, L. E., Engle, D., Mohr, D., Daldrup, R. J., Bergan, J., Meredith, K., et al. (1991). Predictors of differential response to cognitive, experiential, and self-directed psychotherapeutic procedures. *Journal of Consulting and Clinical Psychology, 59*(2), 333–340.

Bohart, A. C., & Associates. (1996). Experiencing, knowing and change. In R. Hutterer, G. Pawlowsky, P. F. Schmid, & R. Stipsits (Eds.), *Client-centered and experiential psychotherapy: A paradigm in motion.* (pp. 199–211). Frankfurt am Main: Peter Lang.

Bohart, A. C., Elliott, R., Greenberg, L. S., & Watson, J. C. (2002). Empathy. In J. Norcross (Ed.), *Psychotherapy relationships that work* (pp. 89–108). New York: Oxford University Press.

Bohart, A. C., & Greenberg, L. S. (1997). *Empathy reconsidered: New directions in psychotherapy.* Washington, DC: American Psychological Association.

Bucci, W. (1985). Dual coding: A cognitive model for psychoanalytic research. *Journal of American Psychoanalytic Association, 33*(3), 571–607.

Burns, D. D., & Nolen-Hoeksma, S. (1992). Therapeutic empathy and recovery from depression in cognitive-behavioural therapy. A structural equation model. *Journal of Consulting and Clinical Psychology, 60,* 441–449.

Cain, D. J., & Seeman, J. (2002). *Humanistic psychotherapies: Handbook of research and practice.* (pp. 3–54). Washington, DC: American Psychological Association.

Carryer, J., & Greenberg, L. S. (2010). Optimal levels of arousal in experiential therapy of depression. *Journal of Consulting and Clinical Psychology, 78*(2), 190–199.

Castonguay, L. G., Goldfried, M. R., Wiser, S., Raue, P. J., & Hayes, A. M. (1996). Predicting the effect of cognitive therapy for depression: A study of unique and common factors. *Journal of Consulting and Clinical Psychology, 64*(3), 497–504.

Clark, A. (1990). *A comprehensive process analysis of focusing events in experiential therapy.* Unpublished doctoral dissertation, University of Toledo, OH.

Coffeng, T., & Vlerick, E. (2008). Focusing en de experiëntiële aspecten van psychotherapie. In G. Lietaer, G. Vanaerschot, H. Snijders, & R. J. Takens (Eds.), *Handboek gesprekstherapie. De persoonsgerichte experiëntiële benadering* (pp. 181–203). Utrecht: De Tijdstroom.

Dierick, P., & Lietaer, G. (2008). Client perception of therapeutic factors in group psychotherapy and growth groups: An empirically based hierarchical model. *International Journal of Group Psychotherapy, 58,* 203–230.

Durak, G. M., Bernstein, R., & Gendlin, E. T. (1996–97). Effects of focusing training on therapy process and outcome. *The Folio. A Journal for Focusing and Experiential Therapy, 15*(2), 7–14.

Elliott, R., Greenberg, L. S., & Lietaer, G. (2004) Research on experiential psychotherapies. In M. J. Lambert (Ed.), *Bergin & Garfield's handbook of psychotherapy and behavior change* (5th ed., pp. 493–540). New York: Wiley.

Elliott, R., & Shapiro, D. A. (1988). Brief structured recall: A more efficient method for identifying and describing significant events. *British Journal of Medical Psychology, 61*(2), 141–153.

Farber, B. A., & Lane, J. S. (2002). Positive Regard. In J. C. Norcross (Ed.), *Psychotherapy relationships that work: Therapist contributions and responsiveness to patients* (pp. 175–194). New York: Oxford University Press.

Gendlin, E. T. (1970). A theory of personality change. In J. T. Hart & T. M. Tomlinson (Eds.), *New directions in client-centered therapy* (pp. 129–173). Boston: Houghton Mifflin.

Gendlin, E. T. (1981). *Focusing.* New York: Bantam Books.

Gendlin, E. T. (1996). *Focusing-oriented psychotherapy: A manual of the experiential method.* New York: Guilford.

Giyaur, K., Sharf, J., & Hilsenroth, M. J. (2005). The capacity for dynamic process scale (CDPS) and patient engagement in opiate addiction treatment. *Journal of Nervous and Mental Disease, 193*(12), 833–838.

Godfrey, E., Chalder, T., Risdale, L., Seed, P., & Ogden, J. (2007). Investigating the active ingredients of cognitive behavioural therapy and counselling for patients with chronic fatigue in primary care: Developing a new process measure to assess treatment fidelity and predict outcome. *British Journal of Clinical Psychology, 46*(3), 253–272.

Goldman, R. N., Greenberg, L. S., & Pos, A. E. (2005). Depth of emotional experience and outcome. *Psychotherapy Research, 15*, 248–260.

Gottman, J. M. (1993). *What predicts divorce: The relationship between marital processes and marital outcomes.* Hillsdale, NJ: Erlbaum.

Greenberg, L. S. (1979). Resolving splits: The two-chair technique. *Psychotherapy: Theory, Research and Practice, 16*, 310–318.

Greenberg, L. S. (1983). Toward a task analysis of conflict resolution in Gestalt therapy. *Psychotherapy: Theory, Research and Practice, 20*(2), 190–201.

Greenberg, L. S. (1991). Research on the process of change. *Psychotherapy Research, 1*(1), 3–16.

Greenberg, L. S. (2002). *Emotion-focused therapy: Coaching clients to work through their feelings.* Washington, DC: American Psychological Association.

Greenberg, L. S. (2007). A guide to conducting a task analysis of psychotherapeutic change. *Psychotherapy Research, 17*(1), 15–30.

Greenberg, L. S., Auszra, L., & Herrmann, I. (2007). The relationship between emotional productivity, emotional arousal and outcome in experiential therapy of depression. *Psychotherapy Research, 17*(4), 57–66.

Greenberg, L. S., Elliott, R., & Lietaer, G. (1994). Research on humanistic and experiential psychotherapies. In A. E. Bergin & S. L. Garfield (Eds.), *Handbook of psychotherapy and behavior change* (4th ed., pp. 509–539). New York: Wiley.

Greenberg, L. S., & Foerster, F. (1996). Resolving unfinished business: The process of change. *Journal of Consulting and Clinical Psychology, 64*, 439–446.

Greenberg, L. S., & Korman, L. M. (1993). Assimilating emotion into psychotherapy integration. *Journal of Psychotherapy Integration, 3*(3), 249–265.

Greenberg, L. S., Korman, L. M., & Paivio, S. C. (2002). Emotion in humanistic psychotherapy. In D. J. Cain (Ed.), *Humanistic psychotherapies: Handbook of research and practice.* (pp. 499–530). Washington, DC: American Psychological Association.

Greenberg, L. S., & Malcolm, W. (2002). Resolving unfinished business: Relating process to outcome. *Journal of Consulting and Clinical Psychology, 70*, 406–416.

Greenberg, L. S., & Paivio, S. (1997). *Working with emotions in psychotherapy*. New York: Guilford.

Greenberg, L. S., & Pascual-Leone, J. (1995). A dialectical constructivist approach to experiential change. In R. Neimeyer & M. Mahoney (Eds.), *Constructivism in psychotherapy* (pp. 169–191). Washington, DC: American Psychological Association.

Greenberg, L. S., & Pedersen, R. (2001, November). *Relating the degree of resolution of in-session self-criticism and dependence to outcome and follow-up in the treatment of depression.* Paper presented at conference of the North American Chapter of the Society of Psychotherapy Research. Puerto Vallarta, Mexico.

Greenberg, L. S., Rice, L. N., & Elliott, R. (1993). *Facilitating emotional change: The moment by moment process*. New York: Guilford.

Greenberg, L. S., & Van Balen, R. (1998). The theory of experience-centered therapies. In L. S. Greenberg, J. C. Watson & G. Lietaer (Eds.), *Handbook of experiential psychotherapy* (pp. 28–57). New York: Guilford.

Greenberg, L. S., Warwar, S. H., & Malcolm, W. (2003). The differential effects of emotion-focused therapy and psychoeducation for the treatment of emotional injury: Letting go and forgiving. Weimar, Germany: Panel Society for Psychotherapy Research.

Greenberg, L. S., & Watson, J. C. (1998). Experiential therapy of depression: Differential effects of client-centered relationship conditions and active experiential interventions. *Psychotherapy Research, 8*, 210–224.

Greenberg, L. S., & Webster, M. C. (1982). Resolving decisional conflict by means of two-chair dialogue: Relating process to outcome. *Journal of Counseling Psychology, 29*, 468–477.

Hendricks, M. (2002). Focusing-oriented/experiential psychotherapy. In D. J. Cain & J. Seeman (Eds.), *Humanistic psychotherapies: Handbook of research and practice* (pp. 221–251). Washington, DC: American Psychological Association.

Henry, W., Schacht, T. E., & Strupp, H. (1990). Patient and therapist introject: Interpersonal process, and differential psychotherapy outcome. *Journal of Consulting and Clinical Psychology, 58*, 768–774.

Henry, W., & Strupp, H. (1994). Therapeutic alliance as interpersonal process. In A. Horvath & L. S. Greenberg (Eds.), *The working alliance: Theory, research and practice* (pp. 51–84). New York: Wiley.

Hill, C. E., & Knox, S. (2002). Self-disclosure. In J. C. Norcross (Ed.). *Psychotherapy relationships that work: Therapist contributions and responsiveness to patients.* (pp. 255–266). New York: Oxford University Press.

Honos-Webb, L., Stiles, W. B., Greenberg, L. S., & Goldman, R. (1998). Assimilation analysis of process experiential psychotherapy: A comparison of two cases. *Psychotherapy Research, 8*, 264–286.

Honos-Webb, L., Surko, M., Stiles, W. B., & Greenberg, L. S. (1999). Assimilation of voices in psychotherapy: The case of Jan. *Journal of Counseling Psychology, 46*, 448–460.

Horowitz, L. M., Rosenberg, S. E., Baer, B. A. Ureno, G., & Villasenor, V. S. (1988). Inventory of interpersonal problems: Psychometric properties and clinical application. *Journal of Consulting and Clinical Psychology, 56*, 885–892.

Horvath, A. O., & Bedi, R. B. (2002). The alliance. In J. C. Norcross (Ed.), *Psychotherapy relationships work: Therapist contributions and responsiveness to patient needs* (pp. 37–69). London: Oxford University Press.

Horvath, A. O., & Greenberg, L. S. (1994). *The working alliance: Theory, research and practice.* New York: Wiley.

Iberg, J. R. (1991). Applying statistical control theory to bring together clinical supervision and psychotherapy research. *Journal of Consulting and Clinical Psychology, 59,* 575–586.

Iberg, J. R. (1996a). Finding the body's next step: Ingredients and hindrances. *The Folio: A Journal for Focusing and Experiential Therapy, 15*(1), 13–42.

Iberg, J. R. (1996b). Using statistical experiments with post-session client questionnaires as a student-centered approach to teaching the effects of therapist activities in psychotherapy. In R. Hutterer, G. Pawlowsky, P. F. Schmid, & R. Stipsits (Eds.), *Client-centered and experiential psychotherapy. A paradigm in motion* (pp. 255–271). Frankfurt: Peter Lang.

Iberg, J. R. (2002). Psychometric development of measures of in-session focusing activity: The focusing-oriented session report and the therapist ratings of client focusing activity. In J. C. Watson, R. N. Goldman & M. S. Warner (Eds.), *Client-centered and experiential psychotherapy in the 21st century* (pp. 221–246). Ross-on-Wye: PCCS Books.

Jaison, B., & Lawlor, M. (Eds.). (1996–97). Focusing and research. *The Folio: A Journal for Focusing and Experiential Therapy (Special issue), 15*(2), 1–84.

Johnson, S. M., & Greenberg, L. S. (1988). *Emotionally focused therapy for couples.* New York: Guilford.

Kennedy-Moore, E., & Watson, J. C. (1999). *Expressing emotion: Myths, realities and therapeutic strategies.* New York: Guilford.

Klein, M. H., Kolden, G. G., Michels, J. L., & Chisolm-Stockard, S. (2002). Congruence. In J. C. Norcross (Ed.), *Psychotherapy relationships that work: Therapist contributions and responsiveness to patients* (pp. 195–216). New York: Oxford University Press.

Klein, M. H.., Mathieu-Coughlan, P. L., & Kiesler, D. J. (1986). The experiencing scales. In L. S. Greenberg & W. M. Pinsof (Eds.), *The psychotherapeutic process: A research handbook* (pp. 21–71). New York: Guilford.

Klein, M. H., Mathieu, P. L., Gendlin, E. T., & Kiesler, D. J. (1969). *The experiencing scale: A research and training manual.* Madison: Wisconsin Psychiatric Institute.

Kolb, D. L., Beutler, L. E., Davis, C. S., Crago, M., & Shanfield, S. B. (1985). Patient and therapy process variables related to dropout and change in psychotherapy. *Psychotherapy, 22,* 702–710.

Lambert, M. J. (2005). Early response in psychotherapy: Further evidence for the importance of common factors rather than 'placebo effects'. *Journal of Clinical Psychology, 61*(7), 855–869.

Lambert, M. J., & Barley, D. E. (2002). Research summary on the therapeutic relationship and psychotherapy outcome. In J. C. Norcross (Ed.). *Psychotherapy relationships that work: Therapist contributions and responsiveness to patients.* (pp. 17–36). New York: Oxford University Press.

Lambert, M. J., De Julio, S. S., & Stein, D. M. (1978). Therapist interpersonal skills: Process, outcome, methodological considerations and recommendations for future research. *Psychological Bulletin, 85,* 467–489.

Leijssen, M. (1996). Characteristics of a healing inner relationship. In R. Hutterer, G. Pawlowsky, P. F. Schmid, & R. Stipsits (Eds.), *Client-centered and experiential psychotherapy: A paradigm in motion* (pp. 427–438). Frankfurt am Main: Peter Lang.

Leijssen, M. (1997). Focusing processes in client-centered experiential psychotherapy. An overview of my research findings. *The Folio: A Journal of Focusing and Experiential Therapy, 15*(2), 1–6.

Leijssen, M. (2000). Die Stärken und Grenzen von Focusing: einige Forschungsergebnisse. In H.-J. Feuerstein, D. Müller, & A. Weiser-Cornell (Eds.), *Focusing in Prozess. Ein Lesebuch* (pp. 217–226). Köln: GwG-Verlag.

Leijssen, M., Lietaer, G., Stevens, I., & Wels, G. (2000). Focusing training for stagnating clients: An analysis of four cases. In J. Marques-Teixeira & S. Antunes (Eds.), *Client-centered and experiential psychotherapy* (pp. 207–224). Linda a Velha, Portugal: Vale & Vale.

Lewin, J. K. (2001). *Both sides of the coin: Comparative analyses of narrative process patterns in poor and good outcome dyads engaged in brief experiential psychotherapy for depression.* Unpublished master's thesis, York University, Toronto, Ontario, Canada.

Lietaer, G. (1992). Helping and hindering processes in client-centered/experiential psychotherapy: A content analysis of client and therapist postsession perceptions. In S. G. Toukmanian & D. Rennie (Eds.), *Psychotherapy process research: Paradigmatic and narrative approaches* (pp. 134–162). Newbury Park, CA: Sage.

Lorr, M. (1965). Client perceptions of therapists: A study of therapeutic relation. *Journal of Consulting Psychology, 29,* 146–149.

Mathieu-Coughlan, P. L., & Klein, M. H. (1984). Experiential psychotherapy: Key events in client–therapist interaction. In L. N. Rice & L. S. Greenberg (Eds.), *Patterns of change: Intensive analysis of psychotherapy process* (pp. 213–248). New York: Guilford.

McMain, S. (1995). *Relating changes in self-other schemas to psychotherapy outcome.* Unpublished doctoral dissertation. York University, Toronto.

McMain, S., Goldman, R., & Greenberg, L. (1996). Resolving unfinished business: A program of study. In W. Dryden (Ed.), *Research and practice in psychotherapy.* (pp. 211–232). Thousand Oaks, CA: Sage.

Miller, W. R., & Rollnick, S. (2002). *Motivational interviewing: Preparing people for change.* New York: Guilford.

Missirlian, T. M., Toukmanian, S. G., Warwar, S. H., & Greenberg, L. S. (2005). Emotional arousal, client perceptual processing, and the working alliance in experiential psychotherapy for depression. *Journal of Consulting and Clinical Psychology, 73*(5), 801–871.

Morikaya, Y. (1997). Making practical the focusing manner of experiencing in everyday life: A consideration of factor analysis. *The Journal of Japanese Clinical Psychology, 15*(1), 58–65.

Najavits, L. M., & Strupp, H. H. (1994). Differences in the effectiveness of psychodynamic therapists: A process-outcome study. *Psychotherapy, 31*(1), 114–123.

Norcross, J. C. (2002). *Psychotherapy relationships that work: Therapist contributions and responsiveness to patients.* New York: Oxford University Press.

Orlinsky, D. E., Grawe, K., & Parks, B. K. (1994). Process and outcome in psychotherapy. Noch einmal. In A. E. Bergin & S. L. Garfield (Eds.), *Handbook of psychotherapy and behavior change* (4th ed., pp. 270–376). New York: Wiley.

Orlinsky, D. E., & Howard, K. I. (1978). The relation of process to outcome in psychotherapy. In S. Garfield & A. E. Bergin (Eds.), *Handbook of psychotherapy and behavior change: An empirical analysis.* (pp. 283–230). New York: Wiley.

Orlinsky, D. E., & Howard, K. I. (1986). The psychological interior of psychotherapy: Explorations with the therapy session reports. In L. S. Greenberg & W. M. Pinsof (Eds.), *The psychotherapeutic process: A research handbook. Guilford clinical psychology and psychotherapy series.* (pp. 477–501). New York: Guilford.

Paivio, S. C., & Bahr, L. M. (1998). Interpersonal problems, working alliance, and outcome in short-term experiential therapy. *Psychotherapy Research, 8*(4), 392–407.

Paivio, S. C., & Greenberg, L. S. (1995). Resolving 'unfinished business': Efficacy of experiential therapy using empty chair dialogue. *Journal of Consulting and Clinical Psychology, 63*, 419–425.

Paivio, S. C., Hall, I. E., Holowaty, K. A. M., Jellis, J. B., & Tran, N. (2001). Imaginal confrontation for resolving child abuse issues. *Psychotherapy Research, 11*, 433–453.

Paivio, S. C., Holowaty, K. A. M., & Hall, I. E. (2004). The influence of therapist adherence and competence on client reprocessing of child abuse memories. *Psychotherapy: Theory, Research, Practice, Training, 41*(1), 56–58.

Paivio, S. C., & Pascual-Leone, A. (2010). *Emotion-focused therapy for complex trauma: An integrative approach.* Washington, DC: American Psychological Association.

Pascual-Leone, A., & Greenberg, L. S. (2007). Emotional processing in experiential therapy: Why 'the only way out is through'. *Journal of Consulting and Clinical Psychology, 75*(6), 875–887.

Patterson, C. H. (1984). Empathy, warmth, and genuineness in psychotherapy. A review of reviews. *Psychotherapy, 21*, 431–438.

Pos, A. E., Greenberg, L. S., Goldman, R. N., & Korman, L. M. (2003). Emotional processing during experiential treatment of depression. *Journal of Consulting and Clinical Psychology, 71*, 1007–1016.

Pos, A. E., Greenberg, L. S., & Warwar, S. H. (2009). Testing a model of change for experiential treatment of depression. *Journal of Consulting and Clinical Psychology, 77*(6), 1055–1066.

Prosser, M., & Watson, J. C. (June, 2007). *An examination of the relationship between affect regulation and empathy.* Paper presented to the 37th annual conference for the International Society of Psychotherapy Research, Madison, WI.

Purton, C. (2004). Objections: Issues of principle and empirical issues. In *Person-centred therapy. The focusing-oriented approach* (pp. 143–162). Basingstoke: Palgrave Macmillan.

Rice, L. N., & Greenberg, L. S. (1984). *Patterns of change. Intensive analysis of psychotherapy process.* New York: Guilford.

Rice, L. N., & Saperia, E. P. (1984). Task analysis and the resolution of problematic reactions. In L. N. Rice & L. S. Greenberg (Eds.), *Patterns of change* (pp. 29–66). New York: Guilford.

Rogers, C. R. (1942). *Counseling and psychotherapy: Newer concepts in practice.* Boston: Houghton Mifflin.

Rogers, C. R. (1959). A theory of therapy, personality and interpersonal relationships as developed in the client-centered framework. In S. Koch (Ed.), *Psychology: A study of science. Vol. III, Formulations of the person and the social context* (pp. 184–256). New York: McGraw-Hill.

Rogers, C. R. (1961). A process conception of psychotherapy. In *On becoming a person* (pp. 125–159). Boston: Houghton Mifflin.

Rogers, C. R., Walker, A., & Rablen, R. (1960). Development of a scale to measure process changes in psychotherapy. *Journal of Clinical Psychology, 16*, 79–85.

Rosenberg, M. (1965). *Society and the adolescent self-image.* Princeton, NJ: Princeton University Press.

Sachse, R. (1990). Concrete interventions are crucial: The influence of the therapist's processing proposals on the client's interpersonal exploration in client-centered therapy. In G. Lietaer, J. Rombauts, & R. Van Balen (Eds.), *Client-centered and experiential psychotherapy in the nineties* (pp. 295–308). Leuven: Leuven University Press.

Sachse, R. (1992a). *Zielorientierte Gesprächspsychotherapie.* Göttingen: Hogrefe.

Sachse, R. (1992b). Differential effects of processing proposals and content references on the explication process of clients with different starting conditions. *Psychotherapy Research, 2*, 235–251.

Sachse, R. (1998). Goal-oriented client-centered psychotherapy of psychosomatic disorders. In L. S. Greenberg, J. C. Watson, & G. Lietaer (Eds.), *Handbook of experiential psychotherapy* (pp. 295–327). New York: Guilford.

Sachse, R., Atrops, A., Wilke, F., & Maus, C. (1992). *Focusing: Ein emotionszentriertes Psychotherapie-Verfahren*. Bern, Switzerland: Verlag Hans Huber.

Sachse, R., & Elliott, R. (2002). Process-outcome research on humanistic therapy variables. In D. J. Cain & J. Seeman (Eds.), *Humanistic psychotherapies. Handbook of research and practice* (pp. 83–116). Washington, DC: American Psychological Association.

Sachse, R., & Maus, C. (1991). *Zielorientiertes Handeln in der Gesprächspsychotherapie*. Stuttgart: Kohlhammer.

Sachse, R., & Takens, R. J. (2004). *Klärungsprozesse in der Psychotherapie*. Göttingen: Hogrefe.

Safran, J. D., Muran, J. C., & Samstag, L. W. (1994). Resolving therapeutic alliance ruptures: A task analytic investigation. In A. O. Horvath & L. S. Greenberg (Eds.), *The working alliance: Theory, research, and practice*. (pp. 225–255). Oxford: Wiley.

Sicoli, L. A., & Hallberg, E. T. (1998). An analysis of client performance in the two-chair method. *Canadian Journal of Counselling, 32*, 151–162.

Siegel, D. J. (1999). *The developing mind: Toward a neurobiology of interpersonal experience*. New York: Guilford.

Stanton, A. L., Kirk, S. B., Cameron, C. L., & Danoff-Burg, S. (2000). Coping through emotional approach: Scale construction and validation. *Journal of Personality and Social Psychology, 78*(6), 1150–1169.

Steckley, P., & Watson, J. C. (2000, June). *Client attachment styles and psychotherapy outcome in cognitive behavioral and process-experiential psychotherapy*. Paper presented to the 31st annual meeting of the Society for Psychotherapy Research Conference, Chicago, IL.

Steckley, P., & Watson, J. C. (2005, June). *An examination of the relationship between clients' attachment experiences, their internal working models of self and others, and therapists' empathy in the outcome of process-experiential and cognitive behaviour therapies*. Paper presented to the 35th Annual Meeting of the International Society for Psychotherapy Research, Montreal, Canada.

Strachan, A. M., Leff, J. P., Goldstein, M. J., Doane, J. A., & Burtt, C. (1986). Emotional attitudes and direct communication in the families of schizophrenics: A cross-national replication. *British Journal of Psychiatry, 149*, 279–287.

Takens, R. J. (2008). Diepgang in het exploratieproces: analyse van de therapeutische interactie. In G. Lietaer, G. Vanaerschot, H. Snijders & R. J. Takens (Eds.), *Handboek gesprekstherapie. De persoonsgerichte experiëntiële benadering* (pp. 181–203). Utrecht: De Tijdstroom.

Timulak, L. (2007). Identifying core categories of client-identified impact of helpful events in psychotherapy: A qualitative meta-analysis. *Psychotherapy Research, 17*, 310–320.

Toukmanian, S. G. (1986). A measure of client perceptual processing. In L. S. Greenberg & W. Pinsof (Eds.), *The psychotherapeutic process: A research handbook* (pp. 107–130). New York: Guilford.

Toukmanian, S. G. (1992). Studying the client's perceptual processes and their outcomes in psychotherapy. In S. G. Toukmanian & D. Rennie (Eds.), *Psychotherapy process research. Paradigmatic and narrative approaches* (pp. 77–107). Newbury Park, CA: Sage.

Toukmanian, S. G. (1996). Clients' perceptual-processing: An integration of research and practice.

In W. Dryden (Ed.), *Research in counselling and psychotherapy: Practical applications* (pp. 184–210). London: Sage.

Toukmanian., S. G., & Gordon, K. M. (2004). *The levels of client perceptual processing (LCPP): A training manual.* Department of Psychology, York University, Toronto.

Truax, C. B. (1962). *A tentative scale for the measurement of depth of intrapersonal exploration.* Wisconsin Psychiatric Institute, University of Wisconsin.

Truax, C. B., & Carkhuff, R. R. (1967). *Towards effective counseling and psychotherapy: Training and practice.* Chicago: Aldine.

Vanaerschot, G., & Lietaer, G. (2007). Therapeutic ingredients in helping episodes with observer-rated low and high empathic attunement: A content analysis of client and therapist postsession perceptions in three cases. *Psychotherapy Research, 17,* 329–342.

Vanaerschot, G., & Lietaer, G. (2010). Client and therapist postsession perceptions of therapeutic ingredients in helping episodes. A study based on three cases. *Person-Centered and Experiential Psychotherapies, 9* (in press).

Warwar, S. H. (2003). *Relating emotional processes to outcome in experiential psychotherapy of depression.* Unpublished doctoral dissertation, York University, Toronto.

Warwar, S. H., & Greenberg, L. S. (2000, June). *Catharsis is not enough: Changes in emotional processing related to psychotherapy outcome.* Paper presented at the International Society for Psychotherapy Research annual meeting, Chicago, IL.

Warwar, S. H., Greenberg, L. S., & Perepeluk, D. (2003). *Reported in-session emotional experience in therapy.* Paper presented at the annual meeting of the International Society for Psychotherapy Research. Weimar, Germany.

Watson, J. C. (1996). An examination of clients' cognitive-affective processes during the exploration of problematic reactions. *Journal of Consulting and Clinical Psychology, 63,* 459–464.

Watson, J. C. (2001). Revisioning empathy: Theory, research and practice. In D. J. Cain & J. Seeman (Eds.), *Handbook of research and practice in humanistic psychotherapies* (pp. 445–473). Washington, DC: APA Books.

Watson, J. C. (2007). Reassessing Rogers' necessary and sufficient conditions of change. *Psychotherapy: Theory, Research, Practice, Training, 44*(3), 268–273.

Watson, J. C., & Bedard, D. (2006). Clients' emotional processing in psychotherapy: A comparison between cognitive-behavioral and process-experiential psychotherapy. *Journal of Consulting and Clinical Psychology, 74*(1), 152–159.

Watson, J. C., Enright, C., & Kalogerakos, F. (1998). *The impact of therapist variables in facilitating change.* Paper presented to the annual meeting of the Society for Psychotherapy Research, Snowbird, UT.

Watson, J. C., & Geller, S. (2005). An examination of the relations among empathy, unconditional acceptance, positive regard and congruence in both cognitive-behavioral and process-experiential psychotherapy. *Psychotherapy Research, 15,* 25–33.

Watson, J. C., Goldman, R. N., & Greenberg, L. S. (2007). *Case studies in the experiential treatment of depression: A comparison of good and bad outcome.* Washington, DC: APA.

Watson, J. C., & Greenberg, L. S. (1996). Emotion and cognition in experiential therapy: A dialectical-constructivist position. In H. Rosen & K. Kuelwein (Eds.). *Constructing realities: Meaning-making perspectives for psychotherapists* (pp. 253–276). San Francisco: Jossey-Bass.

Watson, J. C., Greenberg, L. S., & Lietaer, G. (1998). The experiential paradigm unfolding: Relationship & experiencing in therapy. In L. S. Greenberg, J. C. Watson, & G. Lietaer (Eds.). *Handbook of experiential psychotherapy* (pp. 3–27). New York: Guilford.

Watson, J. C., & Prosser, M. (July, 2007) *The relationship of affect regulation to outcome in the treatment of depression.* Paper presented to the 22nd annual conference of the Society for the Exploration of Psychotherapy Integration, Lisbon, Portugal.

Watson, J. C., & Rennie, D. (1994). A qualitative analysis of clients' reports of their subjective experience while exploring problematic reactions in therapy. *Journal of Counselling Psychology, 41*, 500–509.

Watson, N. (1984). The empirical status of Rogers' hypotheses of the necessary and sufficient conditions for effective psychotherapy. In R. F. Levant & J. M. Shlien (Eds.), *Client-centered therapy and the person-centered approach: New directions in theory research and practice* (pp. 17–40). New York: Praeger.

Weerasekera, P., Linder, B., Greenberg, L. S., & Watson, J. (2001). The development of the working alliance in the experiential therapy of depression. *Psychotherapy Research, 11*, 221–233.

Weissman, A. N., & Beck, A. T. (1978). *Development and validation of the Dysfunctional Attitudes Scale: A preliminary investigation.* Paper presented at the 86th annual convention of the American Psychological Association, Toronto, Ontario, Canada.

Whelton, W. J. (2004). Emotional processes in psychotherapy: Evidence across therapeutic modalities. *Clinical Psychology and Psychotherapy, 11*, 58–71.

Whelton, W. J., & Greenberg, L. S. (2000). The self as a singular multiplicity: A process experiential perspective. In J. Muran (Ed.), *The self in psychotherapy* (pp. 87–106). Washington, DC: American Psychological Association.

Zuroff, D. C., Blatt, S. J., Sotsky, S. M., Krupnick, J. L., Martin, D. J., Sanislow, C. A. III, et al. (2000). Relation of therapeutic alliance and perfectionism to outcome in brief outpatient treatment of depression. *Journal of Consulting and Clinical Psychology, 68*(1), 114–124.

CHAPTER 7

OPERATIONALIZING INCONGRUENCE
MEASURES OF SELF-DISCREPANCY
AND AFFECT REGULATION

JEANNE C. WATSON & NEILL WATSON

In his phenomenological theory of personality and psychopathology, Rogers (1959) stated that the introjection of conditions of worth from significant others causes incongruence within self-concept and between self-concept and affective experience. An incongruent self-concept is one in which there is a substantial discrepancy between the real self and the ideal self. This type of self-concept may lead to it being incongruent with the affective experience of the organism such that the experience of organismic affect is denied or distorted in conscious awareness. The unavailability of certain affective experiences to awareness interferes with effective affect regulation strategies, and the development of conditions of worth may lead to the development of maladaptive affect regulation strategies.

According to Rogers' (1959) theory, incongruence is a personality predisposition that makes a person vulnerable to anxiety and depression. From this perspective, the process of effective therapy is a decrease in self-discrepancy and an increase in awareness and regulation of affect, thereby decreasing anxiety and depression. In this chapter, we describe measures that assess self-discrepancy and affect regulation. Research with these measures is reviewed to provide a basis for their use in the training of person-centred and process-experiential/emotion-focused therapists and for their use in continuing research on Rogers' theory of the interrelationship of self-structure and affective experience, of the relationship of personality to psychopathology, and of the process and outcome of psychotherapy.

ROGERS' THEORY

Rogers (1959) posited that as human organisms interact with their environments, self-structures are formed that consist of perceived characteristics of the self together with the values attached to these perceptions. The values may either emanate from the organism or be internalized from significant others. As infants and children interact with their environments, they acquire concepts and understandings of themselves, their world, and their relationship to the world that they use to guide their behaviour. While recognizing that human functioning is differentiated, nonetheless Rogers saw persons as operating as organized wholes in their environments as they try to actualize themselves and maintain and enhance their experiences. Thus according to Rogers, persons are goal oriented as they attempt to meet various needs. This process is facilitated and guided by feelings and emotions, which alert organisms to the significance of events to them for their maintenance, enhancement, and survival.

Rogers (1959) theorized that fully functioning persons are able to accurately symbolize their feelings or organismic experience and balance these with their own needs as well as those of others so as to live authentically and with satisfaction in the moment. In contrast Rogers saw pathology as occurring when a person was in a state of incongruence. In this state a person experiences a discrepancy between the real self and the ideal self built on the introjected conditions of worth from significant others, together with a discrepancy between what the organism values as positive and beneficial and what is valued according to the ideal self, such that certain organismic experiences are distorted or denied to awareness. According to Rogers, incongruence makes a person vulnerable to anxiety and depression because the self-structure and the needs of the organism are in conflict. Fully functioning persons do not need to distort experience to fit with introjected conditions of worth; rather they are able to be aware of and open to their experience, including their sensations, feelings, perceptions, construals, and emotions, and they are able to accurately symbolize their experience or label it in awareness, accept it, and express it in ways that are responsible both for the individual's well-being, the specific community, and society at large. From this perspective, the process of effective therapy can be conceptualized as a decrease in self-discrepancy and an increase in affect regulation, which is improved organismic functioning with optimal processing of feelings and emotions so that the person can maintain and enhance the organism.

Organismic experience
As described earlier, organismic experience consists of all the ways human organisms experience themselves and their environments through their bodily felt sense. This knowledge comes in part from their senses, like hearing, vision, and touch, as well as construals, feelings, and emotions. Thus experiencing is made up of both inner and outer experience as persons apprehend what is occurring in their environments through their senses, react to that experience with emotions and or feelings, and come to know and understand its impact on the organism. Much of the information that human organisms acquire through their senses is processed out of awareness so that it can be acted upon efficiently and effectively. In this way experiences are recognized, understood, and acted upon appropriately to enhance the organism's survival. However, Rogers recognized that it is by focusing on their inner experience and

feelings that persons are able to make sense of that experience and come to know and understand its organismic impact. Rogers observed that clients were not always conscious of their inner experience. One of the changes he observed when persons were successful in therapy was that they became more aware of their inner experience and became more able to represent and name their feelings (Rogers, 1961). In this process they became more congruent. Gendlin (1972; 1997) developed these ideas further with his Process Model and his philosophical writings on the creation of meaning and focusing.

Congruence

Rogers (1959) suggested that as a result of psychotherapy clients come to acquire multiple perspectives and develop greater flexibility in thinking so that they can increase their range of action and feeling. He characterized healthy functioning as a capacity to be aware of inner experience moment to moment and to use that awareness to guide actions for living that are satisfying and enhancing to the organism. Later Rogers (1961) extended his definition of congruence to include a matching of experience, awareness, and communication. His definition of congruence on the part of both therapist and client requires that persons be aware of their reactions and symbolize or label these so as to know and understand what they are feeling. Once feelings have been identified, persons are able to reflect on those feelings, understand them in relation to both their present context and to past experiences, and express them responsibly in a way that optimizes the process of self-actualization in order to maintain and enhance the organism (J. C. Watson, 2007). These activities are the foundation of effective affect regulation. Rogers' view of congruence is similar to that proposed in current theories of effective affect regulation (J. C. Watson, 2007). However, while theories of affect regulation do not distinguish between emotions and feelings (Gratz & Roemer, 2004; Kennedy-Moore & Watson, 1999) person-centred and experiential theorists are careful to distinguish the two, seeing feelings as representing a fusion of emotion and cognition.

Rogers' view of optimal functioning is perhaps most clearly expressed in his conceptualization of the process of change that clients undergo in psychotherapy (Rogers, 1961).

In his study of change, Rogers (1961, p. 131) hypothesized that persons moved from '… fixity to changingness, from rigid structure to flow, from stasis to process ….' As he became aware of the continuum of change, he distinguished seven stages on which he was able to locate clients in terms of their relationship to their experience. At *Stage 1* clients' engagement in therapy is defined by fixity and remoteness from experience. In this stage persons are unable or unwilling to disclose their internal experience and share it with others, they do not recognize problems, feelings are not acknowledged, and the personal significance of things is not recognized and owned.

At *Stage 2* there is more communication about topics not relevant to the self, feelings are expressed but not owned, constructs are rigid, differentiation of personal meanings is limited, and problems are seen as external to the self.

At *Stage 3* there is more self-disclosure about self as an object and about experiences in the past. Although feelings are expressed, they are not accepted but rather seen as shameful, bad, unacceptable, or abnormal. At *Stage 4* the client discloses more intense feelings about past events with some current feelings expressed in the session, feelings are more differentiated, experience is not as rigidly construed, and the person begins to show some acceptance of feelings and more ownership of problems. At *Stage 5* feelings are expressed openly in the present and associated with an inner referent so that they are clearly owned in a desire to be authentic and acknowledge the 'real' person; experiencing is looser, more flowing and occurs in the present. At this stage persons are concerned with differentiation and a more exact representation of their feelings and a clear recognition of inconsistencies and contradictions as well as a sense of responsibility for the problems they are facing. At *Stage 6,* feelings are fully experienced, expressed, and accepted. It is accompanied by a physiological loosening, including muscular relaxation and other non-verbal indicators of emotion. Persons express themselves more congruently, and the differentiation of experience is clear and sharp. Rogers described it in these words: 'Once an experience is fully in awareness, fully accepted, then it can be coped with effectively, like any other clear reality' (Rogers, 1961, p. 151). At *Stage 7* persons are in the flow of their experiencing; there is a clear self-referent, ownership of feeling, and a trust in the process. At this end stage, Rogers (1961) saw the person as having subjective and reflective awareness of feelings, while constructs are tentatively formulated and validated against experience.

In summary, Rogers regarded persons as functioning optimally when they are aware of their feelings, able to represent them symbolically in awareness, able to think about them in the context of their total experience, able to be hypothetical in terms of how they view their experience, and able to appropriately share their experience with others. These activities are core to effective affect regulation. In order to regulate affect effectively individuals need to be aware of their inner experience, accurately symbolize it, act on it appropriately to meet their individual and social needs and communicate it effectively to others. In developing his theory of personality and dysfunction, Rogers proposed a series of hypotheses that he saw as amenable to empirical testing. He urged psychotherapy researchers to explore and test his hypotheses further in the hope of increasing understanding of psychotherapy process and outcome, just as he hoped that his hypothesis about the necessary and sufficient conditions for personality change to occur would be subject to testing. The latter hypothesis has received much attention by person-centred researchers and practitioners as well as those outside the approach (Freire & Grafanaki, this volume). However, his theory of personality change has received less attention.

MEASURES OF AFFECT REGULATION

Patterson (2000), in his review of Rogerian theory of the self, noted that there has been a problem with operationally defining organismic experience and aspects of the self-concept. Moreover, he argued that it is important to bring organismic experience within the realm of measurement. This is extremely important if we are to adequately test and demonstrate the validity of Rogers' theory of personality development and change. The objective of this chapter is to identify and describe instruments developed to measure organismic experience and self-discrepancy and provide some initial psychometric data from research studies that have used them. A number of measures, including observer-rated measures and self-report measures, have been identified as potentially useful to operationalize some of the constructs relevant to Rogers' theory. Research with these measures is reviewed to provide a basis for their use in research on personality development, psychopathology, and the process and outcome of psychotherapy.

We will review two process measures that have been developed to examine how clients are regulating and using their inner experience in the session: the Experiencing Scale and the Observer Measure of Affect Regulation. Ratings of client in-session behaviour allow researchers to determine the relationships among clients' characteristics, their in-session processing, and psychotherapy outcome, and to study the interactions between therapist and client behaviour to more clearly illuminate the therapeutic process. The development of process measures is useful and necessary in psychotherapy research, as they not only provide ways of operationalizing constructs for research purposes, but they also provide excellent teaching tools, and are clinically valuable in assessing treatment interventions moment to moment in therapy. Process measures can be used to help clinicians tailor their treatments to different clients so that they can be optimally responsive moment to moment in the session.

The Experiencing Scale

Rogers' (1961) delineation of the seven stages in his process model of therapy, which was described earlier, and Gendlin's (1972) recognition of the importance of the felt sense in promoting self-understanding and change in psychotherapy led to the development of the Experiencing Scale (Klein, Mathieu, Gendlin, & Kiesler, 1969). This measure was designed to describe the movement from stasis to flow that Rogers identified in his process model. As such it attempts to identify the extent to which clients are aware of and are referring to their emotional/organismic experience during the therapy hour in order to understand themselves better and resolve personally significant issues. Following Rogers' process model, the Experiencing Scale is a seven-point ordinal measure that raters use to categorize clients' statements in terms of whether they indicate that clients are aware of and disclosing their inner experience or are reflecting on it in order to pose questions and explore their experiences to achieve self-understanding and problem resolution (Klein, Mathieu-Coughlan, & Kiesler, 1986).

At *Stage 1*, clients discuss events, ideas, or speak about others without any reference to themselves or their inner experience, feelings, and emotions; at *Stage 2* clients refer to the self without expressing emotions; at *Stage 3* clients express emotions only as they relate to external circumstances; at *Stage 4* clients focus inwardly on emotions and feelings; at *Stage 5*, clients engage in focused exploration of their inner experience and specific problems and pose questions about their experiencing; at *Stage 6* there is a growing awareness of previously tacit feelings and meanings. At the highest stage, *Stage 7*, clients reference their emotions as part of an ongoing process of in-depth self-understanding that provides new perspectives for solving significant problems (Klein et al., 1986). Interrater reliability coefficients range from .76 to .91, with rating–re-rating correlation coefficients around .80 (Klein et al., 1986).

Ratings of clients' depth of experiencing have been related to good outcome consistently in person-centred and experiential (PCE) psychotherapies (Elliott, Greenberg, & Lietaer, 2004; Hendricks, 2002; Klein et al., 1986; Orlinsky & Howard, 1978). Moreover, clients' emotional processing in the session has been found to be beneficial across a range of therapeutic approaches other than person-centred and experiential, including cognitive-behavioural and psychodynamic (Castonguay, Goldfried, & Hayes, 1996; Giyaur, Sharf, & Hilsenroth, 2005; Godfrey, Chalder, Risdale, Seed, & Ogden, 2007). Supporting the early observations of Rogers and Gendlin, a number of studies have revealed significant differences in the manner in which good and poor outcome cases refer to their emotional experience during the session across different therapeutic approaches (Castonguay et al., 1996; Pos, Greenberg, Goldman, & Korman, 2003; J. C. Watson & Bedard, 2006).

J. C. Watson and Bedard (2006) found that good-outcome clients in both process-experiential, an emotion-focused approach, and cognitive-behavioural therapy for depression, began, continued, and ended therapy at higher modal and peak experiencing levels during the session than did clients with poor outcome. Good outcome clients engaged in deeper exploration, referred to their emotions more frequently, were more internally focused, and examined and reflected more upon their experience to create new meaning and resolve their problems in personally meaningful ways than did poor outcome clients. In contrast, clients with poorer outcomes were not as engaged in processing their emotional experience, nor did they reflect on or pose questions about their experience during the session in order to examine it and try to understand the origins and implications of their experience more fully. As a result poor outcome clients did not report important shifts in perspective or feeling during the session. Similarly, Pos and Greenberg (2007) found that clients' level of experiencing during the working phase of therapy was related to reductions in depression and an increase in self-esteem in short-term emotion-focused therapy. Moreover, clients who were low on experiencing at the beginning of therapy and who had poor alliances with their therapists did the poorest.

In an earlier study of clients' experiencing in emotion-focused psychotherapy, Goldman, Greenberg, and Pos (2005) found that changes in clients' depth of experiencing on core themes over the course of psychotherapy were better than the working alliance in predicting outcome. Other studies have found that higher experiencing scores are related to better immune system responses (Elliott, Greenberg, & Lietaer, 2004). In a study of the impact of therapist experiencing on clients' experiencing in the session, Adams and Greenberg (1996) found that client experiencing could be improved if therapists oriented their responses to client inner experience. When therapists focused on clients' inner experience, clients moved from an external focus to an internal focus. Moreover, the researchers found that the number of times that therapists were able to shift clients in this way was related to positive outcome, with clients reporting fewer symptoms of depression and increased self-esteem (Elliott et al., 2004).

Observer Measure of Affect Regulation (O-MAR; J. C. Watson & Prosser, 2004)

As described earlier, the Experiencing Scale (Klein et al., 1969) measures how clients are behaving in therapy. It provides an indication of their level of engagement with their own experiencing and whether they are disclosing and aware of their organismic and emotional experiencing in the session, but it does not give a sense of how clients process and manage their organismic experience and emotional functioning overall. Consequently there was a need for a measure that would allow researchers and clinicians to rate how clients are processing their affective experience more generally and to provide a measure of outcome. The O-MAR was developed to provide information about the problems that clients may have processing their feelings and emotional experience by assessing their level of awareness, acceptance, and capacity to symbolize and label their affective experience and by assessing their modulation of their levels of arousal and expression of their feelings and emotions (J. C. Watson & Prosser, 2004). External observers rate clients' therapy tapes and transcripts using the measure of affective processing based on clients' descriptions of their behaviour and episodes of experience. These descriptions and episodes are rated on the extent to which clients appear to be aware of their feelings and emotions, are able to label them and symbolize them in awareness, to accept them, and to modulate their levels of arousal and expression. Five aspects of emotional processing are measured: (1) Level of Awareness, (2) Modulation of Arousal, (3) Modulation of Expression, (4) Acceptance of Affective Experience, and (5) Reflection on Experience. Each subscale is rated on a 7-point Likert-type scale, with 1 signifying the lowest level of functioning, and 7 the highest. Average scores are calculated using the subscale scores.

170

Preliminary findings indicate that the O-MAR has high internal consistency: Cronbach's alpha was .86 for ratings early in therapy and .93 for ratings later in therapy. Interrater reliability was also high with Pearson's product–moment correlation on one-third of the data yielding an r of .86 ($p <. 01$) (Prosser & Watson, 2007). Preliminary evidence of its construct and predictive validity is shown with clients' scores on the O-MAR at the end of therapy positively correlated with reports on a post-therapy questionnaire that indicated that they thought about their feelings before acting ($r = .40$, $p < .001$) and negatively correlated with reports that they suppressed their feelings ($r = -.52$, $p < .001$) and were reactive and impulsive ($r = -.51$, $p < .001$). Moreover, clients' scores on the O-MAR towards the end of therapy predicted changes in clients' reports of their level of depression, self-esteem, and difficulties in their interpersonal relationships at the end of therapy. Additional support for the measure's construct validity was provided by its prediction of clients' level of experiencing during the session on the Experiencing Scale (Klein et al., 1969). Clients' levels of affect regulation at the end of therapy ($M = 4.19$, $SD = 1.36$) was significantly higher than at the beginning ($M = 3.17$, $SD = 0.92$), ($t(49) = -6.23$, $p <. 001$) (Prosser & Watson, 2007).

Moreover clients' scores on the O-MAR at the beginning of psychotherapy were positively correlated with clients' levels of experiencing in the early part of therapy ($r = .44$, $p < .001$). The measure provides a way of measuring incongruence and of showing that changes in clients' levels of awareness of their feelings and emotions are valuable, providing support for Rogers' model of personality functioning. However, more work is required to investigate the relevance of the O-MAR to a range of other client difficulties including anxiety, eating disorders, and relationship problems to see whether the current findings are generalizable to these conditions. In future work it will be important to investigate whether clients' capacities to regulate their affective experience continues to differentiate good from poor outcome, and to see whether persons who enter therapy with different capacities to regulate their affective experience improve with different treatments and specific interventions to help them address problems with emotional processing and regulation.

In addition to the observer-rated measures, two self-report measures have been developed to assess clients' capacities to experience and regulate emotion. One of these was derived from person-centred and experiential theories of personality (Behr & Becker, 2002) and the other was developed from theories of affect regulation (Gratz & Roemer, 2004). Person-centred and experiential theorists have noted the similarity of Rogers' views of optimal functioning and congruence to theories of affect regulation (Behr & Becker, 2002; Elliott et al., 2004; J. C. Watson, 2007).

The Scales for Experiencing Emotions (SEE; Behr & Becker, 2002)

The Scales for Experiencing Emotions is a self-report questionnaire designed to measure qualities of emotional processing based on constructs central to Rogers' (1959) view of personality and was originally developed and tested with a German sample. The measure consists of 42 items that measure whether individuals experience, value, regulate, and cognitively process emotions. It comprises seven dimensions: Symbolization of Bodily Experiences, the degree to which persons attend to and represent their emotional experience; Experiencing Overwhelming Emotions, the extent to which persons feel overwhelmed by their emotions; Symbolization by Imagination, the extent to which persons use imagination to know and represent their feelings; Lack of Self-Control, the extent to which persons feel that they cannot control their emotions; Experiencing Congruence, the extent to which persons accept and are comfortable with their emotions; Experiencing Lack of Emotions, the extent to which persons are unaware of what they are feeling; and Regulation of Emotions, the extent to which they feel they are able to modulate and regulate their feelings and emotions. Respondents are asked to indicate whether statements are true or false on a 5-point Likert-type scale, e.g., 'I trust all my feelings,' 'There's no question for me that I have a right to all my feelings,' and 'I consider daydreams to be useful.'

Preliminary studies have found that the SEE has interscale correlations ranging between .22 and .43, suggesting that the scales are measuring different aspects of the experience of affect and the overall reliability of the scales ranging between .80 and .85. The SEE has shown excellent convergent and discriminant validity with other measures of personality, emotional intelligence, and mental health (Behr & Becker, 2002; J. C. Watson & Lilova, 2009).

Recently the cross-cultural validity of the scale was examined with a Canadian sample (J. C. Watson & Lilova, 2009). As in Behr and Becker's original study, the results showed that the SEE has good convergent and discriminant reliability and excellent validity and is related in expected ways to other measures of personality and emotional functioning. Internal consistency was computed for each of the seven dimensions of the SEE. Interscale reliability was within the acceptable range. Cronbach's alpha ranged between .66 and .88; for men it ranged between .50 and .89 ($n = 22$), and for women between .70 and .88 ($n = 103$). The trend to lower reliability among men was also found in the German sample. However, there was a larger difference in reliability between men and women in the Canadian sample. The Canadian sample had lower scores than the German sample on all the subscales. Individuals in the Canadian sample reported that they used their imaginations and dreams less to understand and clarify their emotions, had less need to hide their emotions from others, and were less aware of their feelings than participants in the German sample. These preliminary studies suggest that the SEE is a useful measure to evaluate a person's awareness of their organismic process. It would be important in future studies to see whether the scale captures changes over the course of therapy and to see whether it correlates with client experiencing and affect regulation.

Difficulties in Emotion Regulation Scale (DERS; Gratz & Roemer, 2004)

The Difficulties in Emotion Regulation Scale is a self-report questionnaire developed to provide a comprehensive assessment of emotion dysregulation: awareness and understanding of emotions, acceptance of emotion, the capacity to engage in goal-directed behaviour and refrain from impulsive behaviour when experiencing negative emotions, and access to emotion regulation strategies that are experienced as effective (Gratz & Roemer, 2004). This measure emphasizes the importance of emotional awareness and notes that emotion dysregulation can be as much a function of lack of awareness and of difficulty in labeling and symbolizing the feelings as it can be the expression of impulsivity or the experience of negative emotions.

The DERS is composed of 36 items divided into six subscales: Lack of Emotional Awareness; Lack of Emotional Clarity; Nonacceptance of Emotional Responses; Difficulties Engaging in Goal-Directed Behavior; Limited Access to Emotion Regulation Strategies; and Impulse Control Difficulties. The measure has shown high internal consistency (α = .93) with item-total correlations ranging from r = .16 to r = .69 (Gratz & Roemer, 2004). In addition the authors found preliminary evidence for the convergent validity of the measure with another measure of emotion regulation, the Negative Mood Regulation Scale (Catanzaro & Mearns, 1990). Preliminary construct validity for the measure has been shown by the positive correlations between self-harm behaviours and poor emotion regulation as measured by the DERS. Moreover, self-harm was associated with the subscales that measure nonacceptance of emotion and impulsive behaviours. Gender differences have been reported with men reporting lower emotional awareness than women (Gratz & Roemer, 2004). The role that specific difficulties with emotion regulation play in different conditions was provided by another recent study of a community sample, which showed that individuals' reports of attachment anxiety and attachment avoidance were related to lack of emotional clarity, nonacceptance of emotional responses, and limited access to emotion regulation strategies as measured by the DERS (Lecce & J. C. Watson, 2007). In addition, attachment avoidance was related to lack of emotional awareness.

Other studies have shown that the DERS distinguishes among different populations, for example, college students have scores averaging 75 to 80 (Gratz & Roemer, 2004; Salters-Pedneault et al., 2006) and symptomatic college students, i.e., those reporting self-harm or panic attacks, score higher with an average of 85 to 90 (Gratz & Chapman, 2007; Tull, 2006). In terms of client populations, those diagnosed with general anxiety disorder score between 90 to 95 (Salters-Pedneault,

Roemer, Tull, Rucker, & Mennin, 2006); the average for post-traumatic stress disorder is 105 (Tull, Barrett, McMillen, & Roemer, 2007); and for borderline personality disorder, 120 (Gratz & Gunderson, 2006; Gratz, Lacroce, & Gunderson, 2006).

To the extent that awareness and acceptance of experiencing and feelings are emphasized as important in Rogers' and Gendlin's theories, the DERS, SEE, and O-MAR are well suited to testing their views of psychotherapy and the change process that ensues in good outcome cases. Previous studies that have examined the efficacy of person-centred and experiential psychotherapies have had to use outcome measures that were developed to measure and assess specific types of symptomatology such as depression, anxiety, and trauma. None of these symptom-based measures, for example, the Beck Depression Inventory (Beck, Ward, Mendelson, Mock, & Erbaugh, 1961), the SCL-90 R (Derogatis, Rickels & Roch, 1976), provides a way of measuring the change process that Rogers and his colleagues began to observe and describe during their intensive analysis of psychotherapy process using tapes and transcripts (Rogers, 1961).

MEASURES OF SELF-DISCREPANCY

Rogers and colleagues introduced self-discrepancy as a therapy outcome measure in their research on client-centred therapy (Rogers & Dymond, 1954). The discrepancy between the real self (the self as one sees oneself) and the ideal self (the self as one would like to be in one's own eyes), together with measures of anxiety and depression, was used to assess therapy outcome (Barrett-Lennard, 1962; Rogers & Dymond, 1954). The results of that research showed decreases in the real–ideal discrepancy and decreases in symptoms, as has more recent outcome research on client-centred therapy (Meyer, 1981) and on cognitive-behavioural and interpersonal therapies (Strauman et al., 2001). Higgins (1987; Higgins, Klein, & Strauman, 1985) later introduced the discrepancy between the real self[1] and the ought self (the self as one believes others think one ought or should be), drawing a distinction between the real–ideal discrepancy, which is a negative self-evaluation for not meeting one's own expectations, and the real–ought discrepancy, which is a negative self-evaluation for not meeting one's perception of others' expectations. Associations of the real–ideal and real–ought discrepancies with both anxiety and depression have been shown in research with clinical samples (Fairbrother & Moretti, 1998; Kinderman & Bentall, 1996; Scott & O'Hara, 1993; Strauman, 1989; N. Watson, Bryan, & Thrash, 2010; Weilage & Hope, 1999). These findings support the use of the real–ideal and real–ought discrepancy constructs in continued research on anxiety and depression and

---

1. Higgins' term is 'actual self.' Rogers' earlier term 'real self' is used in the present chapter.

on therapy for these disorders. This research can potentially increase the basis for the use of a self-discrepancy instrument in clinical assessment. Instruments for these purposes are considered in the present chapter.

An early measure of the real–ideal discrepancy was the Butler-Haigh Q-Sort (Butler & Haigh, 1954), which was used in outcome research on client-centred therapy (Rogers & Dymond, 1954; Shlien, 1957). In a review of research on the psychometric properties of this instrument, Wylie (1974) found no studies of its test–retest reliability, though she computed a rho (ρ) of .78 from data for sixteen control cases reported by Butler and Haigh. In reviewing studies relevant to construct validity, Wylie concluded that there was some evidence of convergent validity but only questionable or contradictory evidence of discriminant validity. Wylie expressed concern about the inadequacy of research on the instrument's reliability and validity. A literature search for the present chapter located no studies of the instrument's psychometric properties since Wylie's review. The paucity of research on the reliability and validity of the Butler-Haigh Q-Sort raises the question of its usefulness as a measure of self-discrepancy.

More recently, the Selves Questionnaire (Higgins, 1987; Higgins et al., 1985), which measures both the real–ideal and the real–ought discrepancies, has been used in a number of studies of the relations of the two discrepancies to anxiety and depression (e.g., Higgins et al., 1985; Strauman, 1989, 1992; Strauman & Higgins, 1988). However, the instrument has questionable psychometric properties. Studies of its short-term test–retest reliability (Higgins, 1987; Moretti & Higgins, 1990; Scott & O'Hara, 1993) have found coefficients consistently lower than Joiner, Walker, Pettit, Perez and Cukrowicz's (2005) standard of .70. The discriminant validity of its measures of the real–ideal and real–ought discrepancies has been questioned by researchers who found high correlations between the two discrepancies and suggested that only a single discrepancy exists (Gramzow, Sedikides, Panter, & Insko, 2000; Phillips & Silvia, 2005; Tangney, Niedenthal, Covert, & Barlow, 1998). The instrument also has been faulted for the rationale and difficulty of its scoring (Francis, Boldero, & Sambell, 2006; Scott & O'Hara, 1993; Tangney et al., 1998). These criticisms of the Selves Questionnaire raise questions about its continued use.

Three instruments that measure the real–ideal and real–ought discrepancies have been recently developed: the idiographic Self-Concept Questionnaire – Personal Constructs; the nonidiographic Self-Concept Questionnaire – Conventional Constructs; and the content-free Abstract Measures (http://www.wm.edu/research/ watson; N. Watson, 2004; N. Watson et al., 2010). The present chapter describes these instruments, summarizes a study that evaluates and compares their psychometric properties, and summarizes three studies of anxiety and depression that use the instruments.

The Self-Concept Questionnaire – Personal Constructs

The idiographic personal construct instrument was designed to have phenomenal accuracy (see N. Watson & Welch-Ross, 2000), that is, to measure self-discrepancy using a content that is meaningful to the individual. The content of the instrument was based on Kelly's (1955) theory of personal constructs, which emphasizes individual uniqueness in perceptions. The theory states that a person uses a term and its polar opposite to construe meaning. The polar opposite of a term provides essential information about an individual's unique perceptions of self and others. For example, the term 'friendly' would have different meanings for two individuals who use different terms as the opposites of 'friendly': The opposite for one individual may be 'hostile,' whereas the opposite for the other individual may be 'indifferent.' Accordingly, the personal construct instrument elicits an individual's bipolar constructs to provide the personality characteristics that are its idiographic content. It was expected that this content could be used to increase the therapist's empathic communication.

The idiographic personal construct instrument is an online computer program (http://www.wm.edu/research/watson). The participant lists six characteristics that describe the real self ('yourself as YOU see yourself in your own eyes'), six characteristics that describe the ideal self ('yourself as YOU would like to be in your own eyes'), and six characteristics that describe the ought self ('yourself as OTHERS think you ought or should be'). These 18 characteristics then are presented in a random order, and the participant enters the opposite of each characteristic, yielding an additional six characteristics for each self-component. Thus, the procedure generates a total of 12 characteristics for each of the three self-components. The 36 characteristics then are presented in a random order, and the participant rates them on a scale from 1 (*never or almost never true*) to 7 (*always or almost always true*) in response to each of the definitions of real self, ideal self, and ought self that were used to elicit the characteristics.

The real–ideal discrepancy is scored by calculating the absolute difference between the real-self rating and the ideal-self rating on each of the 12 characteristics of the real self and on each of the 12 characteristics of the ideal self and then calculating the mean of the 24 absolute difference scores. The absolute difference indicates the distance between the real-self rating and the ideal-self rating for a characteristic whether the ideal-self rating is positive or negative. The real–ought discrepancy is scored in a similar way using the 12 characteristics of the real self and the 12 characteristics of the ought self.

Abstract Measures

The abstract instrument also was designed to correspond to the experience of the individual. This content-free instrument is a modification of Shlien's (1962) Abstract Apparatus, which was based on his clinical observation that the person has access to the experience of self-discrepancy. Unlike the personal construct instrument, which uses two-variable difference scores, the abstract instrument uses one-variable measures of the real–ideal and real–ought discrepancies. The instrument uses a single item for each discrepancy, which permits very fast administration, though it may compromise the test–retest reliability and consequently the validity of the scores.

This online instrument (http://www.wm.edu/research/watson) assesses self-discrepancy by using seven pairs of circles, the areas of which intersect 0%, 16.66%, 33.33%, 50%, 66.66%, 83.33%, and 100%. To measure the real–ideal discrepancy, real self and ideal self are defined in the same way as in the Self-Concept Questionnaire – Personal Constructs, and the participant is asked to think of one circle as representing the real self and the other circle as representing the ideal self. The participant then selects the pair of circles with the intersecting area that 'shows how much your real self and ideal self are alike in general.' The discrepancy score is calculated by subtracting the proportion of the intersecting area from 1. The real–ought discrepancy is measured with a similar procedure.

The Self-Concept Questionnaire – Conventional Constructs

The nonidiographic conventional construct instrument uses personality characteristics from Parker and Veldman's (1969) factor analysis of the Adjective Check List (Gough & Heilbrun, 1965). This instrument is presumably less meaningful to the individual than are the other two instruments because its content is a uniform set of characteristics. However, it has the advantages of faster administration than the personal construct instrument and of many more items than the one-item abstract instrument. Its scoring is based on difference scores using a procedure similar to that of the personal construct instrument.

This online questionnaire (http://www.wm.edu/research/watson) measures the real–ideal and real–ought discrepancies using 28 personality characteristics identified by Parker and Veldman (1969) as the four highest-loading items on each of seven factors in a factor analysis of the Adjective Check List (Gough & Heilbrun, 1965). The participant rates the 28 characteristics in response to the same instructions and on the same scale used for the Self-Concept Questionnaire – Personal Constructs that was described earlier. The real–ideal discrepancy is scored by calculating the absolute difference between the real-self and ideal-self ratings on each of the 28 characteristics and then calculating the mean of the 28 absolute difference scores. The real–ought discrepancy is scored in a similar way using the real-self and ought-self ratings.

Research on the self-discrepancy instruments

In an examination of the psychometric properties of these three instruments, N. Watson et al. (2010) evaluated and compared the instruments on their internal consistency coefficients, test–retest reliability coefficients, convergent and discriminant evidence of validity, and predictive validity of test-criterion relationships (American Educational Research Association, American Psychological Association, & National Council on Measurement in Education, 1999). In preliminary analyses, the researchers addressed the criticism that a two-variable difference score is inferior to a one-variable score in reliability and validity (e.g., Cronbach & Furby, 1970; Wylie, 1974). Comparisons of the test–retest reliabilities and the test-criterion validities of the two-variable real–ideal and real–ought discrepancy scores of the personal construct and conventional construct instruments with the same reliabilities and validities of the one-variable real-self, ideal-self, and ought self scores contradicted the criticisms. These results suggest that the criticism of difference scores does not apply to measures of the experiential entity self-discrepancy.

In both a clinical sample and a nonclinical sample, confirmatory factor analysis (Brown, 2006; Kline, 2005) found convergent and discriminant evidence of validity (Campbell & Fiske, 1959) of the three methods for measuring the real–ideal and real–ought discrepancies, indicating that the two discrepancies are distinct theoretical constructs even though they are highly correlated. The real–ideal and real–ought discrepancy latent variables identified in the analysis, which correspond more closely to the underlying theoretical constructs than do the observed variables that comprise them, were found to have test–retest reliabilities over a four week period of .92 for the real–ideal discrepancy and .91 for the real–ought discrepancy. The self-discrepancy latent variables were also found to have test-criterion evidence of validity in predicting latent variables comprised of multiple measures of anxiety and multiple measures of depression.

In a comparison of the psychometric properties of the three instruments, the findings in both samples supported the properties of the personal construct instrument strongly, the conventional construct instrument with qualifications, the abstract instrument's measure of the real–ideal discrepancy with qualifications, but not the abstract instrument's measure of the real–ought discrepancy. The personal construct instrument had strong internal consistency alpha coefficients for both the real–ideal and real–ought discrepancies (.90 to .92 across both samples). It had test–retest reliability coefficients above Joiner et al.'s (2005) benchmark of .70 for the real–ideal discrepancy (.72) and the real–ought discrepancy (.74). It showed convergent and discriminant evidence of validity as described earlier. The personal construct instrument also showed predictive test-criterion validity for both discrepancies in relation to clinical measures of both anxiety and depression. The psychometric properties of the personal construct instrument were stronger than those of each of the other two instruments in multiple respects (for details see N. Watson et al., 2010), providing a stronger basis for its use in clinical practice and research than do the properties of the other two instruments.

Clinical implications of the findings of the N. Watson et al. (2010) study and of other studies of clinical samples (Fairbrother & Moretti, 1998; Kinderman & Bentall, 1996; Scott & O'Hara, 1993; Strauman, 1989; Weilage & Hope, 1999) are that anxiety and depression are associated with a negative self-evaluation for not meeting one's own expectations of oneself and for not meeting one's perception of others' expectations. Rogers (1959) theorized that self-discrepancy is a personality predisposition to emotional distress and that empathic communication by the therapist decreases self-discrepancy and thereby decreases anxiety and depression. The idiographic personal construct instrument assesses self-discrepancy in the individual's own words, which the therapist can use to increase empathic communication.

The findings of N. Watson et al. (2010) also support the real–ideal and real–ought latent variables for use in research. The stronger test–retest correlations of the latent variables as compared to those of the observed variables make statistical tests more powerful than they would be with the observed variables. If a research protocol cannot accommodate all three instruments in order to use the latent variables, the personal construct instrument has the next-strongest psychometric properties for research.

Using the real–ideal and real–ought latent variables, Bryan, Watson, Babel, and Thrash, (2008) did a study of Rogers' (1959) and Higgins' (1987) theories of self-discrepancy as a personality predisposition to anxiety and depression. Although both theories postulate that a high self-discrepancy makes a person vulnerable to emotional distress, they differ on how the two discrepancies develop and how they predispose a person to anxiety and depression.

According to Rogers' (1959) developmental theory, the introjection of conditions of worth from significant others leads to a high real–ideal discrepancy, and this discrepancy is a vulnerability to anxiety and depression. In terminology later introduced by Higgins (1987), conditions of worth can be defined as a high discrepancy between the real self and the ought self. Using this terminology, Rogers' theory can be stated as a high real–ought discrepancy early in development leading to a high real–ideal discrepancy later in development. The theory suggests that after the ideal self develops in late childhood and early adolescence (Katz & Zigler, 1967), there is a structure of self-concept in which the real–ought discrepancy of earlier development underlies the real–ideal discrepancy. The real–ideal discrepancy is experientially the more salient discrepancy that is more directly related to distress, whereas the real–ought discrepancy is the less salient discrepancy that is less directly related to distress. According to this theory, both discrepancies are associated with both anxiety and depression and the real–ideal discrepancy explains variance in both distresses beyond that explained by the real–ought discrepancy.

Greenberg and J. C. Watson's (2006) theory of introjective depression is similar to Rogers' (1959) theory. On the basis of a qualitative study of the experience of depression (Kagan, 2003, as cited in Greenberg & Watson, 2006), Greenberg and

179

Watson theorized that 'Often, deeper examination of an introjective depression reveals the anaclitic depressive themes beneath it. Self-criticism thus may best be understood as an attempt to cope with feelings of dependency, the need to be loved, and attachment needs, rather than as a totally different character subset with unique vulnerabilities to depression' (pp. 52–53; cf. Blatt, 2004). From the perspective of Rogers' self-discrepancy theory, Greenberg and Watson's theory is that introjective depression is characterized by the self-criticism of a high real–ideal discrepancy, which is based on an underlying high real–ought discrepancy of not meeting others' expectations. Thus, like Rogers' theory, Greenberg and Watson's theory of introjective depression suggests that the real–ideal discrepancy is experientially more salient and more directly related to depression than is the real–ought discrepancy.

In contrast to Rogers' (1959) theory that a high real–ought discrepancy leads to a high real–ideal discrepancy in a developmental sequence, Higgins (1987; Strauman, 1996) theorized that the two discrepancies develop in two types of caretaker–child interaction. A high real–ideal discrepancy, which is theoretically a vulnerability to depression, is the result of the caretaker's withholding love and affection when the child does not fulfill the caretaker's hopes and aspirations for the child. A high real–ought discrepancy, which is theoretically a vulnerability to anxiety, is the result of the caretaker's criticism and punishment when the child does not behave in accord with the duties and obligations the caretaker believes the child ought to follow. On the basis of this developmental theory, Higgins hypothesized that the real–ideal discrepancy is uniquely related to depression and the real–ought discrepancy is uniquely related to anxiety. Studies of these hypotheses that used clinical samples or clinical measures with nonclinical samples have yielded inconsistent support (see N. Watson et al., 2010).

Bryan et al. (2008) tested hypotheses based on Higgins' (1987) and Rogers' (1959) theories using clinical measures of anxiety and depression with a nonclinical sample. Results of a confirmatory factor analysis indicated that the real–ideal and real–ought discrepancies are distinct constructs, a finding replicated by N. Watson et al. (2010). Tests of the hypotheses from Higgins' theory, which require control of depression when the two discrepancies are analyzed as predictors of anxiety and control of anxiety when the two discrepancies are analyzed as predictors of depression (Strauman, Vookles, Berenstein, Chaikin, & Higgins, 1991), did not support the hypotheses. The results showed that neither discrepancy was uniquely related to depression, failing to support the hypothesized unique relation of the real–ideal discrepancy to depression. Also, the results supported a unique relation of the real–ideal discrepancy to anxiety, contradicting Higgins' hypothesis of the unique relation of the real–ought discrepancy to anxiety. Tests of the hypotheses from Rogers' theory, unlike the tests of Higgins' hypotheses, maintained the typical comorbidity of anxiety and depression (e.g., Huppert, 2009) by not controlling one distress when predicting the other. Results showed, as hypothesized, that both discrepancies were correlated with depression. However, only the real–ideal discrepancy was correlated with anxiety, failing to support the hypothesized association of the real–ought discrepancy with anxiety. The results supported the hypothesis that the real–ideal discrepancy explains variance in depression beyond that explained by the real–ought discrepancy. Results of analyses of questionnaires about the importance of the ideal self and the ought self showed that the ideal self was rated as more important than the ought self in how the person thinks about the self, feels about the self, and in what the person decides to do. Together these findings support the hypotheses about depression based on Rogers' theory, suggesting that the real–ideal discrepancy is experientially the more salient discrepancy that is more directly related to depression, whereas the real–ought discrepancy is the less salient discrepancy that is less directly related to depression. The findings also indirectly support Greenberg and Watson's (2006) emotion-focused theory of introjective depression, in which anaclitic issues about meeting dependency needs underlie self-criticism.

Using all three self-discrepancy instruments in a naturalistic study at a university clinic, N. Watson and Bryan (2010) tested hypotheses about therapeutic change that are based on Rogers' (1959) theory of personality and psychopathology. Rogers theorized that a high self-discrepancy is a personality vulnerability to anxiety and depression and that a client in effective therapy experiences a decrease in self-discrepancy together with a decrease in symptoms. In the study, results for therapy outcome showed decreases in both the real–ideal and the real–ought discrepancies on all three instruments, with Cohen's d within-subject effect sizes ranging from 0.45 to 0.69. Outcome results also showed decreases in both anxiety and depression, each measured with two instruments, with Cohen's d within-subject effect sizes ranging from 0.67 to 1.09. A hypothesis of the study was that pretest–posttest change scores for the real–ideal and real–ought discrepancies would be correlated with change scores for anxiety and depression. Results confirmed the hypothesis for both discrepancies on all three instruments in relation to the two measures each of anxiety and depression, with the exception of a very strong tendency toward significance for the personal construct measure of the real–ought discrepancy in relation to one of the measures of anxiety. Rogers also hypothesized that a decrease in the real–ideal discrepancy over the course of therapy involves movement of the real self toward the ideal self and movement of the ideal self toward the real self. N. Watson and Bryan added the hypothesis of a movement of the ought self toward the real self. These hypotheses were tested with the personal construct and conventional construct instruments, which, unlike the abstract instrument, yield a score for each self-component. Results confirmed the hypotheses, showing an increase in the real self and decreases in the ideal self and ought self, except for the ought self measured with the conventional construct instrument. These findings provide evidence that therapeutic change in the real–ideal and real–ought discrepancies is concurrent with change in anxiety and depression. Further research is needed in order to test the causal hypothesis that a change in self-discrepancy leads to a change in distress.

In summary, these two studies are examples of the use of the three self-discrepancy instruments and the latent variables for research purposes. Areas of research include personality and clinical studies of Rogers' (1959) and Higgins' (1987) theories of self-discrepancy as a personality predisposition to emotional distress, as well as the theoretical alternatives that the experience of emotional distress leads to the experience of self-discrepancy or that self-discrepancy and emotional distress are respectively cognitive and affective aspects of the same experience. Areas of research also include social psychology translational studies (Tashiro & Mortensen, 2006) and clinical studies of psychotherapy process and outcome. The idiographic personal construct instrument is also useful in clinical practice because it assesses self-discrepancy in the individual's own words, which the therapist can use to increase empathic communication.

USES IN THERAPIST TRAINING AND IN FUTURE RESEARCH

Measures that assess client incongruence are useful in the training of person-centred and process-experiential/emotion-focused therapists. The Observer Measure of Affect Regulation (J. C. Watson & Prosser, 2004) provides a means for student therapists to learn how to observe a client's affect regulation and monitor its change over the course of therapy. The Self-Concept Questionnaire – Personal Constructs (N. Watson, 2004) provides information about a client's self-discrepancy in the client's own words, which student therapists and experienced therapists can use to enhance their empathy with the client's experience of self. In these respects, the measures can be used to teach the implementation of Rogers' (1959) theory.

Research on the measures of self-discrepancy and affect regulation reviewed in this chapter supports their usefulness in testing hypotheses based on Rogers' (1959) theory of incongruence. However, to our knowledge the two types of measures of incongruence have not yet been used in the same study. Future research can integrate both types of measures in studies to test Rogers' theory. On the basis of the theory, the measures of self-discrepancy and affect regulation are expected to be intercorrelated in studies of personality and psychopathology, and they are expected to show parallel changes in process and outcome studies of psychotherapy. In these respects, the measures of incongruence can be used to test more comprehensively Rogers' theory of the interrelationship of self-structure and organismic experience.

REFERENCES

Adams, K. E., & Greenberg, L. S. (1996, June). *Therapists' influence of depressed clients' therapeutic experiencing and outcome.* Paper presented at the 43rd annual convention of the Society for Psychotherapeutic Research, St. Amelia, FL.

American Educational Research Association, American Psychological Association, & National Council on Measurement in Education. (1999). *Standards for educational and psychological testing.* Washington, DC: American Educational Research Association.

Barrett-Lennard, G. T. (1962). Dimensions of therapist response as causal factors in therapeutic change. *Psychological Monographs, 76*(43, Whole No. 562).

Beck, A. T., Ward, C. H., Medelson, M., Mock, J., & Erbaugh, J. (1961). An inventory for measuring depression. *Archives of General Psychiatry, 4,* 561–571.

Behr, M., & Becker, M. (2002). Congruence and experiencing emotions: Self-report scales for the person-centered and experiential theory of personality. In J. C. Watson, R. N. Goldman, & M. S. Warner (Eds.), *Client-centered and experiential psychotherapy in the 21st century: Advances in theory, research and practice* (pp. 150–167). Ross-on-Wye: PCCS Books.

Blatt, S. J. (2004). *Experiences of depression: Theoretical, clinical, and research perspectives.* Washington, DC: American Psychological Association.

Brown, T. A. (2006). *Confirmatory factor analysis for applied research.* New York: Guilford.

Bryan, B. C., Watson, N., Babel, K. S., & Thrash, T. M. (2008, June). *Relations of self-discrepancies to anxiety and depression: Tests of Rogers' and Higgins' theories.* Paper presented at the annual meeting of the Society for Psychotherapy Research, Barcelona, Spain.

Butler, J. M., & Haigh, G. V. (1954). Changes in the relation between self-concepts and ideal concepts consequent upon client-centered counseling. In C. R. Rogers & R. F. Dymond (Eds.), *Psychotherapy and personality change: Coordinated research studies in the client-centered approach* (pp. 55–75). Chicago: University of Chicago Press.

Campbell, D. T., & Fiske, D. W. (1959). Convergent and discriminant validation by the multitrait-multimethod matrix. *Psychological Bulletin, 56,* 81–105.

Castonguay, L. G., Goldfried, M. R., & Hayes, A. M. (1996). Predicting the effect of cognitive therapy for depression: A study of unique and common factors. *Journal of Consulting and Clinical Psychology, 64,* 497–504.

Catanzaro, S. J., & Mearns, J. (1990). Measuring generalized expectancies for negative mood regulation: Initial scale development and implications. *Journal of Personality Assessment, 54,* 546–563.

Cronbach, L. J., & Furby, L. (1970). How we should measure change – or should we? *Psychological Bulletin, 74,* 68–80.

Derogatis, L. R., Rickels, K., & Roch, A. F. (1976). The SCL-90 and the MMPI: A step in the validation of a new self-report scale. *British Journal of Psychiatry, 128,* 280–289.

Elliott, R., Greenberg, L. S., & Lietaer, G. (2004). Research on experiential psychotherapies. In M. Lambert (Eds.), *Bergin and Garfield's handbook of psychotherapy and behavior change* (5th ed., pp. 493–539). New York: Wiley.

Fairbrother, N., & Moretti, M. (1998). Sociotropy, autonomy, and self-discrepancy: Status in depressed, remitted depressed, and control participants. *Cognitive Therapy & Research, 22,* 279–297.

Francis, J. J., Boldero, J. M., & Sambell, N. L. (2006). Self-Lines: A new, psychometrically sound, 'user-friendly' idiographic technique for assessing self-discrepancies. *Cognitive Therapy and Research, 30,* 69–84.

Gendlin, E. T. (1972). Therapeutic procedures with schizophrenic patients. In M. Hammer (Ed.), *The theory and practice of psychotherapy with specific disorders* (pp. 333–375). Springfield, IL: Charles C. Thomas.

Gendlin, E. T. (1997). *Experiencing and the creation of meaning: A philosophical and psychological approach to the subjective.* Evanston, IL: Northwestern University Press.

Giyaur, K., Sharf, J., & Hilsenroth, M. J. (2005). The capacity for dynamic process scale (CDPS) and patient engagement in opiate addiction treatment. *Journal of Nervous and Mental Disease, 193*(12), 833–838.

Godfrey, E., Chalder, T., Risdale, L., Seed, P., & Ogden, J. (2007). Investigating the active ingredients of cognitive behavioural therapy and counselling for patients with chronic fatigue in primary care: Developing a new process measure to assess treatment fidelity and predict outcome. *British Journal of Clinical Psychology, 46*(3), 253–272.

Goldman, R. N., Greenberg, L. S., & Pos, A. E. (2005). Depth of emotional experience and outcome. *Psychotherapy Research, 15,* 248–260.

Gough, H. G., & Heilbrun, A. B., Jr. (1965). *Adjective Check List manual.* Palo Alto, CA: Consulting Psychologists Press.

Gramzow, R. H., Sedikides, C., Panter, A. T., & Insko, C. A. (2000). Aspects of self-regulation and self-structure as predictors of perceived emotional distress. *Personality and Social Psychology Bulletin, 26,* 188–205.

Gratz, K. L., & Chapman, A. L. (2007). *The borderline personality disorder survival guide: Everything you need to know about living with borderline personality disorder.* Oakland, CA: New Harbinger Publications Inc.

Gratz, K. L., & Gunderson, J. G. (2006). Preliminary data on an acceptance-based emotion regulation group intervention for deliberate self-harm among women with borderline personality disorder. *Behavior Therapy, 37,* 25–35.

Gratz, K. L., Lacroce, D., & Gunderson, J. G. (2006). Measuring changes in symptoms relevant to borderline personality disorder following short-term treatment across partial hospital and intensive outpatient levels of care. *Journal of Psychiatric Practice, 12,* 153–159.

Gratz, K. L., & Roemer, L. (2004). Multidimensional assessment of emotion regulation and dysregulation: Development, factor structure, and initial validation of the difficulties in emotion regulation scale. *Journal of Psychopathology and Behavioral Assessment, 26*(1), 41–54.

Gratz, K. L., Rosenthal, M. Z., Tull, M. T., Lejeuz, C. W., & Gunderson, J. G. (2006). An experimental investigation of emotion dysregulation in borderline personality disorder. *Journal of Abnormal Psychology, 115,* 850–855.

Greenberg, L. S., & Watson, J. C. (2006). *Emotion-focused therapy for depression.* Washington, DC: American Psychological Association.

Hendricks, M. N. (2002). What difference does philosophy make? Crossing Gendlin and Rogers. In J. C. Watson, R. N. Goldman, & M. S. Warner (Eds.), *Client-centered and experiential psychotherapy in the twenty-first century: Advances in theory, research and practice* (pp. 52–63). Ross-on-Wye: PCCS Books.

Higgins, E. T. (1987). Self-discrepancy: A theory relating self and affect. *Psychological Review, 94,* 319–340.

Higgins, E. T., Klein, R., & Strauman, T. (1985). Self-concept discrepancy theory: A psychological model for distinguishing among different aspects of depression and anxiety. *Social Cognition, 3,* 51–76.

Huppert, J. D. (2009). Anxiety disorders and depression comorbidity. In M. M. Antony & M. B. Stein, (Eds.), *Oxford handbook of anxiety and related disorders* (pp. 576–586). New York: Oxford University Press.

Joiner, T. E., Jr., Walker, R. L., Pettit, J. W., Perez, M., & Cukrowicz, K. C. (2005). Evidence-based assessment of depression in adults. *Psychological Assessment, 17,* 267–277.

Katz, P., & Zigler, E. (1967). Self-image disparity: A developmental approach. *Journal of Personality and Social Psychology, 5,* 186–195.

Kelly, G. A. (1955). *The psychology of personal constructs* (Vols. 1–2). New York: Norton.

Kennedy-Moore, E., & Watson, J. C. (1999). *Expressing emotion: Myths, realities and therapeutic strategies.* New York: Guilford.

Kinderman, P., & Bentall, R. (1996). Self-discrepancies and persecutory delusions: Evidence for a model of paranoid ideation. *Journal of Abnormal Psychology, 105,* 106–113.

Klein, M. H., Mathieu, P. L., Gendlin, E. T., & Kiesler, D. J. (1969). *The Experiencing Scale: A research and training manual. Two volumes.* Madison, WI: Psychiatric Institute.

Klein, M. H., Mathieu-Couglan, P. L., & Kiesler, D. J. (1986). The Experiencing Scales. In L. S. Greenberg & W. M. Pinsof (Eds.), *The psychotherapeutic process: A research handbook* (pp. 21–71). New York: Guilford.

Kline, R. B. (2005). *Principles and practice of structural equation modeling* (2nd ed.). New York: Guilford.

Lecce, S., & Watson, J. C. (2007, June). *Attachment and affect regulation.* Paper presented to the 37th annual conference of the International Society of Psychotherapy Research, Madison, WI.

Meyer, A. E. (1981). The Hamburg short psychotherapy comparison experiment. *Psychotherapy and Psychosomatics, 35,* 81–207.

Moretti, M. M., & Higgins, E. T. (1990). Relating self-discrepancy to self-esteem: The contribution of discrepancy beyond actual-self ratings. *Journal of Experimental Social Psychology, 26,* 108–123.

Orlinsky, D. E., & Howard, K. I. (1978). The relation of process to outcome in psychotherapy. In S. L. Garfield & A. E. Bergin (Eds.), *Handbook of psychotherapy and behavior change: An empirical analysis.* (2nd ed., pp. 283–330). New York: Wiley.

Parker, G. V., & Veldman, D. J. (1969). Item factor structure of the Adjective Check List. *Educational and Psychological Measurement, 29,* 609–613.

Patterson, C. H. (2000). *Understanding psychotherapy: Fifty years of client-centered theory and practice.* Ross-on-Wye: PCCS Books.

Phillips, A. G., & Silvia, P. J. (2005). Self-awareness and the emotional consequences of self-discrepancies. *Personality and Social Psychology Bulletin, 31,* 703–713.

Pos, A. E., & Greenberg, L. S. (2007). Emotion focused therapy: The transforming power of affect. *Journal of Contemporary Psychotherapy, 37*(1), 25–31.

Pos, A. E., Greenberg, L. S., Goldman, R. N., & Korman, L. M. (2003). Emotional processing during experiential treatment of depression. *Journal of Consulting and Clinical Psychology, 71*(6), 1007–1016.

Prosser, M., & Watson, J. C. (2007, June). *An examination of the relationship between affect regulation and empathy.* Paper presented to the 37th annual conference for the International Society of Psychotherapy Research, Madison, WI.

Rogers, C. R. (1959). A theory of therapy, personality, and interpersonal relationships, as developed in the client-centered framework. In S. Koch (Ed.), *Psychology: A study of a science: Vol. 3. Formulations of the person and the social context* (pp. 184–256). New York: McGraw-Hill.

Rogers, C. R. (1961). The process equation of psychotherapy. *American Journal of Psychotherapy, 15,* 27–45.

Rogers, C. R., & Dymond, R. F. (Eds.). (1954). *Psychotherapy and personality change: Coordinated research studies in the client-centered approach.* Chicago: University of Chicago Press.

Salters-Pedneault, K., Roemer, L., Tull, M. T., Rucker, L., & Mennin, D. S. (2006). Evidence of broad deficits in emotion regulation associated with chronic worry and generalized anxiety disorder. *Cognitive Therapy and Research, 30*(4), 469–480.

Scott, L., & O'Hara, M. W. (1993). Self-discrepancies in clinically anxious and depressed university students. *Journal of Abnormal Psychology, 102,* 282–287.

Shlien, J. M. (1957). Time-limited psychotherapy: An experimental investigation of practical values and theoretical implications. *Journal of Counseling Psychology, 4,* 318–322.

Shlien, J. M. (1962). Toward what level of abstraction in criteria? In H. H. Strupp & L. Luborsky (Eds.), *Research in psychotherapy* (Vol. 2, pp. 142–154). Washington, DC: American Psychological Association.

Strauman, T. J. (1989). Self-discrepancies in clinical depression and social phobia: Cognitive structures that underlie emotional disorders? *Journal of Abnormal Psychology, 98,* 14–22.

Strauman, T. J. (1992). Self-guides, autobiographical memory, and anxiety and dysphoria: Toward a cognitive model of vulnerability to emotional distress. *Journal of Abnormal Psychology, 101,* 87–95.

Strauman, T. J. (1996). Stability within the self: A longitudinal study of the structural implications of self-discrepancy theory. *Journal of Personality and Social Psychology, 71,* 1142–1153.

Strauman, T. J., & Higgins, E. T. (1988). Self-discrepancies as predictors of vulnerability to distinct syndromes of chronic emotional distress. *Journal of Personality, 56,* 685–707.

Strauman, T. J., Kolden, G. G., Stromquist, V., Kwapil, L., Schneider, K., Heerey, E., et al. (2001). The effects of treatments for depression on perceived failure in self-regulation. *Cognitive Therapy and Research, 25,* 693–712.

Strauman, T. J., Vookles, J., Berenstein, V., Chaiken, S., & Higgins, E. T. (1991). Self-discrepancies and vulnerability to body dissatisfaction and disordered eating. *Journal of Personality and Social Psychology, 61,* 946–956.

Tangney, J. P., Niedenthal, P. M., Covert, M. V., & Barlow, D. H. (1998). Are shame and guilt related to distinct self-discrepancies? A test of Higgins' (1987) hypotheses. *Journal of Personality and Social Psychology, 75,* 256–268.

Tashiro, T., & Mortensen, L. (2006). Translational research: How social psychology can improve psychotherapy. *American Psychologist, 61,* 959–966.

Tull, M. T. (2006). Extending an anxiety sensitivity model of uncued panic attack frequency and symptom severity: The role of emotion dysregulation. *Cognitive Therapy and Research, 30*(2), 177–184.

Tull, M. T., Barrett, H. M., McMillen, E. S., & Roemer, L. (2007). A preliminary investigation of the relationship between emotion regulation difficulties and posttraumatic stress symptoms. *Behavior Therapy, 38*(3), 303–313.

Watson, J. C. (2007). Reassessing Rogers' necessary and sufficient conditions of change. *Psychotherapy: Theory, Research, Practice, Training, 44*(3), 268–273.

Watson, J. C., & Bedard, D. L. (2006). Clients' emotional processing in psychotherapy: A comparison between cognitive-behavioral and process-experiential therapies. *Journal of Consulting and Clinical Psychology, 74*(1), 152–159.

Watson, J. C., & Lilova, S. (2009). Testing the reliability and validity of the Scales for Experiencing Emotion with a Canadian Sample. *Person-Centered and Experiential Psychotherapies, 8*(3),189–207.

Watson, J. C., & Prosser, M. (2004). *Observer Measure of Affect Regulation (O-MAR)*. Unpublished observer rated measure of affect regulation, Department of Adult Education and Counselling Psychology, OISE/University of Toronto, Toronto, Canada.

Watson, J. C., & Prosser, M. (2007, July) *The relationship of affect regulation to outcome in the treatment of depression.* Paper presented to the 22nd annual conference of the Society for the Exploration of Psychotherapy Integration, Lisbon, Portugal.

Watson, N. (2004). *Self-Concept Questionnaire – Personal Constructs, Self-Concept Questionnaire – Conventional Constructs, Abstract Measure of Real–Ideal and Real–Ought Discrepancies* [Online questionnaires]. Williamsburg, VA: College of William and Mary, http://www.wm.edu/research/watson.

Watson, N., & Bryan, B. C. (2010, June). *Relations of self-discrepancies to anxiety and depression in change in psychotherapy.* Paper presented at the meeting of the Society for Psychotherapy Research, Pacific Grove, CA, USA.

Watson, N., Bryan, B. C., & Thrash, T. M. (2010). *Self-Discrepancy: Comparisons of the psychometric properties of three instruments.* Manuscript submitted for publication.

Watson, N., & Welch-Ross, M. K. (2000). Measuring phenomenal accuracy. *Journal of Constructivist Psychology, 13*, 181–198.

Weilage, M., & Hope, D. A. (1999). Self-discrepancy in social phobia and dysthymia. *Cognitive Therapy & Research, 23*, 637–650.

Wylie, R. C. (1974). *The self-concept: Vol. 1. A review of methodological considerations and measuring instruments* (Rev. ed.). Lincoln, NE: University of Nebraska Press.

CHAPTER 8

MEASURING THE RELATIONSHIP CONDITIONS IN PERSON-CENTRED AND EXPERIENTIAL PSYCHOTHERAPIES
PAST, PRESENT, AND FUTURE

ELIZABETH FREIRE & SOTI GRAFANAKI

Rogers' hypothesis of the 'necessary and sufficient conditions of therapeutic personality change' (1957) was formulated within the framework of logical positivism, which comprises the view that any construct to be investigated scientifically must be 'operationally defined' (Bickhard, 1992; Green, 1992). Rogers formulated his theory of the role of the therapeutic relationship in the promotion of personality change in a way that he believed would permit his theory to be tested with the traditional scientific methods of quantitative research. Therefore, for each of the relationship conditions, Rogers provided an operational definition that, according to his view, would allow an appropriate 'test' of the theory. These operational definitions of empathy, unconditional positive regard, and congruence, together with the overall positivist framework of Rogers' hypothesis, lured many researchers to the challenging task of developing instruments to measure these constructs. Hence, Rogers' hypothesis opened up an extraordinary new field of scientific exploration and throughout the next two decades the amount of research in the field of psychotherapy inspired by his formulation was unprecedented (Horvath, 1994; Patterson, 1984; Wyatt, 2001).

This chapter will review the instruments that have been developed over the years to investigate the therapist's facilitative conditions postulated by Rogers. There are a large number of instruments that were developed from within psychotherapeutic traditions other than person-centred or experiential that have subscales that relate to more or less of an extent to some of Rogers' relationship conditions (for instance, the 'Warmth' and 'Friendliness' subscales of the Vanderbilt Psychotherapy Process Scales (VPPS), Suh, O'Malley, Strupp, & Johnson, 1989). However, considering the focus of this book and space limitations, we decided to restrict our review to instruments that were developed specifically from within the person-centred and experiential (PCE) traditions.

We will present a brief description of each of these measures, alongside their historical context and psychometric properties. The main strengths and limitations of these measures will also be discussed. As a conclusion of the review, we will suggest future research directions for the investigation of the therapeutic relationship in PCE psychotherapies.

I. INSTRUMENTS THAT MADE HISTORY

Two instruments developed in the 1960s played a fundamental role in the history of the person-centred and experiential psychotherapies: the Barrett-Lennard Relationship Inventory (BLRI) (Barrett-Lennard, 1962) and the scales for Therapist Accurate Empathy, Nonpossessive Warmth, and Genuineness (better known as the Truax Scales, Truax & Carkhuff, 1967). Rogers himself was to some extent involved in the development of both measures, and most of the research that was developed out of Rogers' conditions theory used either one of these instruments (Barrett-Lennard, 1998).

1. Barrett-Lennard Relationship Inventory (BLRI)

In 1956, Barrett-Lennard was a graduate student at the Counseling Center of the University of Chicago looking for a topic for his doctoral thesis, when Rogers first circulated his theoretical formulation of the relationship conditions (one year before its publication). For his doctoral research, Barrett-Lennard decided to test Rogers' theory with actual clients in therapy (Barrett-Lennard, 1959). However, there were as yet no measures of the therapist-to-client relationship conditions and therefore Barrett-Lennard had to 'invent them from the ground up' (Barrett-Lennard, 2002, p. 65).

Barrett-Lennard reasoned that the relationship 'as experienced by the client would be most crucially related to the outcome of therapy' (Barrett-Lennard, 2002, p. 67). Consequently, he decided to focus his instrument on the client's perceptions of the therapist's attitudes in the relationship, supplemented by the therapist's views of his/her own responses.

Description of the instrument

The BLRI comprises four subscales: 'Empathic Understanding', 'Level of Regard', 'Unconditionality', and 'Congruence'. Barrett-Lennard (1962) considered that the concept of unconditional positive regard (UPR) could not be treated as a unitary dimension or single variable, and therefore he separated UPR into two distinct variables: 'Level of Regard' and 'Unconditionality'. In the initial version of the instrument, Barrett-Lennard (1962) had included a fifth variable called 'Willingness to be Known' but the results for this variable were ambiguous and he decided to drop it from later versions of the inventory. However, some elements of this scale were absorbed into the congruence dimension (Barrett-Lennard, 1978, 1986).

The BLRI is structured as a self-report questionnaire, with a six-point bipolar rating scale ranging from –3 ('NO, I strongly feel that it is not true') to 3 ('YES , I strongly feel that it is true'). The 64-item BLRI (Barrett-Lennard, 1978), the version most widely used today (Barrett-Lennard, 1998; 2003), contains 16 items (8 positively worded and 8 negatively worded) for each of the four subscales. Examples of items from the 64-item client form (Other-to-Self, or OS) are presented in the table below.

Clients are asked to mentally insert the name of the therapist in the underlined space in each item.

Table 1. *Examples of items from the 64-item client form*

Subscale	Item
37. Level of Regard (+)	_____ is friendly and warm toward me.
33. Level of Regard (-)	_____ just tolerates me.
30. Empathic Understanding (+)	_____ realises what I mean even when I have difficulty in saying it.
58. Empathic Understanding (-)	_____'s response to me is usually so fixed and automatic that I don't get through to him/her.
51. Unconditionality (+)	Whether thoughts and feelings I express are 'good' or 'bad' makes no difference to _____'s feeling toward me.
11. Unconditionality (-)	Depending on the way I am, _____ has a better (or worse) opinion of me sometimes than at other times.
12. Congruence (+)	I feel that _____ is real and genuine with me.
52. Congruence (-)	There are times when I feel that _____'s outward response to me is quite different from the way he/she feels underneath.

The items in the therapist's form ('Myself-to-the-Other', or MO) are worded in the first person for therapists to describe their response to their clients. These items are equivalent to the items in the client's form (Barrett-Lennard, 1986). However, this equivalence is not exact because that would make some items sound 'unnatural' (Barrett-Lennard, 2002, p. 71). The following examples (see over) of the therapist's form (MO) correspond to like-numbered items in the client's form (OS) listed above.

Revisions
The first version (1962) of the BLRI consisted of 85 items, but since then the instrument has undergone a number of modifications, which have resulted in a considerable reduction in the number of items. These modifications have primarily been directed toward enhancing the wording of the items and reducing response bias by balancing positively and negatively stated items. However, the essential structure and rationale of the various versions are identical to the original (Barrett-Lennard, 2002, 2003).

Table 2. *Examples of items from the 64-item therapist form*

Subscale	Item
37. Level of Regard (+)	I feel friendly and warm toward _____ .
33. Level of Regard (-)	I put up with _____ .
30. Empathic Understanding (+)	I can tell what _____ means, even when he/she has difficulty in saying it.
58. Empathic Understanding (-)	I often respond to _____ rather automatically, without taking in what he/she is experiencing.
51. Unconditionality (+)	Whether _____ is expressing 'good' thoughts and feelings, or 'bad' ones, does not affect the way I feel toward him/her.
11. Unconditionality (-)	Depending on _____'s actions, I have a better opinion of him/her sometimes than I do at other times.
12. Congruence (+)	I feel that I am genuinely myself with _____.
52. Congruence (-)	There are times when my outward response to _____ is quite different from the way I feel underneath.

The only substantial alteration of the BLRI has been the 40-item version, which has 10 items for each subscale (Barrett-Lennard, 2002). In this version, Barrett-Lennard not only dropped some items, but he also merged some others and reversed the positive/negative wording of a few items. These modifications were based more on 'experience and judgment' than on psychometric analysis of the items (Barrett-Lennard, 2002, p. 73).

Moreover, many distinct adaptations of the main 64-item and 40-item forms have been developed for particular uses or for specific populations. There are BLRI forms developed for students/teachers, children, groups, dyads, 'relational life space', supervisory relationships, nurse/patient, and doctor/patient relationships. Other further developments include an observer form (O-64) and a form for group members outside of therapy (OS-G-64) (Barrett-Lennard, 1984, 1998, 2002, 2003).

Other researchers have also added items to the original BLRI for the purposes of their own investigation. For instance, Lietaer (1976) added items related to 'directivity' in his Dutch-language translation, and Cramer (1986a) added an 'advice-given' scale to the BLRI in his study.

Validity

The initial items in the BLRI were derived from Rogers' (1957) paper and from the Relationship Q-Sort (Bown, 1954). The content of these items was revised following discussions with the staff members at the University of Chicago Counseling Center. According to Barrett-Lennard (1962), 'the preparation of items involved constant interaction between theory and operational expression and resulted in a continuous growth and progressive refinement of meaning relating to each concept' (p. 6). The construct validity of the BLRI is also supported by the formal content-validation procedure carried out to eliminate non-differential items. Five qualified judges (Rogers 'might have been' one of them[1]) analyzed and checked carefully each item in order to eliminate items that did not express the variable they were designed to represent (Barrett-Lennard, 1978). The subscales were derived using a combination of item analysis and rational-theoretical considerations (Barrett-Lennard, 1959). Moreover, according to Barrett-Lennard, the considerable range of independent studies that have demonstrated an association between the BLRI and therapy outcome provides substantial evidence of 'predictive construct validity' (Barrett-Lennard, 1998, 2003).

Reliability

In an extensive review of the evidence on the BLRI, Gurman (1977) reported internal reliability data from 14 studies (five in actual therapy settings, four in therapy analogue settings, and five studies on other type of relationships, e.g., teachers, parents, and friends) with differing versions of the instrument. The mean internal consistency reliabilities across these 14 studies (four of them used alpha coefficients, the others used split-half reliabilities) were .91 for Level of Regard, .88 for Congruence, .84 for Empathy, .74 for Unconditionality and .91 for the total score. These results indicate that the 85-item and 64-item forms of the BLRI have high internal reliability.

There are no psychometric data reported on the 40-item version, although the reliability is expected to be a little lower, given the reduced number of items. Thus, Barrett-Lennard recommends the use of the 64-item version 'where length is not a problem' (Barrett-Lennard, 2002, p. 74).

Intercorrelation of the BLRI subscales

Gurman (1977) reviewed 16 studies that reported intercorrelations among the BLRI subscales and concluded that (a) Empathy, Level of Regard, and Congruence present a moderate positive correlation, i.e., these dimensions 'appear to be relatively dependent'; (b) Unconditionality bears a very low (and in one case negative) correlation with the other dimensions (i.e., it is 'quite independent'); and (c) Empathy, Level of Regard, and Congruence are all either moderately or highly correlated to the total score (p. 510).

---

1. Barrett-Lennard, 2010, personal communication.

Factor analysis
Gurman (1977), after reviewing three studies that factor analyzed the BLRI using item intercorrelation, concluded that the BLRI is 'tapping dimensions that are quite consistent with Barrett-Lennard's original work on the inventory' (p. 513). However, he pointed out that more factor-analytic work on the BLRI on actual therapy settings should be undertaken. Almost ten years later, Cramer (1986b) factor analyzed the original version of the BLRI and found that the first four factors accounted for 49.5% of the variance and reflected the four subscales postulated by the instrument. However, according to Cramer, half of the items did not 'clearly distinguish the four factors', and he concluded that 'further refinement of this questionnaire was necessary to improve its factorial validity' (p. 126).

Further comments
The BLRI has been the most extensively used measure in PCE psychotherapies research. It has been considered the most suitable instrument to test Rogers' theory of the relationship conditions since it taps into the client's perceptions of the therapeutic relationship (Asay & Lambert, 2001; Gurman, 1977; Lockhart, 1984; Watson & Prosser, 2002). The BLRI has gained a wide reputation and has been translated into many languages, including Arabic, Dutch, French, German, Greek, Italian, Japanese, Korean, Polish, Portuguese, Slovak, Spanish, and Swedish (Barrett-Lennard, 2002). The usage of the BLRI has expanded beyond the psychotherapeutic context to wider applications in other human service contexts and significant personal life relationships (e.g., family, friendship, work, and classroom relationships). An important strength of the BLRI is its extensive use in clinical settings and its validation primarily in actual counselling interactions, rather than analogue settings. However, the use of different forms, modifications of content and response format, and the use of isolated subscales (usually Empathy) rather than the whole inventory by various researchers have posed significant challenges to its further empirical validation and systematic psychometric assessment (Ponterotto & Furlong, 1985).

2. Scales for Therapist Accurate Empathy, Nonpossessive Warmth, and Genuineness
The Scales for Therapist Accurate Empathy, Nonpossessive Warmth, and Genuineness are observer-rated measures of the relationship conditions. They were developed by Truax and Carkhuff (1967) after they participated in a seminar with Rogers in the early part of 1957. Although the scales were developed 'closely tied to Rogers' statements' on the relationship conditions (Truax & Carkhuff, 1967, p. 43), the identifying labels for the three therapist's conditions were changed from Rogers' original formulation. Empathy was changed to 'Accurate Empathy', which, according to Truax and Carkhuff 'contains elements of the psychoanalytic view of moment-to-

moment diagnostic accuracy' (p. 43); Unconditional Positive Regard was changed to 'Nonpossessive Warmth (NW)' because the authors considered that 'unconditionality of positive regard does not greatly contribute to outcome'; and Congruence was labelled 'Genuineness' (G), since they considered that 'what seemed most related to client improvement was not simply a congruence between the therapist's organismic self and his behaviour or self-concept, but rather the absence of defensiveness or phoniness' (p. 43).

The scales were devised to be applied by trained independent raters, usually to samples of therapy tapes. The 'scoring unit' is typically two to five minutes of therapy interaction randomly extracted from the total therapy session (Bohart, Elliott, Greenberg, & Watson, 2002).

Description of the scales
• *A Tentative Scale for the Measurement of Accurate Empathy (AE)*
This is a nine-point anchored rating scale. The range of this scale extends from a low point where the therapist has no awareness 'of even the most conspicuous of the client's feelings' (Stage 1) through a middle stage of where the therapist responds 'to all of the client's more readily discernible feelings' (Stage 5), to a high point where the therapist 'unerringly responds to the client's full range of feelings in their exact intensity' (Stage 9).

• *A Tentative Scale for the Measurement of Nonpossessive Warmth (NW)*
This is a five-point anchored rating scale. In the lowest level of the scale, the therapist is 'actively offering advice or giving clear negative regard' (Stage 1). At the mid-point, the therapist shows a 'positive caring ... but it is a semipossessive caring' (Stage 3), and at the top level the therapist conveys a prizing of the client uncontaminated by 'evaluations of his behavior or his thoughts' (Stage 5).

• *A Tentative Scale for the Measurement of Therapist Genuineness or Self-Congruence (G)*
This is a five-point anchored rating scale ranging from a very low level where 'there is explicit evidence of a very considerable discrepancy between what he [the therapist] says and what he experiences' (Stage 1) through a mid-point where 'the therapist is implicitly either defensive or professional, although there is no explicit evidence' (Stage 3), to a top level where 'the therapist is freely and deeply himself in the relationship' and 'his verbalizations match his inner experiences' (Stage 5).

Carkhuff revision
The main important revision of these scales was developed by Carkhuff (1969). He shortened the original Accurate Empathy scale to five points with the aim of increasing its reliability. Carkhuff's empathy scale was named Empathic Understanding in

Interpersonal Process Scale (EU) and it is considered a 'truncated version' of the original Accurate Empathy scale (Engram & Vandergoot, 1978, p. 349). According to Engram and Vandergoot (1978), the overall correlation between the AE and Carkuff's EU scales is very high ($r = .89$). Carkhuff (1969) also added other scales to reflect more active therapy strategies. The Carkhuff Scales for Assessing Facilitative Interpersonal Counseling are: Empathy, Respect, Concreteness, Genuineness and Self-Disclosure, Confrontation, and Immediacy.

Validity

The construct validity of the Truax and Carkuff scales has been the object of much controversy. The only published study presented by Truax (1972) as evidence of the construct validity of these scales was a study undertaken by Shapiro (1968), on which the ratings on the scales were correlated with observer ratings on a 7-point 'semantic differential scale' of 18 variables that included understanding–not understanding, accepting–rejecting, genuine–false, and good–bad. The 'Accurate Empathy' ratings correlated significantly ($r = .67$) with the understanding–not understanding variable. However, Rappaport and Chinsky (1972) pointed out that the understanding–not understanding ratings correlated even higher with ratings of therapist warmth ($r = .87$) and genuineness ($r = .73$). Moreover, 'Accurate Empathy' correlated higher ($r = .71$) with the variable good–bad than it did with understanding–not understanding. These results are discussed by Rappaport and Chinsky as evidence that the Accurate Empathy ratings represent a 'more general therapist quality' than accurate empathy (p. 401). Truax (1972) also cited positive correlations between Accurate Empathy and various measures of therapeutic outcome as support for the construct validity of this scale. Chinsky and Rappaport (1970), however, contended that correlational data between outcome and a given variable does not provide evidence of the construct validity of that variable.

Furthermore, the discriminant validity of the Accurate Empathy scale was heavily challenged by the results of a study that compared ratings of tapes with and without client statements (Truax, 1966). In this study, samples of tape-recorded therapeutic sessions were edited so as to remove client's statements. Ratings were then made on both sets of tapes (i.e., the tapes with therapists' and clients' statements, and the edited tapes containing only the therapists' statements). No significant differences were found in the ratings of accurate empathy and nonpossessive warmth between the edited and unedited tapes. Moreover, these two sets of Accurate Empathy ratings were highly correlated ($r = .68$).

Truax (1972) presented these findings to argue that therapist responses can be easily rated independent of the client's responses. According to Truax, the 'Accurate Empathy' raters are specifically trained to listen as much as possible only to the therapist responses and to not be influenced by the patient content' (p. 398). However, the fact that the accuracy of a therapist's empathy could be determined in the absence of client statements seems unreasonable: 'How can one assess the accuracy of a therapist's empathy unless there is someone to whom the therapist is responding?' (Chinsky & Rappaport, 1970, p. 380). According to Chinsky and Rappaport (1970), the most parsimonious explanation for these findings is that 'raters are responding to some quality of the therapist (perhaps voice quality, tone, inflection, or language style) or that more general therapist trait is being measured not implied in the definition of Accurate Empathy ' (p. 380).

Caracena and Vicory (1969) also questioned the construct validity of the AE scale after they found that ratings on AE were significantly correlated to the number of words spoken by the therapist. They concluded that raters on the Accurate Empathy scale depend on superficial objective therapist behaviours, rather than on information about 'an abstract variable such as empathy' (p. 514). Furthermore, Barrow (1977) suggested that ratings on the Truax scales are formulated with the 'aid of ground rules that are not explicitly defined by the scales and that might differ from one rating team to another' (p. 659).

Finally, many studies did not find a significant correlation between client ratings of empathy and the ratings on the Accurate Empathy scale (e.g., Burstein & Carkhuff, 1968; Caracena & Vicory, 1969; Hansen, Moore, & Carkhuff, 1968), and these findings represent a further challenge to the construct validity of the Accurate Empathy scale.

Reliability
Truax and Carkuff (1967) estimated the interrater and inter-item reliability coefficients from 28 studies involving a variety of therapist and client populations. The range of interrater reliability values reported for the Accurate Empathy, Nonpossessive Warmth, and Genuineness scales were .43–.79, .48–.84, and .40–.62, respectively, and the median α reliability values were .95, .77, and .72, respectively. Thus they concluded that the scales showed a moderate to high degree of reliability.

However, these reliability findings were also the object of much dispute. First, Rappaport and Chinsky (1972) pointed out that these reliability scores were 'spuriously inflated' (p. 403) because these studies used a small number of therapists. They considered that if the same therapist was rated more than once by the same rater, then the independence of the ratings was compromised. In addition, they argued that 'the number in the computation of reliability coefficients should be determined by the number of therapists, not the number of patient–therapist interaction samples' (Chinsky & Rapport, 1970, p. 381).

In response to this criticism, Beutler, Johnson, Neville, and Workman (1973) estimated the consistency of therapists' ratings across sessions and patients and found that accurate empathy is not a stable quality of the therapist, but rather a reflection of the therapist–client dyad. They concluded that these findings supported the use of reliability coefficients based on the number of client–therapist pairs (as done by Truax) rather than on the number of therapists (as suggested by Chinsky & Rappaport, 1970).

Interdependence of the scales
There has been considerable divergence in the report of the intercorrelations between the Accurate Empathy, Nonpossessive Warmth, and Genuineness scales. Initially, Truax et al. (1966) found that Nonpossessive Warmth correlated negatively with Empathy and Genuineness. Subsequently, Truax and Carkhuff (1967) and Rogers, Gendlin, Kiesler, and Truax (1967) found moderate levels of positive correlation between the scales. On the other hand, Garfield and Bergin (1971) found that Genuineness correlated negatively with Accurate Empathy and Nonpossessive Warmth. Another study by Barrow (1977) added more divergence to these findings: he obtained very high positive correlations among the three scales (.85 to .93). These large discrepancies could be another indication of the poor reliability and construct validity of the Accurate Empathy, Nonpossessive Warmth and Genuineness scales.

Further comments
The Scales for Therapist Accurate Empathy, Nonpossessive Warmth, and Genuineness have been used in most of the research that grew out of Rogers' conditions theory. The Accurate Empathy scale is the best known of these scales, and it has been one of the most widely used observer measures of empathy in psychotherapy research (Bohart et al., 2002; Feldstein & Gladstein, 1980). However, in spite of its widespread use, it seems that the validity of these scales has not been established.

3. Other measures
During the first two decades after Rogers' publication of the relationship conditions theory, a few other measures were developed, but they were rarely used. Halkides (1958) developed the first observer-rated measure of the relationship conditions, a few years before the Truax and Carkhuff scales. Halkides' scale was developed for her doctoral dissertation at the University of Chicago, but it remained unpublished. Barrett-Lennard (1998) commented that 'although seldom acknowledged, this study opened the way to a plethora of subsequent work employing judges' ratings' on the relationship conditions (p. 264).

Two other observer-rated measures of empathy derived from Roger's theory were developed in the 1970s: Cochrane's (1974) measure of Empathic Communication and Lister's (1970) Scale for the Measurement of Empathic Understanding. Cochrane's measure was only tested through a therapeutic analogue procedure and Lister's study remained unpublished. Truax also developed a client-rated version of his own scales, the Truax Relationship Inventory (TRI) (Truax & Carkhuff, 1967) but this measure has seldom been used in psychotherapy research.

II. FURTHER DEVELOPMENTS

Inspired by the seminal work of these pioneers, other researchers from the 1980s onwards embraced the challenge of creating new instruments in order to promote the development of further process-outcome studies on Rogers' relationship conditions. During the last decades, two new observer-rated measures of empathy, the Multidimensional Response Empathy Scale (Elliott et al., 1982) and the Measure of Expressed Empathy (Watson & Prosser, 2002), and a rating system for studying nondirective client-centered interviews (Wilczynski, Brodley, & Brody, 2008) have been developed.

4. Revised Multidimensional Response Empathy Scale
Elliott, Filipovich, Harrigan, Gaynor, Reimschuessel, and Zapadka (1982) developed a multicomponent rating scale for empathy that focuses on particular counsellor verbal responses. The authors considered that empathic responding is composed of multiple components, and that other measures of expressed empathy 'fail to measure components of empathy that do predict client perceptions [of empathy]' and that these measures have 'inadequate specification of the empathy construct in terms of specific counselor behaviors' (p. 380). Therefore, Elliott et al. constructed an observer-rated instrument, the Response Empathy Rating Scale, that aimed to measure expressed empathy associated with particular counsellor responses and that divided empathy into a number of components. The instrument was originally constructed based on the components of the Lister Empathy Scale (i.e., *Internal Frame of Reference, Perceptual Inference, Accurate Perceptual Inference, Immediacy, Emphasis on Personal Perceptions, Use of Fresh Words, Appropriate Voice,* and *Pointing to Exploration*). Elliott et al. (1982) further defined these components in the development of the Response Empathy Rating Scale. The revised version of the instrument (Elliott, Reimschuessel, Filipovich, Zapadka, Harrigan, & Gaynor, 1981) consists of eight components: *Client Feelings, Perceptual Inference and Clarification, Centrality of Topic, Expressiveness, Collaboration, Verbal Allowing vs. Crowding, Exploration,* and *Impact on Exploration.*
    Examples of items are listed below:

- *Client Feelings*: To what extent does the therapist address the client's feelings?
- *Perceptual Inference and Clarification*: Does the therapist make inferences to tell the client something the client hasn't said yet to add to the client's frame of reference or to bring out implications?
- *Exploration*: Does the therapist actively encourage client's exploration by the content of what the therapist says?

All items are rated on 5-point behaviourally anchored rating scales. The scoring unit is a single therapist's response.

Validity
The validity of the first version (1982) of the instrument was tested using client's ratings on how understood they felt during the session. Client's ratings were obtained with the use of 'Interpersonal Process Recall' technique. Immediately after the session, 28 clients viewed the videotape of their session and rated how understood they felt at particular counsellor responses, using a 6-point scale ranging from 1 ('Not at all understood') to 6 ('Extremely understood'). The correlation between clients' perceptions of being understood and the ratings on Response Empathy Rating Scale was small ($r = .10$ to $.27$). However, when client's ratings where aggregated into episodes or sessions the correlation increased to a medium-sized effects on the total scale ($r = .42$).

Reliability
Psychometric data is available only for the first version of the instrument (Elliott et al., 1982). Five raters participated in the study. Interrater reliabilities (Cronbach's alpha) for all but two components were very good, ranging from .75 to .91. Two components failed to reach the .70 criterion. In the revised version of the instrument one of these components was dropped (*Voice*) and the other (*Manner*) was split into two separate components (*Collaboration* and *Exploration*). Inter-item reliability for the total scale was .82, which indicates that the instrument has a high degree of internal consistency.

Factor analysis
Using a principal component method with Varimax rotation, two factors were extracted, accounting for 62% of the total variance. The first of these factors was described as 'Depth-Expressiveness' and the second factor as 'Empathic Exploration'.

Further comments
The instrument was extensively revised after the publication of these reliability and validity results. However, no further tests were reported on the revised version of the instrument. Although it would be expected that the reliability and validity results would improve in relation to the first version, the fact that these results were not reported is a limitation of the instrument.

5. Measure of Expressed Empathy (MEE)
The Measure of Expressed Empathy is an observer-rated measure of therapist-communicated empathy developed by Watson and Prosser (2002). The construction of the instrument was based on behavioural correlates of empathy identified in previous

research: therapists' verbal and nonverbal behaviours, speech characteristics, and response modes. The MEE uses a nine-point Likert scale ranging from 0 ('Never') to 8 ('All the time'). Items are rated on five-minute videotaped therapy segments. The first version of the instrument (Watson, 1999) had 22 items, but a shorter version of the instrument with nine items was developed subsequently (Watson & Prosser, 2002). Examples of items from the revised MEE are listed below:

- Do the therapist's responses convey an understanding of the client's cognitive framework and meanings?
- Does the therapist look concerned?
- Is the therapist responsive to the client?
- Is the therapist's voice expressive?

Validity

The validity of the scale was tested by correlating the MEE ratings with clients' ratings on the Barrett-Lennard Relationship Inventory (BLRI). However, the original (22-item) scale failed to correlate significantly with clients' BLRI empathy ratings. Therefore, analysis of the correlations of individual components led to a refinement of the instrument. Scores on the MEE were recalculated using only the ratings of the nine items that had correlated with the BLRI at the .36 level or higher (i.e., *Voice conveys concern, Captures intensity of feelings, Emotional words, Attuned, Cognitive understanding, Warmth, Looks concerned, Expressive voice,* and *Responsive*). The revised MEE composed of these nine items showed an overall significant correlation with BLRI empathy ratings of .66 (Watson & Prosser, 2002).

Reliability

The psychometric properties of the 22-item version of the MEE have been tested with the use of archival data from the York Psychotherapy of Depression Research Project (Greenberg & Watson, 1998). Forty videotaped 20-minute segments from the middle of the 7th and 16th sessions of 20 clients (i.e., two sessions for each client) were randomly selected. Each 20-minute segment was further divided into 5-minute segments that were then rated on all 22 items of the scale. In total, eight sets of ratings were collected for each client (Watson & Prosser, 2002).

The interrater reliability for most of the items ranged from .80–.90, although four of the 22 items did not reach the recommended .7 level (*Rate of speech, Interruptions, Clarity,* and *Emotional words*). The inter-item reliability (Cronbach's alpha) for the overall scale (components summed across raters) was .88, which indicates a high degree of internal consistency (Watson & Prosser, 2002).

Further comments

The significant correlation obtained between the revised nine-item MEE and the BLRI client's empathy ratings is a very promising result. However, further replication and testing of this revised version of the MEE with a larger sample is advisable for effectively assessing the psychometric properties of this instrument (Watson & Prosser, 2002). According to Watson and Prosser (2002), the MEE can also be a useful tool in the training of empathy. Learning to use the scale can help trainees to improve their empathy and appreciate different aspects of counsellor behaviour that have an impact on expressed levels of empathy.

6. Nondirective Client-Centered Rating System

The Nondirective Client-Centered Rating System (Wilczynksi, Brodley, & Brody, 2008) is an observer-rated scale that evaluates the therapist's nondirective intention or attitude. This instrument was initially developed by Brodley and Brody (1990) for study of the psychotherapy sessions conducted by Carl Rogers that were available through audio and video recordings, film, and transcripts. The primary aim of this scale is to distinguish the therapist's nondirective intentions or attitudes from the directive ones.

The responses are rated into five major mutually exclusive categories, distinguishing five different apparent therapist's intentions: *Empathic Understanding Response, Therapist Comment, Interpretation/Explanation, Therapist Agreement,* and *Leading Question.* Responses are rated as *Empathic Understanding Response* when the 'therapist's apparent intention is to check his or her understanding of the experience, feelings, or point of view immediately expressed by the client' (Wilczynksi et al., 2008, p. 39); responses are rated as *Therapist Comment* when the therapist's apparent intention is 'to offer his or her observation or opinion, or to express the therapist's own feelings about the client or a general point' (p. 44); responses are rated as *Interpretation/Explanation* when the therapist's apparent intention is 'to explain the client *to* the client' (p. 45); a *Therapist Agreement* is identified when the therapist's apparent intention is to verbally agree with the client; and a *Leading Question* is identifiable by the presence of the therapist's apparent intention, 'in the form of a question, to direct the client's feelings, responses, thoughts, or considerations' (p. 47). The mean percentage of agreement between raters in the latest version of this instrument has been reported 90% (Wilczynski, Brodley, & Brody, 2008); unfortunately, the authors failed to report the reliability values using standard statistics (i.e., Cohen's kappa).

III. DEVELOPMENTS FOR THE FUTURE

In the last few years, new instruments have started to emerge, bringing new perspectives in the investigation of the Rogerian relationship conditions. Geller, Greenberg and Watson (in press) have developed the Therapeutic Presence Inventory (TPI), which aims to measure an overarching relationship condition that goes beyond the three core conditions of empathy, unconditional positive regard, and congruence. Three new measures are currently being developed by the research group of the University of Strathclyde in Scotland: the Relational Depth Inventory (Wiggins, Elliott, & Cooper, 2010) that aims to assess the experience of relational depth in therapy; the Therapeutic Relationship Scale (Sanders & Freire, 2008) that encompasses Rogers' therapeutic conditions and incorporates the dimensions of client's deference and therapist's directivity; and the Person-Centred and Experiential Psychotherapy Scale (Freire, Elliott, & Westwell, 2010), a competence/adherence measure for person-centred and experiential psychotherapies.

7. Therapeutic Presence Inventory (TPI)

Geller, Greenberg, and Watson (in press) developed two self-report measures of the in-session process and experience of therapeutic presence – the Therapeutic Presence Inventory, with a therapist version (TPI) and a client version (TPI-C). These instruments used a model of therapeutic presence developed by Geller and Greenberg (2002) from a qualitative study of interviews with experienced therapists. According to this model, the therapist's presence provides not only a 'foundation' for the relationship conditions of empathy, congruence and unconditional positive regard, but it also 'encompasses' them. According to the authors, the 'therapeutic presence prepares the ground for a therapist to be empathic, genuine, and unconditionally accepting' (Geller et al., in press). Moreover, in this model, therapeutic presence is seen as the 'larger condition by which empathy, congruence, and unconditional regard can be expressed', reflecting a global quality that encompasses all relationship conditions and 'yet goes beyond them'.

Description of the measures

The TPI consists of 21 items presented on a 7-point Likert scale ranging from 'Completely' to 'Not at all'. Ten items reflect the 'Process' aspects of therapeutic presence (e.g., *Receptivity, Inwardly Attending,* and *Extending and Contact*), and 11 items represent the 'Experience' of therapeutic presence (e.g., *Immersion, Expansion, Grounding,* and *Being With and For the Client*). Examples of items on the TPI are listed below:

- I was aware of my own internal flow of experiencing.

- The interaction between my client and me felt flowing and rhythmic.

- I was able to put aside my own demands and worries to be with my client.

- My responses were guided by the feelings, words, images, or intuitions that emerged in me from my experience of being with my client.

The measure of the client perceived therapeutic presence (TPI-C) contains three items with the same 7-point Likert scale used for the therapist TPI:

1. My therapist was fully there in the moment with me.
2. My therapist's responses were really in tune with what I was experiencing in the moment.
3. My therapist seemed distracted.

Intercorrelation between TPI and TPI-C

Geller et al. (in press) found that the relationship between therapists' and clients' ratings on the presence measures was not strong. Although there was a statistically significant correlation between the TPI and the TPI-C, this finding was a result of the large sample size (n = 358), as the correlation was small and not clinically significant (r = .20).

Reliability and validity

The item-total reliability (Cronbach's alpha) computed for the TPI and TPI-C were .94 and .82 respectively, which indicates that these measures have good internal reliability.

Construct validity was established in the process of construction, selection and refinement of the TPI items. The 21 items of the final version of the TPI were selected from an initial pool of 32 items based on ratings of nine experienced therapists. Only items that discriminated between sessions perceived by experienced therapists as having high presence and low presence, and were rated by them as clearly reflecting the experience of presence, were selected.

Convergent validity was further assessed by the relationship between therapists' ratings on the TPI and the therapist's ratings on the Barrett-Lennard Relationship Inventory (BLRI). Correlations between TPI scores and the BLRI subscales of Empathy, Congruence, Level of Regard, and Unconditionality were .59, .41, .34, and .20 respectively (all statistically significant).

In terms of concurrent validity of the TPI-C, Geller et al. (in press) found that clients 'reported a positive change following a therapy session where they felt their therapist was present with them, regardless of theoretical orientation of the therapy'.

Also, when clients rated their therapist as present with them, the therapeutic alliance was also rated as positive.

Factor analysis

Items on the TPI and TPI-C were submitted to a principal-axis analysis. On the TPI, the 21 items fell under one main factor that accounted for 50.01% of the variance. On the TPI-C, the three items resulted in one factor that accounted for 67.59% of the variance. These findings indicated that both the TPI and the TPI-C are unidimensional measures, i.e., they reflect one single factor, as predicted – therapeutic presence – which support the construct validity of the measures.

Further comments

The Therapeutic Presence Inventory represents an important contribution to the development of a new frontier of research on person-centred and experiential therapies. As Rogers pointed out in an interview later in his life (Baldwin, 2000): 'perhaps it is something around the edges of those conditions that is really the most important element of therapy – when my self is very clearly, obviously present' (p. 30). Therefore, an instrument that aims to tap into these 'edges' of the relationship conditions certainly brings a promising contribution to the development of research on person-centred and experiential psychotherapies.

8. Relational Depth Inventory (RDI-C)

The Relational Depth Inventory (RDI-C) is an instrument developed by Wiggins, Elliott, and Cooper (2010) that aims to assess the experience of *relational depth* in therapy, as defined by Mearns and Cooper (2005). The concept of *relational depth* was initially proposed by Mearns (1996, 1997) as the coming together of all six of Rogers' relationship conditions at its best, representing a distinctive hallmark of person-centred therapy. Later on, Mearns and Cooper (2005) defined *relational depth* as 'a state of profound contact and engagement between two people, in which each person is fully real with the Other, and able to understand and value the Other's experiences at a high level' (p. xii).

Description of the measure

The Relational Depth Inventory (RDI-C) consists of 24 items presented on a 5-point Likert scale ranging from 'Not at all' to 'Completely'. Clients are initially asked to describe a 'particularly helpful moment or event' that they had during a therapy session. Then, they are asked to rate 'how accurately' each of the 24 items fits with their experience of this event. Examples of items are listed below:

- I felt I was going beyond my ordinary limits.
- I felt a warm personal bond between myself and my therapist as fellow human beings.
- I felt more alive.
- I felt my therapist and I were equal.

Reliability and validity

The inter-item reliability (Cronbach's alpha) for the RDI-C was .93, which indicates a high degree of internal consistency (Wiggins, 2010). The construct validity of the instrument was sought through the process of construction, selection and refinement of the items. The initial pool of items was developed out of clients' and therapists' descriptions of relational depth experiences in therapy collected by Cooper (2005) and Knox (2008). The pilot version of the RDI contained 64 items and it was responded to online by 189 therapists and 152 clients. The events described by the participants were subsequently rated by three judges to the extent that they represented a 'relational depth' event according to Mearns and Cooper's (2005) definition cited above. The correlations between the RDI items and these ratings of 'relational depth presence' ranged from –.37 to .47. The items whose correlations were ≥ .30 were selected for the second version of the instrument (Wiggins, Elliott, & Cooper, 2010).

Discriminant validity was assessed by the relationship between clients' ratings on the RDI-C and the Working Alliance Inventory (WAI-SR). Wiggins (2010) reported a significant but moderate correlation between RDI-C and WAI-SR of .34, which seems to indicate that 'working alliance' and 'relational depth' are different although related constructs. Moreover, RDI-C scores were found to predict therapeutic outcome, a finding that supports the predictive validity of the instrument (Wiggins, 2010).

Factor analysis

An exploratory factor analysis using principal component method with Varimax rotation found two factors that accounted for 47% of the total variance. The first of these factors was described as 'Therapist genuine/available' and the second factor was described as 'Transcendence'. These factors were named according to their most highly loaded items: the first factor was named after the item '*I felt my therapist was being genuine with me*' and the second factor was named after the items '*The atmosphere was kind of awesome*' and '*I felt a kind of magic happened*'.

Further comments

The RDI-C is an instrument still in development, as part of the PhD studies of Susan Wiggins. A current limitation of the measure that might be addressed in the course of its future development is that it aims to evaluate the 'depth' of one single moment in therapy – a moment defined by the client as helpful – rather than the overall level of 'depth' attained across the relationship. Also, although the process of construction and validation of the RDI-C was very complex and elaborated, it is also not entirely clear what construct the RDI-C is really measuring. The factor analysis would seem to suggest that the RDI-C is not measuring a unidimensional construct, as the definition of 'relational depth' would suggest. In fact, the RDI-C items encompass a width of characteristics that goes from mundane aspects such as 'I felt my therapist respected me' to out-of-the-ordinary experiences such as 'I felt as if time had stopped', some of which are not clearly related to the concept of 'relational depth' as defined by Mearns and Cooper. This observation is supported by the moderate correlations found between the RDI-C items and the ratings of 'relational depth presence'.

9. Therapeutic Relationship Scale (TRS)

Sanders and Freire (2008) are developing a new instrument, the Therapeutic Relationship Scale (TRS), which aims to capture the client's and therapist's experience of the quality of their relationship, focusing particularly upon the core conditions of empathy, unconditional positive regard and congruence, the experience of client's deference, and therapist's directivity. The authors recognize the importance and value of other measures of the Rogerian relationship conditions, particularly the Barrett-Lennard Relationship Inventory, however they consider that the BLRI presents some limitations that they aim to overcome with their new measure. They consider that the BLRI is too long, and many of its items are too complex with some items asking more than one question. Also the type of bipolar rating scale used in the BLRI is no longer recommended in modern theories of measure development (Yorke, 2001). Moreover, the TRS aims to include other dimensions of the therapeutic relationship that go beyond Rogers' core conditions (e.g., 'Dynamics of power', and 'Trust/feeling safe').

The pilot version of the TRS contains 27 items, which aims to cover the following dimensions: *Empathy, Acceptance, Warmth, Collaboration/Partnership, Trust/Feeling Safe, Genuineness, Dynamics of Power,* and *Self-disclosure*. Examples of items of the TRS are listed below:

- I am happy with the way that my therapist and I are working together. (*Collaboration/Partnership*)
- I felt that I could say everything that was in my mind. (*Trust/ Feeling Safe*)
- I felt it was OK for me to correct or disagree with my therapist. (*Dynamics of Power*)
- My therapist revealed something personal about themselves to me. (*Self-disclosure*)

There is also a parallel therapist's form of the TRS.

Some of the items on this instrument were derived from items of the BLRI, and some other items were derived from Rennie's (1994) study on client's experience of deference in psychotherapy. The instrument uses a 4-point rating scale ranging from 'Not at all' (0) to 'A great deal' (3). The reliability and validity of the TRS is currently being tested with clients of the Strathclyde Therapy Research Centre.

10. Person-Centred and Experiential Psychotherapy Scale (PCEPS)

The assessment of 'treatment integrity' is an essential component of psychotherapy trials (Waltz, Addis, Coerner, & Jacobson, 1993). The test of 'treatment' integrity includes both an assessment of therapist adherence to the therapy manual and an assessment that the therapy is being performed competently. Waltz et al. (1993) recommended that integrity checks be undertaken through analysis of audio or video recordings of the therapy sessions by independent researchers/practitioners. In view of the absence of an appropriate adherence/competence measure of person-centred and experiential therapies and given the fundamental importance of this kind of measure in the development of efficacy trials of PCE therapies, Freire, Elliott and Westwell (2010) are developing a new instrument to fill that gap: the Person-Centred and Experiential Psychotherapy Scale (PCEPS). This instrument consists of two subscales corresponding to (a) person-centred process and (b) experiential process.

The Person-Centred Process scale consists of 10 items: *Client Frame of Reference, Client Track, Core Meaning, Client Flow, Warmth, Clarity of Language, Content Directiveness, Accepting Presence, Judgement,* and *Ungenuineness.* Examples of items of this scale are:

- Do the therapist's responses convey an understanding of the client's experiences as the client themselves understands or perceives it? (*Client Frame of Reference*)
- Do the therapist's responses reflect the core, or essence, of what the client is communicating or experiencing in the moment? (*Core Meaning*)
- Do the therapist's responses convey judgements of the client's experiences behaviour? (*Judgement* – reversed item)

The Experiential Process scale consists of 9 items: *Collaboration, Experiential Specificity, Emotion Focus, Articulation of Emotions, Core Client Experiences, Emotion Regulation, Resolution, Client Self-development,* and *Therapeutic Indicators.* Examples of items of this scale are:

- Does the therapist actively try to facilitate client–therapist collaboration and mutual involvement in the goals and tasks of therapy? (*Collaboration*)
- Does the therapist actively try to help the client achieve and maintain an optimal

level of emotional arousal for exploring their feelings? (*Emotion Regulation*)

- Do the therapist's responses aim to help the client identify, persist in, and resolve key goals or tasks, within and across sessions? (*Resolution*)

The reliability and validity of this new measure is currently being tested using 180 audio-recorded 10-minute segments of therapy sessions systematically selected from the archive of taped therapy sessions of the Strathclyde Therapy Research Centre.

IV. MEASURING THE RELATIONSHIP CONDITIONS: A PARADOX?

Since the publication of Rogers' hypothesis of the 'necessary and sufficient conditions' for therapeutic personality change more than five decades ago, many researchers have attempted to tackle the challenge of testing its validity. The development of instruments to 'measure' the therapist-provided conditions of empathy, unconditional positive regard and congruence, and the client's perception of these conditions became the first step or the essential tool for any viable test of Rogers' hypothesis. However, how close have we come to really measuring these 'core conditions'? Or perhaps that is the wrong question; perhaps one should ask: Are these conditions in fact measurable?

In a traditional, positivist approach to psychology there is an omnipresent credo that: 'Whatever exists at all exists in some amount. To know it thoroughly involves knowing its quantity' (Thorndike, 1918, p. 16). However, is it true that all psychological attributes can be measured? In quantitative science, such as physics, attributes such as temperature, length, velocity, etc., are taken to be measurable because they have a distinctive kind of internal structure: a quantitative structure. According to Michell (1997, 2000), there is no logical necessity that any attribute should have a quantitative structure,[2] in fact, conceptualizing an attribute as quantitative is a scientific hypothesis to be tested in itself.

The paradigm that underpins measure development in psychology is characterized by the assumption that measurement is simply 'the assignment of numerals to objects or events according to rule' (Michell, 2000, p. 650). However,

---

2. A 'quantitative structure' is characterized by the following: 'A range of instances of an attribute Q constitutes continuous quantity if and only if for any a and b in Q, (1) One and only one of the following is true: (i) a = b, (ii) There exists c in Q such that a = b + c; (iii) There exists c in Q such that (1) b = a + c; (2) a + b = b + a; (3) a + (b + c) = (a + b) + c, (4) If a > b, there exists c in Q, such that a > c > b; (5) every non-empty subset of Q that has an upper bound has a least upper bound. It is because of this quantitative structure, that magnitudes of a quantity are measurable, that is, they stand in relations to one another that can be expressed as real numbers' (Michell, 1997: 356).

Michell (1997, 2000) points out that this definition of measurement is quite unlike the traditional concept used in the physical sciences. Therefore, he concludes that quantitative psychology is a 'pathology of science', and that psychometrics has a 'methodological thought disorder', since it endorses an anomalous definition of measurement (Michell, 2000, p. 639). Perhaps Michell's criticisms of the concept of measurement in psychology could shed some light on the reasons why the endeavour to measure Rogers' relationship conditions seems to always fall short of a complete success. Perhaps trying to measure the relationship conditions is somewhat like a Sisyphean challenge, an absurd and futile task that will never be fully accomplished?

There is an inherent paradox (Freire, 2009) in Rogers' theory, in that 'it was cast in the objectivism of logical positivism while also encompassing foundational phenomenological constructs and an almost "mystical view" of the therapeutic relationship' (p. 228). Nowadays, we can be critical of the naïve objectivism of Rogers' formulation of the relationship conditions and his search for 'operational definitions' of these conditions. We recognize today that the overall 'if–then' framework of his theory is a 'deterministic, mechanistic, and reductionistic account of the complexity, richness and unpredictability of the therapeutic process' (p. 228).

Perhaps the time has come for a new formulation of Rogers' theory in which the qualities of the therapeutic relationship won't be defined as 'attributes' provided by the therapist regardless or independently of the client's active participation and engagement in the therapeutic process (Butler & Strupp, 1986; Grafanaki, 2001, 2002; Stiles & Shapiro, 1989). In this new framework, the qualities of the therapeutic relationship would certainly be best investigated by qualitative methodologies, on which the individual differences and contextual variations would be seen as the 'very effects' to be investigated, and not excluded as 'error variance' as is the case with quantitative methodologies (Yardley, 2008).

We appreciate the monumental work that has been undertaken by a number of researchers in the development of measures of the relationship conditions that would allow for the testing of Rogers' hypothesis. However, we recognize that this might have been an impossible task, as the therapeutic relationship might not have a quantitative structure that would permit a rigorous mathematical measurement. Therefore, we recommend that a new framework for the investigation of the therapeutic relationship be developed, in which the client wouldn't be considered a passive recipient of the therapist-provided conditions, and in which the uniqueness and singularity of each therapeutic encounter would be considered as the core and essence of any therapeutic process.

V. CONCLUSION

To end this review with the critical tone above would be extremely unfair, with the importance and magnitude of the work developed by Rogers and his successors on the investigation of the therapeutic relationship. Despite the inherent epistemological paradoxes, Rogers' hypothesis of the relationship conditions was a fundamental contribution that revolutionized the field of psychotherapy research. Rogers' theory gave rise to a new paradigm, which emphasized the importance and significance of the therapist's attitudes rather than the application of techniques (Rogers, 1951). In fact, all instruments reviewed in this chapter share this underlying assumption that 'it is the relationship that heals'. These instruments are essential and invaluable tools in the process of gathering evidence of the paramount importance of the Rogerian relationship conditions for effective psychotherapy.

REFERENCES

Asay, T., & Lambert, M. (2001). Therapist relational variable. In D. Cain & J. Seeman (Eds.), *Humanistic psychotherapies: Handbook of research and practice* (pp. 531–558). Washington, DC: American Psychological Association.

Baldwin, M. (2000). Interview with Carl Rogers on the use of the self in therapy. In M. Baldwin (Ed.), *The use of self in therapy* (2nd ed., pp. 29–38). New York: The Haworth Press.

Barrett-Lennard, G. T. (1959). *Dimensions of perceived therapist response related to therapeutic change.* Unpublished doctoral dissertation, University of Chicago.

Barrett-Lennard, G. T. (1962). Dimensions of therapist response as causal factors in therapeutic change. *Psychological Monographs, 76* (43, Whole No. 562).

Barrett-Lennard, G. T. (1978). The Relationship Inventory: Later development and adaptations. *JSAS Catalog of Selected Documents in Psychology, 8,* 68.

Barrett-Lennard, G. T. (1984). The world of family relationships: A person-centered systems view. In R. F. Levant & J. M. Shlien (Eds.), *Client-centered therapy and the person-centered approach: New directions in theory, research and practice* (pp. 222–242). New York: Praeger.

Barrett-Lennard, G. T. (1986). The Relationship Inventory now: Issues and advances in theory, method and use. In L. S. Greenberg & W. M. Pinsof (Eds.), *The psychotherapeutic process: A research handbook* (pp. 439–476). New York: Guilford.

Barrett-Lennard, G. T. (1998). *Carl Rogers' helping system: Journey and substance.* London: Sage.

Barrett-Lennard, G. T. (2002). Perceptual variables of the helping relationship: A measuring system and its fruits. In G. Wyatt & P. Sanders (Eds.), *Rogers' therapeutic conditions: Evolution, theory and practice. Vol. 4, Contact and Perception* (pp. 65–90). Ross-on-Wye: PCCS Books.

Barrett-Lennard, G. T. (2003). *Steps on a mindful journey: Person-centred expressions.* Ross-on-Wye: PCCS Books.

Barrow, J. C. (1977). Interdependence of scales for the facilitative conditions: Three types of correlational data. *Journal of Consulting and Clinical Psychology, 45,* 654–659.

Beutler, L. E., Johnson, D. T., Neville, C. W., & Workman, S. N. (1973). Some sources of variance in 'accurate empathy' ratings. *Journal of Consulting and Clinical Psychology, 40,* 167–169.

Bickhard, M. H. (1992). Myths of science: Misconceptions of science in contemporary psychology. *Theory & Psychology, 2,* 321–337.

Bohart, A. C., Elliott, R., Greenberg, L. S., & Watson, J. C. (2002). Empathy. In J. C. Norcross (Ed.), *Psychotherapy relationships that work: Therapist contributions and responsiveness to patients* (pp. 89–108). Oxford: Oxford University Press.

Bown, O. H. (1954). *An investigation of therapeutic relationship in client-centered psychotherapy.* Unpublished doctoral dissertation.

Brodley, B. T., & Brody, A. (1990, August). *Understanding client-centered therapy through interviews conducted by Carl Rogers.* Paper presented in the panel on Fifty Years of Client-Centered Therapy: Recent Research, at the annual conference of the American Psychological Association, Boston, MA.

Burstein, J. W., & Carkhuff, R. R. (1968). Objective therapist and client ratings of therapist offered facilitative conditions of moderate to low functioning therapists. *Journal of Clinical Psychology, 24,* 233–236.

Butler, S., & Strupp, H. (1986). Specific and non-specific factors in psychotherapy: A problematic paradigm for psychotherapy research. *Psychotherapy, 23,* 30–40.

Caracena, P. F., & Vicory, J. R. (1969). Correlates of phenomenological and judged empathy. *Journal of Counseling Psychology, 16,* 510–515.

Carkhuff, R. R. (1969). *Helping and human relations: A primer for lay and professional helpers, Vol. 2, Practice and research.* New York: Holt, Rinehart, & Winston.

Chinsky, J. M., & Rappaport, J. (1970). Brief critique of the meaning and reliability of 'accurate empathy' ratings. *Psychological Bulletin, 73,* 379–382.

Cochrane, C. T. (1974). Development of a measure of empathic communication. *Psychotherapy: Theory, Research and Practice, 11,* 41–47.

Cooper, M. (2005). Therapists' experiences of relational depth: A qualitative interview study. *Counselling and Psychotherapy Research, 5,* 87–95.

Cramer, D. (1986a). An item factor analysis of the revised Barrett-Lennard Relationship Inventory. *British Journal of Guidance & Counselling, 14(3),* 314–325.

Cramer, D. (1986b). An item factor analysis of the original relationship inventory. *Journal of Social and Personal Relationships, 3(1),* 121–127.

Elliott, R., Reimschuessel, C., Filipovich, H., Zapadka, J., Harrigan, L., & Gaynor, J. (1981). *Revised multidimensional response empathy scale.* Unpublished manuscript, University of Toledo, OH.

Elliott, R., Filipovich, H., Harrigan, L., Gaynor, J., Reimschuessel, C., & Zapadka, J. K. (1982). Measuring response empathy: The development of a multicomponent rating scale. *Journal of Counseling Psychology, 29,* 379–387.

Engram, B. E., & Vandergoot, D. (1978). Correlation between the Truax and the Carkhuff scales for measurement of empathy. *Journal of Counseling Psychology, 25,* 349–351.

Feldstein, J. C., & Gladstein, G. A. (1980). A comparison of the construct validities of four measures of empathy. *Measurement and Evaluation in Guidance, 13,* 49–57.

Freire, E. S. (2009). A quiet revolution ... or swimming against the tide? *Person-Centered and Experiential Psychotherapies, 8,* 224–232.

Freire, E. S., Elliott, R., & Westwell, G. (2010, July). *Development and validation of a competence/*

211

adherence measure for person-centered and experiential psychotherapies. Paper presented at the 9th World Conference for Person-Centered and Experiential Psychotherapy and Counseling, Rome, Italy.

Garfield, S. L., & Bergin, A. E. (1971). Therapeutic conditions and outcome. *Journal of Abnormal Psychology, 77,* 108–114.

Geller, S. M., & Greenberg, L. S. (2002). Therapeutic presence: Therapists' experience of presence in the psychotherapeutic encounter. *Person-Centered and Experiential Psychotherapies, 1,* 71–86.

Geller, S. M., Greenberg, L. S., & Watson, J. C. (in press). Therapeutic presence: The development of a measure. *Psychotherapy Research.*

Grafanaki, S. (2001). What counselling research has taught us about the concept of congruence: Main discoveries and unresolved issues. In G. Wyatt (Ed.), *Rogers' therapeutic conditions, Vol. 1, Congruence* (pp. 18–35). Ross-on-Wye: PCCS Books.

Grafanaki, S. (2002). On becoming congruent: How congruence works in person-centred counselling and practical applications for training and practice. In J. C. Watson, R. N. Goldman, & M. S. Warner (Eds.), *Client-centered and experiential psychotherapy in the 21st century* (pp. 278–290). Ross-on-Wye: PCCS Books.

Green, C. D. (1992). Of immortal mythological beasts: Operationism in psychology. *Theory & Psychology, 2,* 291–320.

Greenberg, L. S., & Watson, J. C. (1998). Experiential therapy of depression: Differential effects of client-centered relationship conditions and process experiential interventions. *Psychotherapy Research, 8,* 210–224.

Gurman, A. S. (1977). The patient's perceptions of the therapeutic relationship. In A. S. Gurman & A. M. Razin (Eds.), *Effective psychotherapy: A handbook of research* (pp. 503–543). New York: Pergamon.

Halkides, G. (1958). *An experimental study of four conditions necessary for therapeutic change.* Unpublished doctoral dissertation. University of Chicago.

Hansen, J. C., Moore, G. D., & Carkhuff, R. R. (1968). The differential relationship of objective and client perceptions of counseling. *Journal of Clinical Psychology, 24,* 244–246.

Horvath, A. O. (1994). Empirical validation of Bordin's pantheoretical model of the alliance: The working alliance inventory perspective. In A. O. Horvath & L. S. Greenberg (Eds.), *The working alliance: Theory, research and practice* (pp. 109–128). New York: Wiley.

Kiesler, D. J. (1973). *The process of psychotherapy: Empirical foundations and systems of analysis.* Chicago: Aldine.

Knox, R. (2008). Clients' experiences of relational depth in person-centred counselling. *Counselling and Psychotherapy Research, 8,* 182–188.

Lietaer, G. (1976). Nederlandstalige revisie van Barrett-Lennard's Relationship Inventory voor individueel-terapeutische relaties. *Psychologica Belgica, 16,* 73–94.

Lister, J. L. (1970). A *scale for the measurement of empathic understanding.* Unpublished manuscript, University of Florida.

Lockhart, W. (1984). Rogers' 'necessary and sufficient conditions' revisited. *British Journal of Guidance and Counselling, 12*(2), 112–123.

Mearns, D. (1996). Working at relational depth with clients in person-centred therapy. *Counselling, 7,* 307–311.

Mearns, D. (1997). *Person-centred counselling training.* London: Sage.

Mearns, D., & Cooper, M. (2005). *Working at relational depth in counselling and psychotherapy.* London: Sage.

Michell, J. (1997). Quantitative science and the definition of measurement in psychology. *British Journal of Psychology, 88,* 355–383.

Michell, J. (2000). Normal science, pathological science and psychometrics. *Theory & Psychology, 10*(5), 639–667.

Patterson, C. H. (1984). Empathy, warmth, and genuineness: A review of reviews. *Psychotherapy, 21,* 431–438.

Ponterotto, J., & Furlong, M. (1985). Evaluating counsellor effectiveness. A critical review of rating scale instruments. *Journal of Counseling Psychology, 32*(4), 597–616.

Rappaport, J., & Chinsky, J. M. (1972). Accurate empathy: A confusion of a construct. *Psychological Bulletin, 77,* 400–404.

Rennie, D. L. (1994). Client's deference in psychotherapy. *Journal of Counseling Psychology, 41,* 427–437.

Rogers, C. R. (1951). *Client-centered therapy.* Boston: Houghton Mifflin.

Rogers, C. R. (1957). The necessary and sufficient conditions of therapeutic personality change. *Journal of Consulting Psychology, 21,* 95–103.

Rogers, C. R., Gendlin, E. T., Kiesler, D. J., & Truax, C. (1967). *The therapeutic relationship and its impact: A study of psychotherapy with schizophrenics.* Madison, WI: University of Wisconsin Press.

Sanders, T., & Freire, E. S. (2008, July). *Researching the relationship: Developing the therapeutic relationship scale.* Paper presented at the 8th World Conference for Person-Centered and Experiential Psychotherapy and Counseling, Norwich, UK.

Shapiro, J. G. (1968). Relationship between expert and neophyte ratings of therapeutic conditions. *Journal of Consulting and Clinical Psychology, 32,* 87–88.

Stiles, W., & Shapiro, D. (1989). Abuse of the drug metaphor in psychotherapy process-outcome research. *Psychology Review, 9,* 521–543.

Suh, C. S., O'Malley, S. S., Strupp, H. H., & Johnson, M. E. (1989). The Vanderbilt Psychotherapy Process Scale (VPPS). *Journal of Cognitive Psychotherapy, 3,* 123–154.

Thorndike, E. L. (1918). The nature, purposes, and general methods of measurements of educational products. In G. M. Whipple (Ed.), *Seventeenth yearbook of the National Society for the Study of Education, Vol. 2* (pp. 16–24). Bloomington, IL: Public School Publishing.

Truax, C. B. (1966). Influence of patient statements on judgments of therapist statements during psychotherapy. *Journal of Clinical Psychology, 22,* 335–337.

Truax, C. B. (1972). The meaning and reliability of accurate empathy rating: A rejoinder. *Psychological Bulletin, 77,* 397–399.

Truax, C. B., & Carkhuff, R. R. (1967). *Toward effective counseling and psychotherapy: Training and practice.* Chicago: Aldine.

Truax, C. B., Wargo, D. G., Frank, J. D., Imber, S. D., Battle, C. B., Hoehn-Saric, R., et al. (1966). Therapist empathy, genuineness, and warmth and patient therapeutic outcome. *Journal of Consulting Psychology, 30,* 395–401.

Waltz, J., Addis, M. E., Coerner, K., & Jacobson, N. S. (1993). Testing the integrity of a psychotherapy assessment of adherence and competence. *Journal of Consulting and Clinical Psychology, 61,* 620–630.

Watson, J. C. (1999). *Measure of expressed empathy.* Unpublished manuscript, Toronto: OISE/UT.

Watson, J. C., & Prosser, M. (2002). Development of an observer-rated measure of therapist empathy. In J. C. Watson, R. N. Goldman, & M. S. Warner (Eds.), *Client-centered and experiential psychotherapy in the 21st century* (pp. 303–314). Ross-on-Wye: PCCS Books.

Wiggins, S. (2010, July). *Relational depth and outcome*. Paper presented at the 9th World Conference for Person-Centered and Experiential Psychotherapy and Counseling, Rome, Italy.

Wiggins, S., Elliott, R., & Cooper, M. (2010). *The prevalence and characteristics of relational depth events in psychotherapy.* Unpublished manuscript.

Wilczynski, J., Brodley, B. T., & Brody, A. (2008). A rating system for studying nondirective client-centered interviews – Revised. *The Person-Centered Journal, 15,* 34–57.

Wyatt, G. (2001). Introduction to the series. In G. Wyatt (Ed.), *Rogers' therapeutic conditions: Evolution, theory and practice. Vol 1: Congruence* (pp. i–vi). Ross-on-Wye: PCCS Books.

Yardley, L. (2008). Demonstrating validity in qualitative psychology. In J. A. Smith (Ed.), *Qualitative psychology: A practical guide to research methods* (2nd ed., pp. 235–251). London: Sage.

Yorke, M. (2001). Bipolarity … or not? Some conceptual problems relating to bipolar rating scales. *British Educational Research Journal, 27,* 171–186.

CHAPTER 9

RESEARCHING IN A PERSON-CENTRED WAY

PAUL WILKINS

INTRODUCTION

Much of what you will have read in this book up to now has been about the ways in which person-centred therapy has been validated and explored by experimental and/ or quasi-experimental quantitative research. These approaches are fundamental to the positioning of person-centred therapy in the existing 'evidence-based practice' framework. It is the evidence from quantitative research that has the most profound effect on the development of policy and funding. These approaches are also of intrinsic value. They tell a valuable story of the efficacy and efficiency of person-centred therapy and substantiate its theory and practice. Indeed, one of the early and proud boasts of the founders of person-centred therapy was that its theory was firmly rooted in the empirical observation of practice and that this was unique.

Rogers and his early students saw themselves as scientists who sought to establish a basis for their beliefs and practices by actively engaging in research and modifying these in its light. Kirschenbaum and Henderson (1990, p. 201) state 'psychological theory and particularly research occupied a central focus for the first thirty-five years of Rogers's career'. However, although this positivistic, 'evidence-based' approach to the investigation of person-centred therapy persisted and is vitally important to the present day, in the 1960s Rogers himself began to experience a tension between two points of view: the desire to understand how people experience themselves and the world subjectively, and an interest in the behaviour of people from the standpoint of a 'neutral' observer (see Kirschenbaum, 2007, pp. 315–317). Rogers (1961, p. 200) wrote of this tension:

> The better therapist I have become (as I believe I have) the more I have been vaguely aware of my complete subjectivity when I am at my best in this function. And as I have become a better investigator, more 'hard-headed' and more scientific (as I believe I have) I have felt an increasing discomfort at the distance between the rigorous objectivity of myself as a scientist and the almost mystical subjectivity of myself as a therapist.

It was only a few years after this that Rogers' output of positivistic research ceased. By 1968, (see Kirschenbaum & Henderson, 1990, p. 270) Rogers was already expressing his valuing of intuition in the research process. He wrote of his belief: 'That the human organism, when operating freely and nondefensively, is perhaps the best scientific tool in existence, and is able to sense a pattern long before it can consciously formulate one.' Although there is no reason to suppose that Rogers doubted the value of positivistic research, this view has important implications for the role of all those involved in person-centred research (see below).

In the view of O'Hara (1995, p. 49), Rogers was as an unwitting postmodernist pioneer. This was because he needed 'a methodology that could elucidate and critically evaluate the link between his own inner reality and the external reality to which he was attending'. She indicates that Rogers' understanding of this need arose too soon – that is, at that time such methods were not available. It was not until much later that Rogers (1985) indicated his 'pleasant surprise' that there were now 'new models of science much more appropriate to a human science' (see Kirschenbaum & Henderson, 1990, pp. 281–282). Many of these models were at least influenced by person-centred principles and they will be discussed below.

So, it is not that positivistic approaches to research are in any sense 'wrong' or 'inferior', more that they represent a particular set of tools designed for a particular kind of task. The growing sense that there were other research tasks to be done *as well* and for which the existing tools were inadequate was what lay behind Rogers move away from positivistic research and the efforts of others to develop new research tools. Some of these new methods more directly articulate a person-centred way of doing research. In this chapter, I explore some of the history of the development of person-centred approaches to research, describe a person-centred research model, examine in detail two approaches stemming directly from the person-centred approach and a few other 'compatible' approaches in less detail. Finally, I give some examples of how person-centred research has been used in practice and what has been found.

WHAT IS RESEARCH?

In order to understand the contribution of the person-centred approach to ways of researching it is perhaps helpful to briefly revisit just what research is. Conventionally, and in the simplest terms, research is systematic study with the intent to answer a question in the hope that this will lead to the establishment of 'fact', increased understanding and/or knowledge – but it can be understood as a lot more complicated than that. McLeod (2003, p. 4) offered a 'useful working definition of research': 'a systematic process of critical inquiry leading to valid propositions and conclusions that are communicated to interested others.'

In a way, this is a conservative definition but is widely accepted and is certainly one that has dominated the exploration and examination of person-centred therapy. Research of this kind has been described by Heron (1996, pp. 48–49) as *informative;* that is to do with the collection and dissemination of information. McLeod (2003, p. 4) distinguishes research from learning in part because the former 'requires the symbolization and transmission of [newly acquired] understandings in the public domain'. McLeod chooses to define public dissemination as an essential element of research and he shares this certainty with many others. However, there are other ideas, broader definitions.

For instance, Heron (1996, pp. 48–49) describes *transformative* research, that is, research that results in changing systems and he explains how informative and transformative research are interdependent. Research can also be developmental – that is, to do with the personal growth of the inquirers (see Wilkins, 2000a, p. 20 and Mitchell-Williams et al., 2004, p. 332). Transformative research is often of the kind known as *action research* or *action inquiry* and may have 'political' aims or the aim of changing social situations. Developmental research occurs when the researchers are investigating aspects of their own experience and are changed by the investigation itself.

Reason and Hawkins (1988, pp. 79–80) also see research as of different types suggesting that there are 'two paths to inquiry'. These are *explanation* and *expression*. Explanatory research is based in one of two methods: observation and description or experimentation. The questions behind such research are usually *what, how* and *why?* Expressive research is to do with understanding the meaning of experience. In expressive research, the inquirer becomes deeply immersed in the experience to achieve an understanding of it. There is no attempt at detached analysis which is often the case in more traditional approaches to research. The idea of deeply understanding human experience from the inside is reflected in approaches to research such as heuristic inquiry and co-operative experiential inquiry (first described in a person-centred journal, see below). These and other alternative approaches to research were developed because old-style, positivistic, informative research did not provide adequate tools to answer the questions which seemed important to people wanting to explore and understand human experience and how human beings make sense of the world. They are based on the premise that if you want to know about human experience, the best thing to do is to ask a human being – and, in some approaches, that the human being each of us knows best is ourselves. Although person-centred attitudes may facilitate effective data collection in informative and explanatory research, person-centred research methodologies are more likely to lead in the direction of transformative, developmental and expressive approaches.

It is also true that for some inquirers there are philosophical (and perhaps ethical) dilemmas in doing research *on* people. This led to the development of a number of methods of inquiry that involve others as co-researchers, that is, that are about research *with* people. Often psychotherapeutic practice with people implies a set of attitudes and values rarely employed in traditional research. Many newer approaches are more directly concerned with these values.

Although these different approaches have come to prominence in recent times, there is nothing new in this (apparent) division in ways of knowing. In classical Greece, there were notions of *logos* and *mythos* as different, complementary and mutually dependent ways of knowing and arriving at 'truth'. Logos equates with the rational, pragmatic and 'scientific' way of thinking which came to dominate Western approaches to inquiry. As the word suggests, it is to do with logic. Mythos, on the other hand, is about meaning rather than practicalities. It is the way cultures, societies and individuals express insight, intuition and deep (but 'irrational'?) understanding. Myths are some of the stories which give form to this understanding. Arguably, shaping, telling and listening to stories can be research in its own right (see Wilkins, 2000b). Western science may be understood to have lost the necessary connection with mythos but newer methods of exploring human experience can be seen as attempts to redress this. To draw together logos and mythos once more is likely to enrich our understanding of human experience, the ways in which we construct meaning and the diversity and universality of our existence. Here again a person-centred approach to research with its emphasis on listening to the stories people have to tell about their experiences and collaborating with them to construct meaning is likely to be helpful.

PERSON-CENTRED APPROACHES TO RESEARCH

Person-centred attitudes and research as a whole

Person-centred attitudes have much to offer when conducting human inquiry of any kind. For example, because one of the main skills of the person-centred therapist is to listen to the stories told by the client in an accepting and empathic way such as to encourage, support or allow deeper exploration they underpin the good interviewing techniques which are the bedrock of most qualitative approaches to research. This is equally important when engaging with research informants. Also, in his exploration of 'authentic science', Hutterer (1990, p. 68) took the view that 'a person-centered philosophy of research should work on overcoming the separation between ... human sciences vs. natural sciences; phenomenological vs. empirical-experimental approach.' For him, a person-centred approach to research meant not getting stuck in any particular way of doing research but supporting 'the use of all human capacity for discovering knowledge'. Although this idea does not seem to have been developed by person-centred researchers in the interim, there has been recent interest in 'pluralistic research' (research combining quantitative and qualitative approaches) by, for example, Cooper and McLeod (2007), both of whom are influenced by the person-centred paradigm. In a way, this brings together logos and mythos – explanation of phenomena and the meaning human beings attribute to those phenomena. Certainly, a person-centred approach to research would mean applying person-centred attitudes much more widely than simply to interviewing technique, but these attitudes are rarely employed in traditional research.

The experienced need to incorporate person-centred values as a researcher

There is a deeply felt need on the part of some people committed to person-centred values to employ these as researchers. For example, Wolter-Gustafson (1990, pp. 221–222) writes: 'I needed a method that would involve my whole being, including intellect, intuition, feelings, and spirit. To honor and reclaim as strengths my emotions, sensitivity, and creativity was to claim my wholeness as a researcher.' She concludes that person-centred theory and practice offer strategies to enable this. Similarly, Ulph (1998, p. 27) states: 'As I unravel it I come to see that I do not want to tamper with other people's experience. I have a sense within me which is enhanced by my commitment to a person-centred way of being that I want to be entirely respectful to the data I have gathered.'

This desire to be 'respectful to the data' is seen by Wilkins and Mitchell-Williams (2002, p. 292) as being about accepting the stories of the research informants – ideally co-researchers – 'with empathic understanding and to represent them in a way which is free from artifice and the imposition of the views and values of the researcher.'

A collaborative approach fostered by the six conditions

Wilkins and Mitchell-Williams (2002, p. 291) take the view that a person-centred approach to research (by definition) values the subjective experience of the participants and depends for its effectiveness upon the communication of Rogers' (1957, p. 96) necessary and sufficient conditions. They go on to say that it involves a willingness of the initiator(s) of the research to share power with everybody else involved and to engage with them, the research question and findings as a whole and present person. That is, the research is not 'led' by any one individual but all are co-researchers. What Wilkins and Mitchell-Williams are getting at here is that, when operating from a person-centred perspective, there are philosophical (and perhaps ethical) dilemmas in doing research *on* people. A preferred stance is to do research *with* people. This is because not only is it human nature to investigate phenomena and to construct meaning but the nondirective stance and an axiomatic belief that expertise does not rest with any one individual means that research into the human condition *must* involve all concerned with the research as equals. Wilkins (2000c, p. 153) links this to the development and empowerment of all involved in the research offering the opinion that 'if the tasks of designing the research, accumulating knowledge and testing validity are shared then all may be empowered.' All this agrees with Rogers' concept of 'authentic science' of which Hutterer (1990, pp. 60–61) writes:

> To be engaged in authentic science means that investigators are involved as subjective human beings, committed to their values and intrinsically motivated to investigate a specific area of interest. Authentic science involves subjects as respected partners in the research process, incorporating their interests and interpretations as part of the investigatory process.

It is when people approach phenomena with an openness to their experience and with minimal reference to their previous knowledge, a willingness to consider anything seemingly relevant however insignificant it may appear to be and with trust in their total sensing (not only what they think about it but their instinct, intuition and emotional reaction as well), paying heed to their tacit knowledge as well as their explicit knowledge, that they are most likely to discover significant meaning. However, such a subjective approach to research immediately raises questions as to the validity and trustworthiness of its findings. These can be addressed from a person-centred perspective.

Issues of validity and trustworthiness

Hutterer (1990, p. 70) discusses the need for 'two distinct views of objectivity'. The first of these is traditionally associated with the stance of a positivistic researcher, while the second 'focuses on an increasingly closer contact with reality, never fully expressed in empirical data but approachable by passionate involvement.' Passion and involvement are necessary to the discovery of hidden and deeper structures of reality. Although Hutterer chose to view this as an alternative form of objectivity, to most people it probably seems subjective. In terms of empirical/experimental research, what is subjective can not be shown to be reliable or (perhaps) valid. However, what is relevant to the findings from qualitative research is their *trustworthiness* (see McLeod, 2003, pp. 93–94). McLeod (2001, p. 188) states that it is the plausibility and the trustworthiness of the researcher which speaks to the validity of findings stating 'if a piece of research is carried out with integrity, then there is almost certainly something of value in it, there is *some truth* [original emphasis] in it.' So what makes person-centred research trustworthy?

Mearns and McLeod (1984, p. 385) argue that it is person-centred behaviours and attitudes per se that minimize 'the chance of distortion and bias' on the part of the researcher. They link their argument to Rogers' assertion that the closer people come to being fully functioning, the more trustworthy they are as discoverers of truth and his declaration that free and nondefensive behaviour increases 'scientific' acuity and the ability to grasp patterns and gestalts (see Kirschenbaum & Henderson, 1990, p. 270). Wilkins and Mitchell-Williams (2002, p. 293) state that it is the necessary and sufficient conditions as they are provided and experienced by all the co-researchers that promote free and nondefensive behaviour so contributing to the trustworthiness of person-centred research. They point out that there are potential limitations to this linking of authenticity to self-acceptance, asserting, 'part of person-centred research therefore must be attention to the personal development of each co-researcher and to the process of the group as a whole, otherwise the [validity of the] research may be limited.' However, they see no need that, for it to be trustworthy, participants in person-centred research must be 'fully functioning'. They argue that 'what is important is that they freely enter into the research, that they are motivated (that is, it has purpose, relevance and meaning for all concerned) and they are encouraged and supported in it by person-centred attitudes' (2002, p. 293).

An approach not a particular method

Papers and chapters proposing a person-centred approach to research can be thought of as principally concerned with precisely that – an *approach* rather than a definitive method. For example, Mearns and McLeod (1984, p. 372) give five characteristics of a person-centred approach to research which 'when taken as a whole, define a distinctive and powerful perspective on the research act.' Similarly, Barrineau and Bozarth (1989, pp. 465–466) not only state that the necessary and sufficient conditions for constructive personality change are likely to be of benefit to qualitative researchers as a whole but (pp. 472–473) characterize person-centred research, per se, as requiring the researcher to hold particular attitudes, essentially the same as those required of a person-centred therapist.

Wilkins (2000c, pp. 160–161) drawing on person-centred theory, previous suggestions as to the nature of person-centred research, and his practical experience as a researcher, listed characteristics of person-centred research. In Wilkins and Mitchell-Williams (2002, pp. 294–295) this is refined in the light of further practical experience. In summary, they state that person-centred research is:

- *Phenomenological:* based in the subjective experience of all those involved. Intuition, emotional reactions and flights of fancy are to be listened to with as much respect and regard as 'rational' thought.

- *Empowering:* the subjects of the research are also co-researchers contributing equally to the discovery and construction of meaning. Because value is placed on the wealth of experience and views of all concerned and products of the research are co-constructed and co-owned, the experience of co-researchers is of empowerment.

- *Permissive and elective:* participation is by invitation and (except in the most extraordinary circumstances) anyone volunteering with understanding of the process and the commitment involved is likely to offer something of relevance.

- *Inclusive:* the views and experiences of all involved are included with co-researchers making deliberate efforts to lay aside their frames of reference when considering the contributions of others (see Mearns & McLeod, 1984, pp. 376–377). Also, co-researchers participate in the data processing, formulation of conclusions and the presentation of findings.

- *Involves empathy, unconditional positive regard and congruence:* this is axiomatic. When co-researchers experience themselves to be deeply understood and accepted by their authentic fellow co-researchers however naïve, wild or silly they may fear their ideas to be they are likely to be encouraged further in their explorations and so to offer more of the totality of their experience. This considerably enriches the 'data'.

- *A 'real world' approach:* it deals with actual situations, complex inter-relationships and commonplace reality. It attempts to achieve an understanding of individual and collective reality.

Wilkins and Mitchell-Williams (2002, pp. 295–296) go on to address the issue of power in person-centred research, making an argument for a collaborative approach as closest to person-centred principles and offering some evidence from a previous research project (see Wilkins et al., 1999) that co-researchers experience collaborative power as enhancing personal power (see Natiello, 1990, p. 272). Also collaborative effort (because it involves the statement of personal views which are then refined in the light of the views of others) results in the co-construction of meaning. Because it evolves from a consensus, this increases the trustworthiness of findings.

What person-centred approaches to research offer
Trustworthy qualitative research provides a deeper, more complex understanding of human experience than is usually achieved using quantitative methods. It therefore follows that a person-centred approach to research in which the emphasis is on listening to the stories the co-researchers have to tell about their experience and the collaborative construction of a meta-story telling the story of all the participants (and involving any additional information about the experience under investigation to which they may have referred) can provide an exceptionally rich account the human condition.

The philosophical position underpinning a person-centred approach to research suggests that *meaning* is socially constructed and that 'truth' is subjective and therefore variable depending upon your point of view. (Even some research physicists now take this line.) The purpose is to seek an understanding of the contexts of truths, to discover meaning, to explore experience and even to construct new meaning, new understanding and to effect social and/or political change. Person-centred research provides a way to contextualize the 'truth'. Only by understanding the context can we understand the viewpoint of the actors in the context which generated the view of truth and so come to some tentative explanation.

STRENGTHS AND LIMITATIONS
OF PERSON-CENTRED RESEARCH

Although person-centred attitudes may very well be appropriate to any research involving human beings (as subjects but also as researchers), the person-centred research paradigm is not one turned to when the desire is for 'evidence-based' demonstrations of efficacy and efficiency. It is most relevant where the aim is to achieve a deep, rich understanding of human experience – and specifically the experience of the participants. It offers a way of comprehending *personal* meaning and of transforming this to achieve a consensus understanding. It is most fitting when the basic questions are 'How?' or 'What' rather than 'Why'. However, policy makers and funders are primarily persuaded by research that provides quantifiable 'evidence' and so, if this is the objective, person-centred approaches to research may not be the answer. Even so, in conjunction with other approaches, they may add convincingly to the richness of information and provide policy makers with some insight into how consumers and stakeholders may receive changes and developments.

Person-centred research depends for its success upon the commitment of the participants to engage with each other in a process of *encounter*. It involves attention to the relationships between participants, group process and *personal* process as well as to the research process per se (hence the importance of the necessary and sufficient conditions). This is demanding of all those involved but, as Mearns and McLeod (1984, p. 384) point out, this personal commitment is likely to be reciprocated. An implication of this is that for those who find encounter difficult or threatening or who for some other reason foresee this level of personal commitment as unlikely, a person-centred approach to research may be unsuitable.

Because of its collaborative nature and the fact that both direction and method are steered by the co-researchers as a whole, it is doubtful that person-centred research is suitable when a definite endpoint is sought or if there is a specific question which must be answered. Even when there is a sole researcher, because person-centred research methods are exploratory and its focus is subject to continual redefinition and redirection, this applies. However, when the aim is to discover the meaning attributed to ways of being in the world then it offers the possibility of rich description and deep understanding. It will never lead to a generalized, objective understanding but it is singularly effective if the intention is to find out what people really think, feel and/or sense in any given situation. It also has a role to play when change is a potential objective whether this is developmental change (as, for example, illustrated by Mitchell-Williams et al., 2004, pp. 341–343) or transformation of the type which may be sought through participatory action research (see Wilkins, 2000a, pp. 18–20). Undoubtedly this list is not definitive, but given the inspiration, dedication and determination of the co-researchers it can be applied to the exploration, explanation and expression of human endeavour of all kinds.

A potential criticism of exploratory approaches to research as a whole (and therefore person-centred approaches) is that there is a risk that, using them, researchers find exactly what they set out to find. Certainly, unless appropriate measures are taken, this is a risk. However, it is also a risk with all other approaches to research. Also, a function of person-centred approaches to research is the emergence of tacit knowledge. In that sense it can be quite explicitly about what the researcher knows and person-centred approaches provide a way of surfacing that knowledge so that it can be reflected on. Thus, they offer a way of transforming (hidden) knowledge to understanding. However, besides the measures deliberately built in to them in order to guard against, for example, co-researcher collusion (for example, the devil's advocate role in co-operative experiential inquiry – see below), the greatest safeguard against the tendency of researchers to find what they want to find offered by person-centred research lies in its collaborative nature. Findings are consensus findings, pooled from the experiences and reflections of all involved.

PERSON-CENTRED RESEARCH METHODS

In the way it is being described here, person-centred research is a paradigmatic approach to research rather than a specific method. It is of the same order as, for example, approaches to research in which the emphasis is on narrative and of which there are many different operational kinds. In a way, any systematic inquiry employing person-centred attitudes and principles — the same or similar to those set out above — could be described as person-centred research. However, the idea of deeply understanding human experience from the inside in a person-centred way is reflected in specific newer approaches to research. Among the best known of these are heuristic and co-operative experiential inquiries, which came to the fore in the mid 1980s (although the former was developed in the 1960s by Clark Moustakas, an early collaborator of Rogers, see Moustakas, 1961, 1967). The descriptions of heuristic inquiry (Douglass & Moustakas, 1985) and co-operative experiential inquiry (Reason

& Heron, 1986 – in the now defunct *Person-Centered Review*) are contemporaneous with one of Rogers' (1985) last papers in which he addresses the need for 'a more human science of the person'. It was also about the same time that specific attempts to devise and describe person-centred approaches to research were made by Mearns and McLeod (1984) and (a little later) by Barrineau and Bozarth (1989). This reflects the zeitgeist the first well-known flowering of which was the volume on 'new paradigm' research edited by Reason and Rowan (1981). Because they are amongst the earliest examples of person-centred research models and because between them they epitomize the characteristics of person-centred approaches to research, each of these is described in more detail below.

There are other approaches to research which sit well with person-centred attitudes. These include phenomenological research, action research and participatory action research (see, for example, Reason, 1988; Reason, 1994a, 1994b; and Wilkins, 2000a), transpersonal research (see Braud & Anderson, 1998) and autoethnography (see Ellis, 2004; Ellis & Bochner, 2000) although the latter is derived from a sociological/anthropological paradigm rather than a psychology paradigm. These are considered more briefly.

Heuristic inquiry

> HEURISTIC *adj.* serving or leading to find out; encouraging desire to find out; (of method, argument) depending on assumptions based on past experience; consisting of guided trial and error. *n.* the art of discovery in logic; the method in education by which the pupil is set to find out things for himself; (in *pl.*) principles used in making decisions when all possibilities cannot be fully explored. (Chambers 20th Century Dictionary)

Heuristics is defined by Douglass and Moustakas (1985, p. 40) as 'passionate and personal involvement in problem solving, an effort to know the essence of some aspect of life through the internal pathways of the self.' This passionate desire to know something from the inside has been well received as a research method by person-centred thinkers. For example, Rogers (in Kirschenbaum & Henderson, 1990, p. 283) saw it thus:

> a heuristic search is characterized as a passionate, highly personal, self-searching commitment to inner truth. It has its own criteria and its own process. It is, in my judgment, a disciplined but intuitive search that explores, by every possible subjective means, the essence of personal experience, thus generating personal truth.

Others writing from a person-centred perspective have also viewed heuristic inquiry favourably. Barrineau and Bozarth (1989, pp. 468–472) compare heuristic inquiry and the person-centred approach. They (p. 468) take the view that the essential similarity between them 'is that the intention of each is to create an atmosphere of open inquiry.' Moreover (p. 469), they see each as promoting the actualizing tendency. The major difference between heuristic inquiry and person-centred therapy is, according to Barrineau and Bozarth (p. 469), that the former involves some sort of data processing and the derivation of meaning whereas the latter ends at the stage of data collection. For O'Hara (1986, pp. 172–184) too, heuristic inquiry and person-centred therapy are close in form and intent. Indeed, she argues that person-centred therapy *is* heuristic inquiry. Moustakas (1990, pp. 103–105) also makes explicit links between person-centred therapy and heuristic inquiry.

From a person-centred perspective, the best-known and most complete description of heuristic inquiry is as it is understood by Moustakas (1990). It is a way of discovering, learning and constructing knowledge through reflecting on experience. An heuristic research question has definite characteristics:

- It seeks to reveal more fully the essence or meaning of a phenomenon of human experience.
- It seeks to discover the qualitative aspects, rather than quantitative dimensions.
- It engages one's total self and evokes a personal and passionate involvement and active participation in the process.
- It does not seek to predict or to determine causal relationships.
- It is illuminated through careful descriptions, illustrations, metaphors, poetry, dialogue, and other creative renderings, rather than by measurements, ratings, or scores.

Moustakas (p. 37) characterizes it as an extremely demanding process because, not only does it involve continual questioning and checking to ensure that personal experience (and that of co-researchers) is fully analyzed and developed, but it also challenges thinking and creating. Moreover, it requires authentic self-dialogue, self-honesty and unwavering diligence in paying attention to and taking note of 'both obvious and subtle elements of meaning and essence inherent in human issues, problems, questions and concerns'. Deep immersion and personal reflection is one of the main characteristics of heuristic research and 'the research question and the methodology flow out of inner awareness, meaning and inspiration' (Moustakas, 1990, p. 11). However, heuristic inquiry is not presented as licence to follow whims and fancies in an unstructured and undisciplined way. It is underpinned by a set of concepts and processes and there are definite and defined phases to it.

226

As they are described by Moustakas (1990, pp. 15–27), the concepts on which heuristic inquiry is based are (briefly):

- *Identifying with the focus of inquiry:* This is the process of 'getting inside the question', to understand something from another perspective. In person-centred terms, perhaps this is moving into another frame of reference.

- *Self-dialogue:* Literally talking to your self – but with a purpose. This is the process of (p. 16) 'entering into a dialogue with the phenomenon allowing the phenomenon to speak directly to one's own experience, to be questioned by it.' Self-dialogue can take many forms. Sometimes it may be an internal debate – 'on the one hand, on the other hand', sometimes there may be a more deliberate evocation of a devil's advocate role or of a question and answer session. What is important is that self-dialogue involves a deep level of personal honesty and a willingness to confront personal experience as it is relevant to the question or problem which is the focus of the study.

- *Tacit knowing:* Tacit knowledge is the knowing we have about something from an understanding of the elements it comprises. Often, this contributes to a sense of knowing more than we think we can know. Douglass and Moustakas (1985, p. 49) describe tacit knowing as giving 'birth to the hunches and vague, formless insights that characterize heuristic discovery.'

- *Intuition:* Intuition is the bridge between 'the implicit knowledge inherent in the tacit and the explicit knowledge which is observable and describable' (Moustakas, 1990a, p. 23). It is the process by which we draw on knowledge we do not 'know' we have to reach conclusions without apparent intervening steps of logic and reason. It is through intuition (which, as a research tool, improves with practice) that people grasp patterns, see relationships and draw inferences – all of this is essential to good research.

- *Indwelling:* According to Moustakas (1990a, p. 24), indwelling is the 'process of turning inward to seek a deeper, more extended comprehension of the nature or meaning of a quality or theme of human experience.' It is conscious and deliberate but not necessarily logical. 'It follows clues wherever they appear; one dwells inside them and expands their meanings and associations until a fundamental insight is achieved.'

- *Focusing:* Moustakas (1990, p. 25) uses this term in a way similar to Gendlin. It is a way of clearing an inward space so that the thoughts and feelings essential to the inquiry can be more easily accessed and understood. It also allows the inquirer to identify qualities of an experience that have been out of consciousness because time has not been taken to pause long enough to examine experience in detail.

- *The internal frame of reference:* A person's frame of reference is the lens through which they see and experience the world. Inherent in heuristic research is the validity of the internal frame of reference of the person 'who has had, is having, or will have' the relevant experience (Moustakas, 1990, p. 26).

Moustakas (1990a, pp. 27–32) describes six phases of heuristic research drawing on these concepts:

- *Initial engagement:* The process by which a question of intense interest to the researcher and one to which they have a passionate commitment is encouraged into consciousness. Important to this phase are tacit knowing and intuition.

- *Immersion:* The process of becoming deeply involved with the issue or problem under investigation. It is about drawing it deeply into one's life so that it becomes entwined with all aspects of existence, waking and sleeping – even in dreaming. It is as the question is lived so the researcher grows in knowledge and understanding of it. Important processes are identifying with the focus of inquiry, self-dialogue, intuition and tacit knowing.

- *Incubation:* The process of withdrawing from the intense concentration of immersion, putting things on the backburner and allowing the internal processes of the mind, those below the threshold of awareness to take over. Important to this phase are tacit knowing and intuition.

- *Illumination:* This is the process of the breakthrough into consciousness of new insights into the research question – it is the sudden switching on of a light, the 'Ah Ha' experience. This occurs naturally when there is openness to tacit knowledge and intuition.

- *Explication:* In this context, explication is the process of fully examining all that has emerged into consciousness as the result of other processes and to reach an understanding of what it may all mean. Focusing and indwelling are particularly relevant.

- *Creative synthesis:* The last stage of heuristic research is to pull together all the discovered components and core themes into a form which exemplifies the experience which has been examined and makes the findings of the researcher clear to others. This is the creative synthesis. Usually a creative synthesis takes the form of a narrative, probably using material taken from, for example, interviews but it could be in any creative form. What is important is that it encapsulates, expresses and explains the researcher's findings.

Moustakas (1990a, pp. 32–37) argues that the rigorous way in which an heuristic researcher constantly re-addresses and reassesses the research question means heuristic research is intrinsically valid. In Moustakas (1990: 38-56) there is an accounts of how to design and carry out a piece of heuristic research.

What has heuristic inquiry been used to do?

Writing of applying the heuristic method to the exploration of psychotherapy, Moustakas (1990, pp. 105–106) offers the opinion that 'living inside a therapeutic relationship opens avenues of knowing that are not possible through formal or external operations'. He (p. 106) says that heuristic inquiry allows the therapist to gain better understanding of the essence of the experience of the other and cites the studies of van Dusen (1973) on hallucination as a good example. According to Moustakas, the meanings discovered by van Dusen through his internal process of encounter and dialogue with visions, sounds, images and symbols ultimately enabled him to help his patients find new ways of being.

Moustakas (1990, pp. 59–90) also exemplifies the stages of heuristic inquiry and (pp. 91–124) its applications including (pp. 91–99) his classic study of loneliness. Of this, he wrote:

> My studies awakened me to the creative power of loneliness, and the resources it offers in the process of searching and studying. I saw the value of being open to significant dimensions of experience in which comprehension and compassion mingle; intellect, emotion, and spirit are integrated; and intuition, spontaneity, and self-exploration are seen as components of unified experience. (p. 97)

This may sound more like personal development than research (but, arguably at least, development is a valid objective of research). However, harking back to McLeod's (2003, p. 4) criterion that one thing that distinguishes research from learning is publication, it is clear from what Moustakas (1990, pp. 97–98) writes about the reaction to his published account of his study of loneliness that others found value in his work and learnt from it.

As well as the work of Moustakas and his students, there is an increasing number of published pieces of research informed by heuristic inquiry. These include the series of papers by West (1996, 1997, 1998a, 1998b, 1998c, 2001) in which he explores the interface between therapy and spirituality (the first of which also details a co-operative experiential inquiry into the use of 'healing' in therapy), Etherington's (2000) book on the experience of adult males who were sexually abused as children and Atkins and Loewenthal's (2004) paper which is about the lived experience of psychotherapists who work with older people. There are also many dissertations produced by students on a variety of 'social science' programmes (undergraduate and postgraduate) for which this has been the research method of choice.

In my experience, heuristic inquiry is usually developmental and/or transformative for those involved in it. Co-researchers report a deeper understanding of their experience and that of others as a result of conducting an heuristic inquiry. This usually leads to increased choices and (personal) skills. This would be a valid and valuable achievement in its own right but Atkins (in Atkins & Loewenthal, 2004, p. 508) sums up the aspect of heuristic inquiry that can transform it from a personal process to a general one (and therefore renders it 'research') when she writes of her findings: 'While this is a very personal outcome, reflection of the meanings and insights presented here may be helpful to other practitioners.'

Co-operative experiential inquiry (aka co-operative inquiry or collaborative inquiry)

Reason and Heron (1986, p. 458) consider two ideas as fundamental to the development of co-operative experiential inquiry. First, people are self-determining, and second, that there are three kinds of knowledge. These are:

- *Experiential knowledge* which is 'gained through direct encounter with persons, places or things.'

- *Practical knowledge* which concerns 'how to do something – it is knowledge demonstrated in a skill or competence.'

- *Propositional knowledge* which is 'knowledge about something, and it is expressed in statements and theories.'

Heron (1992) adds to this the concept of *presentational knowledge*, which Reason (1994a, p. 42) says relates to the way we first order our tacit experiential knowledge into internal imagery and then symbolize our sense of meaning. This may be in words but movement, shape and colour and other express forms are equally valid. Presentational knowledge forms a bridge between experiential knowledge and propositional knowledge.

From these precepts, Reason and Heron (1986) developed a form of participative, person-centred inquiry with a distinctive methodology involving four phases of action and reflection. In brief, these phases are (after Heron, 1996, pp. 54–55; Reason, 1994a, pp. 42–44; Reason & Heron, 1986, pp. 459–461; Wilkins, 2000b, pp. 21–22):

1. An initial phase in which a group of co-researchers decide upon a focus of inquiry and formulate some basic propositions and agree procedures for carrying out the research. This stage is primarily concerned with propositional knowing but it can also draw on presentational knowledge. Wilkins (2000a, p. 23) describes a process from which this first statement of propositional

knowledge may 'bubble up' offering the idea that there is 'pre-propositional knowledge' from which an idea of what and how to research emerges (see also Wilkins & Mitchell-Williams, 2002, p. 297).

2. A second stage in which the group applies their ideas and procedures using a range of special inquiry skills. In informative inquiries, these include being fully present with an openness to imagination and intuition, leaving aside ingrained conceptual frameworks and being prepared to generate new and alternative ways of seeing and interacting with the world. In transformative inquiries, skills include critically appraising all elements of practice both separately and together, interrupting compulsive or conventional behaviours and being prepared to depart from the habitual form of action and incorporating alternative frameworks for action. All of this involves practical belief.

3. The third phase involves the group in total immersion in the activity and experience. This is fundamental to the whole process and may entail excitement, boredom, alienation and even forgetting they are engaged in an inquiry. The openness of the co-researchers to what is happening to and for them and their environment allows them to 'bracket off' their prior beliefs and preconceptions and to see their experience in a new way. This is the phase of experiential knowing and (particularly in the first cycle) experiential belief.

4. The fourth is a second phase of reflection and occurs after an appropriate period of engagement with the second and third stages. In it, the group return to their original propositions and hypotheses and consider them in the light of experience. Their ideas are then subject to modification, reformulation, rejection and so on. There is an interplay between propositional and presentational processes; these are now grounded in practice and experience. New hypotheses may be advanced and new strategies adopted. This constitutes a critical return to propositional knowing.

These four stages constitute one complete cycle of the co-operative inquiry process. Reason and Heron (1986, p. 461) emphasize that this cycle from reflection to action and back needs to be repeated several times so that ideas and discoveries can be clarified, refined, deepened and corrected. They say that it is this research cycling that supports the validity of the co-operative inquiry process. However, they (p. 466) also acknowledge that 'the method is open to all the ways in which human beings fool themselves and each other' and that this threatens the validity of their process. They propose a set of procedures to counteract this:

- *Development of discriminating awareness.* That is, the deliberate cultivation of a watchful and mindful state. This is particularly important in the experiential phase.

- *Research cycling, convergence and divergence.* Research cycling provides a set of corrective feedback loops. Convergent cycling allows for checking and rechecking with more and more attention to detail; divergent cycling is a way of affirming values of heterogeneity and the creativity that comes from taking many different viewpoints.

- *Authentic collaboration.* To ensure effective and real collaboration, deliberate steps must be taken to make sure that no individual or clique dominates the inquiry group which must be both challenging and supportive of all its members. All voices must be heard equally. This involves attention to group dynamics and group processes.

- *Falsification.* In any group, there is a danger of consensus collusion. The deliberate cultivation of a devil's advocate role is an effective countermeasure. The devil's advocate is a group member who temporarily takes on the role of radical critic and who challenges all the assumptions the group seems to make.

- *Management of unaware projections.* Unacknowledged distress and psychological defences may seriously distort inquiry. This must be dealt with systematically either by bringing it into awareness or allowing it creative expression. Any number of approaches to personal growth may be helpful in this context.

- *Balance of action and reflection.* Co-operative experiential inquiry is a combination of action and reflection. These must be appropriately balanced. It is not possible to prescribe an ideal proportionality because the right balance will depend upon the nature of the inquiry and of the co-researchers.

- *Chaos.* A descent into chaos will often facilitate the emergence of a new creative order. There is no guarantee that chaos will occur but the key issue is to be prepared for it, able to tolerate it and be welcoming of it.

All the above is expanded on in Heron (1996) in which (pp. 200–208) the 'arguments for co-operative inquiry' are presented.

What has co-operative experiential inquiry been used to do?

Reason (1988, pp. 102–220) describes a number of 'ventures in co-operative inquiry,' although several of these could easily be classified as participatory action inquiry, while Reason (1994b) includes an account of the practice of participatory research some of which are (or are informed by) co-operative experiential inquiry. These studies include

Traylen's (1994, pp. 59–81) co-operative inquiry with health visitors which led to greater insight into the problems faced by the health visitors, and helped them move towards a more open and constructive relationship with their clients, each other, other agencies and their managers. In other words, they became happier in and better at their jobs. More recent examples of the use of co-operative inquiry include:

- Hills' (2001) evaluation of student nurse practice which led to a reconceptualization of evaluation as an iterative process which allowed teachers access to students' thinking about their clinical experiences and the meaning they attributed to them.

- Douglas' (2002) use of co-operative inquiry with black women managers and how they moved from surviving to thriving.

- Tee's (2005) co-operative inquiry into the participation of mental health service users in clinical decisions made by mental health student nurses in which aspects of professional values and behaviour facilitated power-sharing and which militated against it. It also led to a model of use in evaluating aspects of participation within clinical practice.

Although it does not conform to the paradigm as it is explained here, the work of Morris (2007), Turner (2007) and Rolfe (2007), which is described as a 'collaborative inquiry between a person-centered therapist and a client', also throws light on the possibilities of person-centred research. Although Rolfe (p. 109) points out that the only truly collaborative element of this study was the writing-up process, he says that there is a strong argument that the writing up was the research. He states, 'this is the point at which the raw data of experience is transformed into understanding and at which the research endeavour truly becomes a project of shared learning and discovery between equals.' This fits at least some of the criteria for person-centred research set forth here.

Other person-centred approaches to research

The key characteristics of these two approaches (and person-centred research as a whole) are:

- The emphasis on *systematic* approach.
- The importance of respecting all co-researchers as equal partners in the research endeavour and the climate of congruence, unconditional positive regard and empathy underpinning this respect.
- An acceptance, indeed positive promotion, of the whole of the co-researchers' experience including intuition, creativity and imagination – even to the extent of listening to the wildest flights of fancy. In every sense, they are holistic.

- The valuing of the stories co-researchers have to tell about their experience howsoever these are told.

Of course, these two methods are not the only valid ways of doing person-centred research and others share many or all of the characteristics listed above. For example, Wilkins and Mitchell-Williams (2002, pp. 297–298) and Mitchell-Williams et al. (2004. pp. 331–332) describe an approach to research using co-operative experiential inquiry as a framework rather than a definitive method. Their approach also draws on heuristic inquiry and values 'storytelling' and conversation as a principle strategy for exploring human experience. An important part of their approach is that the focus of inquiry *and* the methods employed in the exploration of human experience arise from the interactions of the co-researchers. As an account of person-centred research in action, Wilkins and Mitchell-Williams (2002, pp. 296–300) describe and detail the experience of a 'human inquiry research group', the focus for which was 'life stages', concentrating more on what happened than what was found. This is taken further in Mitchell-Williams et al. (2004) where (pp. 334–336) some of the research activities undertaken are described and (pp. 341–344) the outcomes are discussed. One of the important elements of this account of person-centred research is that all participants contributed to its writing-up. This was also the case with Wilkins et al. (1999).

Other approaches compatible with person-centred research are listed below.

Action inquiry and action research
Action inquiry (or action research) is a form of research into practice often with a political or social dimension in that an aim is the facilitation of social change. It is concerned with the transformation of organizations and communities to bring about increased effectiveness and greater justice. It is really a way of balancing a problem-solving approach with the achievement of a deep understanding of the organization that is the focus of the study. Action inquiry is:

- *Practical:* it is based in real actions taken in real world situations.
- *Political:* it is intended to promote positive (even radical) social change.
- *Participative:* it is inclusive of the thoughts, impressions and intuitions of all those involved.
- *Collaborative:* its processes and results are co-owned by the whole research community.
- *Egalitarian:* the perspectives of all participants (including the lead researcher) are seen as of equal value.
- *Critical:* the programme of activity and research is carefully evaluated.

Whatever the focus of an action inquiry, there are three essential practical elements involved and required. These are:

- An understanding and continual re-evaluation of the question 'What are we trying to accomplish (in the organization as a whole and in any sub-units)?'
- The setting up of regular systems to test whether the organization's strategies and operations in fact match its vision and to test its effect on the environment (including workforce, users, etc.).
- The facilitation and promotion of the capacity of the participants for exercising 'action inquiry' as a continuous learning from experience.

Participatory action research

Like action inquiry, participatory action research (PAR) is fundamentally political in nature and it has been widely used with oppressed groups. A basic idea is that, in PAR, the researchers seek to establish a dialogue and rapport with the population with which they are working so that they can discover and address their practical, social and political needs. The two main aims of PAR are firstly, like action inquiry, to produce knowledge and action directly useful to the community, and secondly, to raise awareness and empower people through constructive use of their own knowledge. This 'insider knowledge' then becomes a means of transforming their situation for their own benefit. Because PAR is an ideology rather than a method, there is no one way of doing it – by definition it arises from and is shaped by the community doing it. Many methods can be used in any one project and are as likely to include indigenous forms of expression arising from the culture itself (group meetings, song, dance, poetry, drama) as well as or even instead of more conventional investigatory techniques. In this way, a lot more is required of the researcher than technical research skills. Amongst other things, a PAR researcher has to have:

- A commitment to the empowerment of others.
- A clarity of class, culture and gender analysis (and of anything else that may result in privilege, bias or disadvantage such as age and ability/disability).
- Good communication skills.
- An understanding of individual and group dynamics/behaviour.
- An ability and willingness to self-disclose and share personal feelings and experiences.

Transpersonal inquiry

Perhaps similarly to person-centred approaches to research, transpersonal inquiry is paradigmatic rather than a single method. It includes integral inquiry (see Braud, 1998), intuitive inquiry (see Anderson, 1998) and organic inquiry (see Clements, Ettling, Jennett, & Shields, 1998) all of which focus on transpersonal/spiritual dimensions of human experience could also fit within a person-centred research paradigm.

Autoethnography
This is a form of research in which the researcher is the subject – i.e., interviewer and interviewee are the same person – and where the aim is to connect the personal and the cultural. Autoethnography is usually written in the first person and may take a variety of creative/expressive forms. In autoethnographic texts, concrete action, dialogue, emotion, embodiment, spirituality and self-consciousness all have a place as 'relational and institutional stories affected by history, social structure, and culture, which themselves are dialectically revealed through action, feeling, thought and language' (Ellis & Bochner, 2000, p. 739). Ellis and Bochner (2000, pp. 739–743) name the many trends in or variants of autoethnography they recognize and consider the main types.

CONCLUSION

This review of the person-centred approach as a research strategy demonstrates that any approach to research which values personal experience and which is inherently respectful of the people involved may be constructed and run in a person-centred way. Furthermore, there are methods which are explicitly person-centred in intent and operation. These emphasize collaboration, holism, openness to the total experience of all concerned and they are permissive and elective. What is most important is that the research and the (co)researchers are supported by a deliberate fostering of the necessary and sufficient conditions. There is an inherent trustworthiness to such approaches and although they do not lead to 'evidence-based' conclusions that may influence policy and funding their inclusive nature makes them excellent tools when the objective is to change systems either from the inside or by accurately representing the voices of service users and or service deliverers to managers, funders and politicians. Also, they are excellent (if sometimes accidental) agents for developmental and transformative research. All that said, person-centred research is still an emerging method. Its structures and procedures need to be refined in use and its usefulness demonstrated by example.

REFERENCES

Anderson, R. (1998). Intuitive inquiry: A transpersonal approach. In W. Braud & R. Anderson (Eds.), *Transpersonal research methods for the social sciences* (pp. 69–94). Thousand Oaks, CA: Sage.

Atkins, D., & Loewenthal, D. (2004). The lived experience of psychotherapists working with older clients: An heuristic study. *British Journal of Guidance and Counselling, 32*(4), 493–509.

Barrineau, P., & Bozarth, J. D. (1989), A person-centred research model. *Person-Centered Review, 4*(4), 465–474.

Braud, W. (1998) Integral inquiry: Complementary ways of knowing, being and expression. In W. Braud & R. Anderson (Eds.), *Transpersonal research methods for the social sciences* (pp. 35–68). Thousand Oaks, CA: Sage.

Braud, W., & Anderson, R. (Eds.). (1998). *Transpersonal research methods for the social sciences.* Thousand Oaks, CA: Sage.

Clements, J., Ettling, D., Jennett, D., & Shields, L. (1998), Organic research: Feminine spirituality meets transpersonal research. In W. Braud & R. Anderson (Eds.), *Transpersonal research methods for the social sciences* (pp. 114–127). Thousand Oaks, CA: Sage.

Cooper, M., & McLeod, J. (2007), A pluralistic framework for counselling and psychotherapy: Implications for research. *Counselling and Psychotherapy Research, 7*(3), 135–143.

Douglas, C. (2002). Using co-operative inquiry with Black women managers: Exploring possibilities for moving from surviving to thriving. *Systematic Practice and Action Research. 15*(3), 249–262.

Douglass, B., & Moustakas, C. (1985). Heuristic inquiry: The internal search to know. *Journal of Humanistic Psychology, 25*(3), 39–55.

Ellis, C. (2004). *The ethnographic I: A methodological novel about autoethnography.* Walnut Creek, CA: Altamira.

Ellis, C., & Bochner, A. (2000). Autoethnography, personal narrative, reflexivity: Researcher as subject. In N. K. Denzin & Y. S. Lincoln (Eds.), *Handbook of qualitative research* (2nd ed., pp. 733–768). Thousand Oaks, CA: Sage.

Etherington, K. (2000). *Narrative approaches to working with adult male survivors of child sexual abuse: The client's, the counsellor's and the researcher's story.* London: Jessica Kingsley.

Heron, J. (1992). *Feeling and personhood: Psychology in another key.* London: Sage.

Heron, J. (1996). *Co-operative inquiry: Research into the human condition.* London: Sage.

Hills, M. D. (2001). Using co-operative inquiry to transform evaluation of nursing students' clinical practice. In P. Reason & H. Bradbury (Eds.), *Handbook of action research: Participative inquiry and practice* (pp. 340–347). London: Sage.

Hutterer, R. (1990). Authentic science: Some implications of Carl Rogers's reflections on science. *Person-Centered Review, 5*(1), 57–76.

Kirschenbaum, H. (2007). *The life and works of Carl Rogers.* Ross-on-Wye: PCCS Books.

Kirschenbaum, H., & Henderson, V. L. (1990). *The Carl Rogers reader.* London: Constable.

McLeod, J. (2001). *Qualitative research in counselling and psychotherapy.* London: Sage.

McLeod, J. (2003). *Doing counselling research* (2nd ed.). London: Sage.

Mearns, D., & McLeod, J. (1984), A person-centered approach to research. In R. F. Levant & J. M. Shlien (Eds.), *Client-centered therapy and the person-centered approach: New directions in theory, research and practice* (pp. 370–389). New York: Praeger.

Mitchell-Williams, Z., Wilkins, P., McClean, M., Nevin, W., Wastell, K., & Wheat, R. (2004).

The importance of the personal element in collaborative research. *Educational Action Research,* *12*(4), 329–346.

Morris, M. (2007). A collaborative inquiry between a person-centered therapist and a client: Working with an emerging dissociated 'self'. Part one: Adult Mary/Young Mary – one self, two parts. *Person-Centered and Experiential Psychotherapies, 6*(2), 81–91.

Moustakas, C. (1961). *Loneliness.* Englewood Cliffs, NJ: Prentice-Hall.

Moustakas, C. (1967). Heuristic research. In J. Bugenthal (Ed.), *Challenges of humanistic psychology* (pp. 100–107). New York: McGraw-Hill.

Moustakas, C. (1990). *Heuristic research: Design, methodology and applications* Newbury Park, CA: Sage.

Moustakas, C. (1994). *Phenomenological research methods.* Thousand Oaks, CA: Sage.

Natiello, P. (1990). The person-centered approach, collaborative power, and cultural transformation. *Person-Centered Review, 5*(3), 268–286.

O'Hara, M. (1986). Heuristic inquiry as psychotherapy. *Person-Centered Review, 1*(2), 172–184.

O'Hara, M. (1995). Carl Rogers: Scientist and mystic. *Journal of Humanistic Psychology, 35*(4), 40–53.

Reason, P. (Ed.). (1988). *Human inquiry in action: Developments in new paradigm research.* London: Sage.

Reason, P. (1994a). Three approaches to participative inquiry. In N. K. Denzin & Y. S. Lincoln (Eds.), *Handbook of qualitative research* (pp. 324–339). Thousand Oaks, CA: Sage.

Reason, P. (Ed.). (1994b). *Participation in human inquiry.* London: Sage.

Reason, P., & Hawkins, P. (1988). Storytelling as inquiry. In P. Reason (Ed.), *Human inquiry in action: Developments in new paradigm research* (pp. 79–101). London: Sage.

Reason, P., & Heron, J. (1986). Research with people: The paradigm of co-operative experiential inquiry. *Person-Centered Review, 1*(4), 456–476.

Reason, P., & Rowan, J. (Eds.). (1981). *Human inquiry: A sourcebook of new paradigm research.* Chichester: Wiley.

Rogers, C. R. (1957). The necessary and sufficient conditions of therapeutic change. *Journal of Consulting Psychology, 21,* 95–103.

Rogers, C. R. (1959). A theory of therapy, personality, and interpersonal relationships, as developed in the person-centered framework. In S. Koch (Ed.), *Psychology: A Study of a Science. Vol. 3: Formulations of the person and the social context* (pp. 184–256). New York: McGraw-Hill.

Rogers, C. R. (1961). *On becoming a person.* London: Constable.

Rogers, C. R. (1985). Toward a more human science of the person. *Journal of Humanistic Psychology, 25*(4), 7–24.

Rolfe, G. (2007). A collaborative inquiry between a person-centered therapist and a client: Working with an emerging dissociated 'self'. Part Three: Afterword: Therapy as research. *Person-Centered and Experiential Psychotherapies, 6*(2), 107–111.

Tee, S. R. (2005). *A co-operative inquiry: Participation of mental health service users in clinical practice decisions of mental health student nurses.* Unpublished doctoral dissertation, University of Southampton Faculty of Medicine, Health and Life Sciences. Retrieved May 25, 2010, from Eprints.soton.ac.uk/57948.

Traylen, H. (1994). Confronting hidden agendas: Co-operative inquiry with health visitors. In P. Reason (Ed.), *Participation in human inquiry,* (pp. 59–81). London: Sage.

Turner, R. (2007). A collaborative inquiry between a person-centered therapist and a client: Working with an emerging dissociated 'self'. Part Two: The therapist's perspective. *Person-Centered and Experiential Psychotherapies, 6*(2), 92–106.

Ulph, M. (1998). *Stolen lives: The effects of the development of self of men who have experienced sexual abuse in childhood.* Unpublished master's dissertation, University of East Anglia.

Van Dusen, W. (1973). The presence of spirits in madness. In J. Fademan & D. Kewman (Eds.), *Exploring madness: Experience, theory and research* (pp. 59–81). Monterey, CA: Brooks/Cole.

West, W. S. (1996). Using human inquiry groups in counselling research. *British Journal of Guidance and Counselling, 24,* 347–356.

West, W. S. (1997). Integrating psychotherapy and healing. *British Journal of Guidance and Counselling, 25,* 291–312.

West, W. S. (1998a). Passionate research: Heuristics and the use of self in counselling research. *Changes, 16,* 60–66.

West, W. S. (1998b). Critical subjectivity: Use of self in counselling research. *Counselling, 9,* 228–230.

West, W. S. (1998c). Developing practice in a context of religious faith: A study of psychotherapists who are Quakers. *British Journal of Guidance and Counselling, 26,* 365–375.

West, W. S. (2001). Beyond grounded theory: The use of a heuristic approach to qualitative research. *Counselling and Psychotherapy Research, 1,* 126–131.

Wilkins, P. (2000a). Collaborative approaches to research. In B. Humphries (Ed.), *Research in social care and social welfare: Issues and debates for practice* (pp. 16–30). London: Jessica Kingsley.

Wilkins, P. (2000b). Storytelling as research. In B. Humphries (Ed.), *Research in social care and social welfare: Issues and debates for practice* (pp. 144–143). London: Jessica Kingsley.

Wilkins, P. (2000c). On becoming a person-centered researcher. In J. Marques-Teixeira & S. Antunes (Eds.), *Client-centered and experiential psychotherapy* (pp. 151–166). Linda a Velha: Vale & Vale.

Wilkins, P., Ambrose, S., Bishop, A., Hall, R., Maugham, P., Pitcher, C., et al. (1999). Collaborative inquiry as a learning strategy in a university setting: Processes within an experiential group – the group's story. *Psychology Teaching Review, 8,* 4–18.

Wilkins, P., & Mitchell-Williams, Z. (2002), The theory and experience of person-centred research. In J. C. Watson, R. N. Goldman, & M. S. Warner (Eds.), *Client-centered and experiential psychotherapy in the 21st century: Advances in theory, research and practice* (pp. 291–302). Ross-on-Wye: PCCS Books.

Wolter-Gustafson, C. (1990). How person-centered theory informed my qualitative research on women's lived experience of wholeness. *Person-Centered Review, 5*(2), 221–232.

CHAPTER 10

KEY PRIORITIES FOR RESEARCH IN THE PERSON-CENTRED AND EXPERIENTIAL FIELD
'IF NOT NOW, WHEN?'

MICK COOPER, JEANNE C. WATSON,
& DAGMAR HÖLLDAMPF

The aim of this chapter is to draw together themes from previous chapters in this book and to indicate key priorities for future research in the person-centred and experiential (PCE) field. The chapter suggests that there is an urgent need to continue to demonstrate the efficacy of our approach by conducting high quality randomized controlled trials of PCE therapies with specific client groups, qualitative investigations of effectiveness using consumer groups and clients' perceptions and understandings, and to undertake quantitative and qualitative meta-analyses that can draw the findings together. Other areas that are highlighted as key priorities for research include developing process and outcome measures that are consistent with PCE theory and practice, using research to develop the PCE approach, developing PCE research methods, and adopting and developing case study approaches.

The chapters in this book have shown that there is a large and rigorous body of evidence in support of PCE practices, with a wealth of measures and tools that have been applied and can be used further to help develop this evidence base. Experimental and quasi-experimental designs indicate that PCE interventions are efficacious for adults (Elliott & Freire, Chapter 1), and children and adolescents (Hölldampf et al., Chapter 2) across a range of psychological difficulties; and also bring about significant improvements in the domains of education, parenting and management (Cornelius-White & Motschnig-Pitrik, Chapter 3). Qualitative evidence indicates that PCE therapies are associated with a range of positive changes, including smoother and healthier emotional experiencing, greater self-compassion, and improved interpersonal encounters (Timulak & Creaner, Chapter 4). Adding to the evidence base for PCE therapies, a large body of research indicates that clients are the principal agents of change in therapy (Bohart & Tallman, Chapter 5); and that many of the theoretical constructs proposed by PCE therapies including the quality of the therapeutic relationship and clients' experiencing, are associated with successful outcomes (Watson et al., Chapter 6). To help develop this evidence base, a range of tools have evolved from within the PCE community to assess self and organismic functioning (Watson & Watson, Chapter 7), and the quality of the therapeutic relationship (Freire & Grafanaki, Chapter 8); along with specifically PCE research methods (Wilkins, Chapter 9).

This body of work should be a cause for pride and optimism within the PCE community. And yet, as discussed in the Preface, the PCE approach is under severe threat in many parts of the world. So how can this be happening when, as we have seen, so much evidence is available? Is it that policy-making bodies are specifically prejudiced against PCE therapies, are seeking short-term and more cost-effective treatments, or actively ignore the evidence for PCE therapies in favour of other approaches like CBT? All these are possibilities, but a key limitation of the PCE evidence base is that, while there is a lot of it, it is often judged as not of the 'right' sort. For example, many guideline-making bodies, such as the UK's NICE, operate according to a 'hierarchy of evidence', whereby evidence from a range of randomized controlled trials (RCTs), *in relation to a specific 'disorder'*, are given the greatest weight – if not the only weight! Here, experimental trials for PCE therapies tend to fall down because:

1. Some of the studies are outdated, and may lack the degree of rigor that is required in contemporary guidelines, for example, adequate control conditions, use of symptom based measures (see Moher, Schulz, & Altman, 2001).

2. They are often not focused on a specific 'disorder,' but on a more general population.

3. PCE practice is often not clearly defined, or a range of different practices have been used that are hard to define collectively.

4. Therapies are conducted by inexperienced therapists.

5. The lack of follow-up data.

The question of how to respond to this situation creates a very real dilemma for the PCE community (see Elliott, 2002b). On the one hand, to go down the route of conducting ever more controlled, quantitative and nomothetic research may seem, to some, like a betrayal of the very principles of the PCE approach (see Wilkins, Chapter 9) especially our commitment not to pathologize people, or establish rigid ways of working that may not be attuned to each individual client. And even if there was a willingness to do so, many members of the PCE community do not have the experience that is required to conduct such studies, or to obtain the very limited funding that is available. On the other hand, however, if the PCE community is not willing to 'render unto Caesar' (Elliott, 2002b) and to try and provide the kind of evidence that is being asked for, will there be any PCE community left in a few years time? Does not the pragmatic need to ensure the survival of the approach, or the ethical directive to continue to provide clients with non-CBT alternatives, outweigh any desires for epistemological purism?

In the face of this dilemma, one strategy may be to try and convince policy makers to abandon, or revise, their hierarchies of evidence, and to adopt a more inclusive stance towards different types of research – as organizations like the UK's Mental Health Providers Forum (www.mhpf.org.uk) are attempting to do. There may even be a hope that this increased inclusivity will be a natural trend, as policy makers come to see the limitations of RCT-dominated guidelines. And, indeed, there are some glimmers of hope here. In his oft-cited Harveian oration, for instance, Professor Michael Rawlins (2008, p. 2159), Chairman of the UK's National Institute for Health and Clinical Excellence (NICE), stated that 'Hierarchies of evidence should be replaced by accepting – indeed embracing – a diversity of approaches.' Similarly, in the US in 2006, the American Psychological Association developed a broad and inclusive definition of 'evidence-based psychological practice': 'the integration of the best available research *with clinical expertise in the context of patient characteristics, culture, and preferences*' (APA, 2006, p. 273, italics added). However, on the ground, there are few signs that policy-making bodies are moving, or being convinced to move, towards more inclusive perspectives. Indeed, in developments such as the newly revised Scottish Intercollegiate Guidelines Network (SIGN) national guidelines on the non-pharmaceutical management of depression in adults (2010), there is evidence that they are moving in the other direction: with increasingly narrow requirements for inclusion of data. 'Carry on regardless and hope', then, may prove a very high risk strategy.

Indeed, what makes this strategy even higher risk is the fact that, at some point, it may become *too late* to re-establish PCE therapies as efficacious and valid interventions. This is for a number of reasons. First, if there are no longer many therapists 'in the field' delivering PCE interventions, it may become increasingly difficult to find sites where there are enough people practising in a PCE way to adequately test the approach, and supervise people training in the approach. Second, once other therapies, such as CBT, are established as *the* efficacious treatment for a 'disorder', it becomes increasingly difficult to obtain funding for alternative approaches. This is because funders will say, 'Why do we need to test the effectiveness of this therapy when we already have an intervention that we know works for this disorder.' Third, even if funding is obtained, the 'new' therapy now needs to prove, not just that it is better than no intervention, but that it is *as* effective as – or more effective than – the established intervention; and this requires a more extensive and costly research design that offers two bona fide treatments. Funding and ethical bodies will also require this more complex 'equivalence' design because, once another treatment has been shown to be effective with the disorder, it will no longer be considered ethical to offer a no-intervention control. Fourth, as it becomes ever more difficult to practise and research PCE therapies, students and future practitioners will be dissuaded from developing these skills, viewing them as impediments to their career and job prospects. Thus slowly over time our voice may be silenced and eradicated.

RANDOMIZED CONTROLLED TRIALS

Against this background, and despite reservations amongst many members of the PCE community (see Bohart & Tallman, Chapter 5), we think that a key priority for research in the PCE field – both psychotherapeutic and non-psychotherapeutic – must be to conduct randomized controlled trials of a type that have the potential to impact upon policy makers (see, for example, Watson et al., 2003 or King et al., 2000). Such trials will need to:

- Focus on a specific group of clients, such as clients meeting criteria for generalized anxiety disorder or major depression;
- Be conducted and written up according to standardized recommendations for high quality trials (see Moher, et al., 2001);
- Use a standardized PCE intervention.

Although RCTs require a focus on specific populations, this does not, necessarily, entail a sole focus on DSM or ICD clinical classification. For instance, it could be possible to focus on couples experiencing relational difficulties, or young people seeing a counsellor within a school setting. The key issue here is that the client groups are clearly specified and, ideally, are populations for whom policy-making bodies are interested in identifying and developing effective treatments. Indeed, given the problems of demonstrating that a treatment is more effective than one that has already been endorsed as such as discussed above, it may be useful for PCE researchers to specifically focus on client groups for which no therapy has yet been found to be efficacious, for example, students in higher education. However this should not be seen as a substitute for demonstrating effectiveness with clients who may be seen to be suffering from conditions identified according to the criteria specified by the DSM or ICD manuals, as this is essential if our work is to be credible with policy makers.

Without doubt, prioritizing RCTs raises numerous challenges for the PCE community. Aside from the epistemological issues, there is also the question of whether PCE researchers will want, or have the resources and skills, to conduct such studies. Randomized controlled trials are notoriously complex to design and run, and generally require extensive funding, as well as a large research team to undertake all the tasks. However, as with all research methods, an initially steep learning curve is generally followed by a period of competence and then mastery. What this means is that, perhaps, the focus should be less on attempting one-off RCTs, and more on building up the skills and expertise in this method across the PCE community. What may be required are people who are experienced and familiar with this method, and able to support others in developing such trials.

META-ANALYSIS

To fully impact on policy, findings from RCTs should, ideally, be brought together in a systematic, rigorous and accessible way. Hence, there is a continuing need for high-quality meta-analyses of the efficacy of PCE therapies – as well as non-psychotherapeutic interventions – developing and refining the work of Elliott and colleagues (2002a, 2004, 2007; see Chapter 1, this volume) and other members of the PCE community (for an excellent example of a PCE-informed meta-analysis, see Bratton, Ray, Rhine, & Jones, 2005). Here, as with RCTs, what will be particularly important is to focus on the efficacy of PCE therapies with specific groups of clients, such as young people who meet criteria for major depression, or clients with phobias. Even though RCTs of PCE therapies with such groups of clients may be sparse, a meta-analysis can give a more definitive account of what has previously been conducted, lay the groundwork for subsequent studies and, perhaps most importantly, identify areas where further research is required.

A very recent development of meta-analytic methodology, which may also have the potential to impact policy, is Timulak's (2007, this volume, Chapter 4) qualitative meta-analytic approach. This method of analysis may be of particular interest to PCE researchers as it creates a valuable bridge between qualitative research methods that are more consistent with the epistemological assumptions of PCE researchers and clinicians, and more rigorous, systematic methods of analysis. It also provides a very useful means by which findings from individual qualitative studies could be brought together into a more coherent and influential whole. Timulak and Creaner (Chapter 4) use this method to ask the question, 'What are the outcomes of PCE therapies?' but there are many other valuable questions that such a method could be used to ask: such as 'Is PCE therapy helpful?' and 'What are the helpful elements of PCE therapies?'

PROCESS RESEARCH

While both randomized clinical trials and meta-analyses are important for policy makers in terms of demonstrating the effectiveness of psychotherapeutic approaches, another important way of highlighting what works in therapy is with process-outcome research. Rogers and his colleagues were the first to examine client and therapist processes in an attempt to really understand what was going on. To this end Rogers and his colleagues at the University of Chicago listened to audio-taped therapy sessions to try to understand what clients and therapists did during the therapy hour. This led to the development of Rogers' process (1961) conception of therapy in which he identified the different stages that clients go through as they change their personalities.

He described this model as phenomenological to the extent that it remained within the client's frame of reference but based on expressive behaviour that was observable to another. This work was closely tied with that of Eugene Gendlin, a philosopher at the University of Chicago with whom Rogers collaborated. Gendlin was developing a new theory of epistemology that highlighted the felt sense and which he perceived Rogers' work as facilitating. The Experiencing Scale (Klein, Mathieu, Gendlin, & Kiesler, 1969) emerged from this collaboration and intensive study of psychotherapeutic process. During this time a number of other measures were developed to study clients' in-session behaviour, including clients' and therapists' vocal quality, and the quality of therapists' and clients' language.

This intensive study of psychotherapeutic process has continued, particularly within the experiential wing of the PCE approach as reviewed by Watson, Greenberg and Lietaer (Chapter 6). This type of research is necessary and useful, especially if we are to demonstrate that specific client processes as opposed to techniques are integral to change in psychotherapy. As we move forward there is an urgent need for additional process-outcome studies both in the context of large randomized clinical trials as well as case studies (Watson, Goldman, & Greenberg, 2007). In fact, process research in the context of single case studies can be a less expensive and laborious way for researchers and clinicians to begin to build data sets that can demonstrate the efficacy of PCE approaches, thereby building on the pioneering work of Rogers and his colleagues. Process-outcome studies will help us isolate what is specific and special about PCE approaches, differentiating them from other psychotherapeutic practices, and they will provide information about what specific in-session behaviours are effective and helpful to clients.

The other area that requires more focused attention and research is the impact of the therapeutic relationship, as well as the specific behaviours that communicate the relationship conditions as specified by Rogers (1957). It is clear from a review of the research studies that more rigorous testing of Rogers' relationship conditions is required in order for it to remain focal as the most important aspect of treatment, and not be overshadowed by techniques and alternative practices like expressive writing paradigms, pharmaceutical interventions, or more mechanistic-type interactions. In addition to further testing it is also necessary to ask more nuanced questions about the role of the therapeutic relationship and begin to identify and research moderating variables that impact the relationship (for example, client factors), and influence outcome. As noted in the chapter by Freire and Grafanaki (Chapter 8), more attention needs to be paid to how we measure the relationship. There are a number of new measures that have recently been developed or that are under construction that have the potential to push this initiative forward.

MEASURE DEVELOPMENT

As discussed above, to demonstrate – and adequately assess – the efficacy of PCE therapies, it is very important to develop and validate measures that can identify the kinds of changes that PCE therapies would be hypothesized to bring about. At present, for instance, many trials of PCE approaches use outcome measures that are designed by, and aligned with, other therapeutic approaches – such as the Beck Depression Inventory (e.g., King et al., 2000), which has a particular orientation towards clients' reported symptoms of depression. While PCE therapies have been found to be effective in reducing these symptoms, this data does not help to identify and isolate the impact of the specific constructs of PCE theory, like improved congruence, better organismic functioning, and the essential role of the therapeutic relationship in promoting change. To remedy this, in Chapter 7 Watson and Watson identified a number of measures that have been developed to test particular theoretical constructs of PCE theory. It is likely that if PCE researchers considered using them in trials and other studies, a more coherent body of evidence in support of PCE practices could be developed. There are many other aspects of PCE theory for which measures could be developed: for instance, positive self-regard (Rogers, 1957). Here, findings from studies such as Timulak and Creaner's meta-analysis (Chapter 4) may be useful in identifying appropriate outcomes to assess, such as 'Feeling empowered,' 'Appreciating vulnerability,' and 'Healthier emotional experiencing'.

USING RESEARCH TO DEVELOP PRACTICE AND THEORY

While there is an urgent need for research evidence to preserve and promote PCE approaches, it is important to recognize that research can also play a crucial role in helping PCE therapists develop and improve their practice. This was very much the ethos that guided Rogers in his early work (see Wilkins, Chapter 9) but, to a great extent, has been lost in the PCE field, aside from small pockets such as PE-EFT (e.g., Greenberg, 1979, 1980; Greenberg & Malcolm, 2002). Perhaps, as Rogers himself would surely have lamented, hypotheses such as the 1957 conditions for therapeutic personality change have become reified as 'facts' (Rogers, 1957), such that many members of the PCE community no longer feel that these are necessary to question or explore. Yet if we take Rogers' (1961) vision of the fully functioning person as our guide, with its emphasis on openness to experience and a lack of fixidity and rigidity of beliefs, then every element of PCE thinking and practice would be open to critical questioning and development. For instance, we might ask:

- What aspects of PCE therapies do clients find most helpful?
- What aspects of PCE therapies do clients find least helpful?
- What would PCE clients like more/less of?
- Which kinds of clients do best/worse in PCE therapies?
- How do clients make PCE therapies work for them? (see Bohart & Tallman, Chapter 5)

Researching such questions can help PCE therapists to improve and develop their practice, and while they can be addressed through quantitative designs, they are also eminently answerable through the kinds of qualitative and person-centred methods discussed by Wilkins (Chapter 9).

Alongside developing practice through research, there is also an urgent need to conduct research that can help to develop PCE theories of personality and development. Many of the most basic concepts, such as conditions of worth or the development of self-incongruent experiences (Rogers, 1959), were developed over half a century ago, and remain relatively untested. No wonder, then, that they are afforded little weight by those outside of the PCE field. Given, however, that there are so few contemporary psychologists who are likely to explore these person-centred hypotheses, it may be more useful for members of the PCE community to look towards contemporary non-PCE personality and developmental research, and look at how it can be integrated into, and used to inform, PCE thinking and practice. Much of the work on the psychological and social correlates of well-being, for instance, might fall into that category (e.g., Kahneman, Diener, & Schwarz, 1999), or positive change following trauma and adversity (Linley & Joseph, 2004). Contemporary social psychological theories such as self-determination theory (Ryan & Deci, 2000) and self-concordance theory (Sheldon & Elliot, 1999) also provide a wealth of support for person-centred and experiential understandings of human being.

DEVELOPING PERSON-CENTRED RESEARCH METHODS

As suggested above, in developing person-centred practice and theory, person-centred research methods (Wilkins, Chapter 9) may have a particularly important role. While qualitative, small-scale studies may not be capable of proving the efficacy of PCE therapies to policy-making bodies, they may be very useful in helping researchers and practitioners to think about how their own work – or that of the PCE community – could be improved. For instance, Etherington's work on men sexually abused as children (see Wilkins, Chapter 9) may be very useful for therapists working with this client group, helping them to understand some of the difficulties and tensions that such clients are likely to face.

As well as using these approaches, PCE researchers might consider how other elements of PCE theory and practice might be translated into research methods. For instance, is it possible to think of ways of incorporating some of the research methods that have been used by emotion-focused research-clinicians to study specific processes in PCE therapies, or to focus on the establishment of relational depth between researcher and researchee (Mearns & Cooper, 2005)? Not only would the development of such methods help the PCE community, but also have the potential to make a valuable contribution to researchers outside of the PCE field.

CASE STUDIES

In this regard, one research method that may be particularly valuable to adapt and develop is that of case studies. Members of the PCE community, such as Art Bohart and Robert Elliott have been at the forefront of developments in this approach, and it has the capacity to provide rigorous evidence to support, and develop, PCE therapies, while also being based on idiographic, qualitative data. Case studies can be used to test theory by replicating data across a number of different clients. In this way therapists and researchers can build up a bank of data that they can then use to support the effectiveness of their work, as well as use to provide more in-depth knowledge and understanding of the specific processes of PCE psychotherapy. A forthcoming book by John McLeod (2010), reviewing different approaches to case studies, should prove a valuable resource in helping researchers to develop work in this way.

DISCUSSION

In considering key priorities for research in the PCE field, it would seem important to avoid an 'either/or' position and attempt to hold a 'both/and' stance. Person-centred and experiential research methods hold enormous promise, and we would encourage researchers to look towards ways of developing them; and we would also encourage members of the PCE community to continue to critique the 'hierarchy of evidence' that so devalues more qualitative, humanistic, practice-based data (for excellent critiques, see Slife, 2004; Westen, Novotny, & Thompson-Brenner, 2004). Yet, in the current historical context, it would also seem essential to be pragmatic, and to try and provide the kind of high-quality, RCT evidence that may be most likely to ensure the survival of the PCE approach.

Whose responsibility is this? Although university-based academics may be best placed to develop large randomized clinical trials, the reality is that there are too few of them to generate the amount of data that is required. This means that the kind of research priorities identified in this chapter are the responsibility of everyone who wishes to see PCE approaches remain alive and thrive: researcher and practitioner, student and academic, therapist and client. In the words of the Talmud: 'If I am not for myself, who will be for me? And when I am only for myself, what am "I"? And if not now, when?'

WHAT YOU CAN DO

Academics/researchers/research (MA/MSc/PhD) students

- In choosing a subject to research, always consider the likely policy impact – ask yourself, 'Is this going to contribute to the survival/development of the PCE approach?'
- Design, and apply for funding for, a pilot randomized controlled trial of PCE therapies with a particular client group.
- Conduct a meta-analysis of PCE therapies with a particular client group.
- Develop a study which can help to validate a PCE outcome measure.
- Develop an outcome or process measure that assesses a particular aspect of PCE theory or practice.
- Consider how you can use research to help you develop PCE practices.
- Publish a case study of PCE practice.
- Engage in process research.
- Develop rigorous and systematic critiques of positivistic research methods.

Practitioners and non-research students

- Familiarize yourself with the research findings for PCE and other therapies, as well as the critiques of 'evidence-based' assumptions (see, for instance, Cooper, 2008).
- Consider enrolling for a research (MA/MSc/PhD) programme.
- Contact PCE-oriented researchers/academics to see how you can collaborate on research.
- Evaluate your work using outcome measures (such as CORE-OM) at pre- and post-counselling or process measures like the Experiencing Scale.
- Consider writing a case study.

REFERENCES

American Psychological Association. (2006). Evidence-based practice in psychology. *American Psychologist, 61*(4), 271–285.

Bratton, S. C., Ray, D. C., Rhine, T., & Jones, L. (2005). The efficacy of play therapy with children: A meta-analytic review of treatment outcomes. *Professional Psychology-Research and Practice, 36*(4), 376–390.

Cooper, M. (2008). *Essential research findings in counselling and psychotherapy: The facts are friendly.* London: Sage.

Elliott, R. (2002a). The effectiveness of humanistic therapies: A meta-analysis. In D. J. Cain & J. Seeman (Eds.), *Humanistic psychotherapies: Handbook of research and practice* (pp. 57–81). Washington, DC: American Psychological Association.

Elliott, R. (2002b). Render unto Caesar: Quantitative and qualitative knowing in research on humanistic therapies. *Person-Centered and Experiential Psychotherapies, 1*(1&2), 102–117.

Elliott, R. (2007). Person-centred approaches to research. In M. Cooper, P. F. Schmid, M. O'Hara, & G. Wyatt (Eds.), *The handbook of person-centred psychotherapy and counselling* (pp. 327–340). Basingstoke: Palgrave.

Elliott, R., Greenberg, L. S., & Lietaer, G. (2004). Research on experiential therapies. In M. J. Lambert (Ed.), *Bergin and Garfield's handbook of psychotherapy and behavior change* (5th ed., pp. 493–539). Chicago: Wiley.

Greenberg, L. S. (1979). Resolving splits: Use of the two-chair technique. *Psychotherapy: Theory, Research, Practice, Training, 16*(3), 316–324.

Greenberg, L. S. (1980). The intensive analysis of recurring events from the practice of gestalt therapy. *Psychotherapy: Theory, Research and Practice, 17*(2), 143–152.

Greenberg, L. S., & Malcolm, W. (2002). Resolving unfinished business: Relating process to outcome. *Journal of Consulting and Clinical Psychology, 70*(2), 406–416.

Kahneman, D., Diener, E., & Schwarz, N. (Eds.). (1999). *Well-being: The foundations of hedonic psychology.* New York: Russell Sage Foundation.

King, M., Sibbald, B., Ward, E., Bower, P., Lloyd, M., Gabbay, M., et al. (2000). Randomised controlled trial of non-directive counselling, cognitive-behaviour therapy and usual general practitioner care in the management of depression as well as mixed anxiety and depression in primary care. *Health Technology Assessment, 4*(19).

Klein, M. H., Mathieu, P. L., Gendlin, E. T., & Kiesler, D. J. (1969). *The experiencing scale: A research and training manual.* Madison, WI: Wisconsin Psychiatric Institute.

Linley, P. A., & Joseph, S. (2004). Positive change following trauma and adversity: A review. *Journal of Traumatic Stress, 17*(1), 11–21.

McLeod, J. (2010). *Case study research in counselling and psychotherapy.* London: Sage.

Mearns, D., & Cooper, M. (2005). *Working at relational depth in counselling and psychotherapy.* London: Sage.

Moher, D., Schulz, K. F., & Altman, D. G. (2001). The CONSORT statement: Revised recommendations for improving the quality of reports of parallel-group randomised trials. *The Lancet, 357*, 1191–1194.

National Institute for Health and Clinical Excellence. (2009). *Depression: The treatment and management of depression in adults (update).* London: Author.

Rawlins, M. (2008). De testimonio: On the evidence for decisions about the use of therapeutic interventions. *The Lancet, 372*(9656), 2152–2161.

Rogers, C. R. (1957). The necessary and sufficient conditions of therapeutic personality change. *Journal of Consulting Psychology, 21*(2), 95–103.

Rogers, C. R. (1959). A theory of therapy, personality and interpersonal relationships as developed in the client-centered framework. In S. Koch (Ed.), *Psychology: A study of science. Vol. 3 Formulations of the person and the social context* (pp. 184–256). New York: McGraw-Hill.

Rogers, C. R. (1961). *On becoming a person: A therapist's view of therapy*. London: Constable.

Ryan, R. M., & Deci, E. L. (2000). Self-determination theory and the facilitation of intrinsic motivation, social development, and well-being. *American Psychologist, 55*(1), 68–78.

Scottish Intercollegiate Guidelines Network. (2010). *Non-pharmaceutical management of depression in adults: A national clinical guideline*. Edinburgh: Scottish Intercollegiate Guidelines Network.

Sheldon, K. M., & Elliot, A. J. (1999). Goal striving, need satisfaction, and longitudinal well-being: The self-concordance model. *Journal of Personality and Social Psychology, 76*(3), 482–497.

Slife, B. D. (2004). Theoretical challenges to therapy practice and research: The constraints of naturalism. In M. J. Lambert (Ed.), *Bergin and Garfield's handbook of psychotherapy and behavior change* (5th ed., pp. 44–83). Chicago: Wiley.

Timulak, L. (2007). Identifying core categories of client-identified impact of helpful events in psychotherapy: A qualitative meta-analysis. *Psychotherapy Research, 17*(3), 310–320.

Watson, J. C., Gordon, L. B., Stermac, L., Kalogerakos, F., & Steckley, P. (2003). Comparing the effectiveness of process-experiential with cognitive-behavioral psychotherapy in the treatment of depression. *Journal of Consulting and Clinical Psychology, 71*(4), 773–781.

Watson, J. C., Goldman, R. N., & Greenberg, L. S. (2007). *Case studies in the experiential treatment of depression: A comparison of good and bad outcome*. Washington, DC: American Psychological Association.

Westen, D., Novotny, C. A., & Thompson-Brenner, H. (2004). The empirical status of empirically supported psychotherapies: Assumptions, findings, and reporting in controlled clinical trials. *Psychological Bulletin, 130*(4), 631–663.

CONTRIBUTORS

EDITORS

Mick Cooper is a Professor of Counselling at the University of Strathclyde, a Chartered Counselling Psychologist and co-editor of *Person-Centered and Experiential Psychotherapies*. Mick is author of *Essential Research Findings in Counselling and Psychotherapy: The Facts are Friendly* (Sage, 2008), and has been closely involved in research on counselling in schools in the UK. Mick is author, co-author and co-editor of numerous texts on person-centred, existential and pluralistic approaches to therapy, including *The Handbook of Person-Centred Psychotherapy and Counselling* (Palgrave, 2007), *Existential Therapies* (Sage, 2003) and *Working at Relational Depth in Counselling and Psychotherapy* (Sage, 2005, with Dave Mearns). Mick lives in Glasgow with his partner and four children.

Jeanne C. Watson is a professor at OISE / University of Toronto, Canada where she teaches and researches PCE psychotherapy approaches to counselling. She has co-authored and edited six books on counselling, including *Learning Emotion Focused Therapy: The process experiential approach to change* (2003); *Expressing Emotion: Myths, Realities and Therapeutic Strategies* (1999); *Client-Centered and Experiential Psychotherapy in the 21st Century: Advances in Theory, Research and Practice* (2002); *Handbook of Experiential Psychotherapy* (1998); *Process-Experiential Psychotherapy in the Treatment of Depression* (2005); and *Case Studies in Emotion Focused Treatment of Depression* (2007), as well as more than 40 articles and chapters.

Dagmar Hölldampf is a researcher at the University of Education Schwäbisch Gmünd, Germany. Her main research topic is the effectiveness of person-centred work with children and adolescents. As a lecturer she is involved in teacher, kindergarten teacher, and person-centred play therapy training at the same university. As a play therapist she works with traumatized children, young people, and their families in a Counselling Centre against Sexual Violence on Children and Adolescents in Stuttgart, Germany.

AUTHORS

Michael Behr is Professor of Educational Psychology at the University of Education Schwaebisch Gmuend, Germany. His research topics are person-centred counselling, child and adolescent psychotherapy, young people's emotions and parent–school relationship. He has authored and edited several books about school development and person-centred work in education. He is the director of the person-centred play therapy training course at the University of Education in Schwäbisch Gmünd and at the Stuttgart Institute for Person-Centred Therapy and Counselling, which he co-founded and where he works as a therapist, supervisor and facilitator.

Arthur C. Bohart is currently affiliated with Saybrook University in San Francisco, California. He is also Professor Emeritus from California State University Dominguez Hills. He is a fellow of the American Psychological Association. His major work has been on the client as active self-healer, empathy, and experiencing in psychotherapy. He is the co-author of *How Clients Make Therapy Work: The Process of Active Self-Healing* (1999) and co-editor of *Empathy Reconsidered: New Directions in Psychotherapy* (1997).

Jeffrey H. D. Cornelius-White is Associate Professor of Counseling at Missouri State University and Adjunct Assistant Professor of Educational Leadership and Policy Analysis at the University of Missouri. He trained at the Chicago Counseling Center and Pre-Therapy Institute beginning in 1995. Jef has been editor of *The Person-Centered Journal* since 2005. He served as chair of the board of WAPCEPC from 2008–2010. He is the co-editor (with Michael Behr) of *Facilitating Young People's Development* (PCCS, 2008) and author (with Adam Harbaugh) *Learner-Centered Instruction* (Sage, 2010).

Ina Crawford teaches at the University of Education Schwäbisch Gmünd. While she was doing her Master's degree in Educational Sciences she worked in several research projects relating to person-centred play therapy and filial therapy. At present her main research interest focuses on test anxiety.

Mary Creaner commenced her career in education, and subsequently qualified as a psychotherapist and clinical supervisor. She has undertaken various trainings in the person-centred approach and her theoretical orientation is greatly influenced by this tradition, both as a therapist and supervisor, and also as an educator and researcher. She has led person-centred groups and has been involved in person-centred counselling training. Mary is a lecturer and research co-ordinator with the Doctorate in Counselling Psychology and Course Director for the M.Sc./P.Grad. Diploma in Clinical Supervision, Trinity College, Dublin.

Robert Elliott is Professor of Counselling at the University of Strathclyde, and Professor Emeritus of Psychology at the University of Toledo. He has served as co-editor of the journals *Psychotherapy Research*, and *Person-Centered and Experiential Psychotherapies*. He is co-author of three books: Facilitating Emotional Cha*nge, Learning Emotion-Focused Therapy*, and *Research Methods in Clinical Psychology*, as well as more than 100 journal articles and book chapters. In 2008 he received the Distinguished Research Career Award from the Society for Psychotherapy Research and the Carl Rogers Award from the Division of Humanistic Psychology of the American Psychological Association.

Elizabeth S. Freire is a person-centred therapist and researcher. She is Lecturer in Counselling Psychology at the University of Strathclyde, in Scotland. She was one of the directors of Institute Delphos in Brazil until 2004, when she moved to the UK. She is currently involved in the development of several research projects related to the evaluation of the efficacy of person-centred therapy. She has published several articles and chapters in English, and a book in Portuguese about the theory and practice of person-centred therapy.

Soti Grafanaki is Professor of Counselling at St. Paul University (Ottawa, Canada), Certifying Coordinator and trainer of the Focusing Institute (New York), and Chartered Psychologist (BPS). Her Ph.D. research (1997) focused on client and counsellor experience of congruence during significant moments of person-centred therapy. Soti has published research papers and book chapters on the role of congruence in PCE practice. She is member of the editorial board for *Person-Centered and Experiential Psychotherapies*. Her current research examines trainee formative experiences and training effectiveness. She is the editor of the Special Issue of *Counselling and Psychotherapy Research* on 'Counselling and Psychotherapy Training' (2010). Soti is committed to the application of PCE principles in her training, research and practice.

Leslie Greenberg is Professor of Psychology at York University in Toronto and Director of the York University Psychotherapy Research Clinic. He has authored the major texts on emotion-focused approaches to treatment. His latest authored book is *Emotion-Focused Therapy: Coaching Clients to Work through Emotion*. Dr. Greenberg is a founding member of the Society of the Exploration of Psychotherapy Integration (SEPI) and a past President of the Society for Psychotherapy Research (SPR). He recently received the SPR Distinguished Research Career award. He conducts a private practice for individuals and couples and offers training in emotion-focused approaches.

Germain Lietaer is Emeritus Professor at the Catholic University of Leuven, where he has been teaching client-centred/experiential psychotherapy and process research on a master's and postmaster's level. Professor Lietaer has published widely (see http://perswww.kuleuven.be/~u0004824/). He is chief editor of *Client-Centered and Experiential Psychotherapy in the Nineties* (1990, Leuven University Press) and co-editor of *Handbook of Experiential Pychotherapy* (1998, Guilford Press). He is also chief editor of the recent Dutch *Handbook of Person-Centered/Experiential Psychotherapy* (2008, De Tijdstroom). Characteristic of his work is an attempt at integrating different suborientations and related approaches into a broadly conceived paradigm of client-centered/experiential/humanistic psychotherapy. During the years 2000–2003 he was chair of WAPCEPC.

Renate Motschnig-Pitrik is vice-head of the Computer Science Didactics and Learning Research Center at the University of Vienna, Austria. She has held positions at the University of Technology, Vienna, the RWTH Aachen in Germany, the University of Toronto, Canada, and the Masaryk University in Brno, Czech Republic. Renate is deeply interested in the multiple ways in which understanding and whole-person learning happen and is determined to foster a style in higher education that is based on person-centered attitudes, our co-actualizing potential, and thoughtful support by web-based technology. She appreciates synergies between presence and distance, cognition and feeling/meaning, and a multitude of (scientific) disciplines and cultures.

Karen Tallman conducts quantitative and qualitative research to identify successful practices for Kaiser Permanente in Oakland, California. She has published or presented research in the areas of physician–patient communication, therapist communication, palliative care, physician job satisfaction, team leadership, transfer of successful practices, diversity, and patient satisfaction. She coauthored *How Clients Make Therapy Work: The Process of Active Self-Healing* (1999).

Ladislav Timulak is Course Director of the Doctorate/M.Sc. in Counselling Psychology, Trinity College Dublin. He has training in both classical client-centred therapy as well as emotion-focused therapy. He is involved in the training of counselling psychologists and in the past trained person-centred therapists as well. He has published four books, a number of peer-reviewed papers and various chapters in both his native language, Slovak, and in English. His most recent books include *Research in Psychotherapy and Counselling* (Sage, 2008) and forthcoming *Developing Your Counselling and Psychotherapy Skills and Practice* (Sage). He maintains a part-time private practice.

Neill Watson is Research Professor and Professor Emeritus at the College of William and Mary in Williamsburg, VA, USA. He was chair of the Virginia Consortium Program in Clinical Psychology; he taught, practiced, and supervised client-centered therapy; and he published 15 articles and book chapters that included his development of methods to assess self-discrepancy. He retired to focus on his research on Rogers' theory of self-discrepancy.

Paul Wilkins is a person-centred academic, practitioner and supervisor. He has written several books on counselling and psychotherapy and has recently retired from lecturing in the Department of Psychology and Social Change at Manchester Metropolitan University.

INDEX

H

Haigh, GV 175, 183
Halkides, G 197, 212
Hambidge, G 19, 39
Hansen, JC 196, 212
Harbaugh, AP 48, 50, 63
Harding, CM 96, 126
Harris, ZL 16, 39
Hart, JT 123, 127
Harvey, JH 100, 127
Hawkins, P 217, 238
Hedges' *g* effect size statistic 6
Helmeke, KB 106, 127
Hemenover, SH 100, 127
Henderson, VL 215, 216, 221, 225
Hendricks, MN 139, 150, 157, 169, 184
Henry, W 137, 157
Herd, RH 33, 34, 39
Heron, J 217, 225, 230, 231, 237, 238
Hester, R 115, 127
heuristic
    inquiry 217, 224, 225–30, 234
    research, phases of 228
Higgins, ET 174, 175, 179, 180, 182,
        184, 185, 186
Higgins, TE 33, 34, 38
Hill, CE 135, 157
Hills, MD 233, 237
Hoerner, C 109, 127
Holburn, SH 60, 61, 63
Hölldampf, D ii, 16, 20, 21, 25, 36, 39,
        240
Hollon, SD 8, 13, 23, 37
Holton, E 59, 60, 63
Honos-Webb, L 97, 127, 153, 157
Horowitz, LM 136, 157
Horvath, AO 102, 106, 123, 127, 135,
        157, 158, 188, 212
Hough, M 33, 34, 38
House, R 29, 33, 39
Howard, K I 5, 14, 115, 116, 127, 169,
        185
Howe, D 119, 127

human relations management 45, 58, 59,
        61
Hume, K 30, 33, 39
Hunter, JE 6, 13
Huppert, JD 180, 185
Hüsson, D 16, 20, 36, 39
Hutterer, R 218, 220, 237
hypothesis v

I

Iberg, JR 150, 158
ICD-10 (see International Classification of
        Diseases)
incongruence 16, 92, 165
    operationalizing 164ff
Interactive Resonance 20
International Classification of Diseases
        (ICD-10) 25, 26, 31, 243
International Pilot Study of Schizophrenia
        96
Interpersonal Process Recall (IPR) 199
Interpersonal Training 60
Inventory of Interpersonal Problems 136
Iwakabe, S 66, 89

J

Jacobs, MK 103, 118, 127
Jaede, W 19, 39
Jaison, B 150, 158
Jenny, B 29, 31, 33, 40
Jernberg, AM 19, 40
Johnson, DW 49, 51, 63
Johnson, RT 49, 51, 63
Johnson, SM 4, 11, 13, 14, 28, 32, 33,
        40, 158
Joiner, TE 175, 178, 185
Jones, EM 19, 21, 33, 34, 40, 56
Joseph, S 247, 250
Joyce, AS 89

K

Kaczmarek, MG 29, 30, 33, 40
Kagan, F 119, 127, 179

THE LIFE AND WORK OF CARL ROGERS

Howard Kirschenbaum

ISBN 978 1 898059 93 6
  (cased) £29.00, £25.00 online
  pp. 736
ISBN 978 1 898059 98 1
  (with jacket) £50.00, £47.50 online
  pp. 736

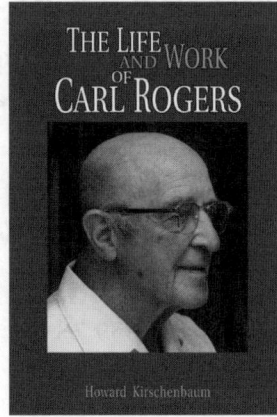

Twenty years after his death, PCCS Books celebrates the life and work of Carl Rogers with the long-awaited second edition of his biography by Howard Kirschenbaum. This completely re-written and re-titled edition includes a more detailed personal and professional history, and a full account of the last decade of Rogers' life. That decade turned out to be one of the most important periods of his career in which he developed peace work all over the world including South Africa and Northern Ireland, culminating in a Nobel Peace Prize nomination just days before his death. Until now this work has not been widely known.

The new edition adds deeper understanding of Rogers' contributions to psychology, the helping professions and society. On a personal level, access to recently revealed private papers tells us much more about Carl Rogers the man than was known to many of his closest associates. Kirschenbaum's own understanding of Carl Rogers, psychotherapy, education, and the human condition has matured over the intervening years. This much-anticipated second edition reflects a wiser and more balanced perspective of his subject. Now fully referenced, this is the life and work of Carl Rogers.

I couldn't put it down. I kept jumping from one part of the book to another and getting absorbed in the close research and the wonderful detail. I know the book took years to research, and now I can see why. Even reading the footnotes is absorbing.
Professor Dave Mearns, Professor Emeritus, University of Strathclyde

Buy direct for free shipping (in the UK) and permanent discounts from
www.pccs-books.co.uk

FIRST STEPS IN PRACTITIONER RESEARCH

A guide to understanding and doing research in counselling, and health and social care

Pete Sanders & Paul Wilkins

ISBN 978 1 898059 73 8

pp. 330

This book is written for complete beginners in social sciences research. It explains research from first principles and takes the reader through to the point at which they will be able to attempt simple research into their own practice. It builds confidence not only by explaining contemporary methodologies in everyday language, but also by looking at how to approach, understand and evaluate a range of research in journal articles and books.

Sanders and Wilkins know that practitioners are often ambivalent about research ... and speak directly to this ambivalence ... they are accomplished writers who know their audience. The book does not avoid complexity, but explains complex concepts plainly ...
Bill Stiles, Professor of Clinical Psychology, Miami University, Ohio

The point is to entertain, draw in, seduce, or somehow lure nervous students into the whole research thing. I'd like to see First Steps in Practitioner Research *left lying around in conspicuous places so that students will come across it and be tempted ...*
Robert Elliott, Professor of Counselling, University of Strathclyde

AUTHORS

PETE SANDERS spent over 30 years practising as a counsellor, educator and clinical supervisor. He has written, co-written and edited a number of books, chapters and papers on many aspects of counselling, psychotherapy and mental health. He is a trustee of the Soteria Network UK.

PAUL WILKINS is a person-centred academic, practitioner and supervisor. He has written several books on counselling and psychotherapy, and until recently was a senior lecturer in the Department of Psychology and Social Change at Manchester Metropolitan University.

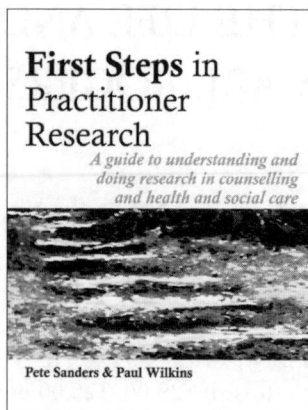

PCCS Books
www.pccs-books.co.uk   sales@pccs-books.co.uk
T: +44 (0)1989 763900   F: +44(0)1989 763901
2 Cropper Row, Alton Road, Ross-on-Wye, HR9 5LA, UK